Microcomputers in Teaching

An Introduction to

Microcomputers in Teaching

ANDREW NASH
*(formerly Teaching and Information Officer,
Computer Laboratory, University of Leicester;
now a freelance writer and editor)*

and

DEREK BALL
*(Lecturer in Education and Mathematics,
School of Education, University of Leicester)*

HUTCHINSON

Hutchinson & Co. (Publishers) Ltd

An imprint of the Hutchinson Publishing Group

17–21 Conway Street, London W1P 6JD

Hutchinson Group (Australia) Pty Ltd
30–32 Cremorne Street, Richmond South, Victoria 3121
PO Box 151, Broadway, New South Wales 2007

Hutchinson Group (NZ) Ltd
32–34 View Road, PO Box 40-086, Glenfield, Auckland 10

Hutchinson Group (SA) (Pty) Ltd
PO Box 337, Bergvlei 2012, South Africa

First published 1982
Reprinted 1983

©Andrew Nash and Derek Ball 1982

Printed in Great Britain by The Anchor Press Ltd
and bound by Wm Brendon & Son Ltd,
both of Tiptree, Essex

Illustrations by Gillies Mackinnon

British Library Cataloguing in Publication Data

Nash, Andrew
   An introduction to microcomputers in teaching.
   1. Microcomputers
   I. Title   II. Ball, Derek
   371.3'9445   QA76.5

ISBN 0 09 149031 6

Contents

1	**Introduction**	7
2	**Learning**	16
	2.1 Freedom to learn	16
	2.2 Teachers	19
	2.3 Learners	22
	2.4 Evaluating learning	26
3	**Programs**	29
	3.1 Background to programming	29
	3.2 Specifying a program	36
	3.3 Obtaining a program	53
	3.4 Using a program on different microcomputers	59
	3.5 Evaluating a program	63
	3.6 AUGURY: an illustration	66
4	**Graphics**	76
	4.1 What are graphics?	76
	4.2 How can they be used?	79
	4.3 Limitations in practice	83
	4.4 Computer graphics versus other means of presenting pictures	87
	4.5 Potential problems and some solutions	91
5	**The role of the computer in teaching**	97
	5.1 Gaining mastery of situations	97
	5.2 The advantages of a computer	100
	5.3 The function of the computer in learning	104
	5.4 Translation	110
	5.5 Achieving your aims	113
6	**Day-to-day use of a computer**	117
	6.1 Protecting your program	117

6.2	Making your programs available	121
6.3	Being flexible in your approach	123
6.4	Being receptive to new ideas	125

7 Case studies in programming 129

7.1	Program code and portability	130
7.2	Structure of code	142
7.3	Condensation of code	152
7.4	Updating tables on the screen	160
7.5	Updating pictures on the screen	169
7.6	Error-trapping	177
7.7	Command and tutorial modes	184

8 Case studies in teaching 202

8.1	Individual and group use	202
8.2	Overt and covert use	208
8.3	Stimulation of discussion	216
8.4	Freedom and constraint	229
8.5	GRAPH: an illustration	240

9 Microcomputers 258

9.1	Computers: what are they?	258
9.2	Processing	261
9.3	Storage	265
9.4	Input	267
9.5	Output	271
9.6	Software	274
9.7	Systems	279
9.8	Choice of microcomputer	283

10 Epilogue 287

Appendices 293

A.1	Program evaluation: a checklist	293
A.2	Program to prevent the stripping of leading blanks from BASIC programs on the RML 380Z microcomputer	294
A.3	Program to aid design of characters on the screen	298
A.4	Addresses	311
A.5	Books	313

Programs in this book 315

Index 316

1 Introduction

This book is an introduction to ways in which microcomputers can be used in teaching. Microcomputers, or 'micros' as they are often called, are becoming increasingly widespread in all kinds of context, and nowhere more quickly than in education – schools, colleges, universities and professional training establishments. The micro is an extra, versatile piece of equipment to be incorporated into teaching in the way that tape recorders, slide projectors and overhead projectors have been.

But microcomputers – and other computers – may also seem to be vaguely disturbing, complex machines, enshrouded in esoteric jargon and threatening to take over rather than assist. Thus we hope that we have explained all the useful jargon, and explained it lucidly. This book will give you ideas about where to use micros, and where not to use them; about what are 'good' programs, and what are not; about how to control the micro, and not be controlled by it.

The book tells you a lot about micros – what they are, for instance, and how they differ from each other. Below is a simple working introduction to the micro: not very detailed, but sufficient, perhaps, for you to understand the larger part of the book. Other aspects of the machine will appear incidentally throughout the book, and Chapter 9 provides a more complete guide to the micro for those who need it.

The book also talks a lot about teaching, especially in Chapters 2 and 5. Indeed, teaching is the central concern of the whole book: by keeping this in mind, we hope to help you in deciding whether micros aid or hamper teaching as you know it.

In this first chapter, therefore, we look at:

- *whether you should read this book;*
- *if you do read it, which parts will interest you most;*
- *our use of pronouns;*
- *whether you need a micro;*
- *what a microcomputer is;*
- *how much jargon you really need to master;*
- *whether you have got to do your own programming;*
- *whether you can understand programs without being a programmer;*
- *who helped us in writing this book.*

Why this book?

We have written this book because we think teachers need a guide to micros which is above all *practical*, a source of ideas about what and how and why, a book which gives examples which are practical and useful (and perhaps amusing or provocative). You will not find exhaustive technical explanations, though you will find a comprehensive basic computer vocabulary, each new word being introduced and defined in context. You will not find a list of approved answers, though you will find a lot of questions raised, some of them difficult in their implications. And you will not find any assumptions about your knowledge at the outset; we wish this book to be useful to those who have none. Our starting premise is that computers are not a panacea for anything, but can often be a great help and a stimulus to teachers and to students alike. At times they can provide flexibility in teaching – at others, they may be totally inappropriate, and other teaching methods superior.

As a teacher learning about microcomputers, you will probably need to retain a sense of humour through your difficulties and misunderstandings! We hope that this book will help you to do that. Micros, though potentially extremely useful, are only machines – servants, indeed. They must not be taken too seriously.

Using the book

We have tried to make the book useful to you in whatever way you choose. While the material is necessarily in one order, you may wish to use it in another, and you are encouraged to skip around it as you please. The index should help you find the information you need, as should the contents pages. Technical terms are printed in **bold face** where they are defined and discussed in detail: having found one in particular, you will probably find it useful to read the whole of the section in which it occurs.

Throughout, we invite you to assess the validity of our ideas. Some of these are far from universally accepted, and you may disagree with us in some respects.

A note about pronouns

In writing this book, 'the authors' could have remained impersonal and addressed 'the reader' only indirectly. But our interest in microcomputers in teaching is personal and we hope that yours will be also, so *we* have chosen to address *you* in a personal way. From time to time, it is useful to introduce the third person into the discussion – 'the teacher', 'the programmer', 'the user' – and she is consistently referred to as 'he'. This is a literary convenience only, and implies no sexist assumptions!

What use are microcomputers to you?

In essence, if you have a need which can be met by text or lines on a television screen (possibly in colour), and if your need can be exactly and completely specified by enough detailed instructions to let a machine get on with it, the microcomputer may be an answer.

A micro can be used in a range of subjects to do tasks such as:
* display text (e.g. facts about historical figures);
* display tabulated data (e.g. annual balance of payments figures);
* perform simple calculations (e.g. statistics such as totals and averages);
* store information and search for individual items as required (e.g. library catalogue);
* draw pictures, including maps and graphs (e.g. geographical distribution of fossil fuels);
* draw successions of pictures, or make rapid alterations to a single picture, to give the illusion of movement (e.g. effects of varying battle formations in early wars);
* combine complex calculations and pictorial display to simulate real processes (e.g. models of traffic flow in towns);
* allow the user to control and direct the progress of a simulation, by varying one or more factors (e.g. rates of chemical reactions, as affected by concentration of reactants and by temperature);
* test the user on his knowledge (e.g. multiple-choice tests) or his skill (e.g. arithmetic exercises) and mark the result;
* produce printed material for photocopying, provided that the micro is connected to a printer (e.g. form lists, sets of exercises, laboratory instructions – this can be particularly helpful, if liable to change each year).

You may or may not be or become a programmer. But there are lots of programs about for you to use, and if you can't find the one you want, and if you can't write the program yourself, there is probably someone you know whose arm you can twist.

Microcomputers – a working definition

Well, what are they, these machines we keep talking about? There is a detailed answer in Chapter 9 for those who want it: here is a simplified account which may remain adequate to your needs.

A **microcomputer** comprises several basic parts. At the centre is a **processor**, the bit that does the actual computing. Attached to it are a means of getting **information** in, usually a **keyboard** (not unlike that on a typewriter), and a means of getting information out, usually a television **screen**. (It is useful to be able to see at any time where on the screen the next character to be printed will appear: this position is marked by a **cursor**, which advances to the next position when a character is displayed.) Many micros use a **printer**, a device similar to the part of the typewriter that does the actual typing, as a means of output in addition to the screen.

Using the keyboard, the user can **instruct** the micro to perform a variety of **operations** and to display the result. Instructions are often grouped together to form a sequence called a **program**. (Programs are known collectively as **software**.) Output is displayed in a form chosen by the user which may be words (**text**) or pictures (**graphics**) or a combination of the two.

The inside of the micro usually has several **boards**, on which are mounted **integrated circuits** or **chips**. One sort of chip, the **CPU chip** ('CPU' for 'central processing unit'), does the processing. Another sort, **memory chips**, store information and instructions as they are used. These memory chips collectively form **core storage**, and this is used to store programs and data as they are being used.

At other times, programs and data are stored outside the machine, on **backing store**. This is most often either **magnetic disc** or **magnetic cassette**. Both comprise a plastic support medium on which is coated a magnetizable material. Cassettes are ordinary domestic cassettes; the storage is on a length of tape, and this is used on a cassette recorder. Discs are flat versions of the same idea: information stored on them can be accessed more easily, however, since the entire surface is available all the time, whereas tape must be wound from one spool to the other. Discs are flexible, but spin continuously while in use; this spinning makes them behave as if rigid. A given micro may be connected to one cassette player or more, and it may be connected to one or more disc drives. (Discs may be used on one side only or both. Thus two disc drives may give access to four disc surfaces.) It may be possible on your micro to transfer information from cassette to cassette, from disc to disc, from cassette to disc, and from disc to cassette.

In the machine and on backing store, information is kept in related groups called **files**; each file is given a **filename**.

All the work which you do with the computer is controlled by a sophisticated program called the computer's **operating system** (or sometimes **monitor**). This allows you to do things or prohibits you from doing things, and tells you what is going on by means of messages. Messages which are issued as the result of an error are known as 'error messages'.

The processor itself works in a **low-level language**, referred to as **machine language**. This is difficult for humans to understand, so they often work in one of several **high-level languages**. (Examples include BASIC and PASCAL.) Conversion between high-level and low-level languages is done automatically by a **translator**. Translators come in two varieties, the one most commonly used with micros being an **interpreter**.

To run a program on a micro, then, you need to have in core storage not only the program itself but the operating system and an interpreter. Core store is of two sorts: some retains its information when the micro is switched off, some

Introduction 11

Cassettes are ordinary domestic cassettes. Discs are flat versions of the same idea.

does not. If the information is lost, it must be loaded anew from backing store each time the micro is used. As a general guide, all teaching programs are kept on backing store and loaded as required. Interpreters are usually treated similarly, but may well be held permanently in the machine. Whether you need to load the interpreter (from tape or disc) will depend upon the make of computer and the language you are using. Operating systems are often stored in the permanent type of core storage. This is especially true of operating systems specially intended for use with cassettes, whereas those for use with discs may need to be loaded each time.

All being well, a program once started continues its **execution** until complete. Sometimes it aborts before the end, a condition known as a **crash** – in such circumstances, the messages will help you to find out what went wrong. Occasionally, the problem will be inside the program instructions – the **code** – and you will have to correct the code: such little problems are called **bugs**.

So much for what a microcomputer is. As you use one, if you do, you will rely heavily on programs produced by other people. To know what is available and to understand how to use it when you have it, you will also rely heavily on their **documentation**. This will naturally be of variable quality; some will be clean and neat and tell you all you need to know, some will be inadequate or missing. Notice if you can what you find helpful in other people's documentation, and try to follow the same path when you come to write your own.

A program when bought does not always arrive by itself. It will usually have instructions on how to use it, and perhaps some ideas about how to alter it if you wish. It may also have materials for practical work – worksheets for your students, perhaps. It may even come as one only of several programs. The whole set – programs, documentation and materials – is known collectively as a **package**.

Programming

In a book about microcomputers, much must be said about programs. Several programming examples are given to illustrate points of design, clarity and sophistication. How much do *you* need to know about programming?

To use a micro, you need programs to do what *you* want done. Programs are created in stages. First, someone (the designer) specifies the nature and details of what they would like the micro to do. Next, someone (the programmer) develops these as instructions which a micro can actually execute: a program. Designer and programmer then work together to check that the program does what it was intended to do, and check that this is indeed a useful thing to do. A program to be used in teaching should be tested with learners to assess its effectiveness: the program may then be refined in the light of experience. This process of testing and refinement is continued until designer and programmer alike are satisfied.

'The designer' and 'the programmer' are often the same person, though they need not be. So you may write programs, though you need not. Even if you do not, it will be helpful for you to have at least a superficial knowledge of programming, of its potential and its constraints; and a well-written program should make a lot of sense even to non-programmers. By itself, this book will not teach you to program, but it will teach you a lot about what sorts of task programs can do, and about how to design and evaluate programs.

The instructions in a program – the **code** – are written in a programming **language**. There are several languages available on micros, and picking one of them is one part of the design stage of each program. The one most commonly used is undoubtedly BASIC; the examples in this book use BASIC also.

As far as possible, code should be intelligible both in its working and in its written forms. Intelligibility of written code is dependent on how nearly the program *code* resembles the *English* in which the original specification was written. Here is one example.

In all sorts of program, it is important to check information supplied by the user ('input'). Suppose that a program at some point invites the user to specify one of four compass directions by giving a single letter – 'N', 'S', 'E' or 'W'. We wish to check his input. Here is one way of doing so:

1 Print a message asking for a direction (PRINT).
2 Input the user's answer (INPUT).
3 Compare the *actual* input with each *valid* letter.
  If the letters match, the answer is valid, so go to the next part of the program (IF ... THEN).
  Otherwise, try the next letter.
4 When the valid letters have been exhausted, the input is known to be in error: tell the user (PRINT) and let him try again (GOTO).

And here is one way of representing the instructions written above in *English* as instructions written in BASIC *code*:

```
3120 REM Ask user for compass direction
3130 REM   and ensure that input is valid
3140 REM
3150     PRINT "Which direction";
3160     INPUT D$
3170 REM
3180     IF D$ = "N" THEN 3280
3190     IF D$ = "S" THEN 3280
3200     IF D$ = "E" THEN 3280
3210     IF D$ = "W" THEN 3280
3220 REM
3230 REM Error found
3240 REM
3250     PRINT "** Please answer with N S E or W"
3260     GOTO 3150
3270 REM
3280 REM (Rest of program)
```

Some points to note about this code:
* Lines begin with numbers ('line numbers') which keep the code in order and can be used to hop around the program (see lines 3200 and 3260).
* Lines which start with the word REM (for 'remark') are there to explain to any reader of the program what is going on. They are ignored by the computer when the program is executed.
* The INPUT instruction when executed will put a '?' on the micro's screen as a prompt to the user: this will appear at the end of the text 'Which direction'.
* If no match is found, the program arrives at 3250, prints a message and then goes back to line 3150.
* The program is carefully laid out. Instructions other than REM are indented. Lines 3140, 3170, 3220, 3240 and 3270 are blank lines which help to make the code readable.
* This is not the only way of doing what was specified, but it is quite a good way, *if* it is clear to you, the reader.
* Lines 3180–3210 inclusive could have been written as a 'loop', in which the line within the loop is executed up to 4 times depending on whether or not the actual input and the current valid letter match:

```
3180     LET VL$ = "NSEW"
3190     FOR J = 1 TO 4
3200       IF D$ = MID$(VL$,J,1) THEN 3280
3210     NEXT J
```

Line 3180 defines a 'string' of valid letters: line 3200 compares the input with each of these in turn. Line 3200 is executed up to 4 times because of lines 3190 and 3210, which mark the beginning and end of the loop.

This is just one small illustration of the relationship between what the programmer wants a program to do and the way in which he writes his instructions. We feel that the instructions in English and the instructions in code should resemble each other very closely; and that it should be possible to read code almost as you might read a book. Ideally, it should not be necessary to refer to other sources as you read someone else's program – the words should be clear from their context, and the logic should be clear from the words. Programs in this book make that assumption: for the most part, we do not explain the individual lines of code, nor the words within them. But we do in each case provide a diagram of the overall structure of the program: this should give you a feel for what the program is doing and you should therefore know what to expect in the code.

If you understood most of that example and the discussion which followed it, you should be able to make a lot of sense of other programs in the book – whether or not you become a programmer.

(All the programs in this book were written originally for one particular microcomputer – the Research Machines Ltd (RML) 380Z, and require RML Extended BASIC Version 5. Some of them can be adapted for other machines quite simply, and we give some advice about these changes: there is general advice in section 7.1, and there are specific notes with each program. The programs may be available for your machine, whether or not it is an RML 380Z, on disc or cassette – details are given on page 315.)

Acknowledgements

We would like to acknowledge two groups of people who have contributed to the publication of this book.

The first group provided the *stimulus* for publication. These are friends and colleagues (or others whose work we have read) who have discussed, experienced, or caused our views.

The second group provided the *means* for publication. These are firstly our close friends and families, who have borne up remarkably well throughout the protracted period of gestation, and who have tolerated our preoccupation and consequent neglect. A particular apology is due to those with whom we have shared meal tables, as the conversation turned inevitably to our book sooner or later, and often sooner. While we *might* have survived without her excellent cooking, Val proved indispensable in keeping the children at bay. We are indebted to Sandy Douglas, who read the script; to Mick Bonsor, who took the photographs; to Gillies Mackinnon, who provided the cartoons. And finally we thank our publishers: Charlotte Orde, who edited the manuscript (though all the mistakes remaining are ours); Sue Lacey who designed the book; and especially Bob Osborne, who published it.

A particular apology is due to those with whom we have shared meal tables.

2 Learning

This book is not just about microcomputers, it is about the use of microcomputers *in teaching*. Your attitude to micros in this context will depend on your view of teaching itself, so this chapter describes some of the issues involved in teaching and considers some of the ways in which computers can be used to help students to learn more effectively.

We look in turn at:

- *freedom as a facet of learning;*
- *the role of teachers;*
- *the needs of learners;*
- *aspects of evaluating success in learning.*

2.1 Freedom to learn

There are two ways of learning. You may decide to learn something, and apply yourself thereafter to learning it. But equally, you may learn something by accident in the course of trying to learn something else, or because you become sidetracked from your original intention. Thus there are also two elements to your learning: motivation and enjoyment. A learner who is highly motivated may learn even if he is not enjoying himself; a learner who is enjoying himself may learn even if he is not highly motivated. Suggestions made in this book seek to make learning more enjoyable; and it may be that motivation, or increased motivation, will follow.

When the going gets rough, the learner's interest may flag. This happens for the motivated learner when learning is simply hard, and for the happy learner when he is restricted. In both cases, what is wanted is freedom; and it is the increased freedom which computers can afford learners which is their most attractive feature in teaching.

The aspects of this freedom include the following:

- ○ *computers as providers of freedom;*
- ○ *difficulties arising from the use of computers;*
- ○ *'attitudes' to learning displayed by computers;*
- ○ *parallels between the freedom offered by a book and the freedom offered by a computer;*

- applications of computers to hard learning;
- the question of who is in control of learning.

Computers in learning: a source of freedom

A computer does not always make learning freer or more enjoyable – this depends on where and how it is used. A computer can improve learning only if its use has been carefully designed to make learning easier.

A computer *can* make learning more enjoyable simply by leaving both you and your students free to concentrate on the most important aspects of what is being learnt. For example, the computer can cope rapidly with as much tedious processing as could possibly be required, so this load can be taken from the learner's shoulders. Where the computer is assisting in the learning of a single student or of a group of students, *you* are freed for other functions. No computer will ever be able to handle all aspects of your task as a teacher: it cannot share enthusiasm, give encouragement or repair lost confidence.

The student also may be freer to concentrate on the important facets of learning. Computers can sort out information quickly and reliably, can perform arithmetical calculations and display results in a form which is easy to read and make sense of. Sometimes a learner must develop his own skills of organization or calculation or presentation of data; at other times these processes simply distract him from his main task: when his energies are no longer diverted, he is free to learn more easily.

Computers in learning: a source of problems?

Advantages to the student are not always welcomed wholeheartedly. Electronic calculators, for example, are regarded by some people with suspicion; it is alleged that they make students 'lazy' and less motivated to become proficient at arithmetic. There may be a threat to the teacher not so much in what a student does *not* learn as in what he is able to learn; a calculator is under the student's control – he can press buttons and see what happens. He can make discoveries, and may then wish to check these with you – 'What's that button for?', 'Why does doing this make that happen?' A computer is more powerful than a calculator, so potentially it can offer the learner a much richer context in which to try things out and see what happens. Yet because the computer can be programmed, it follows that it can be programmed to limit exploration as easily as to facilitate it.

A teacher may sometimes feel threatened when new opportunities of learning are offered to his students. He may feel threatened by the unfamiliarity of computers themselves, especially when some students probably know more about computers than he does, for he may be using the computer simply to assist his teaching. This can feel uncomfortable unless he is content to learn from his students.

18 Learning

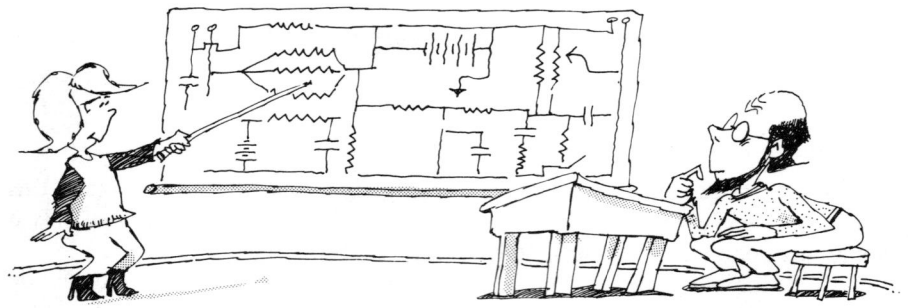

Some students probably know more about computers than the teacher does.

Coupled with the unfamiliarity is the difficulty, even impossibility, of keeping up with the speed of technological change. Innovations may provide new opportunities and exciting new teaching methods, but equally they may seem just like new threats. And shining new machines can distract both you and your students from more important aspects of your tasks.

Computers in learning: how do they appear to the learner?

Computers in learning are often valued as possessing desirable characteristics which even the ablest teacher may lose from time to time; they are supposed to be totally reliable, infinitely patient and completely non-judgemental. Although these characteristics apply strictly only to humans, they describe some of the helpful attributes of computers in teaching and learning. Computer programs certainly can appear to be all of these things, but they can also be written so that they seem to the student to be impatient, patronizing and sarcastic. Programs can time the responses made by students, for example, and goad them if they are 'too slow'; they can make acid comments if students give incorrect answers or press inappropriate keys; they can even store students' errors for subsequent public display. The computer is available to be used in whatever ways you desire; it will adopt helpful 'attitudes' to the students who use it only if those attitudes are valued by you and by whoever designs the programs.

Computers in learning: a comparison with books

There are many parallels between the design of a book and the design of a computer program. To make points about programs, therefore, we say something in this book about the book itself – how we wrote it, why we wrote it, the way it is designed and the way in which you use it. As we wrote, we tried to identify what we were seeking to communicate, which information should go in which chapter and so on. Having done this, we have provided you with summaries of the contents of each chapter and with an index, so that you are not restricted to the sequence of the book but may turn to whichever page you choose, to get the information you want in the order that you want it. We would like you to be as clear as possible about what you are learning from this book: the clearer you are, the freer you are – free to get what you want from it, to decide what not to believe, what to disagree with and what to ignore.

The freedom to choose what to look at next, and to choose how to use and develop it, is crucial in the use of computers; it is well described by the phrase **user authority**. To have authority, the user (the teacher or the student) needs to know what is available and why, and what choices he is free to make; he can then adapt the situation to meet his own needs. It is useful to bear this in mind when evaluating computer programs.

Computers in learning: support for the learner

In some situations, before the learner can be free to develop his understanding in the way he chooses, he needs to put in much disciplined effort to gain some essential facility. For instance, you may find driving anything but fun, yet it is made worthwhile by the mobility which you gain at the end. To suggest that all learning is uniformly exciting would be foolish: hard learning may be made bearable for the learner by the conviction that it is worthwhile. As a teacher, you try not to make this process harder. This is another useful yardstick by which to judge computer programs: if they are designed to assist with tedious, routine learning, are they making such learning as straightforward as possible and are they providing sufficient support?

Who controls the process of learning?

In formal teaching, the learner is never completely free to learn in the way he wishes. In some situations and on some occasions *you* will know best what the learner needs. Even when you do not know, you will often find that you have to provide an environment in which he himself can discover what he needs to learn. When learning is necessarily hard, you provide careful instruction and frequent encouragement lest the learner give up altogether. But ultimately the learner needs to feel in control of his own learning. Computers may sometimes afford a useful means of providing the appropriate combination of instruction, support and freedom.

2.2 Teachers

In designing or assessing computer programs as elements in your teaching, it will help if you are aware of your role as a teacher. Some programs take the place of particular kinds of teaching, some programs facilitate a new approach to teaching, some programs free the learner to work along his own path with

support from the teacher. In examining programs, therefore, we need to think about:
- the fact that teachers are also still learners;
- the order in which material should be taught;
- how teachers and learners react when things go wrong;
- the extent to which computers can help.

Teachers and learners

All teachers are also learners. All teachers can reflect upon their own learning and thus gain greater insight into how they can teach more fruitfully. In this book we say many things about teaching; we have tried to design our book in a way that accords with and illustrates our stated beliefs. In the same way, the learning situation provided by you as a teacher will presumably be influenced by the ways in which you yourself learn most easily.

A teacher continues to learn about the subject he teaches. He is continually discovering what makes it fun, what aspects are difficult, which skills are particularly useful, what is the best way of sorting out a particular idea and so on. What is fun for him may well be fun for his students also.

Every teacher has his own way of learning, and – since one of the things he is learning about is how to teach – every teacher has his own style of teaching. Those who offer resources to teachers (including resources which make use of computers) may overlook this diversity of styles by offering programs designed so that they can be used in one way only, or they may offer programs capable of being used in a variety of ways according to the skills of the teacher and the needs of his students.

What do you learn first?

It is commonly believed that to teach a subject successfully, the order in which topics are dealt with is crucial. This is clearly true of some subjects, but with others there is often more flexibility than may at first appear.

Computers are potentially more flexible than books in this respect. As far as the reading of this book is concerned, you may choose to start your reading wherever you wish, but there is in fact a Chapter 1. Computer programs can be written in such a way that they are utterly free from implied ordering.

Is this lack of implied ordering an advantage? We think it is; we argue elsewhere in the book that it is important for learners to be able to assume responsibility for their own learning. We feel that the job of the teacher is less to impart knowledge than to foster specific attitudes to learning. In recognizing that enjoyable learning is likely to be effective learning, that a motivated student is likely to learn more quickly and more thoroughly than an unmotivated student, we are drawn to the notion that time spent in enticing the student to learn is time well spent.

If students are to be given some say in their own learning, we as teachers must attend not only to the subject matter but to the students themselves. We can learn from them by observing what they can do and what they cannot do; and by listening to them when they tell us where *they* want to begin. Computer programs used in teaching vary considerably in the choice they give the user (teacher or learner) about where to begin; some demand that learning takes place in the set order ordained by their designers. But others give almost complete freedom to the user to determine his own order; and these, we suggest, make it possible for learners to express their own needs and to work in their own ways.

What happens when things go wrong?

We should first try to be clear what we mean by 'going wrong'. The process of learning is not at all a steady one; it is uneven, sudden, capricious and, above all, inefficient. It is unrealistic to expect every student to learn a little every day; it is even less realistic to imagine that all students will learn the same thing. Teachers may know what they are going to teach, but they do not know what their students are going to learn.

It is easy to act as if the opposite were true. The playing of games is an activity from which participants learn a great deal, yet games may be thought to have no value in education unless 'learning objectives' can be clearly enumerated. But learning is diffuse – it is often more important to learn the feel than to learn the facts. Long-jumpers are not trained for the actual competitive event by performing long jumps only; they use a variety of physical and mental exercises designed to give them greater general as well as specific control over what they are doing. And what is true for long-jumping is true also of multiplication and of sheep farming in New Zealand.

So when learners are not learning in a particular way or at an even pace, a lot of what happens is not 'wrong'; it is inevitable. Nevertheless things can go wrong; students may persist in not understanding, they may begin unmotivated or become so, they may lose confidence, they may end up knowing less than when they started. If this happens it is easy to find someone to blame, when it might be more profitable to try a new method, to review the goals or even simply to be honest and give up.

Computers can help by offering new ways of teaching and learning, new flexibility, new approaches; some things that seemed wrong need no longer be regarded in that light, and other things that remain wrong may not matter to the same degree.

Computers will solve all your problems

Well, it would be lovely if they could. But while computers may help, the problems remain to be solved. And computers will not even help unless careful thought is given to their use.

What computers do offer is an opportunity to take a good look at what happens in teaching, so that the best and not the worst methods are incorporated into learning programs and so that new possibilities offered by the computer are not missed. Reviewing the teaching will not only ensure that computer programs are well written, it will help improve teaching away from the computer. And there are still the things that cannot be taught with a computer; being clear about *why* this is so may indicate more effective methods of teaching those things.

2.3 Learners

Microcomputers in teaching are there to assist the learner in his learning. This section considers the needs of the learner, in terms of:

- *growing confidence in himself;*
- *the speed at which he learns;*
- *his need for support while learning;*
- *his choice of what to learn;*
- *the value of competition;*
- *the value of mistakes.*

Building confidence

Imagine a student on a degree course who goes to see his teacher three weeks before the course starts. Ostensibly he is going to discuss whether he has chosen the right option, or what preliminary reading he can most usefully do. He is *really* going to find out whether he will be able to work with the teacher, whether he will be comfortable with the course, whether he will feel confident. When you undertake some difficult task, perhaps for the first time, what is likely to hinder you most is not your lack of knowledge or lack of skill; it is your lack of confidence. Human beings must believe in themselves before they can take responsibility for their own learning.

Most teachers realize the importance in learning of confidence and patiently build it, yet it is all too easy to forget about its importance sometimes when you are teaching. Computers can help build a student's confidence in undertaking some task – they can provide immediate feedback so that he gains encouragement from his early successes; even when he goes wrong, they can perhaps quickly put him back on the right path.

Sometimes success can be assured by making the steps in the learning sufficiently small; at other times this strategy can be counterproductive. Being compelled to take small steps when you feel able to take bigger ones can be very frustrating and there are times when, in order to make progress, a student must plan the route for himself.

Keeping the learner's options open

Establishing the optimal size of step is just one aspect of adapting the learning process to the needs of the student. Some students need more advice or encouragement than others.

There are various ways of dealing with the differing needs of learners. One way is to provide a completely open situation for the learner: to let him do anything he likes. The lack of restriction may mean that he gets little support from the teacher. At the opposite end of the spectrum, the learner may be instructed to perform his task exactly as he is told and maybe even at exactly the given speed. The learner may receive support of a kind, but perhaps to the detriment of his own needs. Obviously it is a balance between these extremes which is likely to be most helpful, although it may be far from easy to see what balance to achieve. And although unexpected contributions from the student may cause problems for the teacher, the learner does need to question, to think for himself, to discuss his own ideas. He needs room to grow.

Well-designed computer programs can help the learner keep his options open. He can be asked whether or not he wants instructions; it can be made possible for him to ask the computer for help whenever he wants it but be left otherwise to cope by himself. Thus he may be given the option of telling the computer to display a result as a graph, while being able to go straight on to the next stage if he prefers. And some programs are designed not so much to teach some particular point as to promote discussion; such programs leave their users with more room for manoeuvre.

Deciding what to learn

During the first three years of his life, a child usually accomplishes two very important and complex pieces of learning – learning to walk and learning to talk. Apparently nobody tells him to learn these skills, nobody suggests that they will be useful. And nobody teaches him; he just learns. He probably receives help and encouragement and approval from his parents, but *he* remains in control of what is going on. During the years before his formal education begins, a child will have learnt a great deal about learning.

In a formal educational setting, who decides what to learn? You may consult with your students, seek their opinions about what your course should contain, yet in the end it is you who decides what to teach. But only the *student* can decide what to *learn*. He may of course decide to learn nothing – or to learn skills which you would prefer him not to learn! But even if he is motivated and interested in the course, what he learns is specific to him.

And what students learn is invariably considerably different from what you intended to teach. When you are planning your teaching, it is almost impossible for you to remember just how complex human beings are. Students learn not only from the content of your course, but also from your style, your manner, your attitudes, your feelings about them, the room, other students, the weather, and so on. It is possible (and probably quite common) to complete, say, a geography course without having learnt much geography, and yet having learnt profitably a great deal.

The same things are true of learning from computer programs. Style, context and the general feel of a program are likely to influence the student as much as, if not more than, the content. One student may take a long while to use a particular program, not because it proves difficult or confusing but because it causes him to pause in the middle for a daydream. And even though daydreams cannot be *evaluated* as achievements, they may on occasions be the most significant parts of learning.

Competition

Some teachers believe that competition is a useful and important aspect of most – if not all – learning situations. Others do not. . . .

Competition has very little to do with daydreaming.

Competition works for learning some things. It works for some students but not for others.

Competition is often viewed ambivalently by people, because as children they are trained both to want to win and to be good losers.

If you wish to use competition as part of your teaching, you will welcome the advent of the computer. Computers can handle statistics with the utmost facility, so you can keep totting up marks and measure thereby your students' progress (if not their learning) against your own criteria. On the other hand, you can if you wish use computers to help to *remove* competition: the learner can take all day, make as many mistakes as he likes, get all the help he needs . . . and no one else need ever know.

Making mistakes

A child who is learning to walk or to talk makes lots of mistakes. Adults enjoy a child's mistakes when he is learning to walk or to talk; instinctively they feel that his trying things out is an essential part of his learning.

In formal education, mistakes are often regarded quite differently. They are counted, accumulated, and used to measure the student's achievement – or lack of it. A more profitable reason for pointing out mistakes is that they can be used to sort out learning.

The game of 'Mastermind' requires one player to identify a hidden code, a code set by the other player. Identification is a gradual process, in which the solver makes guesses at the code, and the setter gives limited information about the closeness of the guess to the code. This information means that each successive guess is more educated than the last, and the actual code is finally 'induced' from the previous attempts. We introduce the game here because it

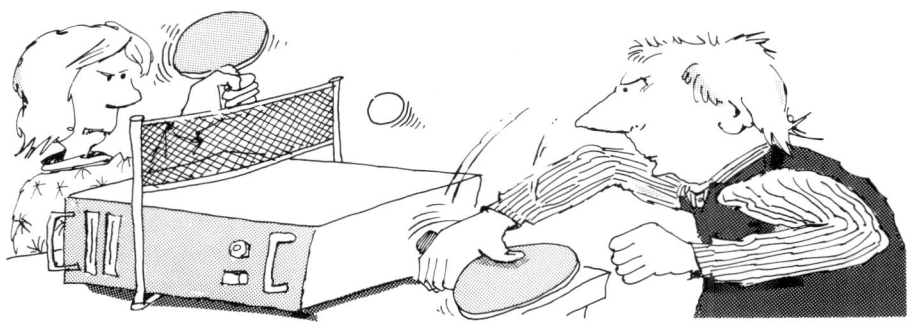

The computer can certainly be used for the playing of games

lends itself to a remarkable strategy: it is often most informative to try a solution which you are sure will be *wrong*. It requires a certain level of maturity in games-playing even to consider adopting such a strategy.

Estimating and approximating are skills which are essential in solving many practical problems, yet they are skills which many people fail to develop. Learning to approximate and learning by making and testing hypotheses have this in common: they are hindered by an obsessive need during formal education to get right answers.

Where trial-and-error methods, approximation and hypothesizing are useful strategies in learning, the computer has a great deal to offer. It can certainly be used for the playing of games (such as 'Mastermind') and is often used in this way. It can also provide more 'serious' learning situations, where hunches are to be followed and where it is valuable for the learner to obtain immediate feedback from following these hunches.

Mistakes made by students are not always wrong! Suppose a teacher asks a question, receives an answer and then says, 'No.' Does he mean 'No, that's incorrect' – or 'No, that's not the answer I wanted'? This distinction is not always appreciated by the learner. Much the same applies to mistakes made by the student at the computer.

The kind of mistake that a student makes when using a computer will depend very much on the way the computer is being used. In one type of use, the situation is largely under the control of the computer. Perhaps the computer is being used to ask the student questions, to give him tasks to complete, to invite him to ask it questions, or to assist him in sorting out some fairly well-defined situation. The mistakes made by the learner are then likely to be predictable for the most part, in which case the computer can be programmed to offer help. A mistake made by the learner in the way he is instructing the computer is not really a mistake in his *learning* at all, and the computer should definitely provide him with sufficient guidance – reminding him which keys he can press, for example – to prevent him being confused for long. And where the learner makes mistakes in his understanding of the topic, these mistakes can enable the computer to offer help, to remind him what sort of response would be appropriate, and so on.

On the other hand, the use of the computer may be to a much greater extent under the control of the learner. Perhaps he is programming the computer; perhaps he is using a program which leaves most of the choices with him and so forces him to plan in advance the way in which he uses it. In either case, the learner's mistakes result in an outcome which he was not expecting. By comparing this with the outcome he *was* expecting, he can locate his mistakes, correct them and profit from the experience. Thus the learner can learn to treat his mistakes not as a source of discouragement or self-judgement, but as an opportunity to learn further. Mistakes should not destroy the learner's confidence in himself, they should increase it.

2.4 Evaluating learning

We look now at the question of what is being learnt. Are the right things being learnt? Is anything being learnt? Do we know what things 'should' be learnt? We ask:
- what are the objectives of learning?
- what is the relationship between 'teaching' and 'testing'?
- how can we evaluate learning?

Objectives of learning

When you are deciding what teaching strategy to use to help your students to learn, you will naturally seek to understand what you are trying to achieve. Here are some possible objectives.
* To keep your students quiet.
* To get your students to complete Exercise 3 on page 34.
* To ensure that your students have memorized the names of the first 20 elements in the periodic table.
* To develop your students' skill in identifying wild flowers.
* To increase your students' understanding of the process of industrialization.
* To foster in your students an enjoyment of English literature.
* To help your students to concentrate.
* To teach your students what it is like to be absorbed in some piece of learning.
* To teach your students how to accept having their ideas criticized.
* To help your students to gain confidence in themselves and in you.
* To help your students to become independent of you in their learning.

These objectives are of different kinds and operate at different levels. Roughly speaking, we feel that the nearer the objective to the top of the list above, the more likely is it to have been considered by a busy teacher while formulating his objectives for teaching. Nevertheless, many teachers would want to give high value to those lower down the list.

When designing a computer program to help students learn, it is vital that you are as clear as you can be about *all* of your objectives. It is relatively easy to decide upon the *content* of the program – what information is to be included, and so on. It may not be too difficult to decide upon the *sequence* of presentation – how much to put on the screen at any one time, and so on. As you get used to it, you will find it increasingly easy to design programs which are simple to use – programs which give clear messages, trap mistakes and provide help where appropriate: we hope that this book gives you some assistance with this.

But perhaps the most difficult and the most important thing is to design a *context* which feels right for the user. Are you aware of the assumptions you are making about the student? Are you communicating these assumptions through the style of the program? Will the program leave the learner feeling more confident, more interested in the subject under study, more able to relate to you as his teacher? Just as these considerations distinguish good teaching from merely adequate teaching, so they distinguish the good teaching program from the merely working program.

Testing

In some situations, testing is natural. If you learn woodwork or car maintenance, the tests of your learning are whether you can make the record cabinet or carry out the 3000-mile service, and whether other people admire the cabinet and you feel safe driving your car.

In other situations, testing is less natural. If you learn about urban geography or the arithmetic of your everyday life, testing may often miss the point. The tests may be of your ability to remember facts or to perform low-level skills; understanding, higher-level skills, confidence and attitudes may be more important. Such less tangible yet more significant aspects of learning are tested automatically in the more natural testing situations.

Computers lend themselves to the testing of students. Most obviously they can be used to test low-level abilities in less natural contexts, but with ingenuity they can also test the intangibles like understanding or the ability to apply principles. Where it is appropriate to test students, computers can often provide a convenient way of doing so.

Testing is not the same as teaching. A program which tests whether a student knows some factual information is not a program which *teaches* that information. If a computer asks a student to complete some subtractions and then tells him how many he completed correctly, it may be valuable for testing the student, but it is teaching him nothing – any more than is a teacher who does the same thing.

Learning evaluated?

How will you evaluate what you have learnt from this book? Your evaluation will be subjective. You may try to *describe* exactly what you have learnt; you could even try to *prove* that you have learnt it. Your evaluation will probably consist in a gut feeling about whether or not the book was useful and why. Your conviction will be diminished not at all for being subjective.

In the same way, the most important guide you will have to the effectiveness of the computer in your teaching is your own instinctive feeling about it. However useful it may be to state and evaluate our objectives as teachers, to consider what factors help teachers to teach and learners to learn, in the end we are probably guided by one consideration only – whether we feel it worked.

3 Programs

A computer **program** may be defined as *a sequence of separate instructions, written in a programming language, which together may be used as and when required to do what is required – clearly, completely and consistently*. A program may be considered good or bad, successful or unsuccessful, in proportion to the degree to which it meets this ideal.

Programs are available ready-written from a number of sources (discussed later in the chapter), and it is by no means necessary for you to do your own programming. But you will gain in your understanding and your enjoyment of computing if you *do* write some programs. This book by itself will not teach you to program: there are many texts on the subject already, usually written with a particular programming language in mind. What we want to do is to provide you with a 'buyer's guide' to programs: to teach you how to look at and assess a program. This chapter talks about the contents of computer programs and about aspects of their design, to demonstrate what sort of things are possible. We hope that this will help you to discriminate between the programs which you see, to help you recognize their strengths and weaknesses, and to provoke ideas for programs of your own. We discuss:
- *the definition of a program;*
- *the specification of a new program;*
- *ways of acquiring programs;*
- *aspects of using a program on a range of microcomputers;*
- *what to look for when assessing programs;*
- *observations made about one illustrative program.*

3.1 Background to programming

The definition given above of a computer program is by no means exhaustive, but it forms a useful basis for discussion. Below, we look at aspects of the definition, illustrating some of these with fragments of program code taken from a program called AUGURY which is discussed fully at the end of the chapter. The aspects dealt with in this section are:
- *a program as a set of instructions;*
- *a program as a sequence of instructions;*
- *the use of programming languages;*

○ clarity in working (for designer, programmer and user alike);
○ completeness in working;
○ consistency in working;
○ the availability of programs when required.

A *program contains instructions*

Instructions in a program tell the computer to do the various things it is capable of doing – which consist fundamentally in adding, subtracting, comparing and shunting data from place to place in computer memory (core) – so as to do what we want done. The manufacturer has provided these **machine operations**, and they are invoked by **machine instructions** which together constitute a **low-level language**.

Instructions to the machine can be difficult to understand, as you can see from this piece of code:

```
            LD HL, ADDRSTR
GETCHAR:    EMT KBDW
            LD (HL), A
            INC HL
            CP 13
            JP NZ, GETCHAR
```

This piece of code is actually asking a person sitting at the keyboard of a micro for a piece of data. To make their thinking simpler and clearer, programmers often use **high-level languages**, in which one instruction automatically generates many low-level instructions. In BASIC, which is a high-level language, the entire piece of code above could be represented by the single, more comprehensible instruction:

```
1790    INPUT R$
```

A *program should be in sequence*

It is not sufficient that we give the computer instructions, we must give them so that they are executed in the correct order. At its simplest, this means writing a list of instructions which is obeyed strictly in order, top to bottom, each instruction once and once only. But this way we would need a lot of instructions, and some of them would be repeated, so one improvement is to be able to **loop** – to specify that a selected group of instructions be executed a chosen number of times, or until some condition is fulfilled.

Here is an example of a loop:

```
7000    FOR A = 1 TO 15
7010        PRINT "*";
7020    NEXT A
```

Background to programming 31

In this piece of code, line 7010 is an instruction to print an asterisk. It is sandwiched between two statements which act as brackets round the loop: the first says that the loop is to be executed 15 times, the second marks the end of the loop.

We may even want to loop (or **iterate**) round some of the instructions which are part of an existing loop, creating a loop within a loop, or a loop within a loop within a loop (a phenomenon known as **nesting**). And we may want to skip over a bunch of instructions – every time we come to them (which is an **unconditional jump**) ...

```
2630      GOTO 2750
```

... or only sometimes (which is a **conditional jump**): in this case we shall get the computer to take a **decision**:

```
2830      IF C$ = "N" THEN 3360
```

The normal thrust of a program's execution is one instruction after another, in a strictly linear fashion: each of the techniques above effects a **transfer of control** to a part of the program other than the next instruction in the sequence.

A program is written in a programming language

We feel that a serious comparison of programming languages is beyond the scope of this book. They are all designed for the same reason: to make the job of a programmer simpler. Different languages are intended for different categories of people. Some languages are expected to help mathematicians: these are precise in numerical work. Some are for business use: these are good at dealing with character data ('string-handling') and require consistent programming practices (or, one might argue, impose bureaucratic restrictions) because this enables several people to work on programs together. Other languages are designed to assist with **information retrieval**: these make it easy to ask questions, to search through banks of data (**databases**) quickly and methodically, and might be used, for example, by public libraries and by airline reservation systems. But all languages are capable of the same basic operations, and if one has a grasp of these essentials, learning a new language is largely a matter of discovering how each of these basic operations is accomplished.

As an illustration of this last point, here are three versions of the same program: the program asks the user for ten numbers and finds their total. The first piece of code is written in the programming language called BASIC, the second in FORTRAN, the third in PASCAL.

32 Programs

```
230     LET T = 0
240     FOR C = 1 TO 10
250        PRINT "ENTER A NUMBER"
260        INPUT N
270        LET T = T + N
280     NEXT C
290     PRINT "THE TOTAL IS"; T
```

```
        TOTAL = 0
        DO 110 COUNT = 1,10
           WRITE (6,*) "ENTER A NUMBER"
           READ (5,*) NUMBER
           TOTAL = TOTAL + NUMBER
110     CONTINUE
        WRITE (6,*) "THE TOTAL IS ", TOTAL
```

```
TOTAL := 0;
FOR COUNT := 1 TO 10 DO
   BEGIN
      WRITELN ('ENTER A NUMBER');
      READLN (NUMBER);
      TOTAL := TOTAL + NUMBER
   END;
WRITELN ('THE TOTAL IS ', TOTAL);
```

Code is a generic term: it is used of anything written in any programming language – including low-level languages – be it a lot of programs, a single program, a piece of program or an individual instruction.

One thing that makes languages seem different is the way in which code is laid out. In some languages, no more than one instruction may be put on a line, and each line must contain an instruction. In others, several instructions may be put on a line (separated in some recognizable manner), and some lines may be left blank, as blank space is left between some paragraphs in this book. Some languages permit the user to indent lines of code; others require each line to begin in the same column. One language (BASIC) needs a number at the front of each line (the **line number**) and makes use of these numbers to keep the program in order and to cross-refer between lines.

All languages permit the programmer to interleave **comments** or **narrative** with the code, to explain to others (and to remind himself) what each bit of the code does, and how the complicated bits work. Such narrative, denoted by words like 'COMMENT', 'REMARK' or 'REM', are not part of the working instructions, and are therefore ignored by the translator (the program which turns high-level instructions into low-level instructions).

In the piece of code below:

```
1130 REM     Deal with user's interruption
1140 REM
1150     TEXT : PRINT CHR$(12) : REM Clear the screen
1160     PRINT CHR$(17) : REM Disable paging
```

the only instructions that are actually translated are:

```
1150     TEXT : PRINT CHR$(12)
1160     PRINT CHR$(17)
```

All languages have rules to govern the way in which instructions or **statements** may be written: the language **syntax**. And all languages use particular words to mean particular things (not the same words in each language, unfortunately!). These **reserved words** may not be used by the programmer for any other reason.

A program should work clearly

This has two facets: its workings must be clear to a user and they must be clear to a programmer.

At any stage of acquiring, preparing to use, using, or examining the results of a program, the user should understand what is going on. He should know what are the facilities of the program, and what are its limitations. This is achieved by documentation. **External documentation** comprises the written material accompanying any program, which explains how to implement it on the computer, gives a statement of the programmer's intentions, supplies examples of its use, and so on. **Internal documentation**, so far as the *user* is concerned, consists in the way in which output from the computer is displayed.

There are basically two kinds of informative output. One sort presents the *results* of the program's execution: like any report about anything, these results should be carefully laid out and should be intelligible to the reader. Ideally, they should be intelligible in themselves, without any further explanation and without the reader needing to have run the program himself. (The person who reads the results is not always the one who operates the computer!) The other sort of output exists when the program is interactive: here the user is continually being asked questions, or invited to supply data, or to select from a list of options (a **menu**). It must be clear to him at all times what he is being asked for.

Both of these sorts of internal documentation are provided by means of whatever instructions in the particular programming language in use deal specifically with output and with its format (instructions like 'PRINT' and

34 *Programs*

Ideally, the results should be intelligible in themselves.

'WRITE', perhaps with tabulation facilities.
    Thus these instructions

```
3010      PRINT "Understood. Parameter values are now"
3020      PRINT
3030      PRINT "PARAMETER"; TAB(22); "NOW"; TAB(31); "TO ALTER"
3040      PRINT " Number of people"; TAB(22); P; TAB(31); "P"
3050      PRINT "   Mode of travel"; TAB(23); M$; TAB(31); "M"
3060      PRINT " Driving livestock"; TAB(23); L$; TAB(31); "L"
3070      PRINT "      Ground state"; TAB(23); G$; TAB(31); "G"
```

produce output such as

```
Understood. Parameter values are now

PARAMETER              NOW TO ALTER
  Number of people      10      P
  Mode of travel         R      M
  Driving livestock      Y      L
  Ground state           W      G
```

These are ways of making the workings clear to the user. But programs must also be clear to *programmers*: to those who write them in the first place and to those who might have to alter them later. The programmer has available to him all the documentation that the user has, and he has extra. He has, for example, a **listing** of the program; the actual sequence of instructions. These may be explained (as noted above) by the use of narrative. Internal documentation can be improved in other ways also. For one thing, the program can be split into sections or **modules**, each of which is relatively self-contained, and which is given a **name** or **identifier**, chosen to reflect its purpose. There are many opportunities to make a program modular, and by isolating pieces of code which deal exclusively with a particular **function** or **procedure**, one makes the overall program easier to test. These isolated pieces of program, often referred to as

subroutines, are used by the **main routine** when required. Modules can be separated by blank lines, so as to highlight the structure of the program.

Data within a program is either **constant** or **variable**. Both sorts are stored in the computer memory (the core) when the program is running, and the program needs to know the **address** in core of each piece of data. High-level languages allow the programmer to give each piece of data a name or identifier. The computer remembers which name corresponds to which address, so the *programmer* need know nothing about the way in which the core is organized.

Identifiers also facilitate internal documentation and should always be chosen to fit the data – for example, a program to convert temperatures might have variables called 'CELSIUS' (or simply 'C') and 'FAHRENHEIT' (or 'F'). A lot of programs use **counts**, which are increased (**incremented**) or decreased (**decremented**) in steps.

Programmers may have external documentation as well. This will usually include a diagram of the way the program operates, the links between the modules, the places where decisions are taken and what are the possible routes in each case: such diagrams chart the flow of control in the program, and are therefore called **flowcharts**. Other external documentation might include a list of the names of identifiers in the program, and notes on what each does; advice on how to test the program; perhaps some sample test data. Examples of these are given in section 3.6 and in Chapters 7 and 8.

A program should work completely

This remark is susceptible to several interpretations – and all are true of a good program! It fulfils the objects of the programmer (or the person who requested it). And all parts of the program work. And finally all parts of the program are actually necessary and are used – it is easy so to construct a program that some instructions are never executed!

A program should work consistently

Whatever you do with it, whatever data you supply to it, whoever uses it, whatever the extraneous circumstances, the workings of the program should be predictable and reproducible. Later in the chapter we give you some ideas on how to check programs to make sure that this is the case.

A program may be used when required

An important aspect of computing is that you develop or acquire programs and keep them ready for the time when you actually need to use them. It is exactly analogous to creating a library: you build your stock as you have time and as you can afford. It is possible to store not only complete programs (in a **program library**) but also fragments of programs, usually complete modules of the sort described above (**library routines**). General-purpose routines can be accumulated gradually, each being tried and tested as it arrives. They can then be incorporated into other programs as required, which saves some of the work of programming, and means that only the new part need be tested and documented.

3.2 Specifying a program

The previous section ignored completely one bit of the definition of a computer program given on page 29: 'a program ... can be used as and when required to do what is required'. 'What is required' is dictated by:
- what you want it to do;
- how the user will use it;
- the response to the user's mistakes;
- helping the user to do what he wants to do;
- your views about the nature of program code;
- what you need other than the program.

What do you want it to do?

Often, the answer to this seems so obvious that the question is never asked. It is as well to check at the outset what you really do want, and to keep checking this at every stage of the design and while using the program. If you are selecting from existing software, you will be unable to influence its design; but the questions posed below should still assist you in deciding whether or not a particular program on offer serves your particular need.

Can you write down your requirements? Is the resulting specification complete? Does it, perhaps, include items which are not the province of the program itself but rather of the situation in which it is to be used? Suppose for instance that you wish to monitor the change in temperature during a chemical reaction. The computer is to be used to plot these temperatures against the time from the start of the reaction, the results being displayed on a screen. Is the *computer* also to measure the temperatures, or will the *user* make these measurements and type the readings at a keyboard, with the time at which each is taken? Are the measurements to be taken at equal intervals or more frequently when the reaction is going fast? Is the *computer* to be used to time these intervals? Can you think of other closely-related aspects of the same subject, which although not part of the problem as you originally envisaged it, might profitably be dealt with in the same program?

It is wise to go through the procedure of asking these questions several times and without referring to the earlier answers. You will gradually appreciate what it is that you really do want your program to do.

Are you to be the only one making use of the program? What about your colleagues: will they use it? Or your counterparts in other institutions? This is of particular importance if you yourself are writing the code, since you are more likely to be interested in offering it (for money!) to others.

For how long do you think this program will be useful to you? And to others? Will your requirements remain the same throughout this period, or will they change? Do you expect to revise it, say annually? Have you allowed for development, for modification in the light of experience?

Repeated examination of questions such as these will probably push you in one of two directions, since it will oblige you to raise fundamental issues about the aims and nature of your teaching – issues like: what are you really trying to teach? why are you trying to teach it? is the computer conferring any real advantage? why use a computer at all? So you may end up either with a very clear and complete idea of the purpose and uses of the program (and that's what you were seeking), or you may be left feeling totally muddled about the whole thing. Maybe the latter attitude is the more productive in the long run!

How does the user use it?

The term 'user', when applied to programs, can include simultaneously several people with quite separate – even conflicting – objectives. In the case of an airline reservation system, for example, the users are the people who wish to travel (who want accurate information quickly), the airline itself (who can fill flights more effectively and so save money, which ought to make seats cheaper), and travel agents.

With programs intended specifically for teaching, 'the user' may be the teacher, a learner or a group of learners. It is the effectiveness of the computer in improving the teaching available that measures the program's worth.

No book could provide a definition of the way in which any user uses any and every conceivable program. Below, however, is a list of some questions which might be asked about programs for teaching. (There is no implication of order of importance.)

* Is the computer's role clear to the user?
* Is the aim of the program clear to you? Is the program a good way to achieve this aim?
* What does the learner bring to the learning process – what skills, what knowledge? Does the program recognize, does it value, these?
* Does the program *involve* the learner?
* Is the program interactive? If so, what contribution does this make to learning?
* Does the program use pictures? If so, do these help to achieve its aims, do they embellish it, do they serve no purpose at all, or do they interfere with learning?
* How long does it take to run the program?
* Who uses it? The teacher? A learner? A group of learners?

* Is any knowledge required of the way in which computers work?
* Can the user affect the speed of operation of the program? Can short-cuts be taken as required?
* Is the learner expected to record anything while the program is running? If so, how?
* What does the program do for you? Does it make you think – about the subject being taught, about the manner in which you are teaching it, about the underlying principles? Does it enable you to do what would otherwise prove more difficult?
* Why use a computer at all?

What happens when the user makes a mistake?

Two points must be made at the outset. First, we are considering programs designed to be used in some sort of teaching context, so it is part of the definition of their suitability or otherwise that *they are intended to help the user*. The user alone is the barometer of a program's success.

Second, what do we mean when we say that the user has 'made a mistake'? Do we mean rather that he has typed something which the computer had not been led to expect? If we do, then the onus is again on the programmer: to make sure that the user knows what he *should* type and to make sure that the computer is prepared for him *not* to type it! Words like 'mistake' and 'error' are convenient when discussing interaction between user and computer, but it is important to remember that the computer is there to serve its users – not the other way round.

Let us consider the specification of one program, from the point of view of the user. We start with a clean sheet: we can do anything we choose: what will help the user? Our sole requirement is that the user is to supply interactively information which will be used by the program: the way in which we satisfy that requirement is at our discretion.

It is simpler to think about this in the context of a practical example, so here is the scenario for a simple program. The place is the village of Slalewic ('muddy dwelling') in Northumbria, records of which have since been unaccountably lost. The year is AD 934. Slalewic, a small village of not more than 50 inhabitants, is very nearly self-sufficient. From time to time, however, it is necessary for some of the villagers to journey to Hahlwud ('corner of a wood') to fetch special goods and to sell their own surplus produce. Hahlwud is fully 12 miles away, a great distance, and there are two routes to it: one is only 15 miles long, but passes through dense woods where ambush is likely; the other is 20 miles long and entails a climb to the top of the scarp where, as it is less densely wooded, the trip is safer.

The villagers have been making this journey regularly for the past four generations, and have derived from their accumulated experience a set of guidelines for those contemplating the trip. These have to do with how many people are going, whether they are riding horses or walking, whether they are driving livestock, and which season it is. The rules give two sorts of information to those wise enough to consult them: they suggest whether or not the journey can be made (by one or other route) in safety, and if made, how long it may be expected to take. For example, a person on horseback who is not driving stock can travel quickly but may not go the short way; six or more people are necessary for the short route to be safe on foot, and at least ten if stock are to be taken this way.

To evaluate all of this takes an hour or so of thought each time, and sometimes a look at some entrails – or at least it did, until the villagers bartered some spare turnips for a microcomputer. They are typical computer users: they just want the answers, they couldn't give a fig how these are arrived at – provided that they are right! And if the machine isn't nice to them, they attack it with double-headed axes (not the sort you draw on graphs). They bought the micro from an itinerant computer salesman, and have detained him until their program, AUGURY, has been proved satisfactory. He is eager to put a lot of careful thought into the way in which he gets data from the villagers.

He doesn't ask questions needlessly. For example, the route taken depends on the number of people travelling, because the short route is through a wood, and is safe only when there are enough people to defend themselves against attack. But if more than twelve go, the village will be undefended, so the journey is inadvisable. It would be easiest, from the programmer's point of view, to ask for all details of the trip and then find the augury; but in fact if the number travelling is more than twelve, there is no point is asking any further questions.

When he *does* ask questions, he tries to keep them short but unambiguous. To the programmer, even to someone familiar with other programs, the purpose of a particular question may appear patently obvious. But to the user it may come as a complete surprise; even worse, he may think that he is being asked one question which seems clear to him when in fact he is being asked something quite different.

And even when the user understands the question, in what form is the answer to be given? Take our example: some of the Slalewic villagers will use the program repeatedly; they will end up knowing more about it than does the programmer. Others will approach it for the first time, timidly, in fear and wonder (and carrying some weapon); for these, instructions must be provided at the beginning of the program. Yet the regular users will become impatient if they have to sit through all that nonsense each time. So it will be helpful if the first question is:

```
Do you require instructions?
```

You do: you've never run the program before. How do you reply? Do you type 'YES'? Or 'Y'? Or 'INSTRUCTIONS'? Or 'I'? Or something quite unrelated – as far as you are concerned – something which is simpler for the programmer to deal with, such as '1' or '–999'? The timorous user will sit for perhaps ten minutes, unresolved in his dilemma, terrified by what may happen if he types the wrong thing. How much better it would be if the programmer (who knows what he wants) told the user what to type:

```
Do you require instructions ('Y' or 'N')?
```

The user is now more likely to get the answer 'right' – that is, to provide what is wanted – first time. This is encouraging for him.

There is still the possibility (virtual certainty) that the user will hit the wrong key even if trying to give the 'right' answer – hence the need for **error-trapping**. A mistake has been defined as the typing of something that the computer has not been prepared to expect. If the programmer has failed to anticipate such a mistyping, the user may see something like this:

```
Do you require instructions (Type '1' for 'YES', '0' for 'NO')? o
ILLEGAL DATA, RETYPE INPUT AT 655
?
```

This is perhaps the worst case: an error (the letter 'o' instead of the figure '0') has not been trapped by the user's program but by the interpreter (the program which converts data into the form needed internally). The message is not helpful to the user, unless he is himself a programmer: *he* doesn't know why the data is 'illegal' (in fact, because the program wanted numeric data but was given character data), nor does the figure '655' have any significance for him (it is the line number of the statement in the BASIC program which sought this piece of data). The programmer should foresee all of this and examine the character(s) actually typed.

```
Do you require instructions (Type '1' for 'YES', '0' for 'NO')? o
INCORRECT RESPONSE
?
```

This is an improvement, but not a substantial one. What action should the user now take? It would be better to return the user to the same question, and to make his answer to it more natural to him.

```
Do you require instructions ('Y' or 'N')? m
INCORRECT RESPONSE
Do you require instructions ('Y' or 'N')?
```

The next improvements are to encourage the user to continue despite his recent 'failure', and to remove the moral judgement from the message – 'm' is not so much 'incorrect' as 'unacceptable' given the way in which the program has been written.

```
Do you require instructions ('Y' or 'N')? m
SORRY, 'M' IS NOT UNDERSTOOD - TRY AGAIN
Do you require instructions ('Y' or 'N')?
```

This kind of dialogue is just as feasible for the computer as the unhelpful sort; yet it is surely more comfortable for the user. Why then is it not more common in marketed software? Until it becomes a habit, it takes a lot of thought on the part of the programmer, and some are lazy in this respect. An argument against this kind of error-trapping is that the space inside the computer – the core size – is limited; and all these extra checks and messages, attractive though they may be, take up valuable space. This argument is valid: space can be a real problem. But if the program is aimed at novice users (such as the general public), adequate error-trapping is essential – there is often some other part of the program which can be trimmed to create space. (In section 7.3 we give alternative ways of condensing one sample piece of code.)

If the user is supplying a sequence of related information and he keeps making mistakes, a problem can arise. The program, let us assume, contributes explanatory messages, spurs him on and reiterates the question: it takes several lines of text to do so. To accommodate new lines of text on the screen, existing lines must be moved, and this is usually achieved by **scrolling** the lines upwards (so that as a new line appears at the bottom, an existing one disappears at the top). The user may therefore lose track of the question sequence, as the previous bit is lost from view.

One solution to this is a facility offered by some microcomputers whereby the keys on the keyboard may be deadened selectively and reversibly. If the answer required is to be 'Y' or 'N', for instance, all keys other than these may be 'switched off' for the duration of this question, so that the user is simply *unable* to type the 'wrong' answer – nothing will happen if he does! The same or different keys may be made available to him for the next question.

If it is accepted that the program should interact with the user, should comment on what he types, reassure him and keep continual contact with him, then this technique is a compromise, and should be used either to retain a lot of material on the screen or to minimize the code size by eliminating error messages and simplifying error-checking.

Answers to questions are not always 'Y' or 'N'; indeed there may be a range of permissible answers. But the same principles apply: the user should know what he is being asked, and what sort of answer he can give. Below is a sample of dialogue between a Slalewic villager and his micro, chosen to illustrate these points.

```
JOURNEY TO HAHLWUD : AN AUGURY
-------------------------------

Do you want instructions ('Y' or 'N')? n

Please answer the following questions
  about your journey

   How many people are travelling
      ('1'..'12')? 15
        * Too many! The village will be
          undefended. Try again

   How many people are travelling
      ('1'..'12')? 10

   Are you riding or walking
      ('R' or 'W')? riding
        * Sorry, 'riding' is not understood.
          Try again

   Are you riding or walking
      ('R' or 'W')? r

   Are you driving livestock
      ('Y' or 'N')? y

   Is the ground wet or dry
      ('W' or 'D')? w

Thankyou

You may safely travel by the short route

Your journey should not take more
  than 4 days
```

Keeping the user's options open

Suppose that you are a stonemason. Your next-door neighbour arrived home last night somewhat the worse for wear, and had a slight *contretemps* with his gatepost, during which the left-hand stone eagle was fragmented. You now have before you the right-hand eagle for reference and a new block of stone, from which you are to create a new eagle. Here are your instructions.

Task 1: reduce the block to roughly the right shape and size: for this you use one set of tools – saws, large chisels, and so on. Task 2: work more carefully with smaller chisels, until the outlines of the two eagles resemble one another. Task 3: refine, using calipers, rules and the like to check your accuracy. Task 4: finish the detail, with very fine chisels, scribers and files. Task 5: brush it all down, check your work, and put the eagles on the gateposts – not forgetting to send your neighbour the bill.

To review: you start with a predefined objective; you carry out the first step with one limited range of tools; you carry out the second step with a second set of tools, the third step with a third set, and so on. An allegory, of course – an allegory for one type of interactive program, the type which operates in **tutorial mode**. Its premises are that the objectives of running the program are defined and known in advance by the programmer, and that he also knows which tools you require at which stage. So as a user you are asked at each stage for data, instructions, but only of a limited kind. The question you are asked now depends on the answer you gave to the last one, and the question you will be asked next depends on your answer to this one.

Tutorial mode has advantages to the user in that it both defines and circumscribes his choice of action at any given moment: true, it presents difficulties to the programmer, who has to provide questions for all circumstances allowable and keep track of what has happened, but the *user* is led by the nose through this labyrinth, and need not be aware of the complexity of the underlying program.

The principle behind tutorial mode is that the purpose of running the program is known in advance, and its structure can therefore be tailored to this end. But there is an alternative approach, known as **command mode**: *its* thesis is that the purpose of the program is *not* known in advance, only the general area in which it operates: all aspects of it must be left under the control of the user (commensurate with his ability to handle the choice), and he must be aware of this. To return to the allegory, we are providing tools for a stonemason, not saying what he is to do with them: our job is to tell him that he has a saw, a coarse chisel, a fine chisel, a scriber and so on, to make sure that each works properly, and to leave the rest to him. We do not make statements like 'you are using them in the wrong order' or 'that's not what it's for'. This approach is said to give the mason **user authority**. It tends also to encourage better programming, since the programmer does not have to keep track in the same way of what has happened; rather, he provides a set of program **modules** (called 'CHISEL', 'SAW', 'BRUSH' and so on) which operate independently. Programs often use both modes – command mode to establish a kind of activity, perhaps, tutorial mode to specify how that activity is to be conducted; command mode to pick a chisel from the range of tools, tutorial mode to say that it is wide rather than narrow. (Examples of command mode are given in sections 7.7, 8.3 and 8.5.)

When working in tutorial mode, it is easy to create a set of parameters which are so interdependent that to alter one the user must restate them all. This is usually due to bad planning by the programmer: if the parameters *are* interdependent, it may be possible to calculate one from the value of another, without the user supplying both. If they are separate, they can be restated separately. One of the great advantages of a computer's gift for fast calculation is that the user can be allowed – even encouraged! – to try things out. The continuity of this is lost if he has repeatedly to retype the same data.

Sometimes, of course, restatement is unavoidable. But the program can at least warn of the implications of a particular course of action. We pay another call on the Slalewic villagers.

44 Programs

```
AUGURY NUMBER 2

Do you wish to alter all parameters or
   just one ('A' or 'J')? J

Understood. You may change number of
   people ('P'), mode of travel ('M'),
   driving livestock ('L'), ground
   state ('G') or none ('N')? g

   Is the ground wet or dry
      ('W' or 'D')? w

Thankyou

You may safely travel by the long route

Your journey should not take more
   than 2 days
```

When this version was tried out on the villagers, it was quickly pointed out that there are only two options to 'ground state' (and indeed to 'mode of travel' and 'driving livestock'). Since the question is phrased 'you may change', there is no need to ask the user for the new state – it is the converse of the current one.

```
Understood. You may change number of
   people ('P'), mode of travel ('M'),
   driving livestock ('L'), ground
   state ('G') or none ('N')? g

   Understood. The ground is wet.

Thankyou

You may safely travel by the long route

Your journey should not take more
   than 2 days
```

As it stands, the program permits the user to alter only one parameter before giving the new augury, but it would be easy to permit as many changes as he wished, simply by looping back to the choice until he typed 'N' for 'none'. Changes can be effected in some cases without asking for the new value, as shown above; but the user needs to know what the current setting is. So it is helpful if the parameters are displayed to the user, perhaps as a table. Where the text is scrolled off the top of the screen, such a table must be printed afresh each time: this can be useful when coupled with a printer, since the results of adopting certain parameters may be linked with those parameters on the printed output.

Specifying a program 45

```
AUGURY NUMBER 4

Do you wish to alter all parameters or
   just one ('A' or 'J')? J

Understood. Parameter values are now

PARAMETER              NOW  TO ALTER
   Number of people     2      P
   Mode of travel       R      M
   Driving livestock    Y      L
   Ground state         W      G
```

In the discussion so far, it has been assumed that each word is printed to the right of the previous word, each line below the previous line, causing the scrolling of text off the screen. But most microcomputers give greater flexibility than this: low-resolution graphics – demonstrated in this connection in section 7.4 – permit the programmer to put characters at chosen points on the screen.

This gives an alternative to the method above: all questions can be posed and answered using the bottom part of the screen, and the table of parameters can be displayed continuously at the top – when the user changes a parameter, its value as shown is updated without rewriting any other part of the table.

This kind of table, which shows the user all options available to him at a given time, is an example of a **menu**. Some programs are controlled by this means exclusively, and are said to be **menu-driven**. Depending on what else the screen is being used for, it may be possible to leave the menu displayed continuously. (This is true of the AUGURY program, for instance, though the code provided for this in section 3.6 does not work in this way.) If it is not possible to leave the menu on the screen all the time, the speed at which it can be written is important. Some computers can completely fill the screen with information in a moment, but most build the display character by character, which may take several seconds. Menus which appear slowly can become very irksome to the user, especially if he is familiar with the program and already knows both the choice he is to be offered and the response which he wishes to give. Text in menus should therefore be kept to the minimum consistent with clarity.

(In the campaign to ease the user's passage through selection of a number of options without becoming irritated by the slowness of questions from the computer, there is a further sophisticated technique available to the programmer: he can allow the user to anticipate. The idea is that the user who is familiar with the program knows in advance that he will be asked certain questions in a certain order, and will have to supply appropriate data in answer to these. Thus it is possible for the computer to be programmed to allow the user to supply these answers, or some of them, *in anticipation* – the computer then works its way through the questions, without actually sending them as messages to the screen, and uses the user's data until this has been exhausted. At this point, it resumes asking questions. This powerful technique is potentially hazardous if the user misremembers the order of the questions!)

There are other ways in which the user may be assisted in the operation of the program, most of which will not be in the least apparent to him if properly implemented.

There are other ways in which the user may be assisted in the operation of the program, most of which will not be in the least apparent to him if properly implemented. One is the assiduous application of consistency by the programmer in all aspects of the program. All questions should be set out in the same form, for example, with the same use of capital or lower-case letters. They should perhaps all appear in the same part of the screen, with the same indentation. Where a range of permissible responses is shown, as advocated above, these should all take the same form: all single letters, maybe; all shown in alphabetical order, if appropriate. All error messages should be in the same style; and in a style differing from that employed (consistently) for the other messages. The user will not note this consciously, but will find questions progressively easier to understand and to answer, and so will grow in confidence. Indeed, the idea of consistency can be carried between several programs.

The foregoing discussion has made the tacit assumption that if the user is offered a choice, and provided that he is sure of both the question being asked and the form which his reply is to take, then he will be able to supply the required answer. This is not always the case! In some cases, the user will be dealing with information totally new to him, and he may be quite incapable of knowing what to do in a certain situation. He could be left to flounder, of course, but we are concerned with helping him to learn: we can assist him by telling him the answer.

At each point where there is a choice, the teacher can suggest which path will be the most easily followed by the unfamiliar traveller. This suggestion can be built into the program as a response 'in default' – the user is asked for a decision and told that 'don't know' is a legitimate reply: 'don't know' invokes the preset default response. In computing, **default** is used as a noun meaning 'that which happens if you don't instruct otherwise', and as an adjective – hence 'default value of a parameter'.

Defaults can be *implemented* in several ways, but how does the user indicate that he wishes to *invoke* the default? Perhaps the simplest way is to give no answer! Conversation between user and computer is conducted in the most polite fashion: each always signals to the other that he has finished speaking before the other starts the next bit. The user often signals by pressing a button on the keyboard marked 'RETURN' (for 'return control') – on such a system, 'don't know' could be indicated by pressing 'RETURN' without having said anything: this is called giving a **null response**. (Beware! On some systems, a null response stops the program!) Alternatively, 'don't know' could be signalled by another character or word chosen by the programmer and offered as one of the permissible answers to this question.

Defaults may greatly assist the user during a first run through the program; on second and subsequent uses he can vary one or more parameters and note the resultant changes in the output. But when he leaves it to the program to make decisions for him in this way, he should in each case be told by the program what decision has been made.

The computer hands over control to the user when it wants some data, and indicates this by a **prompt**, frequently a question mark. Thus in the AUGURY program, each request to the Slalewic villagers for information is terminated by a '?', an 'over-to-you' message.

The same program gave more help to the user, namely the use of upper-case letters to display what the computer said and lower-case letters to display what the user said: this simply makes it easier for the user to see at a glance who said what to whom, and what happened. (The programmer must consider whether the computer sees 'a' and 'A' as the same or as different letters. If the latter, the machine is said to be **case-sensitive**, and the programmer must ensure that responses from the user are understood either way.) The distinction in cases suggests another simple aid to the user, that of **echoing back** his input, but changing the case:

```
Are you riding or walking ('R' or 'W') ? r
R
```

This is trivial but reassuring to the user, who may doubt that the computer really takes any notice of what he says. The reassurance can be reinforced by *doing* something with the data there and then:

```
Are you riding or walking ('R' or 'W') ? r
Understood - you are riding
```

But this can become insufferable.

48   Programs

One final point about helping the user. Some people think that all programs for teaching should contain what are known as **help facilities**. Were this done, the user could type 'H' or 'HELP' at any point where he was asked something, and the program would offer assistance – sample answers, perhaps, or more information about what was going on at the time. This fine ideal is impractical in many contexts because it would make the program too big, too clumsy, or too slow. But as extra memory becomes cheaper, microcomputers will be able to afford the space in which to run programs at this level of sophistication.

Program code

Discussion so far has been about overall design of the program: what it is meant to do, the way in which it does it, how that is tailored to the user. But even with these features crystal clear in his mind, the programmer could still write the actual *code* in any one of several ways. This part of the section deals with a few aspects of the design of the code itself. This is *not* solely the province of the experienced programmer; there are many things which any thoughtful person can check for himself. Programming 'style' is probably the most contentious aspect of computing: opinions tend to be held intractably and argued vehemently.

Let's assume that you know nothing about programming. You do, however, have experience of assessing books on a given subject. What sorts of thing make you describe one book as 'good' and another as 'bad'?

* Content: can you see what the book is about? What topics does it cover? How can you tell? Are the topics related to each other, do they follow in sequence?
* Structure: is the book one long sentence? No: so it is divided – into paragraphs, pages, chapters. Are the ideas in the sections of comparable difficulty or importance? Do the sections in a given chapter have a common thread?
* How do you find your way around the book? By means of contents list and index? How much use is the book without these?
* Readability: an indefinable quality which a book either has (for you) or hasn't. It is a result of the way in which language is used, and determines how hard you, the reader, have to work to get information from the book.
* Layout: a book is attractive or not, according to your tastes, in terms of the use of indentation at the beginnings of paragraphs, of white space between sections, of titles which stand out, of lists clearly separated from the rest of the text, and so on.

So: you can assess a book. In deciding whether you like the design of this book, you probably use criteria like those listed above. And the same criteria apply also to program code, so you can assess that too. In Chapters 7 and 8 are several

Specifying a program

programs: we suggest that you flick through those and identify the sort of thing discussed above.

We introduced these ideas in the part entitled 'A program should work clearly', where we mentioned that you can write comments in your program to explain and annotate the code, and that you can split it into modules. As an example of this, we now tell you how to make grapefruit marmalade.

First we define a set of rules: the **algorithm**. Well, you need to buy the fruit and wash it; you need to cook it (we're going to use a pressure cooker); you need to throw away the pith and put in the rest of the ingredients; you need to finish off the cooking and put the marmalade into pots. Some programming languages (such as PASCAL, used below) make it easy to write the code the same way you think about the process: these are called **algorithmic languages**. You need to know that in PASCAL

   := means 'make equal to'
   * means 'multiplied by'
   / means 'divided by'
   (* ... *) encloses a comment

and then off you go.

```
PROCEDURE  preparefruit;
  BEGIN
    buy grapefruit * oneandahalfpounds;
    IF limesavailable
      THEN buy (2 * lemon + 1 * lime)
      ELSE buy (3 * lemon);
    washallfruit;
    allfruit := allfruit / knife (* cut in half *)
  END    (* preparefruit *);

PROCEDURE  cookfruit   (* requires a pressure cooker *);
  BEGIN
    pcooker := pcooker + allfruit;
    pcooker := pcooker + water * onepint;
    WHILE NOT (pressure = fifteenpounds) DO
      pcooker := pcooker + heat;
    FOR minutes := 1 TO 20 DO
      cook;
    pcooker := pcooker - heat;
    WHILE NOT (pressure = roompressure) DO
      letcoolslowly (* fast cooling will make marmalade froth *);
  END    (* cookfruit *);

PROCEDURE  mixingredients;
  BEGIN
    squeezefruit; discardpith;
    pcooker := pcooker + alljuicestrained + water * furtherhalfpint;
    pcooker := pcooker + granulatedsugar * threepounds;
    REPEAT
      rind := rind / knife
    UNTIL verysmallpieces;
    pcooker := pcooker + rind
  END    (* mixingredients *);
```

```
PROCEDURE  finishcooking;
   BEGIN
      REPEAT
         BEGIN
            fastboil;
            minutes := minutes + 5
         END
      UNTIL atsettingpoint
   END    (* finishcooking *);

PROCEDURE  filljars  (* requires 5-6 1lb jars *);
   BEGIN
      jars := clean + dry + warm;
      WHILE marmaladeleft DO
         BEGIN
            GET (jar);
            REPEAT
               jar := jar + marmalade
            UNTIL jarfull;
            jar := jar + waxeddisc + cover + datelabel
         END
   END    (* filljars *);
```

Each PROCEDURE is a separate module: it can be coded and tested separately. The main program then looks like this:

```
BEGIN  (* main program *)
   preparefruit;
   cookfruit;
   mixingredients;
   finishcooking;
   filljars;
END    (* main program *).
```

Of course, for a machine to be able to *make* grapefruit marmalade, it would need more instructions than this: our program is simply an example of the design and implementation of an algorithm. But it *is* possible to make programs that intelligible, at least at the overall level. And if it is possible for a program to follow exactly these principles, why is it that one finds programs that do not?

The reason is compromise: above we state ideals, but there are practicalities which conflict with them. Many programmers write bad code to start with, to assure themselves that the thing works, as it were, and they then go back at a later stage and tidy up the code. Sometimes they rewrite it completely, paying more attention this time to the design of the code; sometimes they just do a cosmetic job on what they have already; sometimes they go and do something more interesting. Good design is a habit of mind, nothing more; and better in the long run because it saves so much time in amending code, even while this is being developed. Programs which need to be completely rewritten were inadequately planned at the design stage.

Conflicts arise between the ideals of programming style and the practicalities of running a program. Top-quality code annotated throughout by lucid comments tends to be rather long, and so to take up too much space in the computer. 'Too much' should be defined: the size of the core memory is finite: some of it is required to house the operating system, some for a translator, some may be needed for the results from the program when it runs. The program itself must fit into what is left, and on microcomputers this may be insufficient.

So the programmer can be faced with the need to reduce the size of the program. What can he get rid of to save space?

The first thing to go is often the indentation: if you look back at the marmalade example, you will see that one reason it is so clear is that lines are indented in proportion to their level. But in most microcomputers, indentation is stored as actual blank characters which take up room in core: if we remove all the indentation, and reduce any group of blanks in the line to just one, there is a substantial saving. Consider one of the PROCEDUREs from the marmalade example:

```
PROCEDURE cookfruit (* requires a pressure cooker *);
BEGIN
pcooker := pcooker + allfruit;
pcooker := pcooker + water * onepint;
WHILE NOT (pressure = fifteenpounds) DO
pcooker := pcooker + heat;
FOR minutes := 1 TO 20 DO
cook;
pcooker := pcooker - heat;
WHILE NOT (pressure = roompressure) DO
letcoolslowly (* fast cooling will make marmalade froth *)
END    (* cookfruit *);
```

We think that this is relatively hideous, but it has saved space. Many microcomputers strip out any indentation which you may put in, quite automatically, not as a matter of choice, but as a 'feature' imposed by the manufacturer. We deplore their attitude; though some manufacturers are now considering alternatives. (For the RML 380Z microcomputer, we give you in Appendix A.2 a way round the automatic blank stripping.)

Narrative lines take up space, too, but are not necessary to the program (it is argued), so these too can go. Again, we have advocated choosing identifiers which match their use, thus 'pcooker' for 'pressure cooker'. But these are often the longer for being clearer, and we could use shorter ones – such as 'pc' for 'pressure cooker'. And then there is the question of how many statements you put on one line of code: you can always squeeze a few more together. It is doubtful whether this saves much space, except in the case of the BASIC programming language, which uses line numbers – for each line you excise, you save a line number's worth of storage. So let's have a final look at the space-saving marmalade program.

52 Programs

```
PROCEDURE prepfrt;
BEGIN
buy grapefrt*oneandhfpd;
IF limes THEN buy (2*lem+1*lime) ELSE buy (3*lem);
washfrt; allfrt := allfrt/knife
END;
PROCEDURE cookfrt;
BEGIN
pc := pc+allfrt; pc := pc+water*onepint;
WHILE NOT (press=fifteenlbs) DO pc := pc+heat;
FOR mins := 1 TO 20 DO cook; pc := pc-heat;
WHILE NOT (press=rmpress) DO cool
END;
PROCEDURE mix;
BEGIN
sqfrt; dispith; pc := pc+strnju+water*fhfpt;
pc := pc+gsug*threelbs;
REPEAT rind := rind/knife UNTIL small; pc := pc+rind
END;
PROCEDURE fincook;
BEGIN
REPEAT BEGIN fastboil; min := min+5 END UNTIL set
END;
PROCEDURE filljars;
BEGIN
jars := clean+dry+warm;
WHILE marmleft DO
BEGIN
GET (jar); REPEAT jar := jar+marm UNTIL jarfull;
jar := jar+wdisc+datelabel
END
END;
```

and the main program could look like this:

```
BEGIN prepfrt; cookfrt; mix; fincook; filljars END.
```

A magnificent saving, there, and plenty more could go yet: see what you can find. (Clue: 'a := b' can be rendered as 'a:=b'.) It is important to understand that these changes make no difference at all to the way in which the program operates, or indeed to what the *user* sees – only the programmer is affected.

This is not true of the more insidious practice of 'simplifying' error-checking. We have argued above in favour of careful, thorough checking of all data supplied by the user; we have argued that nothing should be allowed to cause the program to fail; we have suggested that the 'wrong' data be exploited for what it is and used in the error message, rather than simply be rejected. But that inevitably makes each data check more specific and so requires specialized code, and so makes the program longer than it could be. Error-trapping, with a little thought, can be turned into one module only and the same module invoked at any point where data is sought from the user.

Think carefully before employing 'shoehorning' techniques such as those described above. They all reduce the size of the code, but they also reduce its readability. Sooner or later, you or someone else is going to need to look at the code again – perhaps to correct flaws (**program maintenance**), perhaps to make improvements (**program enhancement**). And you or they are going to have to understand what you originally wrote, and the way you did things, and the 'clever' short-cuts you introduced. There are three sorts of code – working code (all corners cut), good code (code which works well and is easy to maintain), and code which you are happy to show to others! We give in section 7.3 an example of a piece of code in a full form and in two alternative condensed forms.

What else is required besides the program?

In order to use the program effectively, there will be other needs to be satisfied: needs of the program in its operation, needs of the learner, needs for extra (non-computer) equipment.

The program has to run on a computer. Therefore the computer available has to be adequate to the program which it is required to run. It must be able to support a translator (interpreter or compiler) for the appropriate programming language, and that translator must be suited to the particular version (**dialect**) of the language used. The core store of the computer must be big enough to accommodate the program while running. If the program makes special use of computer hardware other than the processor, this must be available also: typical examples are printers, disc drives and cassette players.

If more than one learner uses the program at a time, can they all see what is happening? Are large monitor screens available? Does the learner have adequate documentation, does he know what is going on, does he have to take notes (is there somewhere for him to write)? Should he have previous knowledge, technical or otherwise? Is he supposed to have come provided with data which he has collected? Is there help available to him before, during and after use?

Is the program being run in support of laboratory work? If so, is the equipment for *this* set up and working? Can the learner get at both sets, is it physically possible for one person to operate the whole lot?

3.3   Obtaining a program

There are two approaches to the accumulation of material goods: considered acquisition, in which the pros and cons are carefully weighed in advance, and impulse buying, in which items are collected because they 'might be useful sometime'. In view of the emphasis placed in the last section on program *design*, you will not be surprised to learn that we favour the 'considered acquisition' approach when building a program library.

Each piece of software which you get should be chosen in answer to a real need, and should be selected to satisfy criteria based on the job it is intended to do. Sources of programs fall neatly into two categories: there are programs written by you, and there are programs written by other people. And as when buying a car, if your requirements include the equivalent of electrically operated windows, headlight wipers, deep-pile carpets and overdrive, you may have difficulty finding the right vehicle and in paying for it if you do. You may also find that such a vehicle proceeds rather slowly or is too big to fit into your garage. So you may have to compromise and get the smaller, less luxurious model – unless, of course, you have the time and competence to build your own.

In this section, we look at:
- the merits and demerits of using other people's programs;
- the merits and demerits of using your own programs;
- the cost to you, in time and money.

Someone else's programs

Some software – **systems programs** – comes with your computer: software written by or for that manufacturer and that model. This is usually quite adequate to your need for an operating system, and may include utilities like text editors, language translators and file management routines. In due course, you will discover the limitations of each of these – after all, they are written for all purchasers in general, not for you in particular – but you are unlikely to be able to do much to alter them, though you could at least make suggestions to the manufacturer.

Other software – **applications programs** – will be acquired according to your needs. In this category are all the programs for specific teaching applications, collected from a variety of sources. Most of these are bought, but some may be offered free with something else you are buying – for example, you can find many programs listed in magazines and books. They may not cost money, but they might cost you in other ways, so you should subject them to the usual assessment. It is very easy to fall into the habit of collecting things just because they are free.

For the most part, you will have to go and look for the program which you want. If *you* want to do something, it is quite likely that someone, somewhere, has had the same idea and has written a program to do it. Locating this person may be difficult if neither of you knows of the other's existence. If you do find the program, it may be on the same theme, but written from so different an angle as to be useless to you. Or it may be perfect.

Various schemes have been devised to help with this problem: they consist in attempts to publicize the existence of programs. You may have access to three or four catalogues of software, the result of trying to centralize the information; and of course dozens are advertised (and some listed) in the computing magazines. Increasingly also there are local groups of like-minded individuals who work together to produce programs for their collective use (and these, as we have mentioned earlier, may actually be consistent in their layout and operation).

Some of the programs thus available are better than others. Sadly, only you can decide which are suited to your purposes. What we can do is to give you some advice on evaluating programs (which we do in section 3.5) and one general recommendation: try never to buy programs which you have not tried yourself – and note that we say 'tried', not 'seen demonstrated'. If you do not try it, you will know what *someone else* thinks it can do, not whether it will do the job that you want done in the way you want it done. And if you buy something that proves inadequate, and cannot adapt it – have the courage to throw it away!

Copyright of programs is discussed briefly in section 6.2. In essence, whatever one may try to do about copyrighting one's program, there is no way of securing either ideas or code against exploitation by others. So some of the software on offer is an adaptation of someone else's work. Be aware also of what you are getting for your money: are you getting any kind of guarantee?

The unsatisfactory conclusion to this is that you should check everything before you pay for it, and that you should build up a network of friends and colleagues who share the interest in computing, and make use of their experience. Be assured that your consumer skills will grow quickly!

Your own programs

The great thing about writing your own programs is that *you* know what you want, and *you* can ensure that the program does exactly that. So the questions to ask are: do you have the ability? Do you have the confidence? Do you have the time?

If you have at your disposal a computer and a few programs to run on it, you will very soon be saying things like 'I wonder if I could do this?' or 'I want to write a program' or 'Even I could do better than this'. So try it. You may find that you do not enjoy programming, you may not be good at it, but it will still enhance your understanding of what goes into someone else's program: you will be better able to assess other programs.

There are many books on programming, each intended to teach one particular language or a general approach to programming through the use of one particular language. There are also courses organized by colleges, schools and businesses, where tutorial help is given to the students. These make a good start to your programming, and may increase your confidence at this early stage. Thereafter, you can practise at your own speed – provided that you have access to a machine of some sort.

Confidence is important to any programmer, and especially to one whose programs are to be hammered by other users. 'Doing' is the only way to acquire it. Write small programs, get your friends to try them out and to comment on them. Be prepared to modify your ideas in the light of their criticisms, remember the things which they praise: as with any other kind of teaching, to see the problems, you must put yourself in the place of the learner.

As regards the choice of programming language, high-level languages include ALGOL, BASIC, COBOL, COMAL, FORTRAN, LISP, PASCAL, PILOT, PROLOG, SIMULA.... Unless you are interested only in tutorial teaching programs, in which case you should consider PILOT, we suggest that you start with either BASIC or PASCAL: both can teach you fundamental concepts of programming which you can then apply to the other languages as you have need or inclination. Although theorists argue various demerits, BASIC remains an excellent teaching and learning language because the syntax and the error messages are clear and specific; and it is almost universally available on micros. It is easy to write a trivial program in BASIC which you understand completely, and gradually to add other bits to it as you try out new constructions. BASIC is also better equipped to deal with strings of characters than most other languages, so it is good for processing text. PASCAL is good for a different reason: you have to supply several pieces of information at the start of even a trivial program, information which forces you to think clearly about what you are trying to do – an excellent habit to acquire.

One concept of programming that is fundamental to any language is the need to give clear structure to each program. A great deal can be achieved in this direction with any language, as for example by careful use of indentation and of blank lines between parts of the program. Some languages, however, take the idea further, and are known as **structured languages** for this reason. (PASCAL is one such.) A simple aspect of the structured approach is the naming of items in the program; early versions of languages restrict you to single letters, perhaps, whereas virtually all high-level languages nowadays allow you more scope – programs, subroutines and variables can all be referenced by names which help the programmer.

A more complicated aspect of structuring is the splitting of a program into **modules**: each module serves a distinct purpose, and may be used by the main program or by other modules. Modules can be written independently and tested independently.

Modules are not all at the same 'level'. For example, suppose there are five such modules in a program: A, B, C, D and E. They will not all call each other:

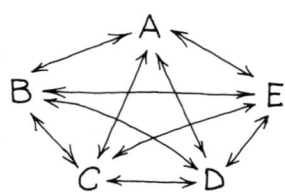

Instead, some modules will be subsidiary to others – rather as this book is divided into chapters, the chapters into sections and the sections into sub-sections. Thus the modules above might be used in this way:

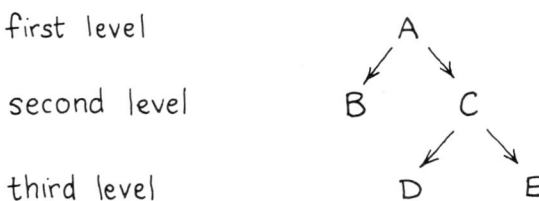

first level

second level

third level

In this structure, C may call D or E, and A may call B or C; but B cannot call C, D or E. The bits of code in A must be available to all modules 'beneath' it: these bits must be **global**. But bits of code in B need not be available outside B at all: they can be **local**. This **block structure** allows one part of a program to be isolated from the others, and so protected from accidental misuse.

(This facility for creating protected blocks is not available in BASIC, though with imagination you can achieve similar ends even in the restricted dialects of BASIC. The lack of block structuring is one of BASIC's principal demerits. But this may not remain so: already COMAL, which began as an extension of BASIC, is becoming widely available, and this offers many of the facilities of a structured language.)

Use may be made of **library** routines: modules of programs which can be kept in their own right and incorporated into other programs as required. In this case, as in the case of block-structured programs as described above, it is necessary for one module to be able to communicate with other modules; to exchange information. But there is a potential problem here. Information in one module is stored in variables with one set of names, yet the library routines must be written (quite independently) with another set of names. When using the routine, how does the program know where to look?

The answer is that although the names are not known, the number of items *is* known. These items are in each case – routine and program – listed after the name of the routine as **parameters** of that routine. Information is then passed between the appropriate paired variables not by name but by position in the list. For instance, a routine to find the largest and smallest items in a list of numbers might be written independently in terms of one set of variable names, and list these thus:

MAXANDMIN (NAMEOFLIST, MAXIMUM, MINIMUM)

and be called by the program in terms of *its* equivalent variable names, thus:

```
CALL MAXANDMIN (CLASSMARKS, HIGHEST, LOWEST)
```

The GRAPH program given in section 8.5 contains many examples of this technique.

A last point about languages. Different languages were developed for different reasons: some were carefully designed from the outset (as was PASCAL); others grew with use (as did FORTRAN). COBOL, designed originally for use on big computers ('mainframes') where space was not the primary consideration, is intended to make commercial programmers state all sorts of things explicitly which other languages might assume; it is necessarily long-winded. Languages available on micros are not always available on mainframes, and vice versa; even if the same language is available on both, it may not be available in the same form. Care must therefore be taken in choosing the most appropriate language. For your own purposes, use whichever language you have. We have recommended BASIC and PASCAL; if you have both, use the one that you prefer.

Finally, a word about time. Programming takes a long time. First you have to learn and practise the skills. Then you have to write the program you need. Then you must test it, trap probable and possible errors by the users, try it out on users, alter it, try it all again, alter it some more, and so on. And you must document it: write up what it does, how it does it, why it does it and for whom.

Can you afford it?

If it is someone else's program, can you afford the money? If it is your own program, can you afford the time?

Cost to you – or to your organization – in money is difficult to assess accurately. Superficially, it is obvious that some programs have a low price and others have apparently a much higher one. But *value* is also related to what the program does for you: how many opportunities it creates for you, how reliable it proves in the long run, how much teaching time it saves you, how many more students you can take on with it than without it. Like any other purchasable commodity, there are occasions when quality pays.

Cost to yourself in time is easier to assess. The demands which programming makes were mentioned above; the testing of programs is also time-consuming if pursued vigorously. Programming can be carried on at any time and anywhere: you can have ideas while washing up, shopping, getting shaved and so on: you can record them on the backs of envelopes and in the margins of your newspaper. The habit grows and can seep into other areas of your life: it is by

Programming can be carried on at any time and anywhere.

no means uncommon for programmers to take their micro home with them. Perhaps you should therefore consider also the cost to your family!

3.4 Using a program on different microcomputers

If you invest in your program as much time, energy and commitment as our discussion implies, you will want to make maximum use of the result. This wish is served by making the program available to others, inside or outside your own institution. The ease with which you can do this will depend in part on the number of different machines which can run it, and this section considers further the practicalities of running the same program on different micros. We investigate:
- the extent to which this is possible;
- what is involved in adapting code to other machines;
- the mechanics of transferring a program from one machine to another.

To what extent is this possible?

It is often useful to develop programs which can run on a range of computers: programs which are **portable**. Aspects of programs which work on any machine are **machine-independent**: those which rely on the facilities of a particular model are **machine-dependent**. There are many exciting features of micros – such as high-resolution graphics, colour graphics and sophisticated text manipulation – which are offered by certain machines only. But in terms of the basic kinds of operation – adding, subtracting, finding square roots, creating loops, making tests on data, sorting things into order and so on – machines are much of a muchness; usually, the various machines do some things well and others badly, but they all do most things somehow. So as a rough generalization, it should be possible to perform the same set of operations on any machine, if you supply the right program. But this is not the same program for all machines!

At its inception, each of the several high-level languages was intended to do something which none of the existing languages did; each was developed for a particular sort of use, a particular sort of user. Thus PILOT for tutorial programs, COBOL for business people, BASIC for learners, ALGOL and PASCAL for programming aesthetes. Each is conspicuously good in some ways and conspicuously bad in others. But each high-level language is itself translated into a low-level machine language, which is entirely machine-dependent. So for each high-level language on each different machine there must be an individual translator. If there was only one version of BASIC (for example), any computer could be made to translate BASIC instructions into the appropriate machine language. But in fact, each manufacturer produces his own dialect of BASIC – it is largely the same as everyone else's, but has a few minor differences: it is better at one thing, worse at another. All such changes consist in trading one facility against another; which result is best for you depends on what you want.

To recapitulate, you have a program, you want to share it with the world, so you have to make it portable. Your program runs on a given machine, in a given dialect of a given language: you want it to run on *any* machine in *any* dialect of that language. As all dialects of a given language are varied extensions of the same core language, you can achieve portability by limiting yourself to those features common to all dialects. The alternative is to alter the program to suit each machine: this is costly in time and makes the program difficult to maintain; any changes to the program must be made to each half-brother as well, and not necessarily identical changes. Thus we arrive at a central tenet of all computational theory, the swings-and-roundabouts principle. Here are some illustrations of it.

Dialects really do offer advantages in respect of the things they are good at: if you do not use the extended facilities of your own dialect, you are wasting them. And your program is not written to exploit the (different) facilities of someone else's dialect, so you are wasting those too. Yet if you do use such extensions, your program is not portable. Again, extensions often make things possible: they increase the 'power' of the language. If you aim for universality, you sacrifice this power. One part-solution to these problems is to confine use of extensions to one or two modules of the program. If anyone who has difficulty because of these extensions needs to make alterations, these alterations can be restricted to a small area – and the alterations may consist in writing in their own dialect something equivalent to yours.

Another aspect of the 'power' of a computer is the amount of core store it requires to be able to run. This can be decreased by use of special language features, but this conflicts with the desire for portability. Program sophistication requires more lines of program, more code, more space in which to store while running – and hence requires all machines on which it is to be run to have an equivalent amount of store. (Not 'the same' amount, possibly, because different machines work in different ways.)

Adapting the program code

If a manufacturer has a program which he wishes to market, he may be assured of sufficient sales to permit of his writing and maintaining several different versions of it – one for RML 380Zs, one for BBC Microcomputers, one for APPLEs and so on. This will put him to a lot of trouble: each program, though it does essentially the same thing, must be developed and tested in its own right. But this may be worthwhile as a commercial enterprise.

For the private individual, perhaps an amateur programmer, this sort of investment is impractical: he will not have the time, resources – machines to test each version – or technical expertise across that range of machines. To take a concrete example, we made use earlier in the chapter of the AUGURY program, and we decided that rather than simply talk about it, we should provide you with code (section 3.6) so that you could – if you wish – try it out and see error-trapping and so on in action. But we do not know what machine (if any) you have to access to: how then are we to supply code which is useful to you? In the event, we have compromised: we have not written one version for each machine, but we have restricted ourselves to the use of BASIC (because it is widely available) and to the constructions in BASIC which are central to most dialects of this language. We have not made use of special features of the particular dialect available to us, for the most part, but in the questionable bits – namely putting more than one statement on a line and converting lower to upper case letters – we have given guidance on what you might have to do instead. We have also taken the deliberate step of printing the code so that you can see its structure, though our painstaking indentation will probably be lost as soon as you type it into your machine. (But see Appendix A.2.) We hope that the structure of the code is sufficiently clear, in conjunction with the comments incorporated in it, that if you have need to alter it (or if you wish to add to it), you will be able to see what is required and how to do it.

Some attempt has been made to control the growth of languages, or at least to monitor their growth. Every so often, for example, ANSI (the American National Standards Institute) issues a new statement of the way in which FORTRAN is encouraged to develop in the next few years. ANSI standards then provide a basis for comparison: manufacturers try to make their own translators do *at least* what ANSI says, and customers can check whether they succeed. (Of course, they all do these things in different ways!)

Hence the idea of **language standards**: if a language has a standard, you can write your program using only the features within that standard, state which standard you referred to (e.g. 'ANSI FORTRAN 77'), and market your program with the knowledge that it is portable, and that potential buyers know in advance whether they will be able to run your program on their machine.

Although ANSI have made recommendations concerning standard BASIC, the BASICs provided by manufacturers continue to differ markedly from this.

You need to look at the documentation (the **manuals**) supplied by manufacturers. The main differences are likely to be in graphics, in input handling and, perhaps most significantly, in the extent to which programs may be structured. But, to repeat what was said earlier, most versions will permit you to do a particular operation in some fashion; you simply have to know what specific command words are required by your dialect to do it.

One thing may have struck you about all this. If one interpreter, from one manufacturer, says 'IF ... THEN ... ' where another interpreter, from a different manufacturer, says 'IF ... GOTO ... ' and the constructions are equivalent, surely it is possible to write a program to work through a piece of code in one style and produce code in the other style? Indeed it is: programs of that type exist, some making quite sophisticated changes. It is even possible in theory to use a program to translate statements in (say) PASCAL into statements in (say) ALGOL 68, just as it is possible in theory to translate English into French by computer – results in the latter case tend to give readable but rather bad French.

Making the move

We have talked about 'portability' of programs: about the ability to create, test and develop a program on one machine, and then to run it on another machine. We concentrated then on the principles of making the code compatible – keeping it machine-independent, using language standards, having it small enough to fit into the memory of the new machine. All these things are helped by well-written, clearly structured code because the code is then easier to adapt if this proves necessary. Such principles affect the likelihood of being able to mount the program on the new machine, and of being able to run it thereafter. What about the actual movement of the program from one machine to another?

The simplest vehicle of transfer is the printed page. We write words on paper, you read them – no special equipment is required. Thus you have programs in this book, to do with as you will. But in order to run them, you must type them into your machine: this will take time and you will make some errors which you must then correct. Wouldn't it be better if we wrote them onto some recording medium, which you could read directly into your machine? That saves time and minimizes errors in transfer. Suitable media are cassette tape and floppy discs; text transferred in this way is said to be **machine-readable**.

Well, yes: it obviously would be better, *provided* that you have the equipment to read the data off the medium and into your machine. It would be no use our sending you a cassette if you have a disc drive only. And even if we know for certain that you have a cassette player, and we have a cassette player, it is not necessarily true that they read and write data in the same way: we might send you a tape which was completely unreadable (or perhaps gave a lot of apparently random characters). So as well as having *language standards* which govern the writing of programs, there are **data transfer standards** which govern the exchange of programs: you and we must agree on a standard in advance of transfer – we then write our tape according to this standard and we know that you can read it. (In practice, so far as the code in this book is concerned, we are providing machine-readable versions of our programs for some machines: details are given on page 315. If your machine is not one of these, we are sorry, but you *will* have to type them in!)

As a general rule, it is easier to transfer material by disc than by cassette: disc operating systems are more standard than are cassette operating systems, so there is a better chance that two machines can both read the same disc. A lot of work has now been done on creating cassette interfaces – adaptors, if you like – so that one cassette system can talk to another. But with cassettes, there are simple mechanical constraints too: for a given tape to be written by one machine and read by another, the tape speeds must be the same, the alignment of the read/write heads must be the same, and the **file marks** (which identify and separate files on a tape) must be understood by both.

3.5 Evaluating a program

Anyone who works with computers of any sort is obliged continually to assess the merits and demerits of programs – programs written by themselves, by friends, by commercial **software houses** or by the manufacturers of the machines. Most of these programs will be capable of alteration by you, provided that you have some programming skills, and the ability to make small changes to applications software is a factor critical in its selection; so the appearance of the code, as well as the ease with which it can be used, is of interest to a potential purchaser. The basic rule is again that the most important person is the user.

Bear in mind that the software supplied by the manufacturer of your machine – the operating system, the translators, the utility programs – will be used more extensively than any applications programs which you may acquire thereafter. It will also largely determine the sort of applications programs which you *can* run, and the speed of running, the response time and the ease of updating. Manufacturer's software should have been **tuned** to the system: any alteration by you may be detrimental, it may **degrade** the system.

This section attempts to give you a 'buyers' guide' to programs: a list of things to check when considering a program with a view to acquisition. The importance of each is perhaps for you to decide; you will undoubtedly think of several that we have overlooked. Appendix A.1 contains a checklist, to which you can add your own selection criteria.

We have been using the word 'acquire' rather than 'buy' because you may be offered programs as presents – from friends, perhaps, or in books or magazines. You may feel that the evaluation process is irrelevant if the program is free. Against this attitude are the philosophical argument that it is important for you, right from the start, to look at everything critically, and the pragmatic argument that your storage space is limited. (Remember, every program you get, every version of every program, is one more thing for you to keep track of.) Contrary to this attitude, we would suggest that you make a point of subjecting to this process a few programs which you definitely do not want to buy – for practice.

There are three stages at which evaluation may be appropriate, though it may not be possible to check in this way in practice:
- *before you use the program;*
- *before you get your own copy;*
- *after you have used it for a while.*

Before use

What do you think of the program design? Do you like the ideas? Why? What do you think are the intentions which underlie this program (that is, those of the designer; not the way in which *you* wish to make use of it)? Are these clear to the learner? Does the program do what *you* want it to do? If so, does it do this in the way you want it done? Does it fit in with other programs which you have? Does it fit in with what you want to teach? Is it intended for individual or for group use? Does it require the learner to have prior knowledge, or to provide collected data? Is it likely to be generally applicable to other subjects, other departments? What skills are required by the learner; what skills does it develop?

Before acquisition

Ideally, never buy a program until *you* have tested it! It can be most informative, as a start, to run the program without looking at any external instructions or to get a colleague with different interests to run it: see if the program instructs you as it goes along – this will give you some idea of how easy it will be to use it. Is it attractive? In what ways? Would they appeal to the learner as well as to you?

Is the program flexible? Does it leave initiative with the user, does it offer options, does it make clear what these are and what are the implications of adopting them? Does it operate in command mode or in tutorial mode? How easy is it to backtrack – must you stop and start again? When you have been through a sequence of choices, are you offered the chance of going through the whole thing again, perhaps making different choices? Can you go through more quickly the second time?

Now test the code to see whether errors have been trapped. There are far too many possibilities for us to discuss them all: you must see whether the response to an error is acceptable to you. There are four cases, roughly: one, the program crashes, and you have to restart from scratch (maybe even reload the program and the interpreter); two, the program loses control to the operating system or interpreter, so that messages bear no specific relation to the aims of the program; three, all errors are caught by the program, but the response is something unhelpful like 'INCORRECT INPUT'; four, all errors are caught, and messages are clear, understandable, relate to what is going on at the time, and tell the user what action to take next.

There are several simple tests you can perform. Hit keys at random: what happens? When the program asks you for something, press the 'RETURN' key without having typed anything else (that is, give a null response). If it asks you for a number, give it characters. Try putting commas in the line (they often, but not always, serve to separate several pieces of data). Try giving it totally inappropriate numbers: decimals when it wants whole numbers, negative numbers when it wants positive, decimals which start with the point (thus '.456' not '0.456'), zero, negative decimals, very large numbers, very small numbers. If it wants a list of numbers in a particular order, give it a list in the wrong order. Give it only one number. Give it more than it asks for. If it is going to sort the numbers into order, give it a list which is already sorted, or which are all the same, or just one number long. If it asks for a character, or for a string of characters, give it a number (the chances are that it will treat this as perfectly acceptable character input). Try punctuation, asterisks, and so on. And try to do each test at least twice in succession, to see if the result is the same – it may not be. Do you always return to a sensible point in the program?

If you are still on speaking terms with the would-be vendor, you could now discuss the requirements of the program. What language is it written in? Do you have a translator which suits? Does it use language features which you don't have? If so, can they be replaced by the equivalent in your dialect? Do you have the skill to do this? What hardware does the program require? How much core storage? Does it need cassette or floppy disc input; if so, how many? Does it use graphics; if so, does it need special high-resolution graphics? Does it use colour?

And now the documentation. What is there? Is there documentation within the code itself, such as 'PRINT' statements to tell the user what is happening or 'COMMENT' or 'REMARK' statements to tell the programmer what is happening? Is there external documentation? Do you get a written statement of what the program is intended to do? Do you get a flowchart? What does the code itself look like: does it look clean, was it thought out carefully? Is it modular? If so, are the breaks clear? And as regards its use for teaching, do you get suggestions on ways to use it: do you get worksheets for the learners?

As with an expensive electrical appliance, you now want to know what sort of guarantee you get and how long this lasts. You want to know about **support** (where to get help and advice in its use) and **maintenance** (what help you get when the thing goes wrong), and whether the cost of this is included in the purchase price. Programs may not so much 'go wrong' as prove to be inadequate: despite your best efforts at testing, problems (**bugs**) in the code may show up only later. Whose responsibility is it to solve these? And then as regards enhancements or updates, new versions of the same thing: is there any prospect of any? Will you get them automatically, will you be invited to get them, will you have to pay again? In what form will the program and any updates be supplied (on cassette, on disc, or simply written)?

66   Programs

After use

When you have used your program for a while, go back and look at it again. Has it done what you wanted? What do your students think of it? Do either you or they want to alter it in some way? If so, in what way, and why? Are you taking note of the things it is actually doing which you had not considered; are you ignoring some new insights into the material being taught? Try it on another group of students: do their comments tally?

If you really do want to alter it, can you? If not, can you (should you) alter your teaching instead? You should feel able to go back to the manufacturer or other supplier of your program with your comments and suggestions.

3.6   AUGURY: an illustration

This chapter has made use of the program called AUGURY. We introduced it for the purpose of illustration, and we are using it again in that capacity in this section. Later in the book, in Chapters 7 and 8, we shall be giving examples of several concepts dealt with in our discussion: we shall be thinking about what happens inside the program, and we shall be thinking about the ways in which it can be used. In each case we shall give an example: a program which we have written and which works in accordance with our intentions at the time.

One of the most important themes in this chapter has been documentation. To illustrate our points, we now present AUGURY as a properly documented program. What is 'proper' documentation is of course a matter of taste, but the following at least are useful elements:

- *a statement of the aims of the program;*
- *a specification of the program;*
- *a diagram of the way in which the program works (a flowchart);*
- *a listing of the complete code of the program;*
- *some typical output from the program;*
- *a discussion of the program – its success, shortcomings, and ideas for its development.*

Aims

AUGURY was conceived to fulfil a number of objectives, all of which are aspects of one main objective – to be a useful example in a book about computing. The aspects included the following:

   * The example must be general and understandable by all readers; it must not be tied to one discipline only. It must be reasonably light-hearted but not too contrived.

* The code will be available to readers so that they can, if they wish, run it on a machine for themselves and modify it. The code must therefore be portable in so far as this is possible.
* As the code is to be supplied to non-programmers, instructions must be used in contexts where their meanings are apparent without further explanation.
* Clarity of code necessarily requires internal documentation, which the program will thus illustrate. Code will be modular, and will include one or more subroutines to show their uses. Variables will be given identifiers which relate to their uses.
* The program will also illustrate the laying out of output.
* A major objective will be to illustrate effective and imaginative error-trapping. This is best done with an interactive program.

Specification

The program will provide auguries for villagers who wish to make a journey by one of two routes, in varying conditions. The villagers will supply data – how many people are going, whether they are riding horses or walking, whether they are driving livestock or not, whether the ground is wet or dry. This data will be used thus: positive numbers (1 to 12) of people may go – more than 12 leaves insufficient in the village to defend it. The shorter route passes through a wood and is more dangerous: it therefore requires more people or faster travel (see diagram below). Livestock is slow-moving, and dictates the speed of travel irrespective of whether the people are riding or walking. Wet ground slows progress by 20 per cent.

Users will be offered new auguries repeatedly until they decline the offer. Each augury will be numbered. Auguries will recommend the best route and estimate the number of complete days required to accomplish it under the stated conditions.

The program will be written in BASIC, this being the most portable language in respect of microcomputers.

Numerical data:
  Distance: 15 miles (short route) or 20 miles (long route)
  Speed: 5 miles/day (with livestock), 10 miles/day (walking without livestock), 15 miles/day (riding without livestock)
  Time taken: distance/speed (multiplied by 1.2 if ground wet) rounded up to the next highest complete day

The rules invented by the Slalewic villagers are shown in the diagram below.

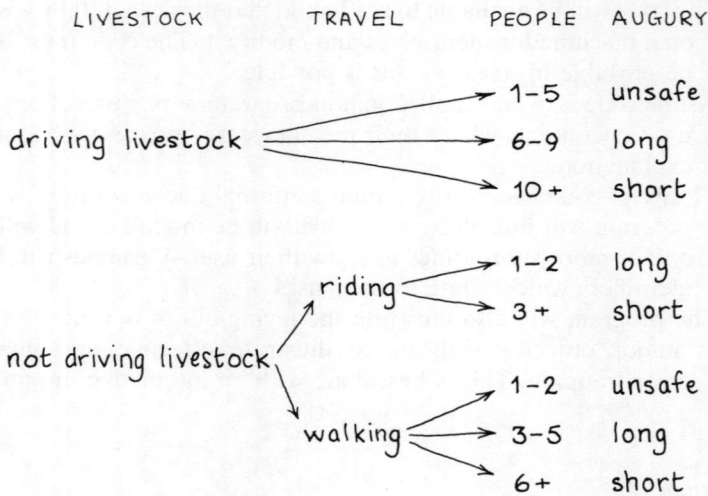

Flowcharts: an introduction

On the previous page is a description of the AUGURY program: what it is to do, how it is to appear to the user, and our objectives in providing such a program at all. On the facing page, there is a diagram of the way in which the program is to function: this is a **flowchart**. It is an 'outline' flowchart, in that it shows general working only: flowcharts can be drawn at differing levels of detail.

As you can see, it uses text in boxes and lines to link these. There are varying conventions about the shapes of these boxes and the points at which lines join them: the important thing is that the flowcharts are *clear*, and this is helped if you are consistent within each such chart. We have used boxes in this way:

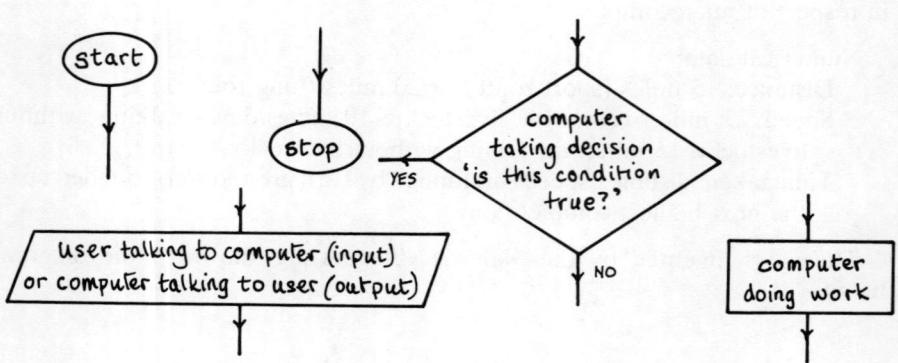

Outline flowchart of AUGURY

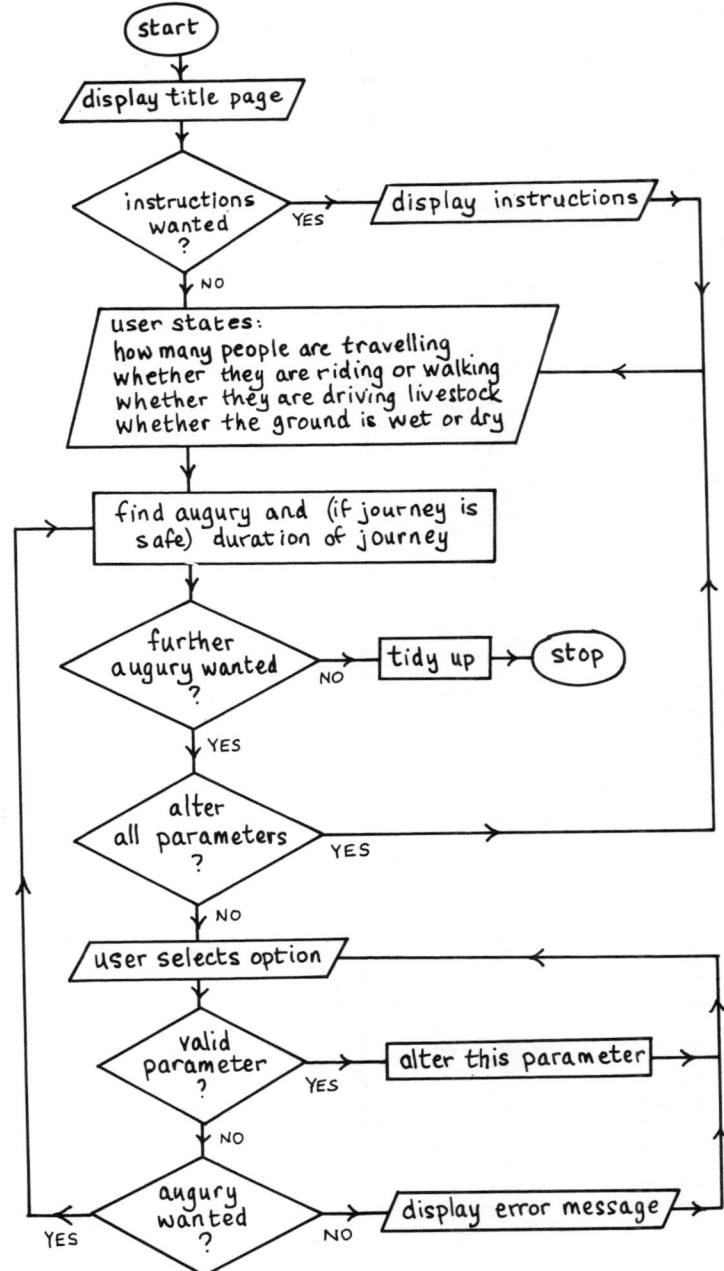

Listing of AUGURY program code

```
1000 REM Program : AUGURY
1010 REM
1020 REM
1030 REM This program gives an augury concerning
1040 REM    the duration of a journey between the
1050 REM    villages of Slalewic ('muddy dwelling')
1060 REM    and Hahlwud ('corner of a wood').
1070 REM
1080 REM
1090      CLEAR 100
1100      DIM V$(5)
1110 REM
1120      ON BREAK GOTO 3370
1130 REM    Deal with user's interruption
1140 REM
1150      TEXT : PRINT CHR$(12) : REM Clear the screen
1160      PRINT CHR$(17) : REM Disable paging
1170 REM
1180 REM
1190      PRINT TAB(17); "AUGURY"
1200      PRINT
1210      PRINT TAB(8); "Give augury for journey"
1220      PRINT : PRINT : PRINT
1230      PRINT TAB(19); "*"
1240      PRINT
1250      PRINT TAB(14); "Andrew Nash"
1260      PRINT
1270      PRINT TAB(15); "Derek Ball"
1280      PRINT
1290      PRINT TAB(19); "*"
1300      PRINT : PRINT : PRINT
1310      PRINT TAB(13); "Copyright 1982"
1320      PRINT
1330      PRINT TAB(10); "Hutchinson Education"
1340      PRINT
1350      FOR D = 1 TO 5000 : NEXT D : REM Delay
1360      PRINT CHR$(12) : REM Clear the screen
1370 REM
1380 REM
1390 REM == TITLE AND INSTRUCTIONS ==
1400 REM
1410      PRINT "JOURNEY TO HAHLWUD : AN AUGURY"
1420      PRINT "--------------------------------"
1430      PRINT
1440 REM
1450      PRINT : PRINT "Do you want instructions ('Y' or 'N')";
1460      INPUT R$
1470      LET V = 2 : LET V$(1) = "Y" : LET V$(2) = "N"
1480      GOSUB 3430 : IF E = 1 THEN 1450 : REM Check character
1490 REM
1500      IF C$ = "N" THEN 1680
1510 REM
1520      PRINT : PRINT
1530      PRINT "This program is written for the"
1540      PRINT "   inhabitants of the village of "
1550      PRINT "   Slalewic who are considering a"
1560      PRINT "   journey to Hahlwud. From information"
1570      PRINT "   supplied by the would-be traveller,"
1580      PRINT "   it assesses whether or not the"
1590      PRINT "   journey may safely be made; and if so,"
1600      PRINT "   how long it may be expected to take."
1610      PRINT
```

```
1620      PRINT "The questions are simple and self-"
1630      PRINT "  explanatory. You may type any answers;"
1640      PRINT "  if they are not understood, you will"
1650      PRINT "  be told."
1660      PRINT : PRINT
1670 REM
1680      LET A = 1
1690 REM
1700 REM
1710 REM == SET ALL PARAMETERS ==
1720 REM
1730      PRINT : PRINT "Please answer the following questions"
1740      PRINT "  about your journey:"
1750      PRINT
1760 REM
1770      PRINT : PRINT "  How many people are travelling"
1780      PRINT "     ('1'..'12')";
1790      INPUT R$
1800      GOSUB 3630 : IF E = 1 THEN 1770 : REM Check number
1810      LET P = N
1820 REM
1830      PRINT : PRINT "  Are you riding or walking"
1840      PRINT "     ('R' or 'W')";
1850      INPUT R$
1860      LET V = 2 : LET V$(1) = "R" : LET V$(2) = "W"
1870      GOSUB 3410 : IF E = 1 THEN 1830 : REM Check character
1880      LET M$ = C$
1890 REM
1900      PRINT : PRINT "  Are you driving livestock"
1910      PRINT "     ('Y' or 'N')";
1920      INPUT R$
1930      LET V = 2 : LET V$(1) = "Y" : LET V$(2) = "N"
1940      GOSUB 3410 : IF E = 1 THEN 1900 : REM Check character
1950      LET L$ = C$
1960 REM
1970      PRINT : PRINT "  Is the ground wet or dry"
1980      PRINT "     ('W' or 'D')";
1990      INPUT R$
2000      LET V = 2 : LET V$(1) = "W" : LET V$(2) = "D"
2010      GOSUB 3410 : IF E = 1 THEN 1970
2020      LET G$ = C$
2030 REM
2040      PRINT
2050 REM
2060 REM
2070 REM == AUGURY : SHORT ROUTE, LONG ROUTE OR UNSAFE ==
2080 REM
2090      IF L$ = "N" THEN 2180
2100 REM
2110 REM ==== Driving livestock (riding or walking)
2120      IF P > 5 THEN 2140
2130         LET A$ = "unsafe" : GOTO 2540
2140      IF P > 9 THEN 2160
2150         LET A$ = "long" : GOTO 2370
2160      LET A$ = "short" : GOTO 2360
2170 REM
2180      IF M$ = "W" THEN 2260
2190 REM
2200 REM ==== Not driving livestock: riding
2210      IF P > 2 THEN 2230
2220         LET A$ = "long" : GOTO 2370
2230      LET A$ = "short" : GOTO 2360
2240 REM
2250 REM ==== Not driving livestock: walking
2260      IF P > 2 THEN 2280
```

```
2270          LET A$ = "unsafe" : GOTO 2540
2280       IF F > 5 THEN 2306
2290          LET A$ = "long" : GOTO 2370
2300       LET A$ = "short" : GOTO 2360
2310 REM
2320 REM
2330 REM == AUGURY : TIME, IF JOURNEY SAFE ==
2340 REM
2350 REM ==== Work out distance (short = 15 miles; long = 20 miles)
2360       LET D = 15 : GOTO 2410
2370       LET D = 20
2380 REM
2390 REM ==== Work out speed (driving livestock = 5 miles/day;
2400 REM           walking = 10 miles/day; riding = 30 miles/day)
2410       IF L$ = "N" THEN 2430
2420          LET S = 5 : GOTO 2470
2430       IF M$ = "W" THEN LET S = 10 ELSE LET S = 30
2440 REM
2450 REM ==== Work out time (distance/speed, rounded to next highest
2460 REM           integer; add 20% if ground is wet)
2470       LET T = D / S
2480       IF G$ = "W" THEN LET T = T * 1.2
2490       LET T = INT (T + 0.999)
2500 REM
2510 REM
2520 REM == GIVE AUGURY ==
2530 REM
2540       PRINT CHR$(12) : REM  Clear the screen
2550       PRINT "Thankyou"
2560       PRINT : PRINT : PRINT
2570       PRINT : PRINT : PRINT
2580 REM
2590       IF A$ () "unsafe" THEN 2650
2600 REM
2610       PRINT "The journey is unsafe by either route"
2620       PRINT "   under these conditions"
2630       GOTO 2750
2640 REM
2650       PRINT "You may safely travel by the "; A$; " route"
2660       PRINT
2670       PRINT "Your journey should not take more than"
2680       PRINT
2690       PRINT TAB(14); T;
2700       IF T = 1 THEN PRINT "day" ELSE PRINT "days"
2710 REM
2720 REM
2730 REM == INVITE FURTHER AUGURY: ADJUST PARAMETERS IF NECESSARY ==
2740 REM
2750       PRINT : PRINT : PRINT
2760       PRINT : PRINT : PRINT
2770       PRINT : PRINT "Would you like a further augury"
2780       PRINT "   ('Y' or 'N')";
2790       INPUT R$
2800       LET V = 2 : LET V$(1) = "Y" : LET V$(2) = "N"
2810       GOSUB 3410 : IF E = 1 THEN 2770 : REM Check character
2820 REM
2830       IF C$ = "N" THEN 3360
2840 REM
2850       PRINT CHR$(12) : REM  Clear the screen
2860 REM
2870       LET A = A + 1
2880       PRINT "AUGURY NUMBER"; A
2890       PRINT
2900 REM
2910       PRINT : PRINT "Do you wish to alter all parameters or"
2920       PRINT "   Just one ('A' or 'J')";
```

AUGURY: an illustration 73

```
2930        INPUT R$
2940        LET V = 2 : LET V$(1) = "A" : LET V$(2) = "J"
2950        GOSUB 3410 : IF E = 1 THEN 2910 : REM Check character
2960 REM
2970        IF C$ = "A" THEN 1750
2980 REM
2990 REM ==== Supply menu
3000        PRINT : PRINT
3010        PRINT "Understood. Parameter values are now"
3020        PRINT
3030        PRINT "PARAMETER"; TAB(22); "NOW"; TAB(27); "TO ALTER"
3040        PRINT "   Number of people"; TAB(22); P; TAB(31); "P"
3050        PRINT "   Mode of travel"; TAB(23); M$; TAB(31); "M"
3060        PRINT "   Driving livestock"; TAB(23); L$; TAB(31); "L"
3070        PRINT "   Ground state"; TAB(23); G$; TAB(31); "G"
3080        PRINT
3090        PRINT : PRINT "Select parameter 'P','M','L' or 'G'"
3100        PRINT "   or type 'A' for augury";
3110        INPUT R$
3120        LET V = 5 : LET V$(1) = "A" : LET V$(2) = "P"
3130        LET V$(3) = "M" : LET V$(4) = "L" : LET V$(5) = "G"
3140        GOSUB 3410 : IF E = 1 THEN 3090 : REM Check character
3150 REM
3160        IF C$ = "A" THEN 2040
3170 REM
3180        IF C$ <> "P" THEN 3250
3190          PRINT : PRINT "  How many people are travelling"
3200          PRINT "          ('1'..'12')";
3210          INPUT R$
3220          GOSUB 3630 : IF E = 1 THEN 3190 : REM Check number
3230          LET P = N : GOTO 3000
3240 REM
3250        IF C$ <> "M" THEN 3290
3260          IF M$ = "R" THEN LET M$ = "W" ELSE LET M$ = "R"
3270          GOTO 3000
3280 REM
3290        IF C$ <> "L" THEN 3330
3300          IF L$ = "Y" THEN LET L$ = "N" ELSE LET L$ = "Y"
3310          GOTO 3000
3320 REM
3330        IF G$ = "W" THEN LET G$ = "D" ELSE LET G$ = "W"
3340          GOTO 3000
3350 REM
3360        PRINT : PRINT "Thankyou.  Good day to you!"
3370        PRINT CHR$(19) : REM Re-enable screen paging
3380        END
3390 REM
3400 REM
3410 REM == S-R: COLLECT AND CHECK CHARACTER RESPONSES ==
3420 REM
3430        LET E = 0
3440 REM
3450        IF LEN(R$) <> 1 THEN 3560
3460 REM
3470 REM ==== If letter, ensure upper case
3480        IF (R$ < "a") OR (R$ > "z") THEN 3500
3490          LET C$ = CHR$(ASC(R$)-32) : GOTO 3530
3500        LET C$ = R$
3510 REM
3520 REM ==== Check that response is a valid letter
3530        FOR I = 1 TO V
3540          IF C$ = V$(I) THEN 3600
3550        NEXT I
3560        LET E = 1
3570        PRINT "      * Sorry, '"; R$; "' is not understood."
3580        PRINT "             Try again"
```

```
3590 REM
3600     RETURN
3610 REM
3620 REM
3630 REM == S-R: COLLECT AND CHECK NUMERIC RESPONSES ==
3640 REM
3650     LET E = 0
3660     FOR I = 1 TO LEN(R$)
3670       LET C$ = MID$(R$,I,1)
3680       IF (C$ )= "0") AND (C$ <= "9") THEN 3720
3690         LET E = 1
3700         PRINT "    * Please give a positive number"
3710         GOTO 3850
3720     NEXT I
3730 REM
3740 REM ==== Response is a number
3750     LET N = VAL(R$)
3760     IF N > 0 THEN 3800
3770       LET E = 1
3780       PRINT "    * Then no traveller will be safe!"
3790       PRINT "       Try again" : GOTO 3850
3800     IF N < 13 THEN 3850
3810       LET E = 1
3820       PRINT "    * Too many! The village will be"
3830       PRINT "       undefended. Try again"
3840 REM
3850     RETURN
```

Sample output

```
Understood.  Parameter values are now

PARAMETER                   NOW    TO ALTER
   Number of people         10        P
   Mode of travel           R         M
   Driving livestock        N         L
   Ground state             W         G


Select parameter 'P','M','L' or 'G'
   or type 'A' for augury? L


Understood.  Parameter values are now

PARAMETER                   NOW    TO ALTER
   Number of people         10        P
   Mode of travel           R         M
   Driving livestock        Y         L
   Ground state             W         G


Select parameter 'P','M','L' or 'G'
   or type 'A' for augury? A
```

Discussion

In comparing the result with our aims (pages 66–7), you as reader are better able to judge whether or not we have been successful in these aims. For the most part, obviously, we think we have achieved our goals – had we not, we might have devised another program, and undertaken all the corrections, alterations and retyping of Chapter 3 which that would have entailed.

The program is longer than we would have wished. But the concepts are important and fundamental: we believe that if you grasp these, you will be relatively well-equipped in building a program library, even if you never write a line of code yourself. We hope that you will want to write programs, and that you will look critically at others – for the same reasons; both pastimes can be stimulating and enjoyable; both pastimes may eventually improve the general standard of code produced by all programmers everywhere, and so ease the problem of those who follow in your steps. Other people, existing programmers, will improve their code only if their clients and customers oblige them to do so.

As regards AUGURY, you may like to tinker with it for practice in programming. It is by no means perfect. It uses tutorial rather than command mode; it scrolls off the screen rather than merely updating its table *in situ*. And it has one or two known logical flaws – for instance, you are asked for your mode of travel even if you are taking livestock, in which case mode of travel makes no difference to the speed and hence to the augury. What else can you find?

AUGURY – like all of the programs in this book – was written originally for a Research Machines Ltd (RML) 380Z or 480Z microcomputer, and you may experience slight difficulties in trying to run it on other machines. But the error messages that you get should assist you in identifying which lines need to be altered. For example, you may be limited to one statement per line, in which case you will have to split some of our lines at the colons which separate statements. Or your micro may use some character other than the colon to separate instructions. You may have to allocate storage at the beginning of the program in a different way or not at all on your micro. You may find that the character handling (the 'string functions') and, for later programs, the graphical display instructions differ for your machine. For AUGURY, modification should be fairly simple: in each case, you need to identify the line that doesn't work, work out what we meant it to do, and replace it with a piece of code which achieves this with your machine: the comments in section 7.1 may help you, particularly with the instructions which open and close each program. Good luck!

4 Graphics

Some computer programs, like some books, contain pictures. We have included pictures in this book because we think that they will help you to understand better some of the points we want to make and to visualize some of the equipment which we are describing; we have also included pictures because we think they will make your use of the book more enjoyable. There are some books where pictures are essential, others where they are useful and still others where they would be quite out of place.

What is true of books is true also of computer programs: some computer programs need pictures (graphics). We are going to look at the use of pictures in computer programs, when to use them, how to use them and how to make the most effective use of them. Topics therefore include:

- *the nature of graphics;*
- *using graphics in teaching;*
- *from theory to practice – some practical considerations;*
- *computer graphics compared with other methods of displaying pictures;*
- *from theory to practice – thoughts about the bits that aren't easy.*

4.1 What are graphics?

For many people, one of the more exciting aspects of micros is that they afford the possibility of using graphics. What are graphics? 'Graphics' means pictures, diagrams and drawings; embellishments of, or alternatives to, the written word. In seeking to understand what computer graphics *do* offer and what they *need* to offer, we consider first how pictures differ from words, and we look also at:

- order in presentation;
- the design of pictures;
- computers as a means of displaying pictures.

Words and pictures

When receiving words – either by reading or by listening – you start at the beginning and go on to the end. If you are listening to someone talking on the radio, the words reach you in a particular order and are then gone. You hear them once, and make of them what you want, while you can. If you read a novel,

What are graphics? 77

the situation is slightly different: you can if you wish go back to the previous page and have another look at it. Nevertheless, the words are (generally speaking) presented in the order in which they are intended to be read. A computer program usually presents words on a television screen in a form which is a compromise between the radio and the book. Words appear first at the bottom of the screen and they gradually move up the screen as more words arrive, so the latest arrivals are always at the bottom. Eventually the words reach the top of the screen and disappear, not to be seen again. This way of presenting words is called **scrolling**: text presented thus is said to be **scrolled**.

When receiving a *picture* – by looking at it – the dynamics are quite different. There is no 'right' place to start looking at a picture; there is no implication of sequence. The relative positions of elements of the picture are very important, but they do not denote sequence; instead, all kinds of other meanings are conveyed in this way – relative significance, association, dominance, intricacy, openness, intimacy and so on. Perhaps this range of meaning explains why a picture is said to be worth a thousand words.

A picture is not usually made up of words, or even of letters or punctuation

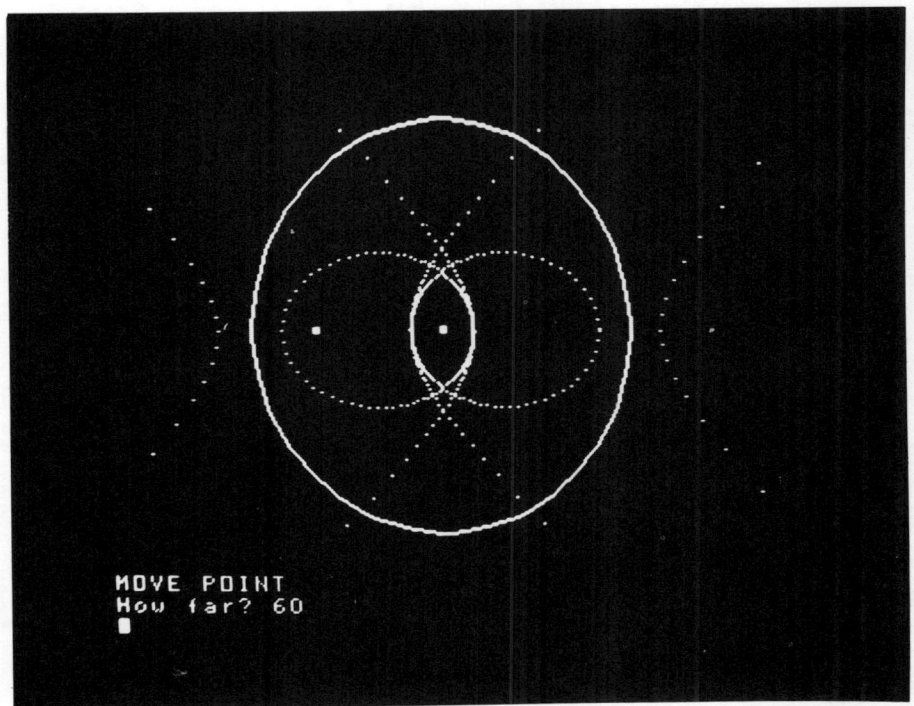

Normally, a picture consists of lines and curves, shading and colour. Graphics on a computer have many of these attributes.

marks, though these may find a place within one. More normally a picture consists of lines and curves, shading and colour. Graphics on a computer have many of these attributes. Drawings may be formed of lines and curves, which may be placed where required. Sometimes it is possible to shade in different parts of the picture, or to use different colours.

What you need to draw a picture

In a computer picture, unlike a picture drawn on paper, elements may be added, subtracted or replaced at will. The arrangement of elements on the screen is chosen to convey a desired meaning and does not necessarily reflect the order in which elements of the picture arrived.

It is useful to be fairly flexible about what is meant by a 'picture'. For example, when reporting experimental findings or other information, a table of results is often displayed: in some senses, such a table is a picture (even if it consists entirely of words and numbers); it is certainly useful to be able to modify individual entries in the table without otherwise disturbing it.

If you are drawing a picture on a piece of paper, the equipment you require depends on what picture you want to draw. You may use just a pencil or a pen; you may need colours. Your colours may be crayons; or they may be paints, in which case you need brushes, which may be fine or coarse. Similarly, if you are creating a picture on a television screen, the facilities you require depend on what picture you want to create: different micros will offer different facilities for creating such pictures and more expensive or more versatile micros will offer you a greater choice. For example, different colours may be available, or the computer may only offer you different shades of grey (or perhaps even white only). It may be possible to choose to draw with the equivalent of a coarse brush or a fine brush.

For each computer there is a lower limit on the width of lines which it enables you to draw on the screen. Lines drawn by a computer are made of many individual points: the size of the smallest point determines the width of the finest line.

If a computer is able to plot very small points, then a large number of them are required to fill the screen, and a lot of information must be stored in the computer to keep track of what is on the screen. Most microcomputers allocate one particular storage location in their core memory to each displayable point of the screen: this is called **memory-mapping** the screen. If memory-mapping is used, more displayable points mean more core memory to map them: it is this memory requirement which places a limit on the number of displayable points, and consequently on the fineness of the lines.

The **resolution** of the graphics is an indication of the number of points required to fill the screen: **high resolution** means a lot of points, so fine lines may be drawn; **low resolution** means fewer and bigger dots, and therefore coarser lines. A resolution of '300 by 200' means that there are 300 displayable dots across the screen and 200 displayable dots up the screen, so there are 60 000 possible positions in which dots may be displayed and which the computer must keep track of. Since storage costs money, high-resolution graphics is a facility which must be paid for. On the other hand, as storage is becoming (and has already become) cheaper, high-resolution graphics is becoming more common and may indeed become a facility integral to microcomputers at the time of purchase, and not one added on later by those who choose to do so.

When people talk about 'low resolution', they usually mean a resolution of '100 by 60' or less; 'high resolution' is usually at least '200 by 100' to qualify for the title, and could be much more than this. The middle ground between these is called **medium resolution**.

Sometimes pictures or diagrams incorporate special symbols. For example, the normal diagrammatic representation of a bridge hand requires the use of playing card suit symbols: many such card games have been programmed successfully, and manufacturers often provide these special symbols to help. They may also provide bomb symbols, shading effects, **reverse-field characters** (black on white instead of white on black) and so on, in much the same way that letters and punctuation are provided. Another idea implemented on some computers is to provide symbols which are thin vertical, horizontal or diagonal lines, judiciously positioned so that they may be strung together to give the illusion of high-resolution graphics – illusory in that choice about the position and direction of the lines which can be drawn is greatly restricted. All such special symbols are known generally as **graphics characters**, because they are normally used in conjunction with pictures and diagrams. On some computers these special symbols are invoked using appropriate keys on the keyboard, in exactly the same way as letters and numbers (which, logically, are therefore 'graphics characters' also, though never called such); on others, the symbols are invoked by some other sequence of keystrokes.

In this book, the term 'graphics' refers to the ability of the computer to draw diagrams or pictures in the sense explained above, and does not refer to the special symbols which may or may not be available to embellish these pictures – useful though these may sometimes be.

4.2 How can they be used?

If a learner is to be free to learn, he needs to be free to develop his insights in his own way and to explore avenues which *he* feels will be interesting or illuminating. It is all too easy to design computer-assisted learning packages which compel the learner to see things in the same way as the package designers, and to learn by making expected responses to fixed questions; it is much harder to design packages which leave initiative with the learner, who is then free to control to a greater or lesser extent the course of his learning.

Words can offer a learner information and are usually intended to convey an unambiguous message: either the learner receives this intended message or he misunderstands. Pictures too can offer the learner information; they allow him to interpret that information in his own way and, sometimes even to gain insights of which the package designer is unaware. Certainly, many teachers see great value in using pictures to support their teaching. This section describes a number of such uses of pictures: particular examples are chosen which illustrate situations where the use of computer graphics is perhaps the most convenient medium through which the material may be presented. It discusses graphics used in:

- *depicting real processes;*
- *exploring models of reality;*
- *stimulating learners' imagination;*
- *explaining difficult concepts;*
- *presenting complex information clearly.*

Simulation

A scientific experiment may be difficult or costly to set up in the laboratory. Alternatively, while it may be possible to run the experiment, it may be too expensive in time or money to run it sufficiently often to explore the effect of changing all the variables in that situation. In either of these cases, it is necessary to *describe* all or part of the experiment rather than to *perform* it. The description will present what is supposed to happen, and will accord with the theory appropriate to the situation. This theory will often take the form of a **mathematical model** – a set of rules from which, given the initial conditions (including the values of relevant variables), the outcome can be calculated. Such a description may simply use static words or pictures, but by using computers, the process can be enlivened.

A program based on the mathematical model can allow the learner to suggest different initial conditions and then to receive information about corresponding outcomes – in other words, it is possible to **simulate** the experiment. Simulation may be of two kinds: the simpler one displays the outcomes on the screen in the form of tables or graphs; whereas the more sophisticated one gives practice in some of the skills involved in the real experiment. For example, the pictures on the television screen might simulate what a student would see if he looked through a microscope, and invite him to respond to what he sees in ways similar to the real experiment. It may be possible to make the speed of the simulated process reflect the speed of the real process: such computer processing is said to occur in **real time**.

(Programs which work in real time run quickly enough for the output to be used at the time. Here we have mentioned programs which simulate experiments at the true speed. Another example of the use of a real-time program is the booking of a seat on an aircraft: the program makes the booking at that time, while the customer is still with the travel agent and still able to supply addi-

How can they be used? 81

Simulation is only a dressed-up description. Wherever possible, the learner should carry out the real experiment for himself.

tional information. Incidentally, real-time programs use graphical output more often than not, since pictures may be assimilated more speedily than words.)

Simulation is only a dressed-up description. Wherever possible, the learner should carry out the real experiment for himself.

Exploration

Pictures or diagrams often help the student to understand the mathematical models themselves. Moving pictures can be considerably more useful if they are made to depend on feedback from the user; for example, in explaining the kinetic theory of gases, animated diagrams representing the behaviour of gas molecules may be modified in response to a request from the user to change the size of the containers, to raise or to lower the temperature, to remove dividing walls and so on.

Stimulation

If a computer can generate pictures to support simulation and explain scientific theories, it can also generate them for quite different purposes. The program designer can present pictures to the learner to excite his imagination rather than his understanding. Thus static and moving pictures can be presented to art students to provoke discussion or creativity. For the *user* (the teacher or one of the students), rather than the program designer, to be able to choose the images which are presented, requires very well-designed software – particularly if the pictures are complex, patterned or moving. And if such software is available, it can be put to good use in learning other subjects too – mathematics, science, geography, history – any subject where pictures can aid learning.

Note that someone who learns to create pictures using this package is solving a problem by instructing a computer – a definition of 'programming'. The commands he uses will probably be more closely tuned to his task than are the commands in a language such as BASIC or PASCAL, but they nevertheless constitute a programming language in just the same way; and this language will be more 'natural' to the user – more 'user-friendly'.

The use of pictures and diagrams in teaching mathematics helps set the learner free from the rigid constraints of prescriptive processes – free to explore mathematics for himself. Geometry films are put to good use in mathematics teaching in stimulating discussion and encouraging thinking and exploration. Transformations, loci and other geometrical situations make beautiful films; the microcomputer is an alternative medium, and although its use may have less aesthetic appeal, it enables the teacher to control the situation interactively, which opens up additional possibilities.

Explanation

You may find that the use of pictures helps you to explain things to learners; computers sometimes offer significant advantages compared with other methods of presenting these pictures. On a computer, diagrams can be animated and the animation fully controlled by the teacher; improvements and adaptations can be made readily; labels or other embellishments can be added to the diagram and subsequently removed.

For instance, suppose that you wish to explain the principle of a canal lock. A working model might be too expensive or take too much time to construct, and might in any case be unsuitable for demonstration to a large group. A film loop, if available, might overcome these problems but would allow you no flexibility in controlling the demonstration. Static pictures – be they overhead projector slides or photographs – might not show clearly enough the *dynamics* of the process. But all of these drawbacks can be overcome with a program on a microcomputer. (Just such a program, CANALOCK, is the subject of section 7.5 later in this book.)

In any like situation, it is for you to weigh the inconvenience of setting up the computer and indeed of finding a suitable program against the real advantages which may be gained in that situation. If you are reasonably competent as a programmer, you can often create simple yet very effective demonstrations of this type fairly quickly – particularly if the programs are to be for your own use only!

Presentation

The examples cited above show uses of graphics which actually *make possible* particular teaching or learning approaches. There are other cases where the use of graphics is not essential, but is very desirable.

Before microcomputers became widely available, learning packages were designed to be run on mainframe computers, and allowed for the fact that they would probably be used with a variety of output devices, especially hard-copy devices (lineprinters and teletypes). This was especially true of the packages intended for use in schools. This range of devices placed certain restrictions on the designer who wanted to make the output attractive and readable: if he left too many blank lines between messages, he contributed to someone else's stationery bill; if the output was changed (for example, if a line was added to a graph or an entry was changed in a table), that whole unit of output had to be repeated. Graphs gave particular problems: most printers can only work down the paper, from top to bottom, whereas a person working with a pencil usually works from left to right: graphs plotted using such printers often have the x-axis vertical and the y-axis horizontal, because this makes the programmer's job much simpler.

These restrictions do not apply to microcomputers, provided that the output is being directed to the screen rather than to a hard-copy device. The designer who wants to make the output look attractive and readable must consider what the *whole screen* is showing at a given time. Blank lines between messages are not expensive; and it may be appropriate to position words in particular places, such as the centre of the screen. The screen can be completely cleared whenever this helps to make what follows more comprehensible, as when there is a natural break in the process. Individual entries in tables may be changed without needing to output the entire table again (as demonstrated in section 7.4). Chosen parameters may be displayed continually on the screen if this clarifies the situation under investigation; when parameters are altered, this can be shown on the screen by adjusting a single item, as with the tables. Graphs may be drawn with the x-axis horizontal (and with more precision than formerly, if high-resolution graphics is available); and extra features may be added to graphs as required without having to redraw the complete graphs on each occasion. Some programs which were originally written for mainframes have been made available for use on microcomputers without any attempt being made to adapt them as described above, but it is likely that good microcomputer software appearing henceforward will ensure that what appears on the screen is both clear and attractive.

In schools, at a time when money available for hardware is limited, graphics afford very practical possibilities for using microcomputers in teaching. Individual access to a computer may be severely restricted, but a class of thirty children can sit round a large television screen and learn from what is being displayed even at a distance, provided that the output consists mainly of pictures rather than words.

4.3 Limitations in practice

The first section of this chapter introduced the term 'graphics', and indicated that it is wide-ranging; the second section demonstrated that the opportunities for the use of graphics in teaching are limited only by imagination – we have given a selection of examples only, to whet your appetite and set you thinking.

84   *Graphics*

But the discussion was of graphics in the abstract, and we turn now to some of the practicalities of their use with real microcomputers.

Our working definition of 'use of graphics' is 'the placing of characters at will in chosen positions on the screen'. Most microcomputers allow the programmer to do exactly this and so offer some graphics capability; but when using computers, it is more important to know whether something is *convenient* than to know whether it is possible. If the programmer needs to write his code in machine language in order to achieve control over the positioning of characters on the screen, he is likely to find this inconvenient and time-consuming. So the programmer will be interested not so much in *whether* he can program graphics as in *how* he can program graphics.

Most microcomputers offer graphics as parts of languages such as BASIC and PASCAL; on some computers, the code used is clearer than on others. Suppose, for example, that you are programming in BASIC and wish to place an asterisk in the 20th position of the 10th row of the screen. On one microcomputer you might achieve this with the code 'PLOT 20, 10, "*"', while on another you might need to write 'POKE 33148,37'. Evaluation of the relative merits of these alternatives in making the situation clear is left as an exercise for you!

In this section, we ask:
- how detailed are the pictures on microcomputer screens?
- can graphics programs be run on different micros?
- what are the implications of using very detailed pictures?

Low-resolution graphics

It is not only in the commands with a language like BASIC that micros differ one from another as regards facilities for graphics. Suppose that you want to construct a picture or a diagram on the screen. You may do this by placing ordinary typewriter characters on the screen where you wish. You may, for example, choose to draw a picture by means of asterisks. If the microcomputer you are using is designed to display 25 lines of text on the screen and 40 characters in each line, then you can choose to place each of the asterisks in any one of 25 rows and in any one of 40 columns. But another computer may allow only 20 lines of text, another 24 lines and perhaps 80 rather than 40 characters in each line. So the number of different locations you can choose from will differ from computer to computer.

What will also differ from computer to computer is the choice of characters to place at a given location. Many microcomputers offer special 'graphics' characters for use in the construction of pictures. On some computers, some of these special characters are deliberately designed to increase the number of locations in which to place individual marks for making up pictures. On one, the space occupied normally by one character is divided notionally into six small squares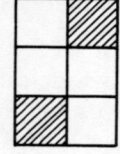

(**pixels**) and special characters are provided which enable you to block in any one or more of these small squares as required. This means that instead of having just 40 positions on each of 20 lines (800 different possible locations), a small square may be placed in any one of 80 (2 × 40) positions on any one of 60 (3 × 20) lines (4800 different possible locations). A similar facility is provided on  another machine, except that the space normally occupied by one character is here divided into only four small squares; in this case, the small square may be placed at any one of 80 (2 × 40) positions on any one of 50 (2 × 25) lines.

Computers differ also in the ease with which the facility just described may be handled. The acid test is this: how easy is it to add a small square at a desired location, without otherwise disturbing the pattern which already exists? Thus, how easy is it to turn  into

when you do not know that it is On some micros the method may entail one simple command, on others it may require a lengthy and tortuous subroutine. 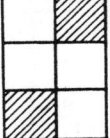 to start with?

Portability of programs with graphics

Since the graphics so far described in this section (low-resolution graphics) are available on most microcomputers, you will wish to make use of them in writing packages for use in teaching and learning. But this creates problems. That there is not just one version of BASIC, that different dialects of the language apply to different machines, has already been discussed in section 3.4. This makes it difficult to write programs which are capable of being run on a range of different computers. In many respects this is not a very serious problem, since the differences between the dialects of BASIC are often small, but in connection with graphics differences are considerable. Here, as we have said, both what can be done and the commands used to do it vary dramatically from machine to machine. One solution to the problem is to avoid the use of graphics in writing packages. This solution is often quite unacceptable.

An alternative is to give very careful thought to the structure of the programs being written, and to isolate those parts of the programming task which involve the use of graphics. It is likely that the uses to which the graphics are to be put in programs are uses which are going to recur repeatedly in different programs. If

86   Graphics

If circles are to look round, if curves are not to be confusingly jagged, if straight lines are to be drawn in any direction with reasonable precision, you need to be able to display more and smaller dots.

these uses are identified and described carefully, it should be possible to write subroutines in such a way that the same effect can be achieved on different microcomputers using comparable subroutines in appropriate dialects. Programmers can then make use of these subroutines in their applications programs: if a program includes graphics and is written for one particular microcomputer, it can be made available on another simply by removing one pre-written subroutine and replacing it by another.

High-resolution graphics facilities

Low-resolution graphics are inadequate for drawing diagrams or pictures in which a lot of detail is required. If circles are to look round, if curves are not to be confusingly jagged, if straight lines are to be drawn in any direction with reasonable precision, you need to be able to display more and smaller dots.

Some microcomputers offer this facility (high-resolution graphics) and allocate a block of memory for keeping track of the large numbers of small dots. Precisely how many small dots are available varies from machine to machine. One microcomputer allows a high resolution of 320×192 (compared with its low resolution of 80×60), a total of 61 440 dots (compared with 4800). To keep track of this many dots requires a lot of memory (especially since each dot may be displayed in one of three shades of grey or undisplayed), and so high-resolution graphics is provided on this machine not as a standard facility but as an additional board containing the necessary extra memory, which can be purchased separately and simply plugged in. Some other manufacturers provide high-resolution graphics as part of the standard machine.

Another facility offered on some microcomputers is colour: like high resolution, colour is standard on some, extra on others and unavailable on a few. Like high resolution also, colour is likely to become cheaper. Whether it is worth the additional expense to you depends upon your own needs.

Other factors affect the usefulness of graphics. It may be helpful to be able to combine high-resolution pictures with text, so that (for example) diagrams and graphs can be labelled. This is possible on some systems, not on others; if possible, the manufacturer's software may make it easy or difficult to use the facility.

Again, you may want to display moving pictures, or to present a number of pictures in quick succession. To make this possible, some systems allow more than one picture to be stored at a time, so that a first picture may be instantly replaced by a second. Other facilities which may be offered include the possibility of fading one picture into another, and of splitting the screen between two pictures or between one picture and text.

Speed can be a problem in making versatile use of a high-resolution graphics facility. If detailed pictures are to be displayed, they must first be specified – a process which requires information about a large number of points and lines, and which may entail time-consuming calculations. The delay involved in specifying pictures may mean that animated graphics are sometimes too slow to be worthwhile. (The last section of this chapter and Appendix A.3 consider ways of overcoming this problem and some of the other problems involving the use of graphics.)

Thus there are a number of factors to take into account if a microcomputer is to be used to display graphics. If you are purchasing a computer, then you should consider exactly what the graphics capability is offering, and whether this capability is part of the standard machine or must be purchased at additional cost. If a system is already available to you, it is worth checking to ensure that, where appropriate, you are using all the facilities offered.

4.4 Computer graphics versus other means of presenting pictures

The previous section considered some of the facilities which might – or might not – be available on microcomputers for drawing pictures on the television screen. The use of pictures in teaching and learning is not, of course, new; pictures have been available for a long time in books, on posters, or drawn on the blackboard or overhead projector. Pictures, whether static or moving, have been available also on the screen through films, film-strips and television programmes.

This section provides:
- *a comparison between computer graphics and films;*
- *thoughts about the ease of creating pictures with a computer;*
- *a comparison between computer graphics and static pictures.*

Films and microcomputers

Films can be used to present pictures which may assist the learner with imagery which helps him to learn. Where moving pictures are most appropriate for this purpose, moving pictures can be presented. Usually, the **definition** (the exactness or precision) and the colour of pictures presented by means of a film are of a high standard. The learner who watches the film as a member of a group may discuss the film when it is over, or may develop, through writing or drawing, some of the ideas which the film has given him. He may generalize the imagery he has developed and conjure up pictures other than those seen in the film.

88 Graphics

Microcomputers may be used to present static or moving pictures.

Microcomputers also may be used to present static or moving pictures to the learner. On the micro available, it may happen that the definition and colour of the pictures presented are not of such a high standard as those of film. The speed at which pictures can be presented may be another limiting factor.

On the other hand, the micro can be programmed so as to allow the learner or the teacher to intervene and control the flow of pictures. This control may be exercised at the beginning: the user may be invited to choose from a number of options, or to set some of the variables which apply to the situation. Or the intervention may be at various fixed points of the presentation. Or the user may be able to intervene at any time during the showing of the pictures, either to change the course of events or to provide feedback information which can be processed and used subsequently.

In presenting pictures, both films and microcomputer programs have much to offer both teacher and learner. Films have an aesthetic appeal; their use is unsullied by interruptions to the rhythm of the presentation. Films allow the film-maker to make a statement and to make it the way he wants. Films are likely to be used by teachers with groups rather than with individual learners.

Computer graphics versus other means of presenting pictures 89

Some teachers need to be fairly confident to use films productively; students discussing the film probably need stimulation without predetermined direction – stimulation which is searching but does not probe restrictively – and this may be difficult to give. In using films, a great deal may be left to the learner's imagination, and this may be very stimulating if teacher and learner can cope with it.

Where teachers are unsure about their confidence in using films, or where something rather different is required, microcomputers allow discussion during, rather than after, the presentation. And when such presentations are used with groups, it is often appropriate for the students to discuss with the teacher choices of what intervention to make or to forecast and describe what will be displayed if the intervention is made. On the other hand, if an individual student is using the microcomputer in this way, the necessity of making interactive decisions may ensure his interest and involvement in the process.

How does the user control the graphics?

Students learn by watching films; they also learn by making films. Making a film requires the exercise of a large number of skills. Some of these skills are technical – choice of camera, film, lighting and so on. Other skills are more conceptual – what is the film desired to show, how is this to be achieved, how are objects or people to be arranged, are moving pictures to be created by shooting sequences or by cartoon-like animation? The technical skills may form an irksome hurdle to cross, but be worth acquiring in their own right; it is the exploitation or enhancement of *conceptual* skills which are the reason for spending time in making films.

Students learn by making films; they learn also by programming computers to produce pictures. If the learner is to create static or moving pictures by means of a microcomputer, there are again technical skills which he will need to exercise, but in this case it is less clear what these skills need be. One possible route is for the learner to acquire the skill of writing a computer program in a standard language such as BASIC or PASCAL, and create his pictures by this means.

Consider a user equipped with a microcomputer with both high-resolution graphics and a BASIC interpreter, who wishes to display an equilateral triangle on the screen. He will probably need to tackle the task like this. First he must calculate the coordinates of the corners of the triangle, in whatever coordinate system is provided by the manufacturer's BASIC for high-resolution graphics: the corners might be at (0,0), (100,0) and (50,87), for example. Then he will write some program code to draw this triangle, code such as this:

```
200     PLOT 0,0
210     LINE 100,0
220     LINE 50,87
230     LINE 0,0
```

90 Graphics

On the other hand, it may not be necessary to use a universal programming language, such as BASIC, indeed it may be much easier not to do so. LOGO is one example of a special picture-drawing language which is becoming available on microcomputers. One way to think about the working of a LOGO program is to imagine an insect with dirty feet crawling about on the screen. In LOGO, a program to draw the same triangle might look like this:

```
TO TRIANGLE
FORWARD 50
LEFT 120
FORWARD 50
LEFT 120
FORWARD 50
END
```

LOGO was invented to introduce young children to geometry, to logical thinking and to programming, rather than to assist in drawing pictures easily (although it may be useful for this purpose also).

More specialized picture-drawing programs may be devised to suit particular contexts. Thus one piece of software might make it possible for a user to request a line to be drawn, and then, by means of a light pen, to 'drag' this across the screen or to rotate it to the required position; it might allow the user to request that two specified points be joined by a straight line, and so on. Another piece of software might permit the user to recall frequently-used shapes or designs, which could then be positioned, rotated or enlarged as desired.

Designing a package which enables a user to do what *he* wants to do, and in a way natural to *him*, which does not make undue demands on his understanding or concentration – a package, in other words, which provides a 'friendly environment' – is a difficult art; and there is much software on the market which is not as good in this respect as it should be. Quite sophisticated 'user-friendly' packages are available on big computers, and work is being done to make these available on microcomputers too. Such programs are useful not only to the student but also to the teacher.

Pictures, posters and microcomputers

As well as films, traditional methods of presenting pictures to the learner include textbooks, the blackboard, the overhead projector and posters. The use of textbooks to present pictures – for example, maps – has the advantage that every student can have one close to hand, and if students are working individually or in pairs on some assignment, this can be highly appropriate. On the other hand, if learning is taking place through direct teaching or discussion in a large group, it is not possible for the teacher or for one of the students to point to one place on everyone's map at the same time! For this purpose, it is more useful to have a map drawn on the blackboard – though if the map is to show reasonable detail, and if the lesson is first in the morning, the teacher will need to get up early; and he may need to repeat his half-hour's map drawing two days later when he teaches another class.

One solution to this problem is to have the map on a poster. Another is the overhead projector, which (arguably) combines the advantages of the blackboard with the advantages of the poster, and has a few more of its own. The map drawn the night before on an acetate sheet can be embellished during the teaching in response to suggestions from students. It can also be put away carefully for next time. But overlays may be used also: detail or particular features (roads, rivers, population densities and so on) may be added or removed so that points may be made. In a limited way, it is even possible to create moving images: overlays may be rotated or pulled across the picture.

A microcomputer used in conjunction with a large television screen (and, in some cases, high-resolution graphics) has all these advantages and some others. Different bits of a map can be added or removed at will and the program designer can contrive various devices for directing the learner's attention to a particular location on the screen or to particular features of the map. Pictures can also be updated easily: thus a political map of the world need not be redrawn completely when affiliations change – boundaries alone can be simply adjusted and names altered. A movable cursor can be used as a means of entering information into the computer: thus, the cursor could be moved to a particular place on the map and then used to record what is at that place. This brings us to a considerable advantage which computers have over other media: not only can additional information be stored in the computer, but the computer can *process* that information and use it in various ways: for instance, on the basis of its new information, it can make additions of its own to a map.

In all the applications described in this section, the advantages of the computer are its *flexibility*, especially in responding to requests from the user, and its ability to *process* information received and to act on the results of the processing. The disadvantages are more diffuse. Expense, and availability of the computer in the right place and at the right time, are obviously two factors. So also is the fact that effective use of the computer in the areas discussed is critically dependent on good software, which is not often readily available. A more subtle disadvantage is that the flexibility of the computer can make it too seductive, so that some teachers come to rely upon it in situations where other teaching methods might be more appropriate. If educational technology is too efficient, it becomes an end in itself, and has the effect of obstructing the process of learning rather than facilitating it.

4.5 Potential problems and some solutions

It is now time to consider problems which arise in connection with using graphics in microcomputer programs. Some of these problems are technical

Graphics

(that is, they relate to available hardware or manufacturers' software); yet technical problems are dangerously enticing, and it is wise to consider first the issues which bear directly upon good teaching. In this section, then, we give:

- *a warning against over-use of graphics;*
- *more thoughts about ease of use;*
- *comments on how graphics programs may be made intelligible to other programmers;*
- *suggestions about using standard chunks of code (subroutines);*
- *another warning, that detailed pictures can take ages to draw.*

Unnecessary use of graphics

Here is the first problem. Using microcomputers at all may be too sophisticated (or ludicrously expensive) a solution to a simple learning problem. Alternatively, although the use of a micro may be appropriate as a strategy in dealing with a specific learning task, use of graphics may detract from it: perhaps graphics has no place at all in a particular situation. It is clear from earlier sections of this chapter that pictures are aids to learning; undoubtedly graphics is sadly missing from many otherwise useful programs, particularly some of those adapted for micros without sufficient care or thought for the potential of the television screens which now replace the original output devices. On the other hand, fancy pictures may be inappropriate or simply put in through self-indulgence on the part of the program writer. Flashing titles, for example, may distract the learner's attention from his learning; they may also help the salesman distract the teacher's attention from the fact that his product is not offering any real help to the learner.

Making graphics feel natural

The second problem is an issue of design rather than a technical one. If programs are to be produced which enable users to create pictures on the screen, considerable thought must be given to the form in which the user conveys his wishes to the computer.

It is important to investigate how people do things when they are *not* using the computer. For instance, if you want someone to go and stand at a particular spot in a room, you say things like 'Go over there', 'No, further to your left', 'Turn to the left', 'No, not as much as that', 'Take a small step forward' and so on. Perhaps you are even more likely to say things like 'Go and stand by Julie', 'No, on her right', 'Not so close – give her room to breathe!' You are most unlikely to say 'Go to a spot 2m in the direction from the door to the window and 3m in the direction from the right-hand wall to the left-hand wall and face in a direction making an angle of 40° with the right-hand wall'. To ponder these and similar situations should be a prerequisite for designers of picture-drawing programs, so that non-specialists may find the programs comfortable to use.

Clarity and portability

The rest of the issues considered here concern the computers themselves. It has already been mentioned that different microcomputers have variations in the way that their hardware makes graphics (both low- and high-resolution) available to the user, and since there are as yet no programming standards relating to programming graphics, different manufacturers have developed very different languages for this purpose. This evidently affects seriously the portability of programs which involve graphics: a program written for one type of computer may need to be altered considerably before it will run on another. The very least any programmer should offer to help anyone reading his program is clear internal documentation explaining exactly what the commands in his program are designed to do. All graphics commands in a program (unless their meaning really is crystal clear to the unfamiliar reader) should be accompanied by comments (such as the 'REM' statement in BASIC) which explain them. Thus, it may be obvious to you that the statement

```
2340    PRINT "♡"
```

has the effect of clearing the screen, but most readers unfamiliar with your machine are likely to be completely mystified by it. So why not put instead

```
2340    PRINT "♡" : REM Clear the screen
```

on each occasion, and so make the situation clear to everyone?

In handling graphics and other facilities, some microcomputers' versions of BASIC make extensive use of the 'POKE' instruction. What 'POKE' does is to store a number at a directly specified location in core store. For example,

```
2570    POKE 32925, 33
```

will store '33' in the core store location whose address is '32925'. Any 'POKE' statement in a program is likely to mystify the reader and its purpose should always be made clear by use of a 'REM' statement.

We have already introduced the idea of memory-mapping, in which a block of memory is used to store information about the display on the screen (one dot on the screen being mapped onto one or more locations in core). This system permits a very crude way of placing a character in a desired location on the screen: to 'POKE' the code for that character into the appropriate position in the block of core which maps the screen. On one micro, the block of memory which maps the screen begins at address '32768'. Thus

```
3680    POKE 32768, C
```

94 Graphics

will place the character with code 'C' at the top left-hand corner of the screen. Since the first 40 memory locations are used to map the top line of the screen (in this particular system),

```
3720      POKE 32808, C
```

will place the character with code 'C' at the left-hand end of the second line down the screen.

```
3770      POKE 32850, C
```

will place the same character in the third position of the third row, and so on. A programmer will probably find it tedious to have to construct a 'REM' statement to explain clearly every such use of 'POKE' in his program. One alternative is to use a subroutine to make life easier for himself and at the same time to make his program clearer to others.

```
2560 REM SUBROUTINE Plot character code C in position J of row I
2570 REM
2580      POKE 32768 + 40*(I-1) + (J-1), C
2590 REM
2600      RETURN
```

This subroutine can be called as follows:

```
1760      I=5 : J=23 : C=65 : GOSUB 2560 : REM Plot a character
```

The first and most important features of a subroutine like this is that it makes the program easier to read. A second very important outcome is that it makes the program more portable: line 1760 will work just as well when the program is used on a different microcomputer, provided that the subroutine at lines 2560–2600 is replaced by a different subroutine which does the same job on the other micro. (Problems may or may not arise if the two micros have differing numbers of characters on a line or differing numbers of lines.) Doing it this way means that only one replacement will be required, rather than several; and that it is much clearer what must be replaced and how.

Library subroutines

Subroutines such as the one just given are likely to be of use not just in one program but in several. If subroutines are written with a clear purpose, are designed to be of general applicability and are well documented, then they may become **library subroutines** – that is, subroutines that you and others keep to be available whenever you need them, and which you use as a matter of course.

There are problems about writing library subroutines in BASIC: perhaps the most significant one is that variables used with a library subroutine cannot be used elsewhere in the BASIC program: this can be a nuisance. Nevertheless, using subroutines in this way is clearly better than not using them.

Where a project is aiming to make a number of programs available on a variety of microcomputers and is writing library subroutines to expedite this, there are good arguments in favour of writing such subroutines in machine code. The advantages are that they will execute more quickly, will take up less room and the problem of variable names will be avoided. If this is done then the subroutines become, in effect, part of the interpreter. There is a logical extension to this suggestion: interpreters for different microcomputers could be fairly easily modified to bring their graphics commands into line with one another, or at least so that there is a common subset of graphics commands available on all microcomputers.

Sometimes the problem in achieving a particular effect by use of graphics is that the programmer's task is very time-consuming. For instance, it is sometimes desirable to be able to draw large representations of letters or numbers on the screen, so that they may be easily recognized by a young child or at a distance. It may prove tedious to set up the machinery which makes a whole alphabet on this basis. However, once the job has been done, the resulting code may be used again and again – and not just by you, but by others. Here then is another situation where there is a strong case for library subroutines, so that someone writing a program using the effect need not spend considerable time in doing something which has been done many times before. (A program to do this, BIGLET, is given and discussed in section 7.2.)

Speeding up graphics programs

Taking up time can also be a problem in quite a different way, especially when using high-resolution graphics. If a microcomputer is used to draw moving pictures, the position of each line on each picture has to be calculated before the picture can be displayed and this is often a lengthy process. It is thus frequently difficult to produce pictures in sufficiently quick succession to give the illusion of smooth continuous movement (as on a film); and it is even more difficult to achieve this if the user is allowed to intervene to influence what is being displayed, since the sequence of pictures cannot then be prepared and stored in advance. One way of improving this situation is to write parts of the program in machine code which makes the program execute considerably more quickly. Many programmers would find this solution too time-consuming or too difficult – again, a case for library subroutines to perform tasks which are done frequently. One example is that of a machine-code subroutine to draw a circle: this could make the running of a program which involves moving circles much more rapid. (This example is given as part of the program CIRCLES, discussed in section 8.3.)

There are several problems here, such as how do we specify the tasks for which subroutines are to be written, and how do we write them in such a way that they will run on a number of different machines or even on different versions of the same machine? It is worth grappling with the problems, so that a large number of programmers may be offered the facilities to write fast graphics programs.

A different approach to speeding up graphics programs is to use a compiler rather than an interpreter (see page 276). Unlike an interpreter, a compiler first takes the program as a whole and produces from it a machine-code program which then does what is required. The translation is made just once; thereafter the program can be run as many times as needed. Programs usually run much faster if they are compiled, because the translation is not being done *while* the program is being run. But compilers are less readily available than interpreters on microcomputers, and more expensive; and it is more tedious to correct mistakes in the program code (though the same reason should encourage careful programming and good programming habits). These drawbacks to using compilers do not preclude the *commercial* production of fast programs in this way.

The way to write the most efficient programs which will run fastest is to write them in machine code; this way the program will not need translating at all and the programmer has complete control over how things are made to happen, so that, after a lot of thought, he can make them happen as fast as possible. Unfortunately, writing machine-code programs requires both considerable expertise and a great deal of time.

In view of some of the difficulties associated with graphics – the variability in provision of both hardware and languages, the ingenuity often required to achieve desired effects – many programmers fight shy of using graphics. But the graphics capability has an important role in the use of microcomputers in learning, and sensible and systematic approaches can minimize, if not eliminate, the trauma involved in using it.

5 The role of the computer in teaching

Computers are used a great deal more in some areas of the curriculum than in others. This may be because they are actually more useful in some subjects than in others, or it may be that most of those people who are equipped to write computer programs are those who have interests in certain subjects, especially the sciences – there are probably more imaginative programs written to teach physics than there are to teach English. English teachers who wish to find out what computers can do for them will naturally look to what is currently available, and may be disappointed. It will take time for computers to become widely accepted as useful educational aids, and for them to be used where they are appropriate and ignored where they are not.

This chapter reviews some of the classroom uses to which computers are currently being put. The examples cited relate necessarily to specific subjects, but they are examples of general points and techniques: it is for you to decide whether these are relevant to your own subject. In some subjects, very little has been done with computers to date; this does not mean that micros have no place in these subjects; rather, it means that there is room for innovation.

In assessing the talents of computers and the uses to which these talents may be put, this chapter examines:
- *the process of attaining mastery of situations;*
- *the things that computers are good at;*
- *different roles of computers in classroom teaching;*
- *various examples of translation;*
- *achieving the result you desire.*

5.1 Gaining mastery of situations

Learning means attaining mastery of a situation or of a set of situations. Driving, football, farming, woodwork, mathematics, art and writing each require different kinds of mastery. One way of assessing the value of the computer in teaching is to discover whether it helps the learner in such situations.

Mastery implies that a person understands not only the constituent parts of that situation but also the subtle and often very complex ways in which these constituent parts interrelate. In learning, however, the student may well need to

Computers are actually more useful in some subjects than others.

focus initially on individual parts of the whole. Thus in this section we look at mastery, in terms of:
- *facts;*
- *skills;*
- *attitudes and feelings;*
- *ideas and principles.*

Facts

In learning almost anything, there are facts which it is useful for the learner to know. The computer can help with such learning in a very straightforward way: it can store facts, ask the learner questions about them and test his memory of them. The spelling programs given in section 8.4 are examples of this use of the computer. Similarly, programs are frequently used which test a student's ability to recall multiplication tables. These are both examples of programs written to teach (or to test) specific facts.

It is also relatively easy to produce general-purpose programs to test students' abilities to recall *any* facts. With such a program, it is necessary only for the teacher to type in the chosen questions and the expected 'right' answers. Problems arise if the answers consist of phrases or of sentences rather than of single words. The computer has to distinguish between correct and incorrect responses, so it might need to decide that the response, though worded differently from the model answer, is in fact equivalent to it. Programs of this sort are difficult to write, especially in general-purpose languages (such as BASIC); but there are specialized languages (such as PILOT) which are designed to make the task easy, and these are known as **author languages**.

The ready availability of computers (and of other electronic devices such as calculators) may in time reduce the need to know so many facts: in some situations, the computer can remember information for you and supply it when required.

Skills

Learning usually requires the acquisition of many skills. Skills vary enormously. Steering a car, sharpening a chisel, subtracting whole numbers, punctuating written English, using perspective, balancing a chemical equation, climbing a rope, icing a cake, training a dog and tuning a cello – each is a skill that differs not only in type but also in complexity and in level from the others.

Most skills are improved by practice. The computer can help with the practice of skills in two different ways. Firstly, it can provide the learner with a situation in which it is possible to practise. For example, suppose that you wish to improve your ability to estimate the size of angles: the computer can display angles on its screen for you to try. Secondly, the computer can provide the learner with assistance. In the same example, the assistance might consist simply in telling you how big the angle shown actually is, leaving you to decide whether your estimates are generally too high or too low, or it might compare your estimate with the actual figure and give you information such as your percentage error.

Provision of assistance is often more difficult than might appear. An important aspect of some skills is that different people develop them in different ways. If you use a program to help a learner with his skill, therefore, the support that you give him in difficulty may not be as helpful as you think; he may not be trying to cope with the situation in the way your advice suggests. For this reason, good programs of this type are difficult to write.

Sometimes programs are written to teach facts, when it might be more appropriate to teach skills. Earlier in this section, we mentioned programs to teach multiplication tables. Facts about multiplication are not isolated facts; it is possible to teach strategies for inferring some facts about multiplication from others. Programs which help the learner to infer (a skill) are probably more helpful to him than those which simply teach facts.

All programs to teach facts, and some programs to teach skills (particularly cognitive skills and where students are advised to perform in one particular way) are called **drill programs**. Essentially, a drill program is one that is designed to modify a student's knowledge or behaviour in a manner completely prescribed by the teacher.

Attitudes and feelings

The attitudes and feelings of a learner towards what he is learning often determine how effectively he learns. Many factors shape a student's attitudes and feelings; it is not easy to offer general prescriptions. Computers may help in some cases.

At one level, computers can perhaps motivate the learner because they are new and exciting. Some students are automatically more interested in anything displayed on a television screen than the same thing displayed on a blackboard.

If the computer addresses the student by name and draws attractive pictures (even though these may have little to do with the teaching), his rather superficial interest may be sustained a little longer. Such motivation is likely to be short-lived; computers will not always seem new.

The interest of students may also be fostered by providing a game structure in which to learn. For instance, computer and learner may each have horses depicted on the screen: if the learner gets his answers right, his horse advances from left to right across the screen; if wrong, the computer's horse advances. Such techniques appeal to some students, if used sparingly.

On the other hand, the computer may provide a student with strong motivation as an intrinsic part of what he is learning. Pictures on the screen may not simply be attractive, they may also make sense of the situation in new ways; a game played on the computer (either against the computer or against other students) may itself teach, as well as motivate. Simulation games, used increasingly in teaching geography, economics, history and science, often come into this category.

Finally, computers may help improve a student's attitude simply because they improve the learning situation. The information available to a student at different stages of his learning may be fuller than might have been possible without the computer; it may also be available more quickly. It may even be possible using the computer to provide tasks for the student which really are more exciting to do than those possible without a computer. This is clearly illustrated in scientific simulations: take for example a simulation of a nuclear reactor. There is much that a student can learn about the effects of varying temperature and speed of reaction, yet the danger of anything approaching the reality is prohibitive. With a model, however, he can actually allow the reactor to overheat, and observe the (simulated) consequences.

Ideas and principles

Before he can attain complete mastery of a situation, the learner needs to be able to make use of the facts and skills he has acquired, to see when and how they are relevant in achieving some goal. Here also the computer can be useful. In situations in which the student is asked 'What is happening here?' or 'How can we make it do that?', he can develop his ability to decide what might be relevant, try it out and so discover what happens. In many of the situations described later in this chapter, the computer is playing exactly this part.

5.2 The advantages of a computer

In assessing what the micro can offer you in your teaching, you may need to look further than the published material already available. You may need to discuss what might be or should be available, and what the micro is capable of doing for

you. To help you, we offer a summary of the more significant talents of the micro:
- *micros can remember a great deal of information;*
- *micros are good at presenting information visually;*
- *micros calculate at high speed;*
- *micros are reliable in their operation;*
- *micros can make choices at random;*
- *micros can control, and be controlled by, other equipment;*
- *micros can be operated by inexperienced users.*

Computer memory

The memory of the microcomputer can store information – information about how to run a program and information which can be used by that program. You can give the computer any facts that you wish it to use, provided that you can specify those facts precisely and provided that you understand how it is to use them.

It is relatively easy to give the computer facts about your subject. It is not so easy to give it facts about what a student may find difficult: how much do you need to say? It is extremely difficult to tell the computer what *most* students are likely to find hard. This is why little progress has yet been made in **tutorial computer-assisted learning**, in which a computer *replaces* a teacher in helping a student to acquire some substantial piece of learning.

Note that if you want to use programs which access a large amount of stored information, you will almost certainly need a disc system rather than a cassette system. These alternative forms of storage are discussed on pages 265–7.

Presentation of information

Most micros can draw pictures, though their versatility in doing this varies. (This was discussed in Chapter 4.) Most micros are also good at presenting information on the screen, clearly and flexibly. For example, it is usually possible to change particular items on the screen without affecting the content of the rest of the screen (as shown in section 7.4). The clarity of information when displayed on the screen depends more on the skill of the designer or programmer than on the limitations of the micro.

One aspect which may prove significant is that the amount of text that can appear on the screen at any one time is limited – most micros are limited to roughly 20 lines of 40 characters. If a particular use requires blank lines between lines of text (as is the case in the program described in section 7.7, for example), there is even less room for text. In some cases, where the screen is not big enough, it may be better to obtain what is required on a printer. The designs of good screen layouts and good printer layouts may be quite dissimilar.

The speed of the computer

On the whole, the micro does what it does very quickly; it is particularly quick at performing the necessary calculations. Sometimes it even works too quickly, and needs to be slowed down to avoid confusing the learner.

Speed is important in finding and displaying information. In this case, speed depends on how much information the computer has to search through before it finds what is sought; it therefore depends also on how the information is structured. This is often thought to be a problem for the programmer, but the program designer (perhaps the teacher) has a vital part to play; it is he who knows how the information will be used, which items will be used most frequently, what are the most useful ways of requesting information, and so on.

Speed is important with pictorial display, too. This is usually quite fast, but not always as fast as the designer might like. Generally speaking, speed is most likely to be a problem if pictures are very detailed, or required to move, or under the control of the user; the more of these are true, the bigger the problem. This issue is discussed in sections 4.3 and 4.5.

Sometimes even operations which the computer carries out rapidly and efficiently may appear painfully slow to the user. Suppose the designer tries to help the user by interrupting the program at various points to fill the screen with information about what is happening and what choices are available at the time. Although it may take only a few seconds to display this information, to the user who knows exactly what to do next and who is waiting to do it, these few seconds can be intensely irritating.

Reliability of programs

Programs on micros are as reliable as are their programmers. Micros virtually never make mistakes. (A programmer may unintentionally tell them to make what he then regards as mistakes!) Micros can be relied upon to get calculations right; they can be relied upon to present the various stages of the program in the appropriate order. This does not mean that programs have to be predictable, far from it; the micro can be programmed to take random decisions.

Chance in programs

One of the major uses of computers in teaching is in providing simulations of real processes and events. Fundamental to so many aspects of life is chance, and for most simulation programs to be of any real value, it must be possible to incorporate this element of the unpredictable.

Almost all micros now include such a facility. It usually consists in a means of generating **random numbers**, numbers between 0 and 1. On successive calls to the random-number generator, the program might be given 0.88732, 0.77737,

0.21358, 0.60104, and so on. These numbers are then utilised in taking a decision which would normally be subject to chance.

Take the simple example of tossing a coin: an unbiased coin might fall showing 'heads' or 'tails'. To simulate this on a micro, one can invoke the random number generator and look at the number thrown up: if it is 0.5 (halfway along the spread of numbers from 0 to 1) or over, the result is treated as 'heads'; if less than 0.5, it is treated as 'tails'.

Any process subject to fate can be simulated in this fashion – the weather, the deal of a pack of cards, the roll of a dice, the distribution of genes in offspring, the outcome of some tactical manoeuvre in a battle, the selection of a question from a list of possible questions in a test, the movement of an animal in a maze. All that is required is a good estimate by the designer of the *probability* of a given outcome – as we supposed that for a fair coin, the probability of getting 'heads' is 1 in 2 – and the decision can be taken randomly by the micro.

Random choices of this sort can be taken quickly by the computer, and find many applications, especially in games. One of their most interesting is in defining a set of initial conditions at the start of a program in which the user must head towards a fixed goal, and in influencing thereafter his progress towards that goal. A typical example would be in the field of economics, in which the user has to manage his stocks for a period of a year and show a profit. A variety of variables could be determined at the outset by means of random numbers – how many commodities he deals in, for instance, what the share prices are at the beginning, whether the price of each goes up or down, whether the price of gold stays constant, and whether there is a national fuel shortage. And chance can be invoked again during the year – a political crisis, a change of government, a national coal strike, a major company takeover, and so on.

Control of other equipment

Micros can be used to control other pieces of equipment. These may be very simple or very complex; they may have all kinds of functions. Some examples: the micro might be connected simply to a bell, which is rung at various times in accordance with what is happening in the program; it might be connected to a synthesizer and loudspeaker to produce music or speech; it might be used to control scientific experiments. One of the most interesting uses is in controlling other teaching aids, such as a tape recorder and film projector: the combination of these can provide some very sophisticated presentations.

The flow of information may be in either or both directions. The tape recorder may tell the micro that the tape has finished. The micro may tell the projector to show the next slide. A photocell may report the level of light as an experiment progresses. A micro may alter the strain exerted upon a piece of metal, record its changing length, take readings more frequently as the metal begins to break, simultaneously plot a graph of these, and start a camera at the moment of breakage.

Communication with the user

A considerable advantage of a computer is the control which it offers to the user. But it is important too for the computer to be able to control the user to some extent; at least to the extent that he is prevented from completely disrupting the smooth operation of the program.

A great deal has been said in Chapter 3 about ways in which communication between computer and user may be designed to help the user. The user must receive the greatest possible assistance from the computer in running the program, and the ease with which this can be offered is affected by the degree of flexibility of the program. The more flexible the program, the more useful it is, usually; yet the more flexible the program, the more difficult it is for the program to support and help the user. If the program does just one thing well, it will be useful only if that is *exactly* what you want done. If the program does many things well, it may be hard for the user to operate the program and he may be spoilt for choice. Precisely because the program is flexible, and because it can be used by different users in different ways, it is difficult to build guidance into the program about what to do with it! If the user is a student, there may be a teacher on hand to provide the guidance required. If the user is a teacher, the problem remains. One kind of solution is to build into the program six examples, say, of its use. The teacher can invoke any one of these six suggestions and thereby gain insight into some of the other uses to which the program may be put. (The GRAPH program given in section 8.5 contains examples in this way.)

It is still important for any program that, whatever the user does with it, he should not be able to produce a situation which requires him to start again from scratch. Programs should be robust enough to deal helpfully with the most idiotic input from the user.

5.3 The function of the computer in learning

There are many different ways in which teaching programs can be classified – by subject, by facilities used, by make of computer, by intended age-range, and so on. One way of highlighting the potential uses of the computer in teaching is to classify programs according to the function of the computer. This is not so much a classification of programs as a classification of program uses; one teacher will use a program in one way, while for another teacher the same program will fulfil a quite different purpose.

Classification in this section is in terms of:
- *the number of students being taught;*
- *the number of students who are looking at the output from the computer;*
- *computers used as sophisticated 'blackboards';*
- *computers used as large stores of information;*
- *computers making new things possible for the learner;*

- computers aiding the teacher to do what he is already doing;
- computers totally in charge of learning.

How many students?

Some programs, such as the drill programs mentioned earlier in this chapter, are clearly designed to be used by individual students; the learner sits at the keyboard, waits for a question, types his response and thus improves his mastery of some facts or some skill. Certain games programs also fall into this category – they are designed for one person to play against the computer. Although it is perfectly obvious that such programs are designed for individual use, they are nevertheless used occasionally with a whole class; and such use is often remarkably successful!

Other programs are specifically designed for use by large groups. Simulation programs in geography or history, for example, may be designed to be played by cooperating or competing groups of students. Other programs (as in art, music, and the sciences) may provide illustrations for a teacher while talking through some topic; although he could do this with one student only, such use is unusual. Yet other programs (in any subject) serve to promote discussion, so it is much easier for a group to benefit from them than for an individual to do so.

In institutions where computers are not plentiful, limited availability encourages teachers to think of group rather than of individual use. There are exceptions to this: primary schools often use drill programs with individuals or very small groups, and computers have valuable applications in remedial work (catching up after an illness, for example) and in teaching students with learning handicaps.

Being able to see output from the computer

In many applications of a computer in class teaching, it is necessary for the students to be able to see output produced by the program. Output is most conveniently displayed on a screen. A single television placed centrally may be sufficient for a class of, say, thirty students. For classes much larger, however, this proves inadequate: the screen cannot be read from a distance. The situation can be improved by using several other television sets (monitors), all connected to the computer and distributed around the room, or by using a single, very large screen. If it is not necessary for the demonstration to be live, with the program available for interaction, there may be a case for pre-recording a demonstration and displaying this (enlarged) on a film projection screen.

Clear visibility to all students is most critical when output comprises large quantities of text: this is the most difficult to read, and students quickly lose interest if they cannot see the display. Pictures are perhaps easier to see, and are often easier to understand than the equivalent text.

It is not always necessary for the display to be visible all the time. Pictures or

At other times, the computer is simply one visual aid among many.

text may be so central to the teaching that students must be able to see them constantly; at other times, the computer is simply one visual aid among many (such as a blackboard or an overhead projector), used for only a part of the lesson; it is still important to be able to see the screen, but only for brief periods; perhaps the students will simply gather round the set. In situations where the computer is providing information (albeit vital) about calculations performed or state-of-play in a game, it may not be necessary for students to see the screen at all, but merely to be told of the output. Even further removed from their sight are the uses of the computer before the lesson begins (to provide data or printed material) or after the lesson has ended (to analyse results). Here students need not see the computer at all; indeed they may not even need to be aware of its existence.

The 'electronic blackboard'

Some advantages of computer screens over other means of visual presentation – blackboards, films and overhead projectors – were discussed in section 4.4. In summary, the computer is likely to be the preferred medium in situations which benefit from the use of pictures which move, pictures in which different features are selectively highlighted, pictures in which detail is added or removed, and pictures whose detailed composition or whose order of presentation is varied in response to decisions taken at the time. In these cases, the computer is used largely as a sophisticated display; a role that has been dubbed the 'electronic blackboard'.

Obvious candidates for this kind of treatment are particular techniques in art and design; maps in geography or history; the interpretation of graphs in geography, economics, science and mathematics; and all diagrams in science and maths. If you glance through textbooks on any subject in which explanation is supported by pictures or diagrams, and if you then reflect on the exact ways in which the diagrams *provide* this support, you will quickly discover where the 'electronic blackboard' may be of use to you. The program CANALOCK (given in section 7.5) is an example of this use of the computer; the program is simple, yet it would be difficult to achieve its effect by any other method.

Even where pictures are not required, the computer may be used to highlight chosen features of a situation, as, for example, in studying textual material. The program HILIGHT (given in section 7.7) provides an instance of this.

Information files

The growing use of computers in educational administration (for storing files of information about students or stock, for example) is beyond the scope of this book. But the computer also has many uses as a source of information *in teaching*. A **database** is a set of information in the computer, structured so that it may readily be accessed in one of several predetermined ways to answer one of a range of expected questions. One example of a database is in the teaching of local history: the database consists of parish registers and similar records, and is used to help research into a variety of questions concerning the local population of the period. Databases may be used in any subject where it is useful to access individual pieces of information from a large quantity.

(Databases are becoming more common as domestic commodities. Devices similar in some ways to electronic calculators can be used in the home to provide information on specialist subjects at the press of a button – gardening, cookery, car repairs, plant identification and the like.)

Databases need not always be created by the teacher for the student. Sometimes students set up their own files of information. For some time there have been in circulation variants of a program called ANIMAL. In essence, the user thinks of an animal, and the program seeks to identify it by asking questions. On occasions, the computer gives up, either because the animal was previously unknown to it, or because the questions were inadequate in identifying it accurately. After surrender, the computer requests the user to supply a question which will help it thereafter to distinguish the new animal from the others which it knows. In this way, the computer can gradually accumulate an impressive amount of knowledge about animals.

ANIMAL can be used equally well with any subject other than animals, especially subjects in which classification is being taught. It can be used by an individual, but group use often provokes interesting discussion when it is necessary to devise a new question: students become aware of the need for appropriate structure in the database. False identifications usually result from inconclusively worded questions, so that students of subjects such as languages and mathematics learn much about the choice of appropriate words through which to communicate their ideas.

There are times when it is useful for the computer itself to act as teacher to the individual student, providing him with a large body of factual information and the tutorial help he needs to assimilate it. This use of **tutorial computer-assisted learning** is fraught with problems (some of which were mentioned in the previous section, under the heading 'Computer memory'*)*.

The computer as enabler

A major component of learning is learning how to solve problems: the computer can assist by posing problems for students to solve. One advantage of using the computer to do this is that the solutions suggested by the students can often be fed into the computer and judged in the light of the results that they produce; feedback obtained from such trials may suggest better ways of tackling the problems. So in economics the student might forecast the combined effect on farm prices over ten years of inflation at 10 per cent, government subsidy of milk products to the tune of 3 per cent and a fall in demand for arable crops of $3\frac{1}{2}$ per cent, the student then having to decide what crops to grow to maximize his profits over the same period. Such problems, and there are many parallels in geography, biology, chemistry and physics, are difficult to conceptualize on paper and require much arithmetic to evaluate. With a computer, the student is free to suggest the strategy and to observe the result as calculated immediately by the computer.

A quite different use of the computer as an enabler is illustrated in the task of essay composition. Many people have difficulty in writing – difficulty in imagining, difficulty in describing, difficulty in creating varied language. All of these can be helped by a computer.

Suppose you want a student with these difficulties to write a story. Instead of sitting him at a desk with pen and paper, you sit him at a computer. The program first offers him the subject – perhaps it simply picks five nouns randomly from its database and the student must somehow combine these to form his story. As he types in the story, the program throws up adjectives at random to go with the nouns he is using (difficult to program, but possible to a limited extent!), and he is in each case invited to accept the one chosen or provide his own. And every time he types a full stop, the program issues a conjunction or an adverb to begin the next sentence – 'although', 'perhaps', 'sometimes' and so on. Apart from making the task of writing enjoyable, the student may gain in confidence; and at the end of the task, the story can be *printed* by the computer's printer, which gives him an attractive piece of work to take away.

In considering the computer as an enabler, we come yet again to its ability to produce pictures. Pictures may stimulate creative work and discussion which would not occur otherwise: the unique benefit of the micro in this context is that it can develop and modify images in the light of continuing work. The program CIRCLES, given in section 8.3, is an example of this.

Support for teachers

Computer programs *may* help you simply by capturing your students' interest and encouraging them to concentrate on what you are teaching. It may also help you in more specific ways.

An earlier part of this section cast the computer in the role of the 'electronic blackboard'; it may also serve as the 'electronic answer book'. In mathematics, science, geography and the social sciences, exercises of a repetitive nature are often set to develop skills in handling structured situations. Students want to check their answers to these exercises, so before the lesson, the teacher works these out (unless they are available in an answer book). While discussing such exercises, you or your students may pose questions of the form 'What would happen if . . . ?' One response, often a useful one, is to say: 'Try it and see.' Yet if you have many students, you may well be deterred from saying this by the need to check all the extra answers. A computer program may free you from this.

A computer may also be useful to the student in checking his answers, even if these are standard answers to standard exercises. Whereas the teacher or the answer book may provide only the end of the chain of reasoning – a number, perhaps, or a diagram – the computer can take the student through the process of solution step by step, so helping him to see why this method works, or where he himself went wrong.

Management of learning

Computers may exert other influences on the organization of learning. Teaching methods in which students work in small groups within a larger class are still not very common, and such groups may be disconcerting to some of the students. Computers may encourage use of this technique by managing simulation games, for example, in which one group competes against another. Students may find this kind of situation less threatening.

Computers often provoke more discussion of the subject than do other methods of teaching it, and may entice teachers into setting open-ended problems where tightly structured exercises are the norm. Shifts of this kind in styles of teaching may be small but significant, and may provide far-reaching possibilities for the teacher.

Computers are occasionally used to manage learning in a more detached, more comprehensive way. Whole courses may be organized in which the computer defines each student's route, marks his work, records his results, and issues a report. Whether the advantages of such **computer-managed learning** outweigh the disadvantages depends on the subject, the objectives of the course, the availability of specialist teachers and so on. This is probably the most contentious role of computers in teaching because it is the one in which the computer is most influential in determining the teaching offered.

5.4 Translation

To some people, the process of translating one language into another appears to be a simple mechanical task of the sort suited to computers, and for some time energy has been devoted to developing suitable programs. The degree of success has varied.

We said in Chapter 3 that translation of one programming language into another, as in the case of the translation of a high-level one to a low-level one, is relatively straightforward; computer programming languages are built round certain known rules which are always followed to the letter. With 'natural' languages, such as English, German or Russian, there are loose rules which are frequently broken in daily usage, and there are idiomatic expressions whose logical forms do not reflect their meanings. ('Before the exam started, he was on edge,' to cite but one example in English.) To be able to program translation more effectively, you need precisely the rules which are missing.

Yet whereas the translation of natural languages is not easily susceptible to the use of a machine, many other forms of translation are. As we have seen, the computer itself relies heavily on translation as when it translates your instructions into machine instructions, and it can perform a similar service in areas such as:

- music (written and played);
- words (written and spoken);
- codes (encoded and decoded);
- language (correct and incorrect);
- text (laid out in different ways);
- numbers (as characters and as pictorial representations).

Musical symbols and sounds

The performer on a musical instrument who wants to learn a new piece buys the sheet music and plays this: in doing so, he translates the symbols written on paper into sounds which can be heard. A record player creates music by translating the irregularities in the record groove into amplified vibrations. Similarly, a microcomputer connected to a loudspeaker can translate instructions given via a program into sounds. The instructions may be in the form of music written in the conventional manner on the screen of the computer, or by touching a keyboard depicted on a touch-sensitive screen, or some other method.

Musicians perform other kinds of translation, too, such as transposition (in which a piece written in one musical key is rewritten in a new key) and transcription (in which a piece arranged for one group of instruments is arranged for a different group). In each of these, the computer can be programmed to do the job – and to produce neat finished copy at the end.

Section 8.1 provides a program which produces a complete major scale on the basis of a chosen keynote.

Written and spoken words

Micros connected to loudspeakers may produce not just music, but speech. The generation of speech needs a special chip in the computer; such chips are now available for several micros. With this facility, the computer can translate words typed at the keyboard into spoken words (provided that they have been programmed to recognize these words). Most of the potential for application of this process has yet to be explored; there is a clear possible use in spelling tests, where the computer will 'say' the word which is to be spelt.

Also being developed are chips to do the reverse activity: to interpret spoken words and use them to control equipment or the flow of the program. Uses of this sort will not be confined to the teaching of languages.

Codes

To record spoken language, you translate it into written symbols. The symbols are used systematically and form an agreed code, understood by those who turn speech into writing and by those who turn writing into speech.

'Code' has also the specialized meaning associated with concealment. Here one set of symbols which are clearly intelligible is translated into another set which hide the content. Computers, since they work quickly and accurately, are ideally suited to this kind of activity: they are perfect for encoding, following a set of predefined rules (see section 8.2 for an example), and for decoding using the same known rules; and they have been successfully applied in code-*breaking* – decoding with unknown rules.

Coding and decoding are not restricted to the field of espionage; the same principles apply to the deciphering of ancient texts and to the interpretation of the mechanisms of genetic inheritance. In other situations, possible states, choices or outcomes are represented symbolically for the purpose of recording or systematizing. This is true, for example, of the moves in chess; and the computer can be used either to teach the notation or to execute the moves as instructed.

Correcting language

Once in the hands of the publisher, the manuscript provided by the author of a book is translated by the editor into language in a form suitable for publication. A similar task is performed by language teachers in correcting the scripts of their students, though the object then is not so much to perfect the final copy as to encourage the student to learn from the corrections. But it may in fact be discouraging to have your masterpiece returned to you with a mass of red ink indicating spelling mistakes, bad punctuation or poorly structured arguments.

Computers cannot of themselves resolve this problem, but they can make it much more palatable, either by remedying errors as they are made or by enabling the student to produce an untarnished printed text of the final version. The second is easier to achieve than the first. The student types his original piece into the computer, and after discussion with the teacher, the piece is amended (which is not too difficult on a micro): when everyone is happy with the current version, this is printed, and provides something worth keeping.

As to the first way of helping, are there ways of getting the computer to advise the student as he produces the first draft? In principle, yes: it is theoretically possible for the computer to correct, say, spelling mistakes automatically, though this requires the program designer to forecast accurately which words are likely to be spelled wrongly and to indicate what the wrong spellings will be. So there is undoubtedly scope for the computer to help in writing, but the area is at present largely unexplored.

Layout of text

Even when the language as written is correct, its layout on the page may look wrong. An attractive appearance is encouraged by indenting all paragraphs to the same extent, by aligning the beginnings (and perhaps the endings) of each line of text, by leaving larger spaces after full stops than after commas, and so on. Computers are good at laying out printed words consistently in accordance with general instructions.

Computers are exceptionally good at substituting certain items in place of others. Suppose, for example, that just prior to publication we had decided to use 'programme' instead of 'program' right the way through this book. We could each have gone through looking for occurrences of the word, but we should probably have missed one or two. A computer could have checked all the way through *and* made the alterations, without overlooking any.

All this and more is involved in **word processing**. While this is already being exploited in administration and business studies, the use by teachers in producing learning materials is growing fast. Many typesetters use computers for their work, and systems are now available to link these with micros; subject to cost, therefore, you may in time be able to prepare your materials – or theses, or reports, or articles – on your micro, and have them typeset directly when you are confident that they are accurate.

The computer is capable of other transformations of text also. We have mentioned the problems associated with a large class looking at text displayed on one television screen. In this context, and with young learners, it may be helpful to be able to display large letters using the graphics capability of the micro. With the program BIGLET, given in section 7.2, the user touches a key and the micro displays a large picture of the appropriate character.

Counting is a fairly mindless activity, and computers are very good at it.

Numbers in computing

All sorts of people need to count things. The whole discipline of statistics is based on counting. Counting is a fairly mindless activity, and computers are very good at it. If you give a computer some information, it will be able to make all sorts of counts for you.

Consider a program which analyses text and produces statistics about its vocabulary and structure – 'lexicostatistics', as they are properly called. How many syllables per word, on average? How many different words? How many spellings of the same word? How many uses of each word? Does one word always occur with another? A single program can be written which counts all of these and more; and with so powerful a tool, the user must be especially aware of what it is he actually wants – in this case, which particular count – and be prepared to disregard the rest. (Numbers, particularly when specified to eight decimal places, seem curiously incontestable!) The program can be designed to help the user with this, as for example by offering him a clear menu. (Such a menu is the subject of the program fragment LEXICAL, given in section 7.3.)

Although numbers are useful in drawing conclusions, interpreting them is not always an easy task. It is often helpful to have the numbers translated into pictures – charts, graphs and the like – and computers can do this with ease.

Computers can translate into pictures other things which are based on numbers. The program called GRAPH, given in section 8.5, translates the written statement of a mathematical function into a graphical illustration of it.

5.5 Achieving your aims

All computer programs are certainly intended to achieve specified aims. Whether or not they do so in practice is a measure of the success of the program in helping the learner to learn. The learner's task may be seen as one of interacting with the micro to attain some known goal, and the program is a good one if it assists the learner in doing so. The success or otherwise of the program is particularly evident in cases where the student is trying out solutions and using feedback from the micro to guide his next attempt in each case.

In the final section of this chapter, we consider the role of the computer in achieving known aims:
- on the screen;
- off the screen;
- in programming;
- in teaching and in learning.

On the screen

One kind of program designed to help students develop some skill or understanding presents a situation on the screen and then invites the student to instruct the micro in such a way that the screen reaches a specified final state. To take an example, suppose that the screen is displaying a maze. You are depicted by some symbol at the centre of the maze, and your task is to move the symbol out of the maze, using instructions such as 'R' for 'turn right', 'F' for 'forward' and 'T' for 'turn around'. If you succeed in leaving the maze, you demonstrate thereby that you have understood the conventions operating in that system.

Alternatively, consider a program which enables pictures to be drawn. Various instructions are available to you – 'square', 'circle', 'down', 'bigger' and so on – and using these you must reproduce the picture on your workcard of a house. If you understand these instructions and think them through clearly, the house will be easy to draw, and the image will confirm the clarity of your reasoning. If not, the picture may be nearly right, so that another try with a minor change may give the desired result.

The program GRAPH, given in section 8.5, contains an option which enables the computer or the teacher to draw the graph of a mathematical function without the students knowing what function is being drawn. The students' task is to identify this function. Each attempt is entered into the computer, which simply draws the new function given: the computer does not decide whether the attempt is right or wrong; that decision is left to the students. The computer merely superimposes the graph of the suggested function on the graph of the unknown function. Discrepancies between the two graphs provide the students with clues, and they can then modify their current suggestion.

Off the screen

Similar analyses may apply to programs which make no use of graphical output. Suppose that in a simulation game you are the manager of a company. You have to make decisions each year about marketing, pricing, investment and so on. Your goal is, let us say, to achieve a steady growth in turnover of 5 per cent. Having made your decisions, you feed them into the micro and this does the calculations. Suppose further that you get it wrong. Perhaps the program allows you to try again. Perhaps it allows you to vary the factors one by one and observe their individual effects. But perhaps it prevents you from doing these things, not because it is badly designed, but because the designer wishes to force you to cope with the *interaction* of the various factors. In either case, the outcome you actually get can be compared with the outcome you desired; you can learn from the differences and from the effect of any adjustment you make.

Programming

Programming is a skill taught to students on many computer studies courses. It is also taught sometimes to students for whom the goal is not to learn about computers at all, but some other subject in which computers figure only incidentally. So in chemistry there may be a phenomenon which can be described by a mathematical model, and in writing a program to exploit that model and thereby simulate the phenomenon, the student may learn more about the model. For whatever reason programming is undertaken, the programmer learns from the outcome of his program. Programs rarely achieve the desired outcome first time, and in comparing the actual outcome with the intended outcome, the programmer continues to learn.

It is difficult in some ways to distinguish this concept of learning through programming from the activities already described in this chapter. The definition of a programming language is itself unclear: any program which offers the user choices at various points is in a sense providing a programming language. The distinction is particularly imprecise when commands to be executed are entered simultaneously and performed later in succession – are you programming or using an applications program?

LOGO is one such program – or language – which provides commands for drawing pictures on a screen. At its lowest level, it can be used directly for that purpose; yet it is in every sense a special-purpose programming language. If there is a moral, it is this: if you wish to introduce your students to programming, if you feel that a concept in mathematics or physics or geography is better understood through the process of writing a program, do not simply assume that this program must be written in BASIC. It may be better to identify a program such as LOGO which provides the command structure of a programming language yet is more closely dedicated to your chosen activity.

Using LOGO, students can draw a house; using BASIC, students can draw a house. But it is much easier using LOGO than BASIC, and students using LOGO may actually learn more about programming!

Teaching and learning

To find the right program for the job you want done is important and may be difficult. As with textbooks, it is easy to make the wrong choice on the first try;

and as with the programs we have been discussing, you must compare what you get with what you wanted and modify your approach next time. By continued trial and error, *you* will achieve the desired outcome!

So we return to the subject of the chapter and the subject of the book. At the beginning of this chapter, we suggested that although a lot of software designed to help in teaching is rapidly becoming available, this is just a start. The program you need may be waiting to be designed.

Perhaps you do not need a computer at all; that is for you to judge. Will it really help you to teach better? Will it help your students to attain mastery of the situations in which you place them?

6 Day-to-day use of a computer

This book began with a discussion of learning, and learning remains throughout the recurrent theme. Any discussion of the use of computers *in* teaching needs to keep clearly in view the *purpose* of teaching.

Sometimes, a computer will be of assistance to you in your teaching; at other times it will be inappropriate or harmful. We hope that this book is helping you to discover which situation is which, and that if a computer *is* of use, you now have some notion of its workings and capabilities.

A computer can be likened to a kitchen: you know what you want to cook; the kitchen is the means of doing so. Unless you are a very keen do-it-yourselfer, you will not want to become bogged down in the mechanics of your kitchen equipment; ideally, you will just use it to cook. But a few of the appliances need a certain amount of routine attention – servicing and maintenance – usually done by a specialist. And you may occasionally need extra equipment. If you want to whip cream, you can make do with a fork, though you could whip it more easily with a hand whisk. If you whip cream often enough, it may be worth investing in an electric whisk; and this may come with other attachments which widen your culinary expertise. So in computing you can get by with very little, or acquire ever more sophisticated special gadgets.

In this chapter, we take a look at some of the practicalities of running a computer system for yourself. They are not all problems! But if you pay them no heed, they will in time *become* problems. If, on the other hand, you look after the system, it will gradually assume an air of comfort and familiarity; its use will become second nature. This in turn will free you from worry about the computer, so that you can concentrate fully on the reason for its use – learning.

This chapter considers ways of:
- *looking after your programs;*
- *offering your programs to other people;*
- *turning problems to advantage;*
- *acquiring new ideas and information.*

6.1 Protecting your programs

Your programs, be they ones which you have bought or ones which you have slaved over for many hours of patient nurture and loving care, are subject

118   *Day-to-day use of a computer*

necessarily to a number of natural hazards. Some of these pertain to the machine itself, some to the way in which you use it, some to the way in which other people use it. All can be avoided by simple precautions.

At all times, programs are stored. If they are in frequent use, they are probably recorded on magnetic disc or cassette; if they are being developed, they may as yet be on paper only. Programs are an investment of your time and money; you should insure them against loss.

Insurance is not a matter of paying a premium – unless it be time – it is a general attitude to computing which can be summed up neatly by two words: **backup copies**. In essence, the first simple rule is: whenever you create something which has value for you, take a copy of it. If it is paper, take a photocopy; if it is machine-readable, take a copy on disc or cassette. This applies to programs you write, programs you buy, programs you steal.

And the second simple rule is: keep your backup copies separately – if anything damages one copy, the other remains intact.

In this section we look at:

- *care of backing store (tapes and discs);*
- *precautions against forgetfulness;*
- *problems caused by large numbers of files;*
- *keeping documentation up to date;*
- *damage to programs caused by other people;*
- *copyright of programs;*
- *care of machinery;*
- *help from manufacturers.*

Protection from natural forces

Programs become corrupted not by moth and rust, but by extremes of environment, especially if they are recorded on magnetic media. They suffer if exposed to high or low temperatures, high or low humidity, radiation, electric or magnetic fields – and (if on disc) being bent, written on or fingered. These conditions do not benefit the machine itself, either: although machines and media are fairly resilient nowadays, there is no point in testing them to destruction.

Use your common sense. Three examples: keep copies; use fireproof cabinets, if you have them; do not site your tape or disc storage by a radiator.

Protection from yourself

You are undoubtedly the greatest natural hazard. You will have accidents. You will upset things, lose things, break things, put things in the wrong places, press wrong buttons, perform operations in the wrong order, become complacent.

Keep copies; *think* about what you are doing, especially if it is familiar to you.

You have one principal disadvantage compared with the machine: you are highly liable to amnesia. So it is a good idea to work systematically; to operate consistently, to do things in a regular order. If you are called away to the phone, for example, your departure will be unplanned; on your return, you may have forgotten what stage you had reached. Habit in this case will be useful in reminding you.

Above all, make the most of the facilities which the computer offers you for keeping notes. Choose your filenames carefully to remind you of what they hold (thus 'EXPTDATA', not 'FILE0074'). Choose your subroutine names to tell you what they do (thus 'FINDMAX', not 'SR5'). Keep written records. Note which cassette or disc holds which file. For cassettes, note the order in which files are kept; for each file, note its position (by means of the counter on the cassette player). For discs, note the length of each file (in bytes – see page 262). Such details are important if you want to run the program or to copy it to another medium. They will also help to reduce the risk of accidental erasure – by cleaning a wanted tape, for instance, or by inadvertently **overwriting** (writing a new file 'on top of') an existing one.

Do not increase your difficulties in keeping track of all your files by throwing nothing away, however useless. Do not create several versions of the same program, for example, all of which have subtle differences that you can't easily recognize, and all of which have the same date on them. Do not keep programs of which you totally disapprove and intend firmly never to use, solely because they 'might come in useful'.

Sooner or later, you will run out of storage space (or simply lose track of it). Sooner or later, you will try to copy a file to a storage medium and there will be insufficient space. This is *not* the time to have a clear-out, though at that stage you will have no choice but to get rid of something. You should do your clearing out when you have time to devote to it, as a careful and deliberate operation, when you are thinking straight. Before you erase *any* file from your filestore, no matter how trivial, no matter how certain you are of its contents, have a look at it: it just might not be the one you think it is. Are you sure you have finished with it? Then get rid of it. Regular removal of obsolete files means that you have fewer to care for: the crucial thing is to act consciously and not in haste. Do not neglect to update your documentation as well.

Erasure of files presents its own problems, even when intentional. Notionally, the removal of a file leaves a gap. When magnetic discs are being used, the system will take advantage of the direct access and will use these gaps: it can even split a file which it is storing, and write bits of the file in different places on the disc. This is not your concern: the computer finds all the bits and reassembles them when you want to retrieve the file; you simply need to know which disc holds which file.

But with magnetic tape, as in cassettes, *serial* access is used: one thing follows another in a line. You can erase a file easily, but you must be very careful if you try to write another file in the space: the new file *must* be smaller than the erased one, or it will partially overwrite the next along. These problems can be reduced by using a different tape for each program, and you may find it helpful to use the shorter of the tapes which are marketed.

Protection from other people

Many programs used by teachers will be used also by their students, students who may have no prior experience of computers. They too may have accidents, may unwittingly damage your program. There is even the possibility of wilful damage. Again, you cannot prevent this damage, but you can ensure that the effects are minimal: every program used by other people should exist also as a copy stored elsewhere. There is no real protection against the very rare person who deliberately alters, rather than destroys, your program; nor is it easy to spot that this has occurred. If a file is especially valuable to you, you could begin each new class with a fresh copy of your master file.

A prickly issue in computing is the subject of copyright. Legally, a program has copyright in the same way that anything else you may write has it; copyright exists from the moment of your rendering material in written form. It is one thing to own copyright, however; quite another to enforce it. The problem exactly parallels that faced by publishers of recorded music: any member of the public with a tape recorder can record music broadcast by radio, despite the fact that such recording is illegal.

Similarly, your program may be plagiarized: someone else may produce a version of your program which they claim to be an original work. Music again provides the exact analogy; many protracted legal cases have been fought concerning just how much new work must be contributed by the plagiarist for it to count as an original work. Money spent in pursuing the matter through the courts is likely to be wasted; in any case, you probably won't even know that your program has been misused in this way.

Manufacturers of computer software are understandably concerned about this problem. They approach it, in some cases, with a very negative attitude: the programs are theirs, nobody must copy them except for his own use, nobody must tamper with them in any way. To prevent these things from happening, some manufacturers intentionally make their code obscure, the idea being that the purchaser will not be able to follow its workings and will therefore be forced to leave it alone. They may use unnecessary jumps in the logic, call routines by confusing names and so on. Sometimes they even try to make it impossible for the user to look at the code – he can load it and execute it, but not look at it.

We have spent much of this book talking about clarity and openness. It will not surprise you, therefore, to learn that we deprecate their attitude. *You* buy the system, it is there to help *you*; so *you* should have access to it, and 'access' includes being able to understand it.

Making your programs available 121

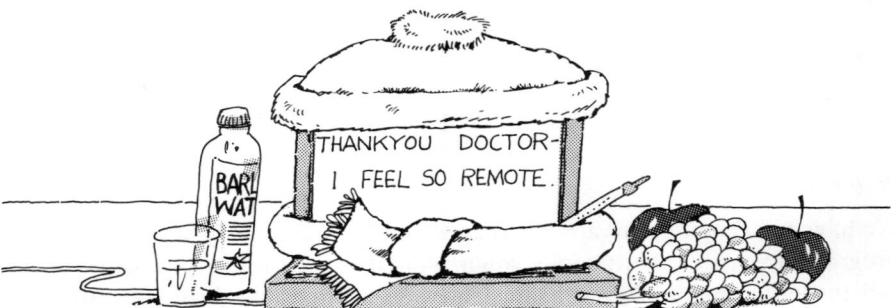

You will in any case have to attend to equipment for other reasons.

Protection of the computer system

This section is about protecting programs. Programs are created on, run on and stored on computer systems, and so to protect your programs you must protect the system also. Common sense is again the rule: ensure that the electric supply is adequate to the system's needs, that the various devices are correctly connected, that equipment stands on level surfaces, is well ventilated and so on. Such aspects must be considered when you first install each device, and may need to be reviewed when you add new equipment.

You will in any case have to attend to equipment for other reasons. It collects dust, for example, and needs to be cleaned (according to the manufacturer's instructions). Devices need servicing occasionally, especially those with moving parts, such as matrix printers; again, consult the instructions which come with the machines. And therefore, do not discard these with the packaging! (In fact, do not discard the packaging either, if you can help it; it may be useful later when transporting the machines.)

Inevitably, faults develop – loose connections, breakages, failures. Manufacturers usually provide fault-finding guidance, and you should check through their lists (especially 'Is the device connected to a power supply? Is the power on?') before seeking outside help. But at the point when help *is* needed, you must know what is available – who to call, where they are based, how quickly they guarantee to come, whether you or they will meet the bill.

6.2 Making your programs available

If you are a programmer, you may produce excellent programs which are of great value and which assist in your teaching. Provided that they are flexible, portable and well documented, you may be able to interest many colleagues in their use also. And *their* programs may be a help to you.

In this section, we consider:
- *transferring programs between micros;*

- using 'standard' features of a language;
- advertising your program, and what information to provide;
- copyright (again);
- liability for the consequences of use of your program.

Portability

We have talked about this already (pages 59-63). In summary, if you want your programs to excite other people, you must make it possible for these people to run the programs. Either you must provide a program which runs on their machine in their dialect of the relevant language, or you must provide clear instructions to them about what aspects may need altering and how. Portability is increased by using only the features of the 'standard' language, and shunning the extensions available in your dialect only; yet the extensions may be paralleled in other dialects, making a translation easy for the other person. But he cannot conveniently modify your program unless its structure and your coding are both clear to him, and it is again *clarity* which is the most important factor of all.

You should also consider how you will pass the program to him (as we did on pages 62-3). On magnetic disc? On cassette? In writing? And if he doesn't like it, or if he finds faults in your logic or things that you've left out, will you be prepared to modify your program?

Advertising

The best advertisement is personal recommendation. On the other hand, your potential market from this source is very limited. So you could submit your program to a journal, or magazine, or newspaper (or you could write a book).

When advertising your programs, think about your own questions as a potential purchaser: what do you need to know? And then answer these questions for *your* customers. What does it do? What could it do? At what level? How flexible is it? Is it for individual or group use? Is it in command or tutorial mode? Where can they get it? How can they get it? In what form can they get it? What micros does it run on? How easy is it to adapt?

Sales and copyright

Back to copyright. Copyright, we have argued (page 120), is yours but indefensible. The negative responses to this are to hide your light under a bushel, to write obscure and convoluted code to confuse people, or to consult a lawyer.

Consider the purpose of copyright. It exists to protect your right to say that the work was originally yours, to take credit for it, and to gain financially from its sale. Yet whether or not you like it, a few unscrupulous people may steal your work and may even pretend it is their own so that *they* can make money or reputation from it, sometimes by adapting it, sometimes not even that.

Here now are the positive responses. Make your programs attractive and clear, make them cheap: more people will want them; most will pay. Make them reliable: people will come back to you. If you publish them in, say, a magazine, you will get a fixed fee (if you are lucky), and as many people will have your program as buy that magazine, and their friends. (*You* may lose your copyright to the publisher – check on this.)

A lot of programs change hands by barter; indeed, there are local groups of computer-using teachers who meet to demonstrate and exchange their programs. No local group near you? Then form one.

So, to spread your programs throughout the educated world, you can sell them for a lot, sell them for a little, or barter them. And there is another method – why not give them away? In this book, *we* give *you* several complete, documented programs. We not only give them away, we invite you to use them, give them to your friends, show them to your colleagues, talk about them at symposia – even review them critically in the press. Help yourself! We go further: you may tamper with them, take them apart, restructure them, add to them, incorporate them into other programs, do what you like with them.

But – if you are a nice, honest, kind and decent person – you will cite us as the original authors, and say where you found them. You will *not* pass them off as your own.

Liability

If you sell a program, it is subject to the normal rules governing the sale of goods. In particular, the program must be fit for the purpose for which it is intended. So if you claim that your program adds twenty numbers and prints out the total, and it doesn't, you are liable at law.

In practice, this aspect of programming is rarely important in the context of teaching. It becomes so when people depend on your program in some way, when its failure may cause them loss. (This would be true of an accounting package, for example.) On such occasions, you might find yourself the defendant in a legal suit.

6.3 Being flexible in your approach

Things don't always work out the way you want; this can be a nuisance. It can also be a source of new ideas, new attitudes, new skills, new interests. You can often turn a setback into an advantage.

Thus in this section we take a look at:
- *restrictive programming;*
- *alternative solutions;*
- *implications of exploiting hardware;*

- *contingency planning;*
- *programs as used in a classroom.*

Flexibility in programming

Use of command rather than of tutorial mode is one example of flexibility; it allows the user to decide how he will use the program. There are many extensions to the same idea: never make avoidable restrictions. Your program will then be of maximum use to the maximum number of people.

Flexibility is also required when you are turning an algorithm into code – you may find that this is not possible in the way you want. Can it be done some other way? If so, is the new way still clear to others, or is it a 'clever' method that they – and you, in six months' time – won't be able to follow? If not, does it matter? Does it instead lead you to think further about what you are trying to achieve, and to find a quite different, perhaps better, way of achieving it?

Keep asking the sort of questions summarized in Appendix A.1, questions designed to help in evaluating other people's programs. You may find ways of improving your own.

Flexibility in hardware

The nature of a program may depend on the hardware available. There are two ways of looking at this: one, if the hardware is restrictive to your method, is there another method where it isn't; two, can you exploit some feature of a particular device and so make a better job of something? If the latter, be aware of the implications for other users of your program who do not have the same device.

One example of this was cited on pages 82–3. We noted that software had been written for mainframe computers, and that the output from these programs had been designed therefore for printers, devices which work in one direction only – down the page. Some of these programs had been adapted, after a fashion, for microcomputers; the programs had been tailored to fit into smaller core sizes, the language had been modified. But *all* micros have screens as their main place of output, and screens are not limited in the same way as printers: text can be written, and *over*written, anywhere on the screen. So it is right, at least in those teaching contexts where students will be looking at screens, to redesign the output to exploit the screens; and the implications for other users are only good, because all micro users have screens.

Do you need extra hardware? Will other people use it? Who will pay?

Flexibility in planning

Since things may go wrong – and they will sometimes – you should plan ahead: coding, procuring, testing and copying all take time.

And if you set out to write a program to do one thing, don't be too surprised if it leads to, or turns into, a program to do something quite different.

Flexibility in teaching

Students often like working with computers, especially if they are allowed to play with them. So if you start them off with a program which enables them to draw architectural plans and elevations, you can assume that they will soon be using that program to draw 'Snoopy' cartoons or play 'Battleships'. Does this matter? Is it more important that they come out of your lesson having learnt exactly that which you had planned for them, or that they have had fun, and perhaps learnt quite a lot incidentally? Perhaps they didn't learn the skill you had in mind; perhaps they learnt another one just as useful. Perhaps they learnt the intended skill by a more enjoyable route.

6.4 Being receptive to new ideas

There are lots of things you can learn about microcomputers; you can spend all the time you have available and more. If you are interested in the equipment, there are books and magazines in abundance; you can learn to talk computerese like a native – you can learn how to strip down boards, isolate faulty chips, take snapshot dumps, inspect output bus drivers, watch graceful degradation and perform crippled leap-frog tests. If you like that sort of thing.

If you are interested in micros simply in terms of their utility in teaching, there is still much to learn. You can learn what programs there are, what your colleagues are doing, and what manufacturers are producing. A lot of time will be well spent in playing with your own computer; there is much to find out about its facilities, its capabilities and its inabilities. Practise its use when you are not actually teaching, so that when you *are* teaching, the equipment and its many idiosyncrasies are familiar to you. Discuss the whole subject with friends who have micros; compare their findings with your own. Write to the manufacturer with your problems: perhaps there is a solution which you have overlooked, perhaps there is a shortcoming which can be cured. Perhaps new equipment is already on the way.

Play with the equipment and play with the ideas. There will be new ways to exploit what you have: new ways to use the machine and its software, new ways to use them to advantage in teaching. Consider novel approaches to education – inter-disciplinary teaching, mixed-ability teaching, games. . . .

Take qualifications in computing or in computer education, if you wish. There are certainly certificates and diplomas and degrees to be had in these subjects of computing and of teaching computing. These may be useful in gaining other people's respect, and thereafter their attention. On the other hand, the subject of this book is neither computing nor the teaching of computing, it is the use of computers in teaching; and this is a subject in which there is little formal education available.

In this section, we deal with a few loose ends by considering:

- *omissions from the book;*
- *micros coupled to other apparatus;*
- *micros coupled to each other and to other computers;*
- *databanks;*
- *sources of information (and some associated problems);*
- *self-reliance.*

New uses of computers in teaching

This book does not cover all aspects of using computers in teaching. Some aspects have been omitted by neglect. But some of our omissions are deliberate: we don't think that this is the place to go into detail about the electronics which underlie the design of your equipment, for example; it doesn't really interest us as *users*, and you can easily find out that sort of thing if you want to.

There remains a grey area: a few items which are a little beyond our present horizons but which will become increasingly relevant to teachers who use computers. So here are three examples; examples of areas now developing which may or may not affect you in your own teaching, examples of the need to keep your eyes and ears open.

Example One concerns the coupling of computers to experimental equipment. The technicalities of this are well outside the scope of this book; suffice it to say that energy and time are now being devoted to designing **interfaces** which make it possible to plug bits of equipment (oscilloscopes, ammeters, sound generators and that sort of thing) into micros. The computer may *monitor* the equipment, perhaps draw graphs or tabulate readings, or it may *control* the equipment – switch bits on and off, perhaps, at set intervals or to keep constant some factor such as temperature. Of course, it can also do any associated calculation as required.

Example Two concerns the coupling of two or more computers to each other. On page 264, we mention that users of 'multiaccess' systems each have a terminal but share the actual processor. The concept can be taken further in that processors can be linked together. Probably the single most important reason for doing so is to be able to transfer files easily from one machine to another. Transfer of a program in machine-readable form not only saves time in typing, it saves errors in transcription. Links between computers may require yet more interfaces, especially if the machines are made by different manufacturers. The result of the linking is a **network**: several computers may be linked to one central computer, or several computers may each be linked to two neighbours so as to form a 'ring' network.

Example Three concerns a particular opportunity arising from the use of works. If users can access material from other machines, there is no need for everyone to have his own versions of everything. Files can be kept centrally, updates can be performed centrally. And one of the most useful applications of this facility is the growth of **databanks**. A databank is simply a collection of data on a given subject set out in a specified format. Thus one might have a list of museum exhibits – type, age, medium, location, place found, estimated value. Or one might have a list of current stock market prices. A databank doesn't do anything, it is simply there to be exploited, in whatever way they choose, by those who have access to it.

Sources of information

Information about these and related matters is disseminated via an overwhelming number of media. Read books and magazines, if you will; listen to the radio, watch television, attend conferences, meet locally and look at what others are doing. Exchange ideas and skills.

Do not, however, believe everything that you hear; doubt especially any claims of miraculous solutions. It should by now be apparent to you that if you improve one aspect of a program (or method of testing, or piece of equipment), something else suffers. And the claimants are unlikely to emphasize the deficiencies of their product.

If you bought this book or found it in a library, you will already have observed that there are many books on the subject of computing. Each new book, presumably, seeks to do something which existing books do not. Not only books: specialist magazines are crammed full of information about computers and computing. There are magazines also for particular disciplines – mathematics, for example, or sociology – magazines which review programs intended to be of use in the teaching of those subjects. And there are quantities of documentation produced by manufacturers in order to sell computers, or to explain their use when sold – documentation which is often either largely incomprehensible or nauseatingly condescending. How on earth can you select which bits of all this to read, how can you find what *you* want?

We cannot say that such-and-such a source is infallibly a reliable one, whereas such-and-such a source is unalterably bad. Not all of the material available is especially good and some very good material is presented in a quite indigestible form. Magazines are particularly problematic in that although they contain many excellent articles, these are not always easy to locate, submerged as they may be among advertisements, commentaries and readers' letters, and less useful articles. It is the sifting process which is so time- and energy-consuming. If you do find something of interest, tear it out or photocopy it immediately – you may never find it again!

The problems are compounded by unclear writing, which causes the reader to work hard at the material simply in order to identify what is being said. Computing is at present an area of fast growth: there are reputations to be

There is nothing magic about computers.

made, quick solutions to be offered, easy money to be made. The market for shoddy goods is considerable.

If this seems negative, here is the positive consequence of it: trust your own common sense. Follow your hunches; heed the 'feeling' you get about a program or a piece of writing. Believe in your own competence to judge a presentation, even if you are ignorant of the subject matter. There is nothing magic about computers. Brilliance results not from the machines, but from accumulated flashes of occasional inspiration among those who program them. Beware of seeing the world as a simple, tidy place with a simple, tidy structure recorded in simple, tidy rules.

7 Case studies in programming

This book has discussed issues in learning (Chapter 2), aspects of programming (Chapter 3), the nature and use of graphics (Chapter 4), and the ways in which these threads may be drawn together when the computer is used in the classroom (Chapter 5). In Chapters 7 and 8 we give a number of practical examples of how these ideas may be put into operation.

The subjects that we have selected as suitable illustrative programs are chosen partly because they exemplify several possible techniques and partly just because they attract us. There are one or two striking omissions: for example, we do not include any simulation programs in the book, but such programs – to simulate a large number of different situations – are readily available from many sources.

Each program illustrates several of our points; most of our principles are illustrated by at least one of the programs. With each program, therefore, there is a limited discussion in which we draw your attention to the aspects of it that we consider most important, and we invite you to develop the program in ways which we think may help you either in your understanding of the programming or in your use of the particular program for teaching.

Chapter 7 concentrates on the practicalities of individual programming techniques. These techniques are then used as required in the programs in Chapter 8, which examines different roles of the computer in teaching. Discussion in Chapter 8 emphasizes the teaching philosophy depicted by the programs, and ways of using them with students.

It may be that you do not intend to do much programming. Some of the content of these two chapters may strike you as over-technical for your needs – this is particularly true of the sections that deal with the portability of our programs. But it will still be useful to you to type in the programs (or obtain them on magnetic media – see page 315) and to *run* them. Several of the programs deal with screen layout and speed of operation: you cannot appreciate these fully unless you have working versions of the program to try. When you have run them, even if you are not a practising programmer, glance through the discussions. These will give you ideas about what is possible, and prompt you to ask related questions when you buy software or see it demonstrated.

We cannot escape the problem of portability. Our programs were written for one particular machine – the Research Machines Ltd (RML) 380Z. This has some attractive features, and we have exploited them. Its younger sibling, the cassette-based 480Z, has all the facilities of the 380Z and some additional ones. Any program which runs on the 380Z may be expected to run on the 480Z also, a phenomenon known in the jargon as 'upward compatibility'.

The 380Z is a versatile machine and common in schools, so it is a good choice; but it is by no means the only machine. If this is not what you have, you may need to adapt the code to your own machine. While we cannot provide versions of every program to run on every machine, we have tried to make our programs easy to adapt (that is, relatively portable), and we have remarked upon the parts that you will need to check and perhaps to change. In many cases, the change will be a simple substitution of one command for another. If your machine is not a 380Z or a 480Z, and if it is you who are going to make the adaptation, you may find it helpful to read through section 7.1. If not, you may care to skip directly to section 7.2.

In Chapter 7, we look at these aspects of programming:
- *the nature of program code and of its portability;*
- *the structure of code (and how to make it clear);*
- *the condensation of code (in which clarity is maintained despite a reduction in the length);*
- *ways of updating tabulated material on the screen;*
- *ways of updating pictures displayed on the screen;*
- *error-trapping;*
- *command and tutorial modes of controlling an interactive program.*

7.1 Program code and portability

This section introduces some general issues of programming style which are common to all or many of the programs given in this chapter and the next. It also explains some of the instructions used with BASIC on the RML 380Z and 480Z, to aid you in following what each program is doing. We elected to program in the language BASIC because it is the language most commonly used with micros; we elected to use the 380Z because it is versatile, common in schools – and because we have one. This section should help you if you need to convert our programs to another machine, even to another language; or if you are simply interested in understanding how they work. If you are interested solely in what the programs do, and not in the way in which they do it, then you are advised to skip to section 7.2. This section looks at:
  ○ *programming style;*
  ○ *portability of RML 380Z programs, and hence the way in which some of their commands operate.*

Programming style

We consider first the issues which apply to code produced for any micro, and indeed to code produced in most programming languages.

Code should look good on the page: this makes it easy to read and to understand. To this end, we indent the beginnings of most lines of program code. In this book, though not necessarily elsewhere, we have indented all lines which are not 'REM' (comment) lines; additional 'REM' lines can therefore be used to provide otherwise blank lines, and so provide a visual break between sections:

```
1560      LET T = T1 + T2
1570      PRINT "TOTAL IS"; T
1580 REM
1590      LET A = T/N
1600      PRINT "AVERAGE IS"; A
```

The extent to which blank lines are used to break the code in this way is dictated partly by program length, and varies from program to program.

'REM' statements are also used as headings for sections of the program or its subroutines:

```
4020 REM *** SUBROUTINE TO FIND MAXIMUM FIGURE ***
```

'REM' statements may be used to give a description of the program at the start of its code. Sometimes it is useful to include with this description a list of the variables employed in the program, and notes on their purposes.

A further use of 'REM' statements is in annotating what may otherwise not be clear, either as an introduction to a whole section of code, or as a note on the end of an individual line whose purpose is not self-evident:

```
7880      PRINT CHR$(12)
```

for example, becomes

```
7880      PRINT CHR$(12) : REM Clear the screen
```

Indentation is used to separate code from comments; it is also used to clarify the code itself. One use is in marking out a block of code which may be skipped over following some conditional test:

```
1360      IF N > 100 THEN 1390
1370          PRINT "* Value too large - reset to 100"
1380          LET N = 100
1390      FOR I = 1 TO N
```

Another use is in marking out the lines of code which fall within a loop, which shows clearly the extent of the loop:

```
1390      FOR I = 1 TO N
1400        LET T = T + A(I)
1410        PRINT A(I)
1420      NEXT I
```

The same principle can be extended to nested loops (loops within loops):

```
1390      FOR I = 1 TO N
1400        LET T = T + A(I)
1410        PRINT A(I); TAB(5);
1420        FOR J = 1 TO A(I)
1430          PRINT "*";
1440        NEXT J
1450        PRINT
1460      NEXT I
```

In some cases, we have placed spaces round the 'equals' sign ('='); in others we have not. In general we have spaced the 'equals' signs in 'FOR' loops in this way

```
1390      FOR I = 1 TO N
```

rather than in this way

```
1390      FOR I=1 TO N
```

because we feel that the '1' (the 'lower bound' of the loop) belongs logically with the 'N' (the 'upper bound' of the loop), and not with 'I' (the loop counter). The spaced form makes the meaning apparent more immediately.

'Equals' signs are also used in assignments and in testing conditions, and we space some of them but not others. Where the spaces are omitted it is usually to minimize the length of the code, and only where they are not absolutely critical for clarity. We have tried to be consistent within a given program.

Most of our programs contain a line of code such as

```
4430      FOR D = 1 TO 5000 : NEXT D : REM Delay
```

which provides a loop containing no statements at all. It is used to delay the execution of the program, by forcing the machine to count up to (in this case) 5000. The length of the delay may be varied by changing the value of the upper bound of the loop. Delays are useful in giving the user time to read the output on the screen before it is removed or replaced, and in slowing down movement in pictures.

Each delay loop forms a unit which is self-contained: it is therefore written in just one line, although it contains three separate statements. In BASIC as implemented on the RML 380Z, statements on one line are separated by colons. Again, there are differing views about spacing round the colons: we consistently space them in all of our programs. The only valid reason for omitting spaces is an absolute need to reduce the program length. If this is the case, then it is silly to space the line thus:

```
4430    FOR D = 1 TO 5000:NEXT D:REM Delay
```

since the breaks in the sense of the line are greater at the colons than within the component statements. An alternative, therefore, is:

```
4430    FOR D=1TO5000 : NEXT D : REM Delay
```

Which do you think is clearer? Many programmers would use:

```
4430 FORD=1TO5000:NEXTD
```

which would *execute* in exactly the same way.

In BASIC, values may be assigned to variables by means of the 'LET' statement, yet almost all implementations of BASIC allow the programmer to omit the word 'LET' itself. Sometimes the use in the code of 'LET' makes the code easier to read (especially for those new to programming); in other programs, the continued use of 'LET' can make the code look untidy or clumsy. Some programs in this book include 'LET', others omit it; but again we regard consistency within a given program as important.

In this book we have tried by and large to maintain a consistency of style between our programs, in respect both of their code and of their output. Consistency of code is reassuring to other programmers; consistency of output is reassuring to the program's users. Once the reader has become accustomed to the ways in which the programmer signifies his intentions in one program, he will more easily understand another program by the same author. But consistency carried to the extreme means that the style of code chosen for one program will dictate that used for another, which may be very different. This strict adherence to convention may obscure the meaning, or simply take up too much space. Because this is not a book which advocates 'right answers', we have deliberately varied our approach to some matters so that you may see what is

134 *Case studies in programming*

possible and select that which you prefer. As a general rule, consistency is useful wherever there are no strong reasons against it.

Portability

We now consider BASIC instructions which apply specifically to the RML 380Z microcomputer. If you have a different micro, you may find that there are already versions of our programs which have been adapted for your micro – see page 315. If no such versions are available, you will have to make the necessary modifications yourself. Many such changes are of a general nature, applying to all the programs given in the book; though in each case, only a few lines will need to be altered. This section should help you to identify where changes need to be made, and there are additional comments with each individual program.

At the beginning and near the end of each program are groups of instructions containing the words 'CLEAR', 'TEXT', 'PRINT' and 'ON BREAK'. At the beginning, they define the conditions under which the program will operate; at the end, they reset these conditions to those which are encountered when the machine has just been switched on. Each program performs the resetting operation when it finishes execution *and* when it is interrupted by the user.

One condition which must be stated when using the RML 380Z is the amount of storage reserved for holding the characters contained in string variables. This is defined by the 'CLEAR' instruction followed by a number, thus:

1170   CLEAR 250

This reserves space for 250 characters in string variables; an error will be reported if the user attempts to store more than this number of characters. Once stated, the number remains in force until a new 'CLEAR' instruction is issued, so that a reservation made in one program may affect the execution of a program run subsequently, unless this contains its own instruction. It is therefore good practice to declare at the start of each program how much space is required in that program – not too much, since this may make the program too big to run; not too little, since the program may crash if the allocation is exceeded. 'CLEAR' has another effect: it sets the values of all numeric variables to zero, and makes all string variables **null** (empty). Your micro may have the same instruction, or something similar, perhaps with a different name; or it may not require such an instruction at all.

At the start of each program, and at various points during execution, it is useful to clear the screen: to wipe off any material displayed by a previous program, by your interaction with the operating system or by an earlier part of the same program. With the RML 380Z, this is achieved by the instruction:

```
3390    PRINT CHR$(12) : REM Clear the screen
```

Your interpreter may use a different instruction to clear the screen, but it should be easy to discover what this is.

When you display many lines of text, as for example when listing a program, you have more lines of output than can be fitted on the screen. Each new line is printed at the bottom of the screen, and the ones above it are each shunted up (**scrolled**) one line. At some point, the screen is full: what happens then?

One possibility is that the text simply continues to scroll off the top of the screen, but that is of little assistance if you wish to read it – text is printed much faster than you can conveniently read. So the 380Z, in common with some other micros, offers a facility called **paging**, whereby printing is halted each time the screen is full. On the 380Z, the screen can hold 24 lines of text, so it prints 23 and displays a flashing cursor on the bottom line, to indicate that there is more to come. This 'page' is displayed until the user presses any key: the next 23 lines are then displayed, with the cursor at the bottom.

This facility is very useful when not executing programs, and indeed when executing some programs which produce large blocks of output. But for most interactive programs, paging is a nuisance and it is useful to be able to switch it off: thereafter, each line is printed and scrolled up to accommodate the next. Programs in this book switch off paging at the beginning of their execution:

```
2030    PRINT CHR$(17) : REM Disable paging
```

and switch it back on at the end:

```
5660    PRINT CHR$(19) : REM Re-enable paging
```

It is important that paging be switched on again even when the program's execution is interrupted. Interruption is common: most micros allow the user to bring the program to a premature end. Some micros have a special key for this purpose marked 'BREAK'; the user of the 380Z must press the 'CTRL' ('control') and the 'Z' keys simultaneously to interrupt the program. Control is then transferred out of the program and back to the operating system.

As we have pointed out, however, it is helpful after setting up unusual conditions to be able to reset them at the end of a program. Although this can be done using the statements given above, these are not normally executed when the program is interrupted: control simply goes straight back to the system. To overcome this problem, the programmer can make use of the 380Z's 'ON BREAK' instruction. The statement

```
1100    ON BREAK GOTO 3050
```

ensures that if execution is interrupted, control is transferred not to the system but to a chosen line in the program, from which the execution can continue to tidy up and end neatly. Your micro may or may not offer a comparable facility: if it does, the code may be different.

Output is usually sent to the screen by means of the 'PRINT' instruction. The instruction

```
3260    PRINT "This is added at the bottom"
```

displays the message in quotes on the bottom line of the screen, incidentally causing each line above it to be scrolled upwards so that the top line disappears from the screen. As we have mentioned elsewhere in the book, the 'PRINT' instruction is not always flexible enough: the programmer may wish to place text on the screen in some place other than the bottom line and to leave unaltered what is currently being displayed (as is illustrated by the program in section 7.4) or to draw and alter pictures (as in section 7.5). Both requirements are met by the 'PLOT' instruction.

On the 380Z, the top 20 lines of the screen are designated as the plotting area. Each character position in this area is divided into six smaller positions, called **pixels**: each character cell is two pixels wide and three pixels high. The pixels in the whole plotting area are given coordinates starting at (0,0) in the bottom left-hand corner. The *character* (not pixel) positions along the line are numbered (0,0), (2,0), (4,0) and so on (counting the pixels rather than the characters). The character positions up the screen are numbered (0,0), (0,3), (0,6) and so on. Thus the diagonal starting at the same place would be (0,0), (2,3), (4,6) and so on.

To display text using this system, the 'PLOT' instruction includes the x-coordinate (along the screen) and the y-coordinate (up the screen), as well as the text to be printed. The instruction

```
2830    PLOT 34, 57, "TITLE"
```

displays the word 'TITLE' on the top line, 17 characters from the left (just about in the middle of the line).

Textual characters each occupy their normal cell-size, equivalent to six pixels. The coordinate system counts in pixels, so the numbers may appear a little complicated for handling text. But they are very useful when drawing pictures, since individual pixels may be plotted. In the black-and-white system, pixels may be shaded grey ('1'),

```
3400    PLOT 34, 25, 1
```

or white ('2'):

3420   PLOT 67, 14, 2

Pixels are erased by plotting them again, this time shading them black ('0'):

3460   PLOT 34, 25, 0

In addition, straight lines may be drawn using the 'LINE' instruction. First a pixel is displayed, then a 'LINE' instruction with a second pair of coordinates marks the end of the line. So

3480   PLOT 23, 13, 2 : LINE 65, 13

produces a horizontal white line.

You can see from the examples above that there are two forms of the 'PLOT' instruction: they differ in the nature of the last parameter. The instruction

3500   PLOT 36, 27, "word"

causes 'word' to be displayed somewhere near the middle of the screen, while

3520   PLOT 36, 27, 2

produces a white pixel because code 2 is used. There are many different codes which may be used as the third parameter of the 'PLOT' instruction: '2' is just an example. Some of these other codes are employed in the programs in this chapter, so we now give a brief description of their functions.

Each character in the core memory is stored as a number. The system of coding characters as numbers varies from micro to micro; the RML 380Z and 480Z both use a **character code** called **ASCII code**, and this code is fairly widespread in its use. In ASCII, upper-case letters are represented by the numbers 65 ('A') to 90 ('Z') and lower-case letters by the numbers 97 ('a') to 122 ('z'): each lower-case letter has a code which is 32 greater than the code for the corresponding upper-case letter. Digits are represented by the numbers 48 ('0') to 57 ('9'); the space by 32; and other punctuation by numbers between 33 and 126 which have not already been allocated. 'Delete' is itself a character, coded by 127.

138   *Case studies in programming*

The numbers 1 to 31 are reserved for various control characters. For example, we have already mentioned the use of

```
3540      PRINT CHR$(12)
```

in clearing the screen: this is the function of code 12. Similarly, the 'RETURN' key actually issues code 13.

The ASCII codes 32 to 126 may be used in 'PLOT' statements to display the characters that they represent. So

```
3560      PLOT 30, 36, 67
```

has the same effect as

```
3580      PLOT 30, 36, "C"
```

though the intention is clearer to the reader if the latter form is used.

It is not meaningful to 'plot' control characters, so the codes 0 to 31 are available for other purposes when plotting. We have already noted the functions of 0, 1 and 2 in plotting individual pixels in black, grey and white respectively. The codes 3 to 31 are used to plot a variety of graphics symbols (of which no use is made in this book).

That explains the codes from 0 to 127. As we said on page 262, however, with eight-bit bytes, 256 different characters can be stored. The codes from 128 to 255 are used to plot pixels also – but in groups of six, not individually.

A single character position on the screen corresponds to six pixels: these pixels are numbered as shown in the diagram:

1	2
4	8
16	32

To code the pattern of pixels shown here: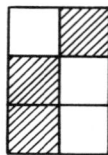

the numbers which correspond to the shaded pixels are totalled: in this case, we get 2+4+16 = 22. That takes care of the pattern, but we must also record the shading, so this total is added to 128 if the pattern is to be in grey or to 192 if it is to be white. To display in white the combination shown, therefore, we use the graphics code 214 (192+22). It follows from all this that the single instruction

```
3600      PLOT 40, 24, 214
```

has the same effect as the three instructions

```
3600      PLOT 40, 24, 2
3610      PLOT 40, 25, 2
3620      PLOT 41, 26, 2
```

but takes one-third of the time to execute.

The plotting area is confined to the top 20 lines of the screen. However, repeated uses of 'PRINT' to issue text at the bottom of the screen will cause text to scroll up into the plotting area. This problem is overcome by the 'GRAPH' instruction, which splits the screen into two portions: the top 20 lines for plotting, the bottom 4 lines for printing. When a fifth line of text is printed, the first disappears as if at the top of the screen; in this way, 'PRINT' and 'PLOT' instructions may be interspersed without spoiling the plotted part. When the instruction

```
2910      GRAPH
```

is executed, the plotting area of the screen is cleared; and thereafter, the instruction

```
4670      PRINT CHR$(12)
```

(introduced above) clears only the bottom four lines, and not the whole screen as before.

Of course, there is an instruction which reverses the effect of 'GRAPH', and this is

```
7220      TEXT
```

When this is executed, all 24 lines again become available for scrolling text (as produced by 'PRINT').

At the start of each program, we do not know what state the micro is in, and we follow the general rule of stating the required conditions explicitly. The opening group of statements in each of our programs therefore contains a 'TEXT' instruction; and if at any point in the program we use 'GRAPH', we also reset to 'TEXT' as part of the general tidying up at the end of execution.

Almost all micros have instructions equivalent to 'PLOT', although on some micros these instructions are less convenient to use. But not all micros allow the screen to be split in the manner described; if yours does not, you will have to identify programs in which 'PLOT' and 'PRINT' are interspersed, and convert all the 'PRINT' instructions to 'PLOT' equivalents. You may also have to obtain your input from the keyboard in such a way that the screen display is not spoiled: read on to the description of the 'GET' instruction given below.

In addition, you may have to take account of a different number of pixels. At low resolution, the plotting area of 40 characters wide and 20 lines up becomes 80 pixels wide and 60 pixels up: on your micro, these numbers may be different. Two of our programs use high resolution, for which the pixels are smaller – 320 pixels across and 192 pixels up. The coordinate system is again numbered with (0,0) in the bottom left-hand corner. High-resolution graphics use subroutines in the interpreter, and each subroutine is invoked by the word

```
CALL
```

Thus lines which deal with high-resolution graphics (and which may need to be altered) are easily recognizable.

Information supplied by the user during execution of the program is normally obtained via the 'INPUT' instruction. The word 'INPUT' is accompanied by the name of a variable, which may be either numeric or string. If the variable is numeric, the system performs various checks of its own on the data that is entered during execution – for example, it checks that no letters are supplied by the user. These checks may lead to system-generated error messages, and these are usually aimed at the programmer rather than the user. To circumvent this problem, it is often helpful to take numeric input as string data initially, and to convert it to a number only when it has been validated. Thus the single instruction

```
1540    INPUT N
```

is replaced by two instructions

```
1540    INPUT N$
1590    N = VAL(N$)
```

and between these instructions, checks can be made by the program. This can be done with most micros.

This is still not entirely satisfactory: since BASIC allows input of more than one piece of data at a time, individual items are separated, usually by commas. Too many or too few pieces of data may also lead to system-generated error messages, and to guard against these one must override the data separator in some way. On the RML 380Z and 480Z, this is done by the instruction

```
1540    INPUT LINE R$
```

which takes the whole line as one item of string data, irrespective of any commas that it may contain. The program can then be made to work through this string in search of the data that it requires.

The 'INPUT' instruction has certain characteristics. For one thing, it permits the user to answer with an indeterminate number of characters, so that the end of the response must be indicated in some way, namely by pressing a key called 'RETURN', 'ENTER' or something similar: when this key is pressed, the cursor is moved to the beginning of the next line on the screen. As characters are typed, they are displayed on the screen: they are said to be **echoed**.

In some situations, these characteristics are undesirable. One situation is mentioned above, in connection with the display of a picture while the user is being asked for information. Most micros offer an alternative which can be used in these situations, this alternative being an instruction called 'GET', 'INKEY' or something of the sort. This instruction causes the micro to look to the keyboard for input of a single character – it does not wait for 'RETURN', nor does it automatically echo the character to the screen. Several of our programs use 'GET': your micro probably provides an instruction to produce the same result, but the form may be quite different.

To close this section, here is a brief discussion of the way in which core memory is used on the RML 380Z and 480Z.

We have drawn the distinction between the two types of store known as RAM and ROM: ROM holds firmware, RAM is used for temporary storage. On the RML machines, the cassette operating system (COS) is held in ROM, but the disc operating system (DOS) is held in RAM. (Other machines may have the disc operating system in ROM also.) In saying that a machine has 32 K RAM, therefore, it does not follow that 32 K RAM is available for the running of applications programs.

In the case of the 380Z, the disc operating system occupies about 4 K bytes of storage: this space is available to you if you are using a cassette operating system instead. But COS requires some of the RAM as storage while operating: this may amount to 1 K bytes. And the BASIC interpreter itself may take up 14–15 K bytes, if one of the high-resolution graphics versions is used.

RAM may thus be divided into **workspace** (the memory used by COS) and **user memory** (the amount available to you to use as you please). User memory normally contains BASIC and perhaps DOS, so that the amount of RAM left over for applications programs and for the storage that *they* require while running (for data) is only about 13 K (that is, 32 K −14 K −4 K −1 K). So a program which only just fits into 32 K (as do CIRCLES and GRAPH, for instance) is not as long as may seem. You should bear all this in mind when estimating the amount of memory that these programs will require on your machine. If you have a cassette-based operating system and if your BASIC interpreter is in firmware (so that it does not take up user memory), a 16 K system should suffice for all the programs in this book. In section 7.3, where we give three versions of the same program, we state the number of bytes of storage that each requires.

7.2 Structure of code

The aim of this section is to provide an example of a program whose method of working is easy to understand *only* because the program is clearly structured and neatly written.

A subsidiary aim is to offer you the data necessary for the production on the screen of enlarged characters, so that you can make use of these in your own programs if you wish.

Specification

The program, BIGLET, will draw big characters on the screen. The characters will be designed so that each fits into a rectangle 8 pixels wide and 12 pixels high. (On the RML 380Z and on the RML 480Z, each normal character occupies a position which is 2 pixels wide and 3 pixels high, so a big character will occupy an area equivalent to 4 character positions across and 4 character positions high.) A space of one character position will be left between adjacent big characters; there will therefore be room on the screen for 4 lines each of 8 big characters. The characters provided will be: upper-case letters, digits, punctuation marks, arithmetic operators and a space.

The program will enable the user to select easily the big characters that he wishes to display and the positions on the screen at which they are to be placed. The current plotting position will at all times be indicated by a cursor, and control characters will be used to facilitate the movement of the cursor round the screen.

The program code will be written in such a way that it is clear to the reader how the program is fulfilling its function. This is particularly important in this program for two reasons. One is that this is the first program we provide in this chapter for you to study. The other is that the program contains blocks of code which you may wish to incorporate into other programs of your own, so it will be useful if you can discover easily which blocks of code are which.

Structure of code 143

Outline flowchart of BIGLET

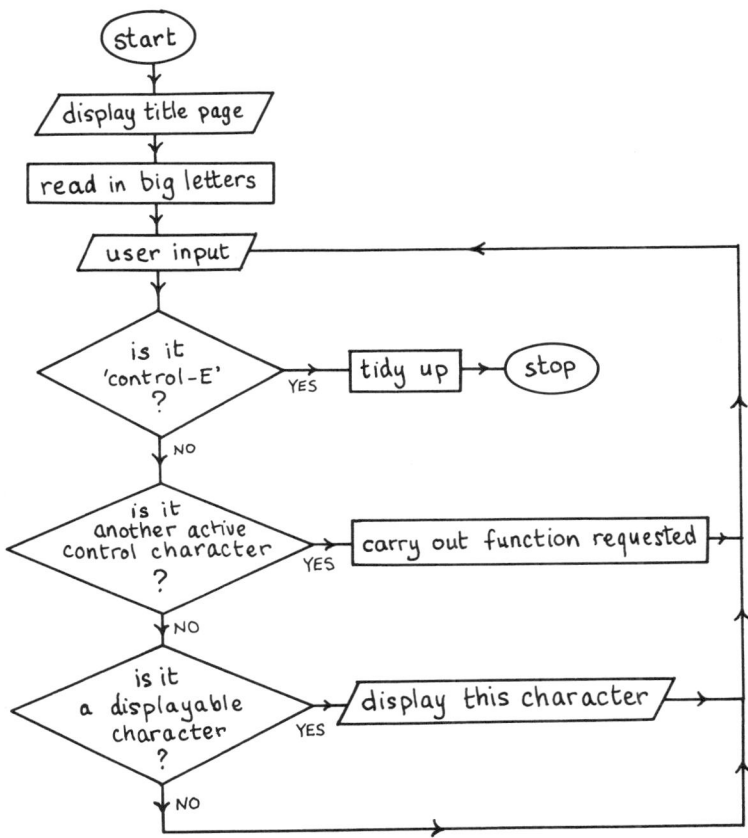

Listing of BIGLET program code

```
1000 REM     Program : BIGLET
1010 REM
1020 REM
1030 REM
1040 REM This program shows how enlarged characters may be displayed
1050 REM     on the screen, in response to the input of characters
1060 REM     at the keyboard.  The graphics codes used to produce the
1070 REM     large characters may be of use in other programs.
1080 REM
1090 REM Three diferent coordinate systems are used in the program.
1100 REM     The coordinate system used by the PLOT command is the one
1110 REM     provided by the system; it starts at the bottom left
1120 REM     of the screen and counts pixels.  The coordinate system
1130 REM     (X,Y) used for the graphics codes for each large character
```

```
1140 REM       starts at the bottom left of the large character and
1150 REM       counts normal character positions. The coordinate system
1160 REM       (R,C) used for the cursor starts at the top left of
1170 REM       the screen and counts large character positions.
1180 REM
1190 REM
1200 REM
1210      CLEAR 500
1220 REM
1230      ON BREAK GOTO 3010
1240 REM   Deal with user's interruption
1250 REM
1260      TEXT : PRINT CHR$(12) : REM Clear the screen
1270      PRINT CHR$(17) : REM Disable paging
1280 REM
1290 REM
1300      PRINT TAB(  7); "BIGLET"
1310      PRINT
1320      PRINT TAB(3); "Produces big letters on the screen"
1330      PRINT : PRINT : PRINT
1340      PRINT TAB(19); "*"
1350      PRINT
1360      PRINT TAB(15); "Derek Ball"
1370      PRINT
1380      PRINT TAB(14); "Andrew Nash"
1390      PRINT
1400      PRINT TAB(19); "*"
1410      PRINT : PRINT : PRINT
1420      PRINT TAB(13); "Copyright 1982"
1430      PRINT
1440      PRINT TAB(10); "Hutchinson Education"
1450      PRINT
1460 REM
1470 REM
1480 REM SET UP COMPUTER
1490 REM
1500 REM Allocate storage for graphics codes which produce big characters
1510 REM
1520 REM   L stores codes for letters
1530 REM   N stores codes for numbers
1540 REM   P stores code for punctuation
1550 REM   C stores code for cursor
1560 REM   P$ stores list of displayable punctuation
1570 REM
1580      DIM L(26,3,3), N(9,3,3), P(14,3,3), C(3,3), P$(14)
1590 REM
1600 REM Allocate storage for recording current screen display
1610 REM
1620      DIM S$(8,5)
1630 REM
1640 REM
1650 REM Read graphics codes for big letters into L
1660 REM
1670      FOR I = 1 TO 26
1680        FOR X = 0 TO 3
1690          FOR Y = 0 TO 3
1700            READ L(I,X,Y)
1710          NEXT Y
1720        NEXT X
1730      NEXT I
1740 REM
1750 REM
1760 REM A - L
1770 REM
1780      DATA 63, 63, 63, 56, 0, 60, 0, 31, 0, 60, 0, 47, 63, 63, 63, 48
```

```
1790      DATA 63, 63, 63, 63, 60, 3, 48, 15, 62, 11, 56, 47, 7, 61, 31, 52
1800      DATA 11, 63, 63, 56, 61, 0, 0, 31, 62, 0, 0, 47, 7, 48, 3, 52
1810      DATA 63, 63, 63, 63, 60, 0, 0, 15, 62, 0, 0, 47, 7, 63, 63, 52
1820      DATA 63, 63, 63, 63, 60, 3, 48, 15, 60, 3, 48, 15, 60, 0, 0, 15
1830      DATA 63, 63, 63, 63, 0, 3, 48, 15, 0, 3, 48, 15, 0, 0, 0, 15
1840      DATA 11, 63, 63, 56, 60, 0, 0, 15, 60, 40, 0, 47, 31, 60, 3, 52
1850      DATA 63, 63, 63, 63, 0, 3, 48, 0, 0, 3, 48, 0, 63, 63, 63, 63
1860      DATA 0, 0, 0, 0, 58, 42, 42, 43, 53, 21, 21, 23, 0, 0, 0, 0
1870      DATA 11, 48, 0, 0, 61, 0, 0, 0, 60, 0, 0, 0, 7, 63, 63, 63
1880      DATA 63, 63, 63, 63, 0, 10, 62, 0, 11, 61, 7, 56, 61, 0, 0, 31
1890      DATA 63, 63, 63, 63, 60, 0, 0, 0, 60, 0, 0, 0, 60, 0, 0, 0
1900      DATA 63, 63, 63, 61, 0, 42, 47, 16, 0, 21, 31, 32, 63, 63, 63, 62
1910 REM
1920 REM M - Z
1930 REM
1940      DATA 63, 63, 63, 61, 0, 0, 47, 16, 2, 47, 20, 0, 47, 63, 63, 63
1950      DATA 11, 63, 63, 56, 61, 0, 0, 31, 62, 0, 0, 47, 7, 63, 63, 52
1960      DATA 63, 63, 63, 63, 0, 3, 48, 15, 0, 3, 56, 47, 0, 0, 31, 52
1970      DATA 11, 63, 63, 56, 61, 0, 0, 31, 63, 16, 0, 47, 55, 63, 63, 52
1980      DATA 63, 63, 63, 63, 0, 43, 48, 15, 11, 55, 56, 47, 61, 0, 31, 52
1990      DATA 11, 50, 63, 56, 61, 3, 52, 31, 62, 3, 48, 47, 7, 63, 19, 52
2000      DATA 0, 0, 0, 15, 42, 42, 42, 47, 21, 21, 21, 31, 0, 0, 0, 15
2010      DATA 11, 63, 63, 63, 61, 0, 0, 0, 62, 0, 0, 0, 7, 63, 63, 63
2020      DATA 0, 10, 47, 63, 43, 61, 20, 0, 23, 62, 40, 0, 0, 5, 31, 63
2030      DATA 42, 63, 63, 63, 23, 58, 42, 42, 43, 53, 21, 21, 21, 63, 63, 63
2040      DATA 63, 32, 2, 47, 1, 30, 45, 16, 2, 45, 30, 32, 63, 16, 1, 31
2050      DATA 0, 0, 2, 47, 42, 42, 61, 16, 21, 21, 62, 32, 0, 0, 1, 31
2060      DATA 63, 56, 0, 15, 60, 31, 32, 15, 60, 1, 62, 15, 60, 0, 7, 63
2070 REM
2080 REM
2090 REM Read graphics codes for big numbers into N
2100 REM
2110      FOR I = 0 TO 9
2120        FOR X = 0 TO 3
2130          FOR Y = 0 TO 3
2140            READ N(I,X,Y)
2150          NEXT Y
2160        NEXT X
2170      NEXT I
2180 REM
2190 REM 0 - 9
2200 REM
2210      DATA 11, 63, 63, 56, 61, 0, 0, 31, 62, 0, 0, 47, 7, 63, 63, 52
2220      DATA 0, 0, 0, 0, 62, 42, 42, 62, 61, 21, 21, 21, 0, 0, 0, 0
2230      DATA 63, 56, 3, 56, 60, 31, 32, 31, 60, 1, 56, 47, 60, 0, 31, 52
2240      DATA 11, 48, 3, 56, 61, 2, 32, 31, 62, 11, 56, 47, 7, 61, 31, 52
2250      DATA 0, 62, 32, 0, 0, 61, 31, 32, 42, 62, 42, 62, 21, 61, 21, 21
2260      DATA 11, 48, 47, 63, 61, 0, 61, 15, 62, 2, 60, 15, 7, 63, 52, 15
2270      DATA 11, 63, 63, 62, 61, 1, 60, 15, 62, 2, 60, 15, 7, 63, 16, 61
2280      DATA 40, 0, 0, 15, 31, 58, 0, 15, 0, 23, 62, 47, 0, 0, 5, 63
2290      DATA 11, 63, 43, 56, 61, 1, 61, 31, 62, 2, 62, 47, 7, 63, 23, 52
2300      DATA 47, 2, 63, 56, 60, 15, 16, 31, 60, 15, 32, 47, 31, 63, 43, 52
2310 REM
2320 REM
2330 REM Read punctuation list into P$
2340 REM
2350      FOR I = 0 TO 14
2360        READ P$(I)
2370      NEXT I
2380 REM
2390      DATA "+", "-", "/", "*", "=", ".", "_", ","
2400      DATA ":", ";", "?", "!", "(", ")", " "
2410 REM
2420 REM
2430 REM Read graphics codes for big punctuation into P
```

Structure of code 145

```
2440 REM
2450     FOR I = 0 TO 14
2460       FOR X = 0 TO 3
2470         FOR Y = 0 TO 3
2480           READ P(I,X,Y)
2490         NEXT Y
2500       NEXT X
2510     NEXT I
2520 REM
2530 REM    + - / * = , _ , ; ; ? ! ( ) space
2540 REM
2550     DATA 0, 2, 32, 0, 0, 43, 58, 0, 0, 23, 53, 0, 0, 1, 16, 0
2560     DATA 0, 2, 32, 0, 0, 3, 48, 0, 0, 3, 48, 0, 0, 1, 16, 0
2570     DATA 0, 2, 32, 0, 0, 35, 50, 0, 0, 19, 49, 0, 0, 1, 16, 0
2580     DATA 0, 32, 2, 0, 0, 6, 36, 0, 0, 9, 24, 0, 0, 16, 1, 0
2590     DATA 0, 0, 0, 0, 0, 3, 12, 0, 0, 3, 12, 0, 0, 0, 0, 0
2600     DATA 0, 0, 0, 0, 15, 0, 0, 0, 0, 0, 0, 0, 0, 0, 0, 0
2610     DATA 0, 3, 48, 0, 0, 3, 48, 0, 0, 3, 48, 0, 0, 3, 48, 0
2620     DATA 0, 0, 0, 47, 0, 0, 0, 0, 0, 0, 0, 0, 0, 0, 0, 0
2630     DATA 0, 0, 0, 0, 15, 15, 0, 0, 0, 0, 0, 0, 0, 0, 0, 0
2640     DATA 0, 0, 0, 0, 47, 15, 0, 0, 0, 0, 0, 0, 0, 0, 0, 0
2650     DATA 0, 0, 3, 56, 10, 10, 32, 31, 5, 7, 56, 47, 0, 0, 63, 52
2660     DATA 0, 0, 0, 0, 10, 10, 47, 62, 5, 5, 31, 61, 0, 0, 0, 0
2670     DATA 0, 0, 0, 0, 43, 21, 21, 58, 16, 0, 0, 1, 0, 0, 0, 0
2680     DATA 0, 0, 0, 0, 32, 0, 0, 2, 23, 42, 42, 53, 0, 0, 0, 0
2690     DATA 0, 0, 0, 0, 0, 0, 0, 0, 0, 0, 0, 0, 0, 0, 0, 0
2700 REM
2710 REM
2720 REM Read graphics codes for cursor into C
2730 REM
2740     FOR X = 0 TO 3
2750       FOR Y = 0 TO 3
2760         READ C(X,Y)
2770       NEXT Y
2780     NEXT X
2790 REM
2800     DATA 3, 21, 21, 48, 3, 0, 0, 48, 3, 0, 0, 48, 3, 42, 42, 48
2810 REM
2820 REM
2830 REM Prepare screen for big letters
2840 REM
2850     PRINT CHR$(12) : REM Clear the screen
2860     GOSUB 4170 : REM Set up new screen
2870 REM
2880     PRINT "Use the following control keys:"
2890     PRINT "  R  right     L  left        U  up"
2900     PRINT "  D  down      N  Normal      B  backwards"
2910     PRINT "  C  clear screen    E  end";
2920 REM
2930 REM
2940 REM MAIN PROGRAM
2950 REM
2960     R$=GET$()
2970     IF ASC(R$)=5 THEN 3010 : REM CTRL+E means end
2980     GOSUB 3090 : REM Process input
2990     GOTO 2960
3000 REM
3010     TEXT
3020     PRINT CHR$(12) : REM Clear the screen
3030     PRINT CHR$(19) : REM Enable paging
3040     CLEAR 100
3050 REM
3060     END
3070 REM
3080 REM
```

Structure of code 147

```
3090 REM SUBROUTINE: PROCESS INPUT
3100 REM
3110     C0=C1 : R0=R1 : REM Record old cursor position
3120 REM
3130     IF ASC(R$)>31 THEN 3470 : REM Jump if not a control character
3140 REM
3150 REM Response is a control character
3160 REM
3170     A=ASC(R$)
3180     C1=C0 : R1=R0 : REM Provisionally set new cursor position
3190     IF A=12 THEN C1=C1-1 : GOTO 3370 : REM CTRL+L moves cursor left
3200     IF A=18 THEN C1=C1+1 : GOTO 3370 : REM CTRL+R moves cursor right
3210     IF A=21 THEN R1=R1-1 : GOTO 3370 : REM CTRL+U moves cursor up
3220     IF A=4 THEN R1=R1+1 : GOTO 3370 : REM CTRL+D moves cursor down
3230     IF A<>13 THEN 3270 : REM Check for RETURN
3240      IF R1=5 THEN R1=1 ELSE R1=R1+1
3250      IF D$="backwards" THEN C1=8 ELSE C1=1
3260      GOTO 3370
3270     IF A=2 THEN D$="backwards" : GOTO 4140 : REM CTRL+B sets direction
3280     IF A=14 THEN D$="normal" : GOTO 4140 : REM CTRL+N sets direction
3290     IF A=3 THEN GOSUB 4170 : GOTO 4140 : REM CTRL+C clears screen
3300 REM
3310 REM It's none of these so do nothing
3320 REM
3330     GOTO 4140
3340 REM
3350 REM Prevent control character pushing cursor off screen
3360 REM
3370     IF C1=0 THEN C1=1
3380     IF C1=9 THEN C1=8
3390     IF R1=0 THEN R1=1
3400     IF R1=5 THEN R1=4
3410 REM
3420 REM Find what kind of character to put in place of cursor
3430 REM If R$ is a displayable character use that
3440 REM If R$ is a control character use appropriate character from
3450 REM     current screen display store
3460 REM
3470     IF ASC(R$)>31 THEN C$=R$ ELSE C$=S$(C0,R0)
3480 REM
3490 REM Is it a letter?
3500 REM
3510 REM Convert response from lower case to upper case
3520     IF R$>="a" AND R$<="z" THEN C$=CHR$(ASC(R$)-32)
3530 REM
3540     IF C$>="A" AND C$<="Z" THEN T$="letter" : GOTO 3710
3550 REM
3560 REM Is it a number?
3570 REM
3580     IF C$>="0" AND C$<="9" THEN T$="number" : GOTO 3710
3590 REM
3600 REM Is it punctuation?
3610 REM
3620     FOR I = 0 TO 14
3630      IF C$=P$(I) THEN T$="punctuation" : GOTO 3710
3640     NEXT I
3650 REM
3660 REM Character is none of these, so do nothing
3670 REM
3680     GOTO 4140
3690 REM
3700 REM
3710     IF ASC(R$)<31 THEN 3920 : REM If R$ is a control character skip
3720 REM                                              next bit
3730 REM
```

```
3740 REM Update screen display store when live character pressed
3750 REM
3760     S$(CO,RO)=C$
3770 REM
3780 REM Move forwards
3790 REM
3800     IF D$="backwards" THEN 3870
3810     IF CO=8 THEN C1=1 : R1=RO+1 ELSE C1=CO+1 : R1=RO
3820     IF R1=5 THEN R1=1
3830     GOTO 3920
3840 REM
3850 REM Move backwards
3860 REM
3870     IF CO=1 THEN C1=8 : R1=RO-1 ELSE C1=CO-1 : R1=RO
3880     IF R1=0 THEN R1=4
3890 REM
3900 REM Plot character on the screen in position of cursor
3910 REM
3920     FOR X = 0 TO 3
3930       FOR Y = 0 TO 3
3940 REM
3950 REM       If T$ is a number or a letter use its ASCII code to find
3960 REM          appropriate graphics code in store
3970 REM
3980         IF T$="letter" THEN I=ASC(C$)-ASC("A")+1 : C=L(I,X,Y)
3990         IF T$="number" THEN I=ASC(C$)-ASC("0") : C=N(I,X,Y)
4000 REM
4010         IF T$="punctuation" THEN C=P(I,X,Y)
4020 REM
4030 REM     Plot next part of character in white
4040 REM
4050         PLOT 10*(CO-1)+2*X,15*(4-RO)+3*Y,C+192
4060 REM
4070 REM     Plot next part of cursor in grey
4080 REM
4090         PLOT 10*(C1-1)+2*X,15*(4-R1)+3*Y,C(X,Y)+128
4100       NEXT Y
4110     NEXT X
4120 REM
4130 REM
4140     RETURN
4150 REM
4160 REM
4170 REM SUBROUTINE: SET UP NEW SCREEN
4180 REM
4190 REM At start or when CTRL+C is pressed subroutine sets
4200 REM    current screen display store to spaces, resets
4210 REM    direction flag to "normal", repositions cursor
4220 REM    at top left of screen, clears screen and redisplays cursor
4230 REM
4240     FOR C = 1 TO 8
4250       FOR R = 1 TO 4
4260         S$(C,R)=" "
4270       NEXT R
4280     NEXT C
4290 REM
4300     D$="normal"
4310 REM
4320     C1=1 : R1=1
4330 REM
4340     GRAPH
4350 REM
4360     FOR X = 0 TO 3
4370       FOR Y = 0 TO 3
4380         PLOT 2*X,45+3*Y,C(X,Y)+128
```

```
4390       NEXT Y
4400       NEXT X
4410 REM
4420       RETURN
```

Sample output

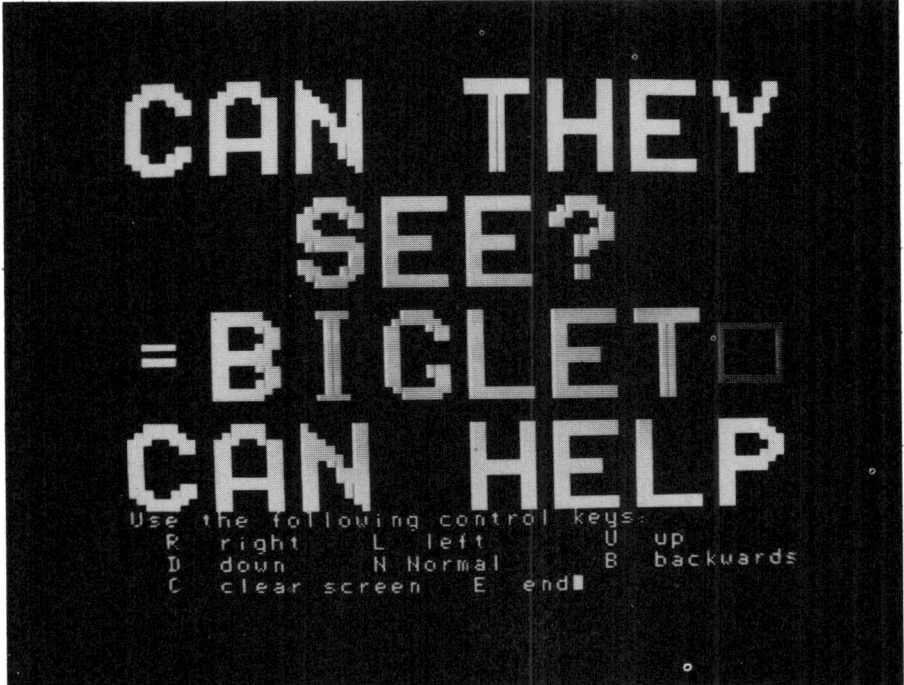

Discussion

What to notice: Since the program stores a lot of information about the character designs, it takes up a good deal of core memory. If you are using an RML 380Z, you need to use the BASICS interpreter rather than BASICSG: the latter, which caters for high-resolution graphics, is substantially longer.

The program neutralizes the effect of the 'CAPITALS LOCK' key. Any letter when input is treated as if in upper case.

The '*' is used as a multiplication symbol; the '/' as a division symbol.

The cursor may be moved backwards as well as forwards: the direction, once set, remains in force until switched explicitly. This enables you to do silly things like writing your name backwards, and may have more serious uses in arithmetic. For micros whose keyboards contain blocks of keys specifically intended for cursor control (as does the RML 480Z), it would be sensible to adapt the program to make use of these keys.

The format of the 'title page' shown when the program is run is used also with all the other programs in this book. This is an example of the consistency we believe may be helpful to the user.

Program code: Since one of the purposes of this program is to illustrate many of the points made in section 7.1, we are drawing your attention to a lot of them in this section. Few of these will be mentioned again in the other programs where they also apply.

The code has been split into sections to make its purpose clear to you. This is achieved using 'REM' statements, which label the sections, label individual lines and provide blank lines in the program at suitable points. The structure is made even clearer by the use of indentation: this is of particular assistance in clarifying the loops, some of which are nested.

Each program begins with a 'title page': a display of the program's title and purpose, our names and that of our publisher, and the copyright notice. It is our intention that in each case this title page should remain visible for a few seconds. We usually achieve this by building in a simple delay loop. In this program, however, it takes some time to read all the data into the arrays before the program can proceed, and this time is sufficient to display the title page; in this program, therefore, there is no delay loop at this point. When the program proper is about to start, the screen is cleared.

There is in this program a considerable quantity of data, and if you are going to make use of it in other programs, it is important that each block of data is clearly associated with its function. We achieve this partly by sectioning the program code, and partly by reading data into arrays whose names and structure clearly indicate their functions. Choosing appropriate names for variables is one of the easiest and most powerful ways of helping both reader and programmer. The meaning of the graphics codes (the manner in which they are calculated) is explained in section 7.1.

The main program is short, as might be expected from the simplicity of the flowchart. The structure of the main program and of the principal subroutine reflect the structure of the flowchart.

In this program, it is helpful to the programmer to keep a note of the kind of character which was input – whether it was a letter, a number or a punctuation symbol. Such notes can be recorded as so-called **flags**. In this case, the character type *could* be recorded in a numeric variable, say 'T', with '0' to represent a letter, '1' a number, and '2' a punctuation symbol. But it is much clearer if the flag is a *string* variable, in this case 'T$', because a string variable can record the actual names: 'letter', 'number' or 'punctuation'. Use of these words makes the entire program clearer, and especially the places where there is a choice of route depending on the value of the flag.

There is a difference of opinion concerning the destination of a jump from a

'GOTO' or 'IF ... THEN' statement. Some people hold that the destination should always be an 'active' line of code, not a 'REM' statement: if this were the case, the user could remove all the 'REM' statements from his code, and the program would continue to function. This deletion of comments is a practice which we deplore, especially if the comments provide headings to subroutines or sections of code, so this is not a rule which *we* follow. An alternative view is that jumps should always be to a 'REM' line, preferably a title of a section, because this makes the logic clearer to the reader. It has the added advantage that if extra code is added into that section, it is not necessary to hunt through the code for 'GOTO' and 'IF ... THEN' statements so as to adjust the line numbers which they cite. We do a bit of both: generally speaking, where the program calls a subroutine, the line number given is that of the title 'REM' line, whereas jumps within a subroutine and within the main program are to active lines of code.

Error-checking: The error-checking within this program is minimal. Each keystroke is examined to see whether the character typed is displayable or an active control character; if it is neither of these, it is simply ignored. The issuing in this situation of error messages would oppress the user without actually helping him much. The list of commands displayed continuously at the bottom of the screen should provide all the information required.

What you could do: You could design your own program to make effective use of the data we provide for the big characters.

You might want to improve on some of our characters. In particular, we feel that some of the punctuation marks might be improved if they were allowed to expand into the pixels adjacent to the edges of the permitted rectangle. For example, the tails of the comma and semicolon could be extended below the base of the letters.

You could produce your own lower-case letters to go with the capitals already provided. In this case, you might find that the program DESIGN, given in Appendix A.3, is helpful.

You could produce an alphabet of which each character is contained in a smaller rectangle – 5 pixels across and 7 pixels up is a size worth considering. If the characters were smaller, you would be able to display more on a line, and more lines on the screen.

Portability: This program makes use of low-resolution graphics, and is therefore tailored very specifically to the machines on which it runs, namely the RML 380Z or 480Z. On the other hand, we hope that the code is laid out clearly enough for you to be able to adapt it to another micro as easily as possible. The data for the program was produced using a design tool, the program DESIGN (see Appendix A.3); this program may be of assistance to you also once adapted to your own micro.

Many of the ways in which BIGLET would need to be changed in order that it might run on a different micro are aspects of portability which apply to most of the programs in the book. (These were described in detail in section 7.1.) Below, therefore, we mention only those points to which specific attention needs to be given in connection with this program.

As has already been pointed out, the blocks of data would have to be replaced by data corresponding to the pixel system on your micro. This might involve changing the size of the data blocks, since the number of pixels per character position may be different on your micro, and this would entail a change to the upper bound in many of the loops.

The program contains three 'PLOT' statements, all towards the end of the program: these would need to be changed to suit your machine.

7.3 Condensation of code

The aim of this section is to show different approaches to the need to shorten a program. This need is usually occasioned by the shortage of space in core memory. Memory is required for various purposes – not just the applications program that you wish to run, but also the systems software that you need in order to be able to run it, and storage for the data that you supply or the data that you create during the running of the program.

Some programmers always make their program code as short as possible, on the principle that the code will then stand the best chance of running in whatever memory is available. Some programmers write code which is short because their only interest is in making it work, not in documenting it clearly; they may or may not add comments at a later stage. Other programmers write code as they think it *should* be written, comments and all, and reduce the length only if they find that they have to; that has been our approach in writing the programs in this book.

Given that a program has been written which is too long, for some reason, there are different ways of cutting it. In this section we illustrate two ways of cutting one program.

Specification

The program will concern lexical analysis – the study of the frequencies, juxtapositions, contexts and vocabulary range in text. The program will be incomplete, but may provide a skeleton suitable for development of the complete program. The complete program would be in command mode, offering a set of options each of which was coded as an independent subroutine. The fragment will comprise only the menu of options and the transfers to the subroutines requested; no action will be taken beyond issuing a message to say that the chosen subroutine was selected successfully.

There will be three versions of this fragment. The first, LEXICAL1, will be a good working version of this program, adequately coded and commented. The others will be condensed forms of this: LEXICAL2 will be condensed as much as possible consistent with operating in the same way; LEXICAL3 will be condensed less severely while making every effort to retain clarity despite the constraint of space. LEXICAL2 will also demonstrate some of the ways in which space can simply *appear* to have been saved.

Outline flowchart of LEXICAL

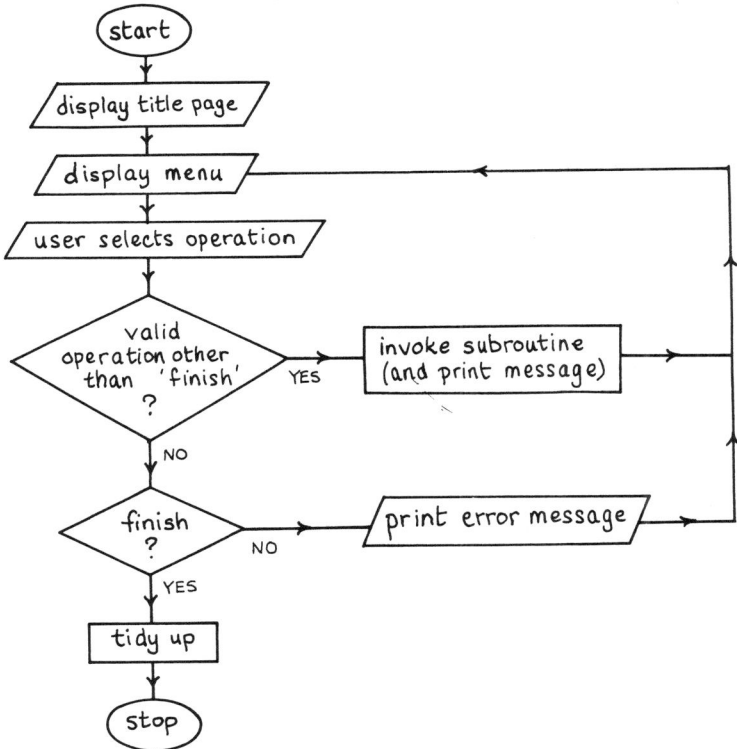

154 *Case studies in programming*

Listing of LEXICAL1 program code

```
1000 REM Program : LEXICAL1
1010 REM
1020 REM
1030 REM This program forms a fragment only of
1040 REM     a lexical analysis program. Here it
1050 REM     consists simply in the menu which
1060 REM     will offer the user the choice of
1070 REM     various courses of action, each of
1080 REM     which courses will be represented by
1090 REM     a subroutine which contains only a
1100 REM     PRINT instruction to show that it
1110 REM     was invoked.
1120 REM
1130 REM
1140     CLEAR 100
1150 REM
1160     ON BREAK GOTO 2020
1170 REM    Deal with user's interruption
1180 REM
1190 REM
1200     TEXT : PRINT CHR$(12) : REM Clear the screen
1210     PRINT CHR$(17) : REM Disable paging
1220     PRINT TAB(16); "LEXICAL1"
1230     PRINT
1240     PRINT TAB(6); "Condensation of program code"
1250     PRINT : PRINT : PRINT
1260     PRINT TAB(19); "*"
1270     PRINT
1280     PRINT TAB(14); "Andrew Nash"
1290     PRINT
1300     PRINT TAB(15); "Derek Ball"
1310     PRINT
1320     PRINT TAB(19); "*"
1330     PRINT : PRINT : PRINT
1340     PRINT TAB(13); "Copyright 1982"
1350     PRINT
1360     PRINT TAB(10); "Hutchinson Education"
1370     PRINT
1380     FOR D = 1 TO 5000 : NEXT D : REM Delay
1390     PRINT CHR$(12) : REM Clear the screen
1400 REM
1410 REM
1420 REM /PRINT THE MENU FOR THE USER/
1430 REM
1440     PRINT
1450     PRINT
1460     FOR I = 1 TO 4
1470        PRINT "-";
1480     NEXT I
1490     PRINT TAB(7);
1500     FOR I = 1 TO 33
1510        PRINT "-";
1520     NEXT I
1530     PRINT
1540     PRINT
1550     PRINT
1560 REM
1570     PRINT "CODE"; TAB(7); "OPERATION"
1580     PRINT
1590     PRINT TAB(2); "LF"; TAB(7); "List word frequencies"
1600     PRINT TAB(2); "PF"; TAB(7); "Plot word frequencies"
1610     PRINT TAB(2); "GC"; TAB(7); "Generate concordance"
```

```
1620      PRINT TAB(2); "LC"; TAB(7); "List collocations"
1630      PRINT TAB(2); "SF"; TAB(7); "Specify output format"
1640      PRINT TAB(2); "FA"; TAB(7); "Finish analysis"
1650 REM
1660      PRINT
1670      PRINT
1680      FOR I = 1 TO 4
1690         PRINT "-";
1700      NEXT I
1710      PRINT TAB(7);
1720      FOR I = 1 TO 33
1730         PRINT "-";
1740      NEXT I
1750      PRINT
1760      PRINT
1770      PRINT
1780 REM
1790 REM
1800 REM /INVOKE THE APPROPRIATE SUBROUTINE/
1810 REM
1820      PRINT "Enter code for operation required";
1830      INPUT R$
1840 REM
1850      IF R$ <> "LF" THEN 1880
1860         GOSUB 2080 : REM List word frequencies
1870         GOTO 1440
1880      IF R$ <> "PF" THEN 1910
1890         GOSUB 2120 : REM Plot word frequencies
1900         GOTO 1440
1910      IF R$ <> "GC" THEN 1940
1920         GOSUB 2160 : REM Generate concordance
1930         GOTO 1440
1940      IF R$ <> "LC" THEN 1970
1950         GOSUB 2210 : REM List collocations
1960         GOTO 1440
1970      IF R$ <> "SF" THEN 2000
1980         GOSUB 2240 : REM Specify output format
1990         GOTO 1440
2000      IF R$ <> "FA" THEN 2040
2010         PRINT : PRINT "   >> Analysis complete"
2020         PRINT CHR$(19) : REM Re-enable paging
2030         END
2040      PRINT "Code not understood - try again"
2050      GOTO 1440
2060 REM
2070 REM
2080 REM /SUBROUTINE TO LIST WORD FREQUENCIES/
2090      PRINT : PRINT "   >> List word frequencies"
2100      RETURN
2110 REM
2120 REM /SUBROUTINE TO PLOT WORD FREQUENCIES/
2130      PRINT : PRINT "   >> Plot word frequencies"
2140      RETURN
2150 REM
2160 REM /SUBROUTINE TO GENERATE CONCORDANCE/
2170      PRINT : PRINT "   >> Generate concordance"
2180      RETURN
2190 REM
2200 REM /SUBROUTINE TO LIST COLLOCATIONS/
2210      PRINT : PRINT "   >> List collocations"
2220      RETURN
2230 REM
2240 REM /SUBROUTINE TO SPECIFY OUTPUT FORMAT/
2250      PRINT : PRINT "   >> Specify output format"
2260      RETURN
```

Listing of LEXICAL2 program code

```
5 CLEAR 100
10 ONBREAKGOTO180
15 TEXT:? CHR$(12)
20 ?CHR$(17)
25 ?TAB(16);"LEXICAL2":?
30 ?TAB(6);"Condensation of program code"
35 ?:?:?:? TAB(19);"*":?
40 ?TAB(14);"Andrew Nash"
45 ?:? TAB(15);"Derek Ball":PRINT
50 ?TAB(19);"*":?:?:?
55 ?TAB(13);"Copyright 1982"
60 ?:? TAB(10);"Hutchinson Education"
65 ?:FORD=1TO5000:NEXTD:? CHR$(12)
70 ?:?:FORI=1TO4
75 ?"-";:NEXTI
80 ?TAB(7);:FORI=1TO33
85 ?"-";:NEXTI:?:?:?
90 ?"CODE";TAB(7);"OPERATION":?
95 ?TAB(2);"LF";TAB(7);"List word frequencies";?TAB(2);"PF";
100 ?TAB(7);"Plot word frequencies";?TAB(2);"GC";TAB(7);
105 ?"Generate concordance";?TAB(2);"LC";TAB(7);"List ";
110 ?"collocations";?TAB(2);"SF";TAB(7);"Specify output ";
115 ?"format";?TAB(2);"FA";TAB(7);"Finish analysis"
120 ?:?:FORI=1TO4
125 ? "-";:NEXTI
130 ?TAB(7);:FORI=1TO33;? "-";
135 NEXTI:?:?:?
140 ? "Enter code for operation required";:INPUTR$
145 IFR$ = "LF"THEN GOSUB190:GOTO70
150 IFR$ = "PF"THEN GOSUB195:GOTO70
155 IFR$ = "GC"THEN GOSUB200:GOTO70
160 IFR$ = "LC"THEN GOSUB205:GOTO70
165 IFR$ = "SF"THEN GOSUB210:GOTO70
170 IFR$ () "FA"THEN185
175 ?:? "   )) Analysis complete"
180 ? CHR$(19):END
185 ? "Code not understood - try again":GOTO70
190 ?:? "   )) List word frequencies":RETURN
195 ?:? "   )) Plot word frequencies":RETURN
200 ?:? "   )) Generate concordance":RETURN
205 ?:? "   )) List collocations":RETURN
210 ?:? "   )) Specify output format":RETURN
```

Listing of LEXICAL3 program code

```
1000 REM Program : LEXICAL3
1010 REM
1020 REM Fragment of lexical analysis program.
1030 REM Provides menu of options; demonstrates
1040 REM that these are invoked.
1050 REM
1060     CLEAR 100
1070     ON BREAK GOTO 1570
1080 REM Deal with user's interruption
1090 REM
1100 REM
1110     TEXT : PRINT CHR$(12) : REM Clear screen
1120     PRINT CHR$(17) : REM Disable paging
1130     PRINT TAB(16);"LEXICAL3"
```

```
1140        PRINT : PRINT TAB(6);"Condensation of program code"
1150        PRINT : PRINT : PRINT
1160        PRINT TAB(19);"*"
1170        PRINT : PRINT TAB(14);"Andrew Nash"
1180        PRINT : PRINT TAB(15);"Derek Ball"
1190        PRINT : PRINT TAB(19); "*"
1200        PRINT : PRINT : PRINT
1210        PRINT TAB(13);"Copyright 1982"
1220        PRINT : PRINT TAB(10);"Hutchinson Education"
1230        PRINT
1240        FOR D = 1 TO 5000 : NEXT D : REM Delay
1250        PRINT CHR$(12) : REM Clear screen
1260 REM
1270 REM /MENU/
1280 REM
1290        GOSUB 1830 : REM Line of dashes
1300        PRINT "CODE"; TAB(7);"OPERATION" : PRINT
1310        PRINT TAB(2);"LF"; TAB(7);"List word frequencies"
1320        PRINT TAB(2);"PF"; TAB(7);"Plot word frequencies"
1330        PRINT TAB(2);"GC"; TAB(7);"Generate concordance"
1340        PRINT TAB(2);"LC"; TAB(7);"List collocations"
1350        PRINT TAB(2);"SF"; TAB(7);"Specify output format"
1360        PRINT TAB(2);"FA"; TAB(7);"Finish analysis"
1370        GOSUB 1830 : REM Line of dashes
1380 REM
1390 REM
1400 REM /INVOKE APPROPRIATE S-R/
1410 REM
1420        PRINT "Enter code for operation required";
1430        INPUT R$
1440 REM
1450        IF R$="LF" THEN GOSUB 1620 : GOTO 1290
1460 REM List word frequencies
1470        IF R$="PF" THEN GOSUB 1660 : GOTO 1290
1480 REM Plot word frequencies
1490        IF R$="GC" THEN GOSUB 1700 : GOTO 1290
1500 REM Generate concordance
1510        IF R$="LC" THEN GOSUB 1740 : GOTO 1290
1520 REM List collocations
1530        IF R$="SF" THEN GOSUB 1780 : GOTO 1290
1540 REM Specify output format
1550        IF R$<>"FA" THEN 1590
1560          PRINT : PRINT "   >> Analysis complete"
1570          PRINT CHR$(19) : REM Re-enable paging
1580          END
1590        PRINT "Code not understood - try again"
1600        GOTO 1290
1610 REM
1620 REM /S-R LIST WORD FREQUENCIES/
1630        PRINT : PRINT "   >> List word frequencies"
1640        RETURN
1650 REM
1660 REM /S-R PLOT WORD FREQUENCIES/
1670        PRINT : PRINT "   >> Plot word frequencies"
1680        RETURN
1690 REM
1700 REM /S-R GENERATE CONCORDANCE/
1710        PRINT : PRINT "   >> Generate concordance"
1720        RETURN
1730 REM
1740 REM /S-R LIST COLLOCATIONS/
1750        PRINT : PRINT "   >> List collocations"
1760        RETURN
1770 REM
1780 REM /S-R SPECIFY OUTPUT FORMAT/
1790        PRINT : PRINT "   >> Specify output format"
```

```
1800      RETURN
1810 REM
1820 REM
1830 REM /S-R LINE OF DASHES/
1840      PRINT : PRINT
1850      FOR I = 1 TO 40
1860        IF (I)4 AND I(8) THEN PRINT " "; ELSE PRINT "-";
1870      NEXT I
1880      PRINT : PRINT : PRINT
1890      RETURN
```

Sample output

```
    ----   ----------------------------------------

    CODE    OPERATION

     LF     List word frequencies
     PF     Plot word frequencies
     GC     Generate concordance
     LC     List collocations
     SF     Specify output format
     FA     Finish analysis

    ----   ----------------------------------------

    Enter code for operation required? ■
```

Discussion

Program code: All three versions offer exactly the same facilities and produce exactly the same output on the screen. LEXICAL1 is, for the most part, the clearest version; it is certainly the longest. LEXICAL2 is equally certainly the shortest, but is not the easiest to read.... LEXICAL3 is not as short as LEXICAL2, which we had hoped it would be, but it *is* a good deal shorter than LEXICAL1 – not just because there are fewer lines, but because these lines are shorter. The actual lengths of the three versions are: LEXICAL1, 3042 bytes; LEXICAL2, 1232 bytes; and LEXICAL3, 2356 bytes.

LEXICAL1 begins with a longish explanation of the purpose of the program. After the title page, there is a group of instructions which print a line of dashes (with a gap in it). Next comes the printing of the menu itself, with one line of code for each line of the table; and after this is another line of dashes. The next group of statements deal with the user's choice of operation: if he supplies a code (in upper case) which corresponds to one of the permitted operations, this operation is invoked by means of a call to the appropriate subroutine; if his input does not match the options available, he is invited to try again. At the end of the program are would-be subroutines, one for each operation. (All that is actually done is to print a message saying which subroutine was invoked.)

LEXICAL2 presents just about the ultimate in condensation of the same program; incredibly, the appearance to the *user* is identical. Note the quick ways of saving space in core memory: leave out all the 'REM' statements and all the 'unnecessary' blanks. One way of using less blanks than are used in LEXICAL1, for example, is to omit the blanks round the statement separator (in our case, the colon). Consider lines 145–165 in LEXICAL2: there are blanks round the 'equals' signs, but not round the colons; the code would be clearer if this were reversed. Notice how difficult the program is to read simply as a result of running instructions and variable names together, as for instance in the case of 'FORD' instead of 'FOR D'. Every subroutine ends with the word 'RETURN', and in well laid out programs, this is printed on a separate line: this helps to show the programmer where the routine ends.

If you are obliged to condense program code, and inevitably you sometimes are (we were forced to shorten GRAPH, for instance, in section 8.5), do make sure that the changes you are making are actually saving space in core. Things are not always as they seem! We have made a practice in our programs of numbering the lines from 1000 upwards: in this way, we can ensure that all line numbers are of four characters, and the statements can be lined up neatly. In LEXICAL2, though, we have 'saved space' by starting at 5 and going up in increments of 5: this is clearly a saving of characters, as is apparent from the listings.... Well no, it isn't: each line number is stored in four bytes, regardless of the line number. (Two bytes store the number; two bytes point to the address in core of the beginning of the next line.) So '5' takes the same amount of storage as does '1000', and the longer numbers are clearer. Line numbers in, for example, 'GOTO' statements are stored as individual characters: minimal savings may therefore be made in these if low numbers are used.

On the same theme, notice the use of question marks in place of the word 'PRINT'. Most micros offer '?' as shorthand for the programmer, and this is clearly a saving in each case of four characters! No, it isn't: when the program is stored, the computer does not actually record the five letters of the word 'PRINT' or the one character that is '?', it stores in each case a code which *corresponds* to the instruction – and the codes for 'PRINT' and for '?' are each one byte long, so there is no saving.

(Savings are sometimes attempted by stringing statements together on one line; as we say elsewhere in the book, we think that this is valid only if the statements form a self-contained unit. Note that in running together two statements, you save the four bytes of storage used for the deleted line number, but you incur new storage requirements because of the colon which separates the statements, and the blanks which you might put around this. Is the saving really worthwhile?)

Particularly unpleasant, we think, is the running on of the text which forms the menu – lines 95–115. This has made the magnificent saving of one line number (setting aside the savings made by deleting blanks). The structure of the program is also obscured by the way in which the loops are set out: consider lines 130 and 135, for instance.

LEXICAL3 represents a halfway house. Savings are made by shortening the explanation at the front of the program; by reducing (but not completely removing) the blank 'REM' lines; by shortening (but not deleting) the headings to sections of the program such as subroutines; by removing blanks between 'TAB' and 'PRINT' and around 'equals' signs. There are two other major changes. One is the use of a single subroutine to print the two lines of dashes: while this makes little difference to the overall length, it makes the program clearer (especially as the call to the subroutine is explained by a 'REM' statement). The same is true of the other major change: the condensation of the section which tests the user's choice and invokes the appropriate subroutine. Compare the two versions in LEXICAL1 and LEXICAL3: the LEXICAL3 version is certainly shorter and (we think) much clearer.

Error-checking: The only input from the user is the choice of option: if this is inappropriate, he is invited to try again.

What you could do: You could extend (say) LEXICAL3 by filling in the subroutines. You could then set up pieces of text (on the screen, as in HILIGHT in section 7.7, or in data files on backing store) and analyse these using your program.

You could take one of our other programs, or one of your own, and condense the code elegantly. And you could bear these concepts in mind when looking at very compressed programs, whatever their sources.

Portability: Apart from the code which opens and closes each program, the code for all three should be portable.

7.4 Updating tables on the screen

The aim of this section is to illustrate two alternative ways of updating a table displayed on a screen, and to show the differences in the code needed to effect them. One way of updating a table is to rewrite it completely; the other is to alter individual parts of it without disturbing the rest.

Specification

The table under discussion will concern a catalogue of museum exhibits. The user is to supply four items of data concerning the exhibits – type of object, material of object, earliest and latest dates of object – and these items form the basis of a search of a hypothetical database, yielding a list of those exhibits in the catalogue which conform to the details supplied. Since the technique being illustrated here is solely that of updating tables, no catalogue will actually be used, and no search will actually be performed.

There will be two versions of the program: one, EXHIBIT1, will rewrite the complete table each time any element of it is altered; the other, EXHIBIT2, will update only the individual element that has been altered. The two versions will be similar in all other respects, to facilitate comparison. Error-checking will be minimal to keep the code short. Entries longer than 20 characters will simply be truncated.

162 *Case studies in programming*

Outline flowchart of EXHIBIT1

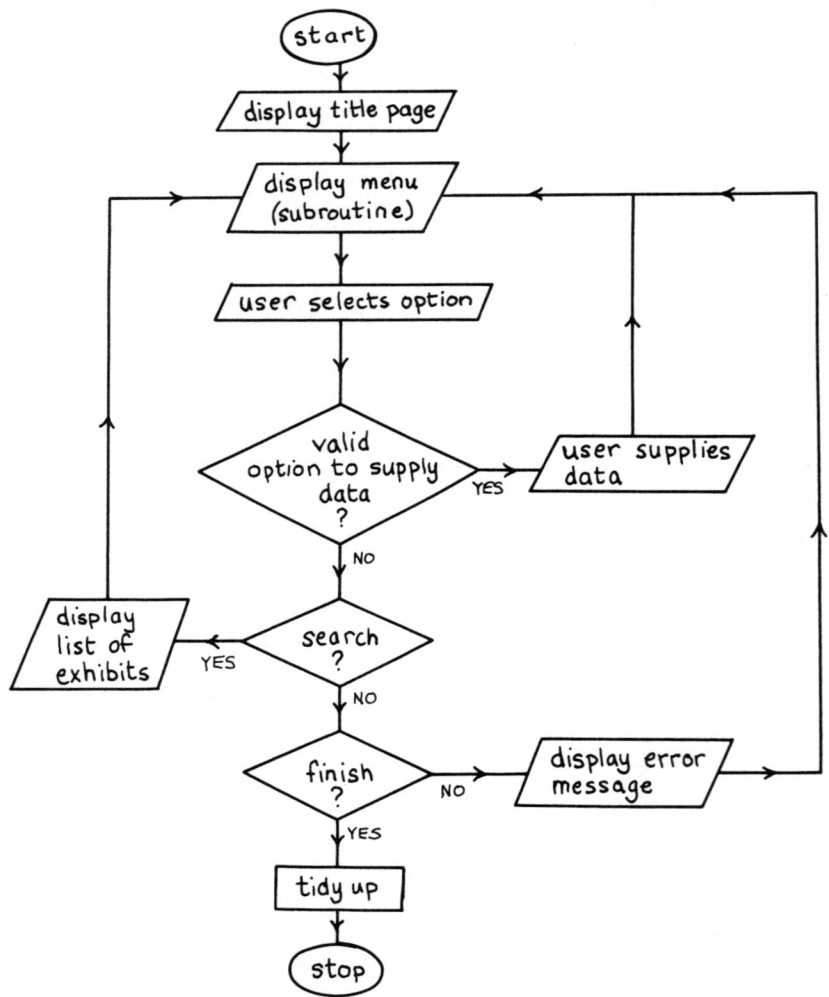

Outline flowchart of EXHIBIT2

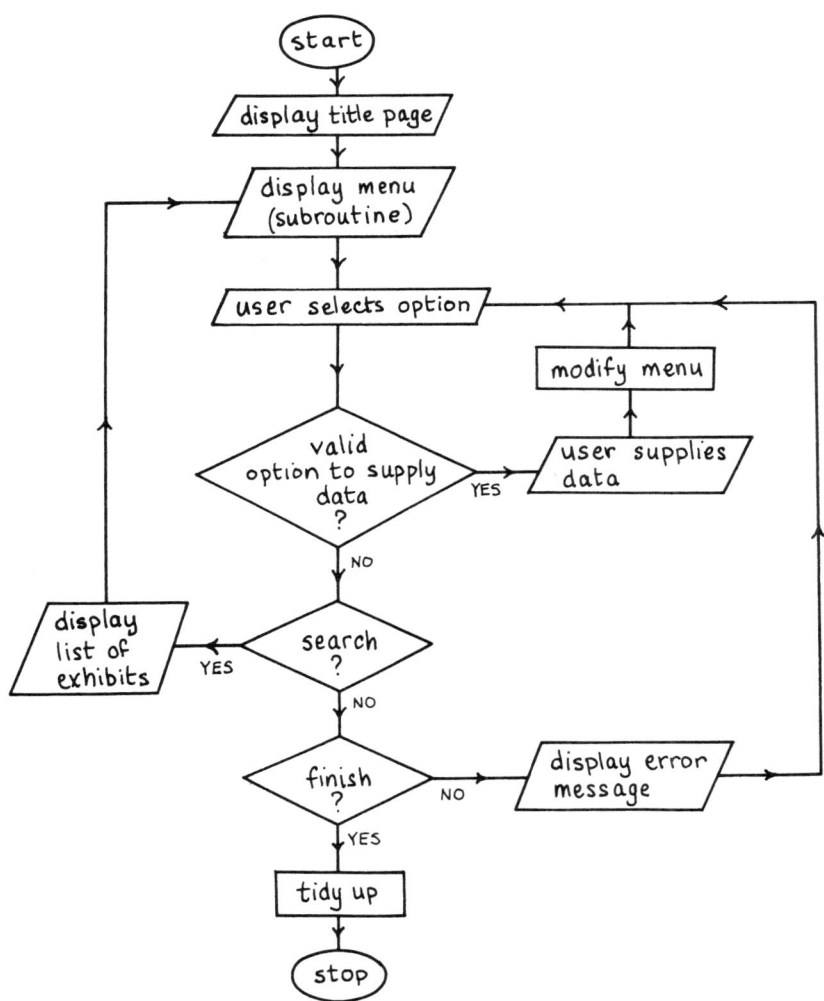

Listing of EXHIBIT1 program code

```
1000 REM Program : EXHIBIT1
1010 REM
1020 REM
1030 REM This program fragment represents one use of a
1040 REM      museum catalogue.  The user supplies details
1050 REM      of objects in which he is interested.  (The
1060 REM      full program would then search for objects
1070 REM      which fitted this description.)
1080 REM
1090 REM This fragment illustrates the method of updating
1100 REM      a table by rewriting it in its entirety - the
1110 REM      technique of scrolling.
1120 REM
1130 REM
1140      CLEAR (100)
1150 REM
1160      ON BREAK GOTO 1850
1170 REM      Deal with user's interruption
1180 REM
1190      TEXT : PRINT CHR$(12) : REM Clear the screen
1200      PRINT CHR$(17) : REM Disable paging
1210 REM
1220 REM
1230      PRINT TAB(16); "EXHIBIT1"
1240      PRINT
1250      PRINT TAB(7); "Update table by scrolling"
1260      PRINT : PRINT : PRINT
1270      PRINT TAB(19); "*"
1280      PRINT
1290      PRINT TAB(14); "Andrew Nash"
1300      PRINT
1310      PRINT TAB(15); "Derek Ball"
1320      PRINT
1330      PRINT TAB(19); "*"
1340      PRINT : PRINT : PRINT
1350      PRINT TAB(13); "Copyright 1982"
1360      PRINT
1370      PRINT TAB(10); "Hutchinson Education"
1380      PRINT
1390      FOR D = 1 TO 5000 : NEXT D : REM Delay
1400      PRINT CHR$(12) : REM Clear the screen
1410 REM
1420 REM
1430 REM
1440      LET O$="" : LET M$="" : LET ED$="" : LET LD$=""
1450 REM
1460      GOSUB 1950 : REM Display table
1470      PRINT : PRINT "Selection (O, M, E or L), search (S)"
1480      PRINT "  or finish (F)";
1490      INPUT R$
1500      PRINT
1510      IF R$ () "O" THEN 1550
1520          PRINT "Objects (e.g. POTS)";
1530          INPUT O$ : LET O$ = LEFT$(O$,20)
1540          GOTO 1460
1550      IF R$ () "M" THEN 1590
1560          PRINT "Material (e.g. CLAY)";
1570          INPUT M$ : LET M$ = LEFT$(M$,20)
1580          GOTO 1460
1590      IF R$ () "E" THEN 1630
1600          PRINT "Earliest date (e.g. BC 500)";
1610          INPUT ED$ : LET ED$ = LEFT$(ED$,20)
```

Updating tables on the screen 165

```
1620        GOTO 1460
1630   IF R$ () "L" THEN 1670
1640        PRINT "Latest date (e.g. BC 250)";
1650        INPUT LD$ : LET LD$ = LEFT$(LD$,20)
1660        GOTO 1460
1670   IF R$ () "S" THEN 1820
1680        PRINT CHR$(12) : REM Clear the screen
1690        PRINT "Here is a list of"
1700        PRINT TAB(3); O$
1710        PRINT "made of"
1720        PRINT TAB(3); M$
1730        PRINT "dated between"
1740        PRINT TAB(3); ED$
1750        PRINT "and"
1760        PRINT TAB(3); LD$
1770        FOR I = 1 TO 10 : PRINT : NEXT I
1780        PRINT "Press SPACEBAR to continue"
1790        LET R$ = GET$() : IF R$ () " " THEN 1790
1800        PRINT CHR$(12) : REM Clear the screen
1810        GOTO 1460
1820   IF R$ () "F" THEN 1880
1830        PRINT
1840        PRINT "Thankyou. Good day to you."
1850        PRINT CHR$(19) : REM Re-enable paging
1860        TEXT
1870        END
1880   PRINT "** '"; R$; "' not understood - try again"
1890   PRINT "Press SPACEBAR to continue"
1900   LET R$ = GET$() : IF R$ () " " THEN 1900 ELSE 1460
1910 REM
1920 REM
1930 REM Subroutine to display the table
1940 REM
1950        PRINT CHR$(12) : REM Clear the screen
1960        PRINT "MUSEUM CATALOGUE"
1970        PRINT
1980        FOR I = 1 TO 40 : PRINT "-"; : NEXT I : PRINT
1990        PRINT "   ITEM"; TAB(20); "SUPPLIED DATA"
2000        PRINT
2010        PRINT "O Objects"; TAB(20); O$
2020        PRINT "M Material"; TAB(20); M$
2030        PRINT "E Earlest date"; TAB(20); ED$
2040        PRINT "L Latest date"; TAB(20); LD$
2050        PRINT
2060        FOR I = 1 TO 40 : PRINT "-"; : NEXT I : PRINT
2070 REM
2080        RETURN
```

Listing of EXHIBIT2 program code

```
1000 REM Program : EXHIBIT2
1010 REM
1020 REM
1030 REM This program fragment represents one use of a
1040 REM     museum catalogue. The user supplies details
1050 REM     of objects in which he is interested. (The
1060 REM     full program would then search for objects
1070 REM     which fitted this description.)
1080 REM
1090 REM This fragment illustrates the method of updating
1100 REM     a table by altering individual
1110 REM     items in situ.
1120 REM
```

166 *Case studies in programming*

```
1130 REM
1140     CLEAR (300)
1150 REM
1160     ON BREAK GOTO 1970
1170 REM    Deal with user's interruption
1180 REM
1190     TEXT : PRINT CHR$(12) : REM Clear the screen
1200     PRINT CHR$(17) : REM Disable paging
1210 REM
1220 REM
1230     PRINT TAB(16); "EXHIBIT2"
1240     PRINT
1250     PRINT TAB(6); "Update table by overwriting"
1260     PRINT : PRINT : PRINT
1270     PRINT TAB(19); "*"
1280     PRINT
1290     PRINT TAB(14); "Andrew Nash"
1300     PRINT
1310     PRINT TAB(15); "Derek Ball"
1320     PRINT
1330     PRINT TAB(19); "*"
1340     PRINT : PRINT : PRINT
1350     PRINT TAB(13); "Copyright 1982"
1360     PRINT
1370     PRINT TAB(10); "Hutchinson Education"
1380     PRINT
1390     FOR D = 1 TO 5000 : NEXT D : REM Delay
1400     PRINT CHR$(12) : REM Clear the screen
1410 REM
1420 REM
1430     LET O$="" : LET M$="" : LET ED$="" : LET LD$=""
1440 REM
1450     GRAPH
1460 REM
1470     GOSUB 2070 : REM Display table
1480     PRINT : PRINT : PRINT "Selection (O, M, E or L), search (S)"
1490     PRINT " or finish (F)";
1500     INPUT R$
1510     PRINT
1520     IF R$ <> "O" THEN 1580
1530        PRINT "Objects (e.g. POTS)";
1540        INPUT O$
1550        LET O$ = O$ + "                    "
1560        LET O$ = LEFT$(O$,20)
1570        PLOT 38,36,O$ : GOTO 1480
1580     IF R$ <> "M" THEN 1640
1590        PRINT "Material (e.g. CLAY)";
1600        INPUT M$
1610        LET M$ = M$ + "                    "
1620        LET M$ = LEFT$(M$,20)
1630        PLOT 38,33,M$ : GOTO 1480
1640     IF R$ <> "E" THEN 1700
1650        PRINT "Earliest date (e.g. BC 500)";
1660        INPUT ED$
1670        LET ED$ = ED$ + "                    "
1680        LET ED$ = LEFT$(ED$,20)
1690        PLOT 38,30,ED$ : GOTO 1480
1700     IF R$ <> "L" THEN 1760
1710        PRINT "Latest date (e.g. BC 250)";
1720        INPUT LD$
1730        LET LD$ = LD$ + "                    "
1740        LET LD$ = LEFT$(LD$,20)
1750        PLOT 38,27,LD$ : GOTO 1480
1760     IF R$ <> "S" THEN 1940
1770        TEXT
```

```
1780        PRINT CHR$(12) : REM Clear the screen
1790        PRINT "Here is a list of"
1800        PRINT TAB(3); O$
1810        PRINT "made of"
1820        PRINT TAB(3); M$
1830        PRINT "dated between"
1840        PRINT TAB(3); ED$
1850        PRINT "and"
1860        PRINT TAB(3); LD$
1870        FOR I = 1 TO 10 : PRINT : NEXT I
1880        PRINT "Press SPACEBAR to continue"
1890        LET R$ = GET$() : IF R$ () " " THEN 1890
1900        PRINT CHR$(12) : REM Clear the screen
1910        GRAPH
1920        GOSUB 2070 : REM Display table
1930        GOTO 1470
1940     IF R$ () "F" THEN 2000
1950        PRINT
1960        PRINT "Thankyou. Good day to you."
1970        PRINT CHR$(19) : REM Re-enable paging
1980        TEXT
1990        END
2000     PRINT "** '"; R$; "' not understood - try again"
2010     PRINT "Press SPACEBAR to continue"
2020     LET R$ = GET$() : IF R$ () " " THEN 2020 ELSE 1480
2030 REM
2040 REM
2050 REM Subroutine to display the table
2060 REM
2070        PRINT CHR$(12) : REM Clear the screen
2080        PLOT 0,51,"MUSEUM CATALOGUE"
2090 REM
2100        FOR I = 0 TO 38 : PLOT (2*I),45,"-" : NEXT I
2110        PLOT 4,42,"ITEM" : PLOT 38,42,"SUPPLIED DATA"
2120 REM
2130        PLOT 0,36,"O Objects" : PLOT 38,36,O$
2140        PLOT 0,33,"M Material" : PLOT 38,33,M$
2150        PLOT 0,30,"E Earliest date" : PLOT 38,30,ED$
2160        PLOT 0,27,"L Latest date" : PLOT 38,27,LD$
2170 REM
2180        FOR I = 0 TO 38 : PLOT (2*I),21,"-" : NEXT I
2190 REM
2200        RETURN
```

Sample output

```
          MUSEUM CATALOGUE
      ..................................../
          ITEM              SUPPLIED DATA

      D Objects           Example of EXHIBIT
      M Material          Photograph
      E Earliest date     1982
      L Latest date       Who knows?
      ....................................

      Selection (D, M, E or L), search (S)
         or finish (F)? ■
```

Discussion

What to notice: By running both versions – and only by running them – you can see how much quicker, more pleasant and less distracting is the process of updating tables *in situ*. Thus the user is encouraged to proceed: results are immediate and clear. Rewriting the whole table can be slow, irritating and off-putting, especially when the user realizes as he presses the 'RETURN' key that he has mistyped his entry, yet must wait for the table to be rewritten.

Compare this with AUGURY (section 3.6), where the table is rewritten each time any part of it is altered.

Note that this method is of use only with programs in which output is sent to the screen – not with those in which output is sent to a printer.

Program code: The code for the two programs is different in one respect: output from EXHIBIT1 is *printed*; that from EXHIBIT2 is *plotted*. Look at the lines in EXHIBIT2 which contain the word 'PLOT', and compare them with the equivalent lines in EXHIBIT1.

The table is displayed by means of a subroutine. In EXHIBIT1, this subroutine is invoked in one place only, and therefore need not be a subroutine in terms of the working of the code. Nevertheless, the use of a subroutine for this purpose makes the working of the code clearer to the reader.

Error-checking: Only the most important errors (those potentially most disruptive) have been trapped: an incorrect option and an over-long entry (which would not fit the table). We have *required* upper-case input, yet not checked for it. The letters in such catalogues are frequently all capitals, and the data used to search the catalogue would need to match its entries in this respect. It would be fairly easy to convert lower-case input into upper-case text automatically, as the entry is typed in; it would also be possible to preserve the input in its mixed-case form but to ignore the case of the letters when performing the actual search (the search would not then be 'case-sensitive').

Over-long entries from the user are merely truncated to the maximum allowable length; the user could instead be advised of the problem and invited to recast his input. In practice, there would be much more important constraints on the wording, in that it would need in some sense to match the kind of entries in the catalogue itself.

What you could do: You could improve the error-checking, by allowing the user to specify either upper- or lower-case text and by converting this to upper-case text only. You could improve it also by advising the user of over-long entries. You could add another line to the table – value of object, for example.

If you want to spend considerably more time and have the ability, you could create a small database and adapt the program to do a real search and to list the results, with the option of directing this list to the printer.

An allied exercise would be to adapt AUGURY (section 3.6) so that its table is updated *in situ* – this is not too difficult if you understand the coordinate system of your micro (see section 7.1) and if you pay attention to the differences in coding between EXHIBIT1 and EXHIBIT2.

Portability: These programs were originally written for an RML 380Z micro. If you have a different micro, you will need to modify the lines which contain the words 'TEXT', 'GRAPH' or 'PLOT'. You *may* also need to turn some of the 'PRINT' statements into 'PLOT' instructions, so that messages to the user do not interfere with the table.

7.5 Updating pictures on the screen

The aim of this section is to show how low-resolution graphics can be used to produce a sequence of pictures on the screen, and how the pictures may be combined with text.

A subsidiary aim is to illustrate how graphics in computer programs may be used to demonstrate principles which would be difficult to teach effectively in any other way.

Specification

The program, CANALOCK, will depict the successive stages in the operation of a canal lock. The lock will be shown both in plan and in elevation. The picture will in each case show a section of canal above the lock, the lock itself, a section of canal below the lock, and the lock gates. The opening and closing of the gates, the movement of the barge and the rise and fall of water in the lock will all be animated (simply).

The user will specify the direction in which the barge moves through the lock (from top to bottom, or from bottom to top): the direction chosen will be recorded on the screen. The user will be able to go in either direction through the lock, irrespective of the state of the lock (full or empty) at the start. After each stage of the operation, the program will pause until the user presses the space-bar: the user will therefore be able to control the speed at which the process is displayed.

The program will demonstrate clear layout of the screen, including messages about the direction of movement and the state of the lock gates; the code to achieve this will also be intelligible.

Outline flowchart of CANALOCK

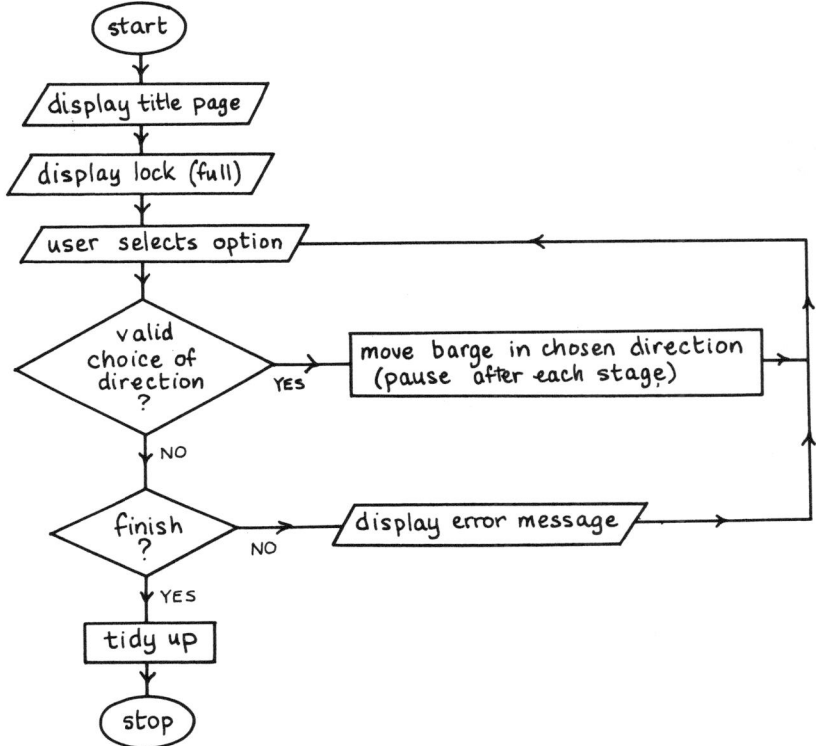

Listing of CANALOCK program code

```
1000 REM Program: CANALOCK
1010 REM
1020 REM
1030 REM This program demonstrates the workings of a canal lock.  The
1040 REM     graphics depict successive stages in moving a barge through
1050 REM     a lock in either direction.
1060 REM
1070 REM The program illustrates how the screen can be laid out and
1080 REM     modified to create a sequence of pictures.
1090 REM
1100 REM
1110     CLEAR 100
1120 REM
1130     TEXT : PRINT CHR$(12) : REM Clear screen
1140 REM
1150     ON BREAK GOTO 2210
1160 REM     Deal with user's interruption
1170     PRINT CHR$(17) : REM Disable paging
```

```
1180 REM
1190 REM
1200     PRINT TAB(16); "CANALOCK"
1210     PRINT
1220     PRINT TAB(2); "Demonstrates working of a canal lock"
1230     PRINT : PRINT : PRINT
1240     PRINT TAB(19); "*"
1250     PRINT
1260     PRINT TAB(14); "Andrew Nash"
1270     PRINT
1280     PRINT TAB(15); "Derek Ball"
1290     PRINT
1300     PRINT TAB(19); "*"
1310     PRINT : PRINT : PRINT
1320     PRINT TAB(13); "Copyright 1982"
1330     PRINT
1340     PRINT TAB(9); "Hutchinson Education"
1350     PRINT
1360     FOR D = 1 TO 5000 : NEXT D : REM Delay
1370     PRINT CHR$(12) : REM Clear the screen
1380 REM
1390 REM
1400 REM * LIST OF VARIABLES *
1410 REM
1420 REM         R$ - User's response
1430 REM         L$ - State of lock
1440 REM         W$ - Water level
1450 REM         M$ - Movement
1460 REM         T$ - Title string
1470 REM         G$ - Gate position
1480 REM
1490 REM     X0, Y0 - Old position of barge
1500 REM     X1, Y1 - New position of barge
1510 REM     X3, Y3 - Position of barge for plotting
1520 REM         Y4 - Coordinates of barge in top lock
1530 REM Y5,Y6,Y9,S - Used for lowering and raising in lock
1540 REM       X, Y - Coordinates for plotting
1550 REM      B, B9 - Brightness for plotting points
1560 REM
1570 REM
1580 REM * PREPARE FOR START *
1590 REM
1600     GRAPH
1610     X0=-99 : REM Barge not on screen
1620     L$="no barge" : REM Barge not in lock
1630     W$="high" : REM Water in lock high
1640     GOSUB 2260 : REM Set up screen
1650 REM
1660 REM
1670 REM * WHICH DIRECTION? *
1680 REM
1690     PRINT "Up, down or finish (U, D or F)";
1700     INPUT R$
1710     IF R$="D" OR R$="d" THEN M$="down" : GOTO 1790
1720     IF R$="U" OR R$="u" THEN M$="up" : GOTO 1790
1730     IF R$="F" OR R$="f" THEN 2210
1740     PRINT " Not understood" : GOTO 1690
1750 REM
1760 REM
1770 REM * NOW GO *
1780 REM
1790     PRINT CHR$(12) : REM Clear bottom of screen
1800 REM
1810     IF M$="down" THEN T$="DOWN" ELSE T$="UP"
1820     PLOT 28,57,"GOING "+T$ : REM Display heading
```

Updating pictures on the screen 173

```
1830      IF M$="down" THEN X1=4 : Y1=15 ELSE X1=56 : Y1=6
1840      B9=0 : GOSUB 2900 : REM Move barge
1850      GOSUB 3130 : REM Pause
1860 REM
1870      IF M$="down" AND W$="high" THEN 1980
1880      IF M$="up" AND W$="low" THEN 1980
1890      G$="close" : GOSUB 2590 : REM Close gate
1900      GOSUB 3130 : REM Pause
1910 REM
1920      GOSUB 2760 : REM Alter level
1930      GOSUB 3130 : REM Pause
1940 REM
1950      G$="open" : GOSUB 2590 : REM Open gate
1960      GOSUB 3130 : REM Pause
1970 REM
1980      IF M$="down" THEN X1=28 : Y1=15 ELSE X1=28 : Y1=6
1990      B9=0 : GOSUB 2900 : REM Move barge
2000      L$="barge"
2010      GOSUB 3130 : REM Pause
2020 REM
2030      G$="close" : GOSUB 2590 : REM Close gate
2040      GOSUB 3130 : REM Pause
2050 REM
2060      GOSUB 2760 : REM Alter level
2070      GOSUB 3130 : REM Pause
2080 REM
2090      G$="open" : GOSUB 2590 : REM Open gate
2100      GOSUB 3130 : REM Pause
2110 REM
2120      IF M$="down" THEN X1=56 : Y1=6 ELSE X1=4 : Y1=15
2130      B9=0 : GOSUB 2900 : REM Move barge
2140      L$="no barge"
2150      GOSUB 3130 : REM Pause
2160      X1=-99
2170      B9=0 : GOSUB 2900 : REM Move barge
2180      PLOT 28,57,"          " : REM Remove heading
2190      GOTO 1690
2200 REM
2210      TEXT : PRINT CHR$(12) : REM Clear screen
2220      PRINT CHR$(19) : REM Re-enable paging
2230      END
2240 REM
2250 REM
2260 REM * SUBROUTINE: SET UP SCREEN *
2270 REM
2280 REM Bottom picture first
2290      PLOT 0,2,2 : LINE 79,2
2300      PLOT 24,3,2 : LINE 24,20
2310      PLOT 25,3,2 : LINE 25,20
2320      PLOT 52,3,2 : LINE 52,20
2330      PLOT 53,3,2 : LINE 53,20
2340      FOR Y = 3 TO 14
2350        PLOT 0,Y,1 : LINE 17,Y
2360        PLOT 18,Y,2 : LINE 23,Y
2370        PLOT 26,Y,1 : LINE 51,Y
2380        IF Y<6 THEN PLOT 54,Y,1 : LINE 79,Y
2390      NEXT Y
2400 REM Now top picture
2410      PLOT 0,38,2 : LINE 79,38
2420      PLOT 0,48,2 : LINE 79,48
2430      FOR Y=39 TO 47
2440        PLOT 0,Y,1 : LINE 79,Y
2450      NEXT Y
2460      PLOT 52,37,2 : LINE 52,49
2470      PLOT 53,37,2 : LINE 53,49
```

```
2480      PLOT 24,37,2 : PLOT 24,49
2490      PLOT 25,37,2 : PLOT 25,49
2500 REM Lastly the messages
2510      PLOT 22,30,"TOP"
2520      PLOT 48,30,"BOTTOM"
2530      PLOT 18,27," (open) "
2540      PLOT 46,27,"(closed)"
2550 REM
2560      RETURN
2570 REM
2580 REM
2590 REM * SUBROUTINE: OPEN OR CLOSE GATE *
2600 REM
2610      IF W$="high" THEN X=24 ELSE X=52
2620      IF G$="close" THEN B=2 ELSE B=1
2630      PLOT X,39,B : LINE X,47
2640      PLOT X+1,39,B : LINE X+1,47
2650      B=3-B
2660      FOR Y=3 TO 14
2670         IF Y=6 AND B=1 AND W$="low" THEN LET B=0
2680         PLOT X-6,Y,B : LINE X-1,Y
2690      NEXT Y
2700      IF W$="high" THEN X=18 ELSE X=46
2710      IF G$="open" THEN PLOT X,27," (open) " ELSE PLOT X,27,"(closed)"
2720 REM
2730      RETURN
2740 REM
2750 REM
2760 REM * SUBROUTINE: ALTER LEVEL *
2770 REM
2780      IF W$="high" THEN S=-1 : B9=0 : Y5=14 : Y6=6 : Y9=0
2790      IF W$="low" THEN S=1 : B9=1 : Y5=6 : Y6=14 : Y9=1
2800      FOR Y = Y5 TO Y6 STEP S
2810         PLOT 26,Y,B9 : LINE 51,Y
2820         IF L$="barge" THEN X1=28 : Y1=Y+Y9 : GOSUB 2900
2830         FOR D = 1 TO 200 : NEXT D : REM delay
2840      NEXT Y
2850      IF W$="high" THEN W$="low" ELSE W$="high"
2860 REM
2870      RETURN
2880 REM
2890 REM
2900 REM * SUBROUTINE: MOVE BARGE *
2910 REM
2920      IF X0=-99 THEN 2940
2930      X3=X0 : Y3=Y0 : B=B9 : GOSUB 3010
2940      IF X1=-99 THEN 2960
2950      X3=X1 : Y3=Y1 : B=2 : GOSUB 3010
2960      X0=X1 : Y0=Y1
2970 REM
2980      RETURN
2990 REM
3000 REM
3010 REM * SUBROUTINE: DRAW BARGE *
3020 REM
3030      PLOT X3,Y3,B : LINE X3+12,Y3
3040      PLOT X3+3,Y3+1,B : LINE X3+9,Y3+1
3050      IF B=0 THEN B=1
3060      FOR Y4 = 42 TO 44
3070         PLOT X3,Y4,B : LINE X3+12,Y4
3080      NEXT Y4
3090 REM
3100      RETURN
3110 REM
3120 REM
```

Updating pictures on the screen 175

```
3130 REM * SUBROUTINE: PAUSE *
3140 REM
3150     PRINT "Press SPACE BAR to continue"
3160     R$=GET$()
3170     IF R$()" " THEN 3160
3180     PRINT CHR$(12) : REM Clear bottom of screen
3190 REM
3200     RETURN
```

Sample output

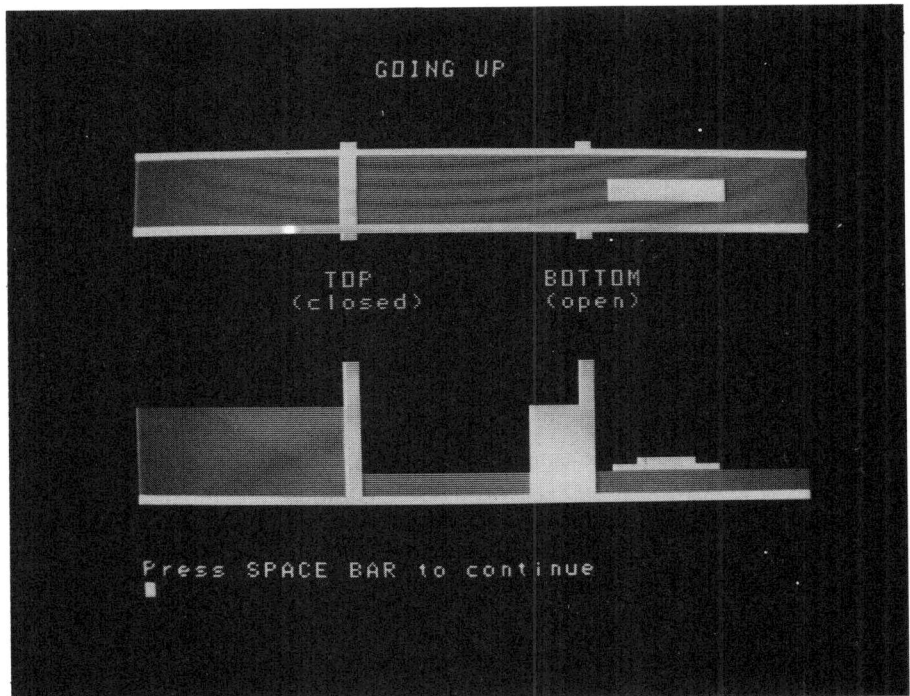

Discussion

What to notice: Nice, isn't it?

Program code: The program contains a list of the variables used, stating their names and purposes. This is the only program in which we have listed these specifically; in other programs, the names are introduced as they are first used, some with 'REM' statements to explain them, others simply occurring in a clear context.

CANALOCK uses a lot of messages to record the current state of various components. Such messages, **flags**, can be anything chosen by the programmer: numbers are often used. We prefer words (stored in string variables), because they help to document the program. Flags can thus be exploited to make it easy for the programmer to keep track of the program's operation.

Note that the program is coded to show canal lock operation as *one* sequence, the sequence being independent of the starting state of the lock and of the direction of movement. By using the flags properly, however, it is possible to use this single generalized sequence to perform *four* different demonstrations (lock full, barge going down; lock empty, barge going up; lock full, barge going up; and lock empty, barge going down).

For a detailed explanation of 'PLOT' and 'LINE', see section 7.1.

Error-checking: There are two types of user response. In one, he exercises an option about the direction of movement of the barge: this input is checked, and if it is not understood, the user is invited to try again. The other sort of response is the control of the speed: when the program has paused, the user must press the space-bar to continue with the next stage; any input other than a space is ignored.

What you could do: You could develop your own sequence of pictures to demonstrate something different. You could modify CANALOCK so that the sequence of operations is not mandatory: at the moment, the user controls only the direction and the speed, but you could allow him to specify the state of each lock gate. In this case, you might find it helpful to modify the picture to show water in the canal above the river: you could then show that this level will drop if both the gates are left open.

Portability: Remarks made in this context about EXHIBIT (see section 7.4) apply to CANALOCK also, only more so. CANALOCK makes use of the specific numbers of pixels across and up the screen, of the distinction between white and grey, and of the grouping of pixels.

7.6 Error-trapping

The aim of this section is to show a particular kind of error-checking, that of numeric input. (The checking of string input is demonstrated by many of the other programs in this book.)

BASIC interpreters permit two kinds of variable: string variables and numeric variables. The two types are distinguished by the fact that the names of string variables end with dollar signs, '$'. When a program is executing, therefore, the data supplied by the user in response to, say, 'INPUT N' can be checked to ensure that it is a number. The check performed by the system is a simple one, and the error message produced (if there is an error) is not very helpful to users who are not programmers. This section demonstrates a sophisticated check done by the *program* rather than by the system: in order that this is possible, the data must be entered first as *string* data (to bypass the system's own numeric check) and converted to a number only when the input has been validated.

Specification

The program will concern an airline seat-reservation system, and there will be two versions of it. In addition to specifying the name of the flight, the user will supply the number of seats that he requires. In AIRLINE1, this number will be checked by the interpreter only. In AIRLINE2, the number will be checked exhaustively to ensure that it is not too small, or too large, or negative, or fractional, or spelt as letters, or mis-typed. Any error will be reported to the user in a very specific, helpful message, and he will be invited to try again.

Outline flowchart of AIRLINE

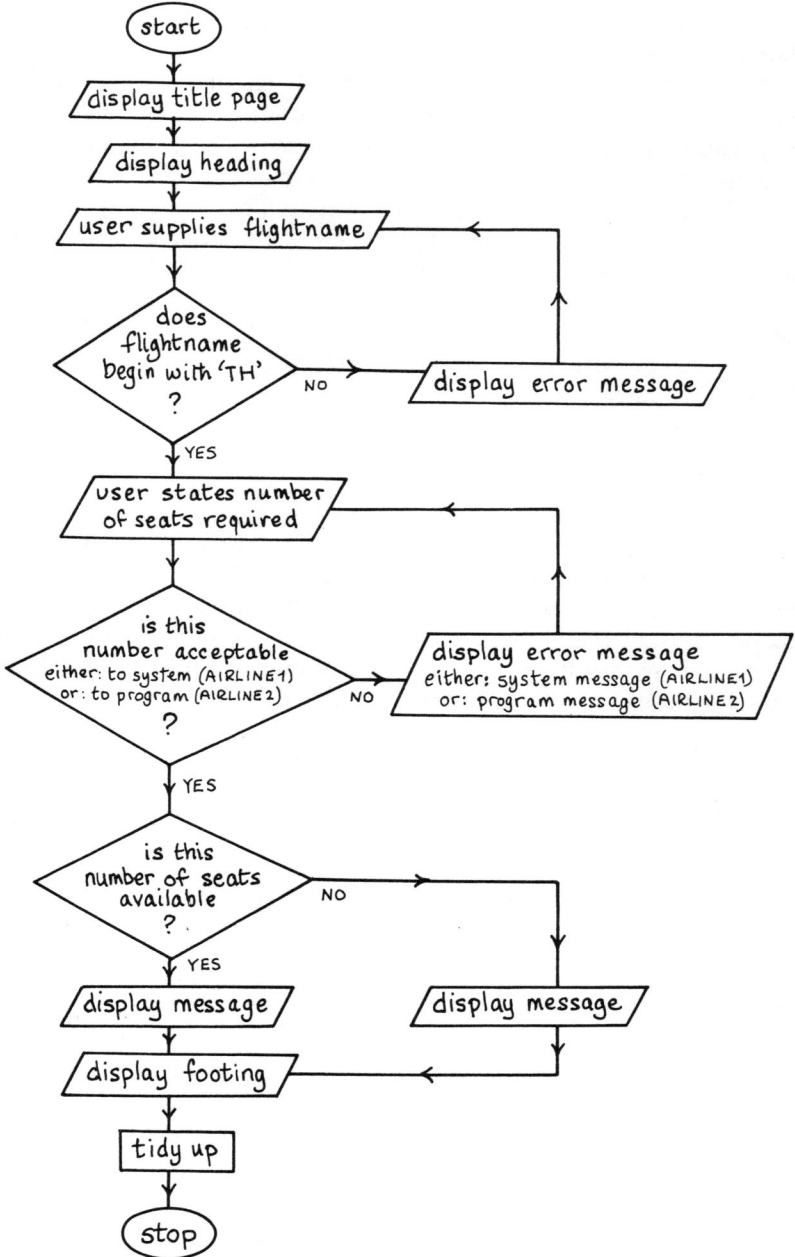

Listing of AIRLINE1 program code

```
1000 REM Program : AIRLINE1
1010 REM
1020 REM Part of a seat reservation program.
1030 REM    Illustrates inadequate checking of
1040 REM    an input number.
1050 REM
1060 REM
1070      CLEAR 100
1080 REM
1090      ON BREAK GOTO 1610
1100 REM  Deal with user's interruption
1110 REM
1120      TEXT : PRINT CHR$(12) : REM Clear the screen
1130      PRINT CHR$(17) : REM Disable paging
1140      PRINT TAB(16); "AIRLINE1"
1150      PRINT
1160      PRINT TAB(9); "Checking numeric input"
1170      PRINT : PRINT : PRINT
1180      PRINT TAB(19); "*"
1190      PRINT
1200      PRINT TAB(14); "Andrew Nash"
1210      PRINT
1220      PRINT TAB(15); "Derek Ball"
1230      PRINT
1240      PRINT TAB(19); "*"
1250      PRINT : PRINT : PRINT
1260      PRINT TAB(13); "Copyright 1982"
1270      PRINT
1280      PRINT TAB(10); "Hutchinson Education"
1290      PRINT
1300      FOR D = 1 TO 5000 : NEXT D : REM Delay
1310      PRINT CHR$(12) : REM Clear the screen
1320 REM
1330 REM
1340      PRINT TAB(5); "Titus Hardman's INland AIRways"
1350      PRINT
1360      PRINT TAB(16); "THINAIR"
1370 REM
1380      PRINT : PRINT "Enter flight name, please (e.g. TH434L)"
1390      INPUT F$
1400      IF LEFT$(F$,2)="TH" THEN 1430
1410         PRINT "** Not one of our flights!" : GOTO 1380
1420 REM
1430      A=7 : REM No. of seats available on this flight
1440 REM
1450      PRINT : PRINT "Enter number of seats, please (e.g. 2)"
1460      INPUT N
1470 REM
1480      IF N<=A THEN 1530
1490         PRINT "Sorry, not enough seats available"
1500         PRINT " on flight ="; F$; "="
1510         GOTO 1560
1520 REM
1530      PRINT "Seats are available on flight ="; F$; "="
1540      PRINT " Please book quickly"
1550 REM
1560      PRINT : PRINT
1570      PRINT TAB(8); "People like to travel in"
1580      PRINT
1590      PRINT TAB(16); "THINAIR"
1600 REM
1610      PRINT CHR$(19) : REM Re-enable paging
1620      END
```

Listing of AIRLINE2 program code

```
1000 REM Program : AIRLINE2
1010 REM
1020 REM Part of a seat reservation program.
1030 REM    Illustrates thorough checking of
1040 REM    an input number.
1050 REM
1060 REM
1070      CLEAR 100
1080 REM
1090      ON BREAK GOTO 1740
1100 REM  Deal with user's interruption
1110 REM
1120      TEXT : PRINT CHR$(12) : REM Clear the screen
1130      PRINT CHR$(17) : REM Disable paging
1140      PRINT TAB(16); "AIRLINE2"
1150      PRINT
1160      PRINT TAB(9); "Checking numeric input"
1170      PRINT : PRINT : PRINT
1180      PRINT TAB(19); "*"
1190      PRINT
1200      PRINT TAB(14); "Andrew Nash"
1210      PRINT
1220      PRINT TAB(15); "Derek Ball"
1230      PRINT
1240      PRINT TAB(19); "*"
1250      PRINT : PRINT : PRINT
1260      PRINT TAB(13); "Copyright 1982"
1270      PRINT
1280      PRINT TAB(10); "Hutchinson Education"
1290      PRINT
1300      FOR D = 1 TO 5000 : NEXT D : REM Delay
1310      PRINT CHR$(12) : REM Clear the screen
1320 REM
1330 REM
1340      PRINT TAB(5); "Titus Hardman's INland AIRways"
1350      PRINT
1360      PRINT TAB(16); "THINAIR"
1370 REM
1380      PRINT : PRINT "Enter flight name, please (e.g. TH434L)"
1390      INPUT F$
1400      IF LEFT$(F$,2)="TH" THEN 1430
1410         PRINT "** Not one of our flights!" : GOTO 1380
1420 REM
1430      A=7 : REM No. of seats available on this flight
1440      M=200 : REM Max. no. of seats on any flight
1450      D$="0123456789"
1460      LC$="abcdefghijklmnopqrstuvwxyz"
1470      UC$="ABCDEFGHIJKLMNOPQRSTUVWXYZ"
1480 REM
1490      PRINT : PRINT "Enter number of seats, please (e.g. 2)"
1500      INPUT N$
1510 REM
1520      GOSUB 1780 : REM Check number
1530      IF E$ = "in error" THEN 1490
1540 REM
1550      N=VAL(N$)
1560 REM
1570      IF N<=M THEN 1610
1580         PRINT "No flight has more than"; M; "seats"
1590         GOTO 1490
1600 REM
1610      IF N<=A THEN 1660
```

```
1620       PRINT "Sorry, there are only";A; "seats available"
1630       PRINT "  on flight =";F$; "="
1640       GOTO 1690
1650 REM
1660       PRINT "Seats are available on flight =";F$; "="
1670       PRINT "  Please book quickly"
1680 REM
1690       PRINT : PRINT
1700       PRINT TAB(8); "People like to travel in"
1710       PRINT
1720       PRINT TAB(16); "THINAIR"
1730 REM
1740       PRINT CHR$(19) : REM Re-enable paging
1750       END
1760 REM
1770 REM
1780 REM SUBROUTINE TO CHECK NUMBER
1790 REM
1800       NC=LEN(N$) : REM Number of characters
1810       ND=0 : REM Number of digits
1820       NL=0 : REM Number of letters
1830       NP=0 : REM Number of decimal points
1840       P$="" : REM String of error pointers
1850       FOR I = 1 TO NC
1860         C$=MID$(N$,I,1)
1870         FOR J = 1 TO 10
1880           IF C$<>MID$(D$,J,1) THEN 1900
1890             ND=ND+1 : P$=P$+" " : GOTO 1990
1900         NEXT J
1910         IF C$<>"." THEN 1930
1920           NP=NP+1 : P$=P$+"^" : GOTO 1990
1930         FOR J = 1 TO 26
1940           IF C$=MID$(LC$,J,1) THEN 1960
1950           IF C$<>MID$(UC$,J,1) THEN 1970
1960             NL=NL+1 : P$=P$+"^" : GOTO 1990
1970         NEXT J
1980         P$=P$+"^" : REM (Other character)
1990       NEXT I
2000 REM
2010       IF (ND=NC) THEN E$="valid number" : GOTO 2360
2020 REM
2030 REM Response contains one or more digits
2040 REM    Identify and report error
2050 REM
2060       E$="in error"
2070       PRINT
2080       PRINT "  ** I need a positive whole number"
2090       PRINT
2100 REM
2110       IF (NL<NC) THEN 2160
2120         PRINT "  ** You have given letters -"
2130         PRINT "        perhaps you spelt the number"
2140         GOTO 2360
2150 REM
2160       IF NOT ((ND=NC-1) AND (NP=1)) THEN 2200
2170         PRINT "  ** You have given a decimal number"
2180         GOSUB 2390 : GOTO 2360
2190 REM
2200       IF NOT ((ND=NC-1) AND (LEFT$(N$,1)="-")) THEN 2240
2210         PRINT "  ** You have given a negative number"
2220         GOSUB 2390 : GOTO 2360
2230 REM
2240       IF NOT ((ND=NC-2) AND (NP=1) AND (LEFT$(N$,1)="-")) THEN 2290
2250         PRINT "  ** You have given a negative decimal"
```

```
2260        PRINT "        number"
2270        GOSUB 2390 : GOTO 2360
2280 REM
2290     IF (ND<NC-1) THEN 2330
2300        PRINT "   ** Your response contains a non-digit"
2310        GOSUB 2390 : GOTO 2360
2320 REM
2330        PRINT "   ** Your response contains"; (NC-ND); "non-digits"
2340        GOSUB 2390
2350 REM
2360        RETURN
2370 REM
2380 REM
2390 REM SUBROUTINE TO DISPLAY POINTERS
2400 REM
2410     PRINT
2420     T=INT((40-NC)/2)
2430     PRINT TAB(T); N$
2440     PRINT TAB(T); P$
2450 REM
2460     RETURN
```

Sample output

```
Enter flight name, please (e.g. TH434L)
? TH2134

Enter number of seats, please (e.g. 2)
? five

   ** I need a positive whole number

   ** You have given letters -
         perhaps you spelt the number
Enter number of seats, please (e.g. 2)
? -123.456

   ** I need a positive whole number

   ** You have given a negative decimal
         number

              -123.456
               ↑    ↑

Enter number of seats, please (e.g. 2)
? ■
```

Error-trapping 183

Discussion

Error-checking: Run both programs, and when you are asked for the number of seats required, try answers such as 'eight', '0.8', '−8', '−0.8', '.8', '−.8', 'z.z', '−eight' and so on. Note the different messages given by the interpreter (in AIRLINE1) and the program (in AIRLINE2).

The error-checking process in AIRLINE2 is more thorough and more specific than would be necessary in many programs. Its messages are also more precise: instead of telling the user simply that his input is 'INVALID DATA', it tries to work out what he did and tell him that − 'decimal number', 'negative number' and the like. It also displays a series of pointers underneath what he typed, so as to indicate which characters were in error.

The process of checking in AIRLINE2 is done by taking the number in as a string and examining it closely. The program counts the number of digits ('ND'), the number of letters ('NL'), and the number of decimal points ('NP'). These are used to draw logical inferences: for example, if the number of digits is one less than the total number of characters, and if there is one decimal point in the string, the input must be a decimal number. (This is true wherever the point occurs in the string, except that a point at the end might have been intended simply as a full stop; but the arrow underneath the point will quickly show the user where the problem lies.) Note that a dash ('−') is treated as a minus sign only if it is at the left end of the string.

Program code: Perhaps the most interesting feature of the code of AIRLINE2 is the use that it makes of **logical operators** − words like 'AND', 'OR' and 'NOT'. Study the logic involved, which is fairly simple, and try to understand why the particular sets of operators (and brackets) do the tests that are required. (In each case, the bit in brackets defines the characteristics of a particular kind of input, such as those of a negative number, and the program goes to the next test in the sequence if these characteristics are *not* true of the input actually supplied.)

Also of interest in AIRLINE2 is the way in which the string of arrows is built up. If a digit is found, a space is added to the string; if anything else is found, an arrow is added.

Finally, note the use of the subroutine to display and centre both the user's input and the string of arrows underneath it.

What you could do: There is one major flaw still in the error-checking in AIRLINE2: the program does not trap responses such as '3,5' which contain a comma: this kind of input will be treated by the system as two separate pieces of data. On the RML 380Z, you can easily cure this using the 'INPUT LINE' instruction instead of 'INPUT' (see section 7.1); there may be something similar on other machines, but if not, you will need to use the 'GET' command.

Portability: Both versions of AIRLINE use simple BASIC constructions which should be available on all micros. Problems may arise, as we say of all these programs, with the instructions which open and close the program.

7.7 Command and tutorial modes

The aim of this section is to illustrate two alternative ways of controlling the execution of an interactive program. Tutorial mode, on the one hand, leads the user by the nose through the entire run, stating the possibilities at each stage and circumscribing his options, whereas command mode offers the user a set of facilities and leaves to him the choice of how to use them. Command mode frequently offers more freedom, but is often unable to give as much guidance as would be possible with tutorial mode, since the programmer is less aware of the user's intentions.

The Hertfordshire County Council Advisory Unit for Computer-Based Education has been in the forefront in developing the use of command structure in programs for schools. It has made helpful recommendations concerning this use in teaching programs, and command structures similar to the one proposed are being employed increasingly by writers of software. ITMA ('Investigations into Teaching using Microcomputers as an Aid') is a group, based in Plymouth, which designs and evaluates teaching programs. In giving control of the program to the user, their approach is to provide 'drivecharts' which indicate the 'decision points' and 'routes' available. At different points in the program, different sets of options may be available, and options are often concealed from the viewers (the students) so that they are not distracted from the task in hand. There are striking differences between the approaches of Hertfordshire, ITMA and other groups. Some people argue in favour of standardization, suggesting that all teaching programs should have a common structure implemented in the same way and should all make use of the same command keywords – always using 'FINISH' to end the program, for example. Our own view is the same as on several other issues: consistency is useful, but standards which take the form of inviolable rules should be resisted; what works well in one program may prove a hindrance in another.

This section contains a program in two versions. In the command version all commands other than the one used to terminate the program have equal status, and the structure of the program is in consequence as simple as the flowchart implies. The relative complexity of the flowchart for the tutorial version of the program reflects the complexity of the program itself: it is fairly typical of such programs, though a good deal simpler than many. Tutorial programs imply order: activities are allowed in a predefined sequence, and are usually coded in the same sequence. Attempts to allow the user to return to individual parts of the sequence (as compared with restarting the entire sequence) frequently result in a labyrinth of tests and transfers of control in the program. While none of this need be apparent to the user, it can be nightmarish for the programmer.

In contrast, programs controlled by commands often comprise a set of more-or-less self-contained operations, each of which can be catered for in an independent module. Again, this is not apparent to the user but makes an enormous difference to the programmer in designing, coding and testing the program – each module can be dealt with independently, if required – and in altering the program at a later stage. In many cases, 'command-mode programs' use commands only at the overall level: within a given module, information is obtained from the user by 'tutorial' means.

A subsidiary aim of the section is to demonstrate how text can be entered and amended (edited), and how the occurrences of particular strings of characters can be identified within a file of text.

Specification

The user will type in text which will be displayed on the screen in well-spaced lines; when the text has been entered, the user will be able to change it – to correct errors, for example. The user will then be able to choose individual letters or strings of letters whose occurrences within the text are to be highlighted. The letters when found will be highlighted by printing them again on the otherwise blank line immediately below them, a form of 'echoing'.

There will be two versions of the program. The first, HILIGHTC, will operate in command mode and will leave with the user the initiative in deciding what action to take next. The second, HILIGHTT, will be in tutorial mode and will continually remind the user of the options available and imply an order in which these actions might best be performed. To aid comparison, each program will provide the same facilities; the programs will differ only in their modes of control.

186 *Case studies in programming*

Outline flowchart of HILIGHTC

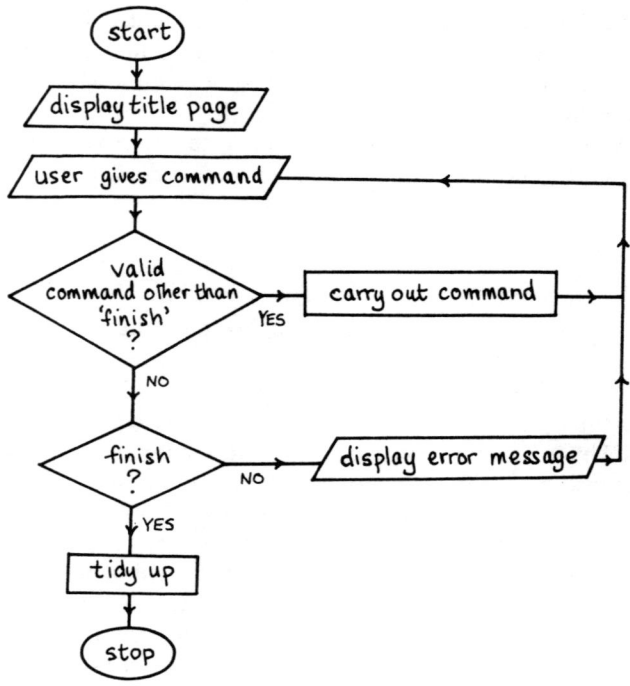

Outline flowchart of HILIGHTT

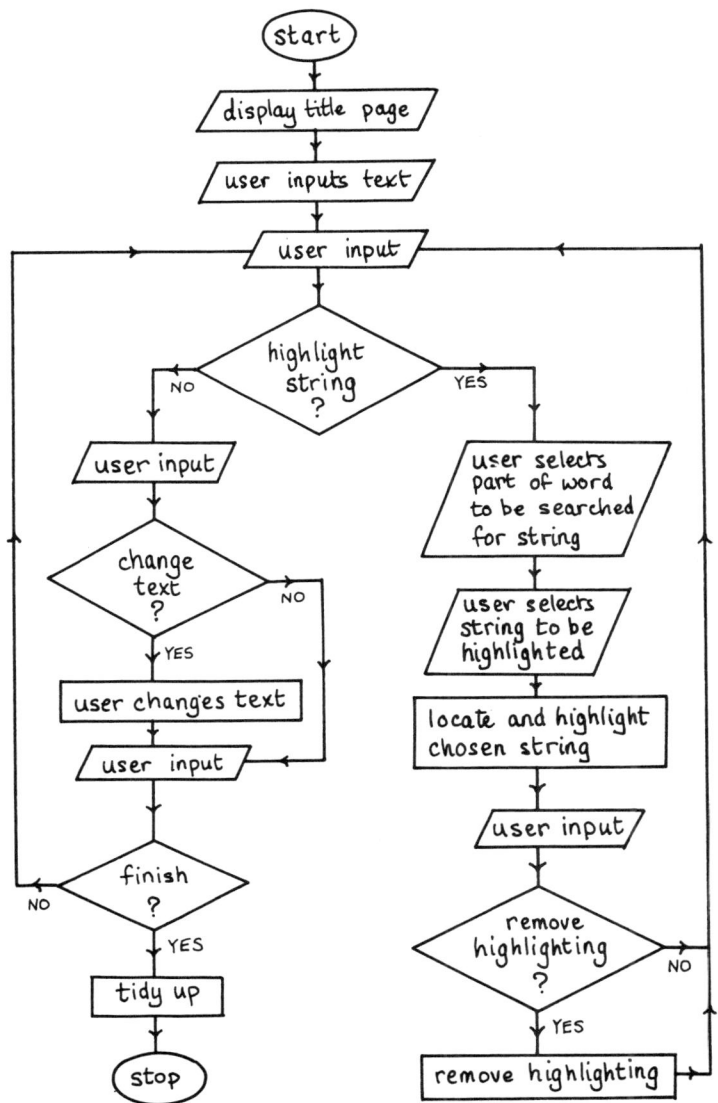

Listing of HILIGHTC program code

```
1000 REM Program : HILIGHTC
1010 REM
1020 REM
1030 REM This program illustrates how text stored in the computer
1040 REM     can be searched for the occurrence of a string of
1050 REM     characters. The string is supplied by the user and
1060 REM     its occurrences within the text displayed on the screen
1070 REM     are highlighted by echoing them below the text line.
1080 REM     The program also illustrates (in a modest way) how stored
1090 REM     text can be edited by the user.
1100 REM
1110 REM Lines of text are stored in the array T$. An extra
1120 REM     undisplayed blank is inserted at the beginning and end
1130 REM     of each stored text line; this is used in testing
1140 REM     for the beginnings and ends of words.
1150 REM
1160 REM This version of the program is in command mode. The user
1170 REM     is given considerable freedom over the order in which
1180 REM     events occur.
1190 REM
1200 REM
1210     CLEAR 1000
1220     TEXT : PRINT CHR$(12) : REM Clear the screen
1230 REM
1240     ON BREAK GOTO 1770
1250 REM     Deal with user's interruption
1260 REM
1270     PRINT CHR$(17) : REM Disable paging
1280 REM
1290 REM
1300     PRINT TAB(16); "HILIGHTC"
1310     PRINT
1320     PRINT TAB(1); "Highlighting strings (command version)"
1330     PRINT : PRINT : PRINT
1340     PRINT TAB(19); "*"
1350     PRINT
1360     PRINT TAB(15); "Derek Ball"
1370     PRINT
1380     PRINT TAB(14); "Andrew Nash"
1390     PRINT
1400     PRINT TAB(19); "*"
1410     PRINT : PRINT : PRINT
1420     PRINT TAB(13); "Copyright 1982"
1430     PRINT
1440     PRINT TAB(10); "Hutchinson Education"
1450     PRINT
1460     FOR D = 1 TO 5000 : NEXT D : REM Delay
1470     PRINT CHR$(12) : REM Clear the screen
1480 REM
1490 REM
1500     DIM CM$(9), T$(6)
1510 REM
1520 REM
1530 REM MAIN PROGRAM
1540 REM
1550 REM Read commands into array CM$
1560 REM
1570     FOR I = 1 TO 9 : READ CM$(I) : NEXT I
1580     DATA FINISH, COMMANDS, INPUTTEXT, DISPLAYTEXT, CHANGETEXT
1590     DATA FIRSTLETTERS, LASTLETTERS, ANYLETTERS, CLEAR
1600 REM
```

```
1610      GOSUB 1840 : REM Get a command
1620 REM
1630 REM Execute command
1640 REM
1650      IF CM$="FIN" THEN 1770 : REM Finish
1660      IF CM$="COM" THEN GOSUB 2150 : REM Commands
1670      IF CM$="INP" THEN GOSUB 2330 : REM Inputtext
1680      IF CM$="DIS" THEN GOSUB 2870 : REM Displaytext
1690      IF CM$="CHA" THEN GOSUB 3430 : REM Changetext
1700      IF CM$="FIR" OR CM$="LAS" OR CM$="ANY" THEN GOSUB 3010
1710      IF CM$="CLE" THEN GOSUB 3310 : REM Clear
1720 REM
1730      GOTO 1610 : REM Go back for another command
1740 REM
1750 REM Finish
1760 REM
1770      TEXT
1780      PRINT CHR$(19) : REM Enable paging
1790      CLEAR 100
1800 REM
1810      END
1820 REM
1830 REM
1840 REM SUBROUTINE : GET A COMMAND
1850 REM
1860      PRINT
1870      PRINT "Type a command"
1880      PRINT "For a list of commands, type COMMANDS"
1890 REM
1900 REM Input command and remove leading blanks
1910 REM
1920      INPUT LINE ":",R$
1930      IF LEFT$(R$,1)=" " THEN R$=MID$(CM$,2) : GOTO 1930
1940 REM
1950 REM Convert command to upper case
1960 REM
1970      CM$=""
1980      FOR I = 1 TO 3
1990        C$=MID$(R$,I,1)
2000        IF C$=>"a" AND C$<="z" THEN C$=CHR$(ASC(C$)-32)
2010        CM$=CM$+C$
2020      NEXT I
2030 REM
2040 REM Match input command against commands available
2050 REM
2060      CM=0
2070      FOR I = 1 TO 9
2080        IF CM$=LEFT$(CM$(I),3) THEN CM=I : I=9
2090      NEXT I
2100      IF CM=0 THEN PRINT R$; " not recognised" : GOTO 1870
2110 REM
2120      RETURN
2130 REM
2140 REM
2150 REM SUBROUTINE : COMMANDS
2160 REM
2170      TEXT : PRINT CHR$(12) : REM Clear the screen
2180      PRINT "Available commands are"
2190      PRINT "======================"
2200      PRINT
2210      FOR I = 1 TO 9
2220        PRINT CM$(I) : REM Print   command
2230        IF I=1 OR I=3 OR I=7 THEN PRINT : REM Leave blank line to
2240 REM                                     divide commands into groups
2250      NEXT I
```

```
2260      PRINT
2270      PRINT "Only the first 3 letters need be typed"
2280      PRINT
2290 REM
2300      RETURN
2310 REM
2320 REM
2330 REM SUBROUTINE : INPUT TEXT
2340 REM
2350      GRAPH : PRINT CHR$(12) : REM Clear the screen
2360      PRINT "Press * to finish"
2370      R=1 : C=1 : REM Position cursor at top left of screen
2380 REM
2390      P$="on text"
2400      C$=CHR$(207) : GOSUB 4250 : REM Plot cursor on text line
2410 REM
2420      T$(R)=" " : REM Start each stored text line with undisplayed
2430 REM                                                          space
2440 REM Get a character which is not a control character
2450 REM
2460      R$=GET$() : IF ASC(R$)<32 AND ASC(R$)<>13 THEN 2460
2470 REM
2480 REM Plot character or, if character is DELETE or RETURN, plot
2490 REM                                                        space
2500      IF R$="*" OR ASC(R$)=13 OR ASC(R$)=127 THEN C$=" " ELSE C$=R$
2510      GOSUB 4250 : REM Plot
2520 REM
2530      IF R$="*" THEN 2790 : REM '*' brings text input to end
2540 REM
2550 REM Deal with RETURN
2560 REM
2570      IF ASC(R$)<>13 THEN 2640
2580      GOSUB 4330 : REM Complete line
2590      IF R<6 THEN R=R+1 : T$(R)=" " : C=1 ELSE 2790
2600      GOTO 2750
2610 REM
2620 REM Deal with DELETE
2630 REM
2640      IF ASC(R$)<>127 THEN 2710
2650      IF C>1 THEN C=C-1 : T$(R)=LEFT$(T$(R),C) : GOTO 2750
2660      IF C=1 AND R=1 THEN 2750
2670      C=40 : R=R-1 : T$(R)=LEFT$(T$(R),40) : GOTO 2750
2680 REM
2690 REM Deal with displayable character
2700 REM
2710      T$(R)=T$(R)+R$
2720      IF R=6 AND C=40 THEN 2750 : REM Screen full of text
2730      IF C=40 THEN T$(R)=T$(R)+" " : C=1 : R=R+1 : T$(R)=" " ELSE
2740 REM                                                        C=C+1
2750      C$=CHR$(207) : REM cursor
2760      C$=CHR$(207) : GOSUB 4250 : REM Plot cursor
2770      GOTO 2460
2780 REM
2790      L=R
2800      FOR R = L TO 6
2810         GOSUB 4330 : REM Complete line
2820      NEXT R
2830 REM
2840      RETURN
2850 REM
2860 REM
2870 REM DISPLAYTEXT
2880 REM
2890      GRAPH : PRINT CHR$(12) : REM Clear the screen
2900      P$="on text"
```

```
2910      FOR R = 1 TO 6
2920          C=1 : REM Text line begins at left of screen
2930          C$ = MID$(T$(R),2,40) : REM Strip undisplayed space from
2940 REM                                      start of text line
2950          GOSUB 4250 : REM Plot text line
2960      NEXT R
2970 REM
2980      RETURN
2990 REM
3000 REM
3010 REM SUBROUTINE : HIGHLIGHT
3020 REM
3030      P$="below text" : REM Characters echoed below text line
3040      PRINT CHR$(12) : REM Clear bottom of screen
3050      PRINT "Please give letter or string"
3060      PRINT "   (followed by RETURN)"
3070      INPUT LINE S$
3080      SL=LEN(S$)
3090      IF SL=0 THEN 3280 : REM Take no action if no string given
3100 REM
3110 REM Remove trailing blanks from string given (system removes
3120 REM    leading blanks)
3130 REM
3140      IF RIGHT$(S$,1)=" " THEN S$=LEFT$(S$,SL-1) : GOTO 3080
3150 REM
3160 REM
3170 REM Check text to find occurrence of string in position specified
3180 REM
3190      FOR R = 1 TO 6
3200        FOR C = 1 TO 41-SL
3210          IF CM$="FIR" AND ASC(MID$(T$(R),C,1))>64 THEN 3250
3220          IF CM$="LAS" AND ASC(MID$(T$(R),C+SL+1,1))>64 THEN 3250
3230          IF S$=MID$(T$(R),C+1,SL) THEN C$=S$ : GOSUB 4250
3240 REM        Plot string if match found
3250        NEXT C
3260      NEXT R
3270 REM
3280      RETURN
3290 REM
3300 REM
3310 REM SUBROUTINE : CLEAR HIGHLIGHTING
3320 REM
3330      P$="below text" : REM Characters below text line are cleared
3340      FOR R = 1 TO 6
3350        FOR C = 1 TO 40
3360          PLOT 2*(C-1),63-9*R," " : REM Clear text by plotting space
3370        NEXT C
3380      NEXT R
3390 REM
3400      RETURN
3410 REM
3420 REM
3430 REM SUBROUTINE : CHANGE TEXT
3440 REM
3450      C=1 : R=1 : REM Position cursor at top left of screen
3460 REM
3470      PRINT CHR$(12) : REM Clear bottom of screen
3480      PRINT "Type U (up), D (down),"
3490      PRINT "     L (left), R (right),"
3500      PRINT "     S (start edit) or E(end changetext)"
3510 REM
3520      P$="belowtext"
3530      C$=CHR$(207) : GOSUB 4250 : REM Plot cursor
3540 REM
3550      GOSUB 4410 : REM Input character
```

192 *Case studies in programming*

```
3560 REM
3570      IF R$="E" THEN C$=" " : GOSUB 4250, : GOTO 4220 : REM End change
3580      IF R$="S" THEN 3700 : REM Start edit                         text
3590 REM
3600      C$=" " : GOSUB 4250 : REM Black out cursor
3610 REM
3620      IF P$="U" AND R>1 THEN R=R-1 : REM Move cursor position up
3630      IF P$="D" AND R<6 THEN R=R+1 : REM Move cursor position down
3640      IF P$="L" AND C>1 THEN C=C-1 : REM Move cursor position left
3650      IF R$="R" AND C<40 THEN C=C+1 : REM Move cursor position left
3660 REM
3670      C$=CHR$(207) : GOSUB 4250 : REM Plot the cursor
3680      GOTO 3550
3690 REM
3700      PRINT CHR$(12) : REM Clear bottom of screen
3710      PRINT "Type R (replace text)"
3720      PRINT "      I (insert text)"
3730      PRINT "   or D (delete text)"
3740      GOSUB 4410 : REM Input character
3750      IF R$="R" THEN 3820
3760      IF R$="I" THEN 3990
3770      IF R$="D" THEN 4110
3780      GOTO 3740
3790 REM
3800 REM Replace text
3810 REM
3820      PRINT CHR$(12);"Type text to replace"
3830      PRINT "   or press RETURN to finish replacing"
3840      R$=GET$()
3850      IF ASC(R$)=13 THEN 3470 : REM Replacement ends when RETURN
3860      IF ASC(R$)<32 OR ASC(R$)=127 THEN 3840                    pressed
3870 REM   Ignore control characters and DELETE
3880      T$(R)=LEFT$(T$(R),C)+R$+MID$(T$(R),C+2)
3890 REM   Replace text in stored text line
3900      P$="on text"
3910      C$=R$ : GOSUB 4250 : REM Plot replacement character   reached
3920      IF C=40 THEN 3470 : REM End replacement if right of screen
3930      P$="below text" : C$=" " : GOSUB 4250 : REM Black out cursor
3940      C=C+1 : REM Move one position to right
3950      C$=CHR$(207) : GOSUB 4250 : REM Plot cursor
3960 REM
3970 REM Insert text
3980 REM
3990      PRINT CHR$(12);"Type text to insert"
4000      PRINT "   or press RETURN to finish inserting"
4010      INPUT LINE I$
4020      T$(R)=LEFT$(T$(R),C)+I$+MID$(T$(R),C+1)
4030 REM   Add inserted text to stored text line
4040      GOSUB 4330 : REM Complete line
4050      P$="on text"
4060      C$=MID$(T$(R),C+1) : GOSUB 4250 : REM Plot line to right of
4070      GOTO 3470                                              cursor
4080 REM
4090 REM Delete text
4100 REM
4110      PRINT CHR$(12);"Delete how many characters"
4120      INPUT R$
4130      N=VAL(R$)
4140      IF N<=0 THEN 3470
4150      T$(R)=LEFT$(T$(R),C)+MID$(T$(R),C+N+1)
4160 REM   Delete N characters from stored text line
4170      GOSUB 4330 : REM Complete line
4180      P$="on text"
4190      C$=MID$(T$(R),C+1) : GOSUB 4250 : REM Plot part line to delete
4200      GOTO 3470
```

```
4210 REM
4220     RETURN
4230 REM
4240 REM
4250 REM SUBROUTINE : PLOT
4260 REM
4270     IF P$="on text" THEN O=0 ELSE O=3
4280     PLOT 2*(C-1),66-9*R-O,C$
4290 REM
4300     RETURN
4310 REM
4320 REM
4330 REM SUBROUTINE : COMPLETE LINE
4340 REM
4350     FOR I=1 TO 42 : T$(R)=T$(R)+" " : NEXT I
4360     T$(R)=LEFT$(T$(R),42)
4370 REM
4380     RETURN
4390 REM
4400 REM
4410 REM SUBROUTINE : GET CHARACTER (UPPER CASE)
4420     R$=GET$()
4430     IF R$>"Z" THEN R$=CHR$(ASC(R$)-32)
4440 REM
4450     RETURN
```

Listing of HILIGHTT program code

```
1000 REM Program : HILIGHTT
1010 REM
1020 REM
1030 REM This program illustrates how text stored in the computer
1040 REM    can be searched for the occurrence of a string of
1050 REM    characters. The string is supplied by the user and
1060 REM    its occurrences within the text displayed on the screen
1070 REM    are highlighted by echoing them below the text line.
1080 REM    The program also illustrates (in a modest way) how stored
1090 REM    text can be edited by the user.
1100 REM
1110 REM Lines of text are stored in the array T$. An extra
1120 REM    undisplayed blank is inserted at the beginning and end
1130 REM    of each stored text line; this is used in testing
1140 REM    for the beginnings and ends of words.
1150 REM
1160 REM This version of the program is in tutorial mode. The user
1170 REM    is led by the nose in making his choices.
1180 REM
1190 REM
1200 REM
1210     CLEAR 1000
1220 REM
1230     ON BREAK GOTO 2110
1240 REM    Deal with user's intteruption
1250 REM
1260     TEXT : PRINT CHR$(12) : REM Clear screen
1270     PRINT CHR$(17) : REM Disable paging
1280 REM
1290 REM
1300     PRINT TAB(16); "HILIGHTT"
1310     PRINT
1320     PRINT TAB(1); "Highlighting strings (tutorial version)"
1330     PRINT : PRINT : PRINT
1340     PRINT TAB(19); "*"
```

```
1350      PRINT
1360      PRINT TAB(15); "Derek Ball"
1370      PRINT
1380      PRINT TAB(14); "Andrew Nash"
1390      PRINT
1400      PRINT TAB(19); "*"
1410      PRINT : PRINT : PRINT
1420      PRINT TAB(13); "Copyright 1982"
1430      PRINT
1440      PRINT TAB(9); "Hutchinson Education"
1450      PRINT
1460      FOR D = 1 TO 5000 : NEXT D : REM Delay
1470 REM
1480 REM
1490 REM                      PRELIMINARIES
1500 REM
1510      DIM T$(6)
1520      GRAPH
1530 REM
1540 REM                      MAIN PROGRAM
1550 REM
1560      PRINT "First input the text"
1570      GOSUB 2180 : REM Input text
1580 REM
1590 REM
1600      PRINT CHR$(12) : REM Clear bottom of screen
1610      PRINT "Do you want to highlight a letter or"
1620      PRINT "    a string (Y/N)";
1630      GOSUB 4110 : REM Get a character
1640      IF R$="Y" THEN 1680
1650      IF R$="N" THEN 1960
1660      GOTO 1630
1670 REM
1680      PRINT CHR$(12) : REM Clear bottom of screen
1690      PRINT "Do you want strings which are"
1700      PRINT "         anywhere (A)"
1710      PRINT "         at beginnings of words (B)"
1720      PRINT "    or at ends of words (E)";
1730      GOSUB 4110 : REM Get a character
1740      IF R$="A" THEN CN$="all" : GOTO 1790
1750      IF R$="B" THEN CN$="first" : GOTO 1790
1760      IF R$="E" THEN CN$="last" : GOTO 1790
1770      GOTO 1730
1780      PRINT R$
1790      GOSUB 2710 : REM Highlight
1800 REM
1810      PRINT CHR$(12) : REM Clear bottom of screen
1820      PRINT "Do you want to clear this (Y/N)";
1830      GOSUB 4110 : REM Get Y or N response
1840      IF R$<>"Y" AND R$<>"N" THEN 1830
1850      IF R$="Y" THEN GOSUB 3010 : REM Clear highlighting
1860 REM
1870      PRINT CHR$(12) : REM Clear bottom of screen
1880      PRINT "Do you want to hightlight another"
1890      PRINT "    letter or string (Y/N)";
1900      GOSUB 4110 : REM Get Y or N response
1910      IF R$="Y" THEN 1680
1920      IF R$="N" THEN 1960
1930      GOTO 1900
1940 REM
1950 REM
1960      PRINT CHR$(12) : REM Clear bottom of screen
1970      PRINT "Do you want to change the text (Y/N)";
1980      GOSUB 4110 : REM Get Y or N response
1990      IF R$<>"Y" AND R$<>"N" THEN 1980
2000      IF R$="Y" THEN GOSUB 3130 : REM Change text
```

```
2010 REM
2020 REM
2030     PRINT CHR$(12) : REM Clear bottom of screen
2040     PRINT "Do you want to finish (Y/N)";
2050     GOSUB 4110 : REM Get Y or N response
2060     IF R$="Y" THEN 2110
2070     IF R$="N" THEN 1600
2080     GOTO 2050
2090 REM
2100 REM
2110     TEXT
2120     PRINT CHR$(19) : REM Enable paging
2130     CLEAR 100
2140 REM
2150     END
2160 REM
2170 REM
2180 REM SUBROUTINE : INPUT TEXT
2190 REM
2200     PRINT "Press * to finish"
2210     R=1 : C=1 : REM Position cursor at top left of screen
2220 REM
2230     P$="on text"
2240     C$=CHR$(207) : GOSUB 3950 : REM Plot cursor on text line
2250 REM
2260     T$(R)=" " : REM Start each stored text line with undisplayed space
2270 REM
2280 REM Get a character which is not a control character
2290 REM
2300     R$=GET$() : IF ASC(R$)<32 AND ASC(R$)<>13 THEN 2300
2310 REM
2320 REM Plot character or, if character is DELETE or RETURN, plot space
2330 REM
2340     IF R$="*" OR ASC(R$)=13 OR ASC(R$)=127 THEN C$=" " ELSE C$=R$
2350     GOSUB 3950 : REM Plot
2360 REM
2370     IF R$="*" THEN 2630 : REM '*' brings text input to end
2380 REM
2390 REM Deal with RETURN
2400 REM
2410     IF ASC(R$)<>13 THEN 2480
2420     GOSUB 4030 : REM Complete line
2430     IF R<6 THEN R=R+1 : T$(R)=" " : C=1 ELSE 2630
2440     GOTO 2590
2450 REM
2460 REM Deal with DELETE
2470 REM
2480     IF ASC(R$)<>127 THEN 2550
2490     IF C>1 THEN C=C-1 : T$(R)=LEFT$(T$(R),C) : GOTO 2590
2500     IF C=1 AND R=1 THEN 2590
2510     C=40 : R=R-1 : T$(R)=LEFT$(T$(R),40) : GOTO 2590
2520 REM
2530 REM Deal with displayable character
2540 REM
2550     T$(R)=T$(R)+R$
2560     IF R=6 AND C=40 THEN 2590 : REM Screen full of text
2570     IF C=40 THEN T$(R)=T$(R)+" " : C=1 : R=R+1 : T$(R)=" " ELSE C=C+1
2580 REM
2590     C$=CHR$(207) : REM cursor
2600     C$=CHR$(207) : GOSUB 3950 : REM Plot cursor
2610     GOTO 2300
2620 REM
2630     L=R
2640     FOR R = L TO 6
2650        GOSUB 4030 : REM Complete line
2660     NEXT R
```

```
2670 REM
2680     RETURN
2690 REM
2700 REM
2710 REM SUBROUTINE : HIGHLIGHT
2720 REM
2730     P$="below text" : REM Characters echoed below text line
2740     PRINT CHR$(12) : REM Clear bottom of screen
2750     PRINT "Please give letter or string"
2760     PRINT "   (followed by RETURN)"
2770     INPUT LINE S$
2780     SL=LEN(S$)
2790     IF SL=0 THEN 2980 : REM Take no action if no string given
2800 REM
2810 REM Remove trailing blanks from string given (system removes
2820 REM    leading blanks)
2830 REM
2840     IF RIGHT$(S$,1)=" " THEN S$=LEFT$(S$,SL-1) : GOTO 2780
2850 REM
2860 REM
2870 REM Check text to find occurrence of string in position specified
2880 REM
2890     FOR R = 1 TO 6
2900        FOR C = 1 TO 41-SL
2910          IF CN$="first" AND ASC(MID$(T$(R),C,1))>64 THEN 2950
2920          IF CN$="last" AND ASC(MID$(T$(R),C+SL+1,1))>64 THEN 2950
2930          IF S$=MID$(T$(R),C+1,SL) THEN C$=S$ : GOSUB 3950
2940 REM        Plot string if match found
2950        NEXT C
2960     NEXT R
2970 REM
2980     RETURN
2990 REM
3000 REM
3010 REM SUBROUTINE : CLEAR HIGHLIGHTING
3020 REM
3030     P$="below text" : REM Characters below text line are cleared
3040     FOR R = 1 TO 6
3050        FOR C = 1 TO 40
3060          PLOT 2*(C-1),63-9*R," " : REM Clear text by plotting space
3070        NEXT C
3080     NEXT R
3090 REM
3100     RETURN
3110 REM
3120 REM
3130 REM SUBROUTINE : CHANGE TEXT
3140 REM
3150     C=1 : R=1 : REM Position cursor at top left of screen
3160 REM
3170     PRINT CHR$(12) : REM Clear bottom of screen
3180     PRINT "Type U (up), D (down),"
3190     PRINT "     L (left), R (right),"
3200     PRINT "     S (start edit) or E(end changetext)"
3210 REM
3220     P$="belowtext"
3230     C$=CHR$(207) : GOSUB 3950 : REM Plot cursor
3240 REM
3250     GOSUB 4110 : REM Input character
3260 REM
3270     IF R$="E" THEN C$=" " : GOSUB 3950 : GOTO 3920 : REM End change te
3280     IF R$="S" THEN 3400 : REM Start edit
3290 REM
3300     C$=" " : GOSUB 3950 : REM Black out cursor
3310 REM
3320     IF R$="U" AND R>1 THEN R=R-1 : REM Move cursor position up
```

```
3330      IF R$="D" AND R<6 THEN R=R+1 : REM Move cursor position down
3340      IF R$="L" AND C>1 THEN C=C-1 : REM Move cursor position left
3350      IF R$="R" AND C<40 THEN C=C+1 : REM Move cursor position left
3360 REM
3370      C$=CHR$(207) : GOSUB 3950 : REM Plot the cursor
3380      GOTO 3250
3390 REM
3400      PRINT CHR$(12) : REM Clear bottom of screen
3410      PRINT "Type R (replace text)"
3420      PRINT "      I (insert text)"
3430      PRINT "   or D (delete text)"
3440      GOSUB 4110 : REM Input character
3450      IF R$="R" THEN 3520
3460      IF R$="I" THEN 3690
3470      IF R$="D" THEN 3810
3480      GOTO 3440
3490 REM
3500 REM Replace text
3510 REM
3520      PRINT CHR$(12);"Type text to replace"
3530      PRINT "  or press RETURN to finish replacing"
3540      R$=GET$()
3550      IF ASC(R$)=13 THEN 3170 : REM Replacement ends when RETURN pressed
3560      IF ASC(R$)<32 OR ASC(R$)=127 THEN 3540
3570 REM     Ignore control characters and DELETE
3580      T$(R)=LEFT$(T$(R),C)+R$+MID$(T$(R),C+2)
3590 REM     Replace text in stored text line
3600      P$="on text"
3610      C$=R$ : GOSUB 3950 : REM Plot replacement character
3620      IF C=40 THEN 3170 : REM End replacement if right of screen reached
3630      P$="below text" : C$=" " : GOSUB 3950 : REM Black out cursor
3640      C=C+1 : REM Move one position to right
3650      C$=CHR$(207) : GOSUB 3950 : REM Plot cursor
3660 REM
3670 REM Insert text
3680 REM
3690      PRINT CHR$(12);"Type text to insert"
3700      PRINT "  or press RETURN to finish inserting"
3710      INPUT LINE I$
3720      T$(R)=LEFT$(T$(R),C)+I$+MID$(T$(R),C+1)
3730 REM     Add inserted text to stored text line
3740      GOSUB 4030 : REM Complete line
3750      P$="on text"
3760      C$=MID$(T$(R),C+1) : GOSUB 3950 : REM Plot line to right of cursor
3770      GOTO 3170
3780 REM
3790 REM Delete text
3800 REM
3810      PRINT CHR$(12);"Delete how many characters"
3820      INPUT R$
3830      N=VAL(R$)
3840      IF N<=0 THEN 3170
3850      T$(R)=LEFT$(T$(R),C)+MID$(T$(R),C+N+1)
3860 REM     Delete N characters from stored text line
3870      GOSUB 4030 : REM Complete line
3880      P$="on text"
3890      C$=MID$(T$(R),C+1) : GOSUB 3950 : REM Plot part line to delete
3900      GOTO 3170
3910 REM
3920      RETURN
3930 REM
3940 REM
3950 REM SUBROUTINE : PLOT
3960 REM
3970      IF P$="on text" THEN O=0 ELSE O=3
3980      PLOT 2*(C-1),66-9*R-O,C$
```

Case studies in programming

```
3990 REM
4000     RETURN
4010 REM
4020 REM
4030 REM SUBROUTINE : COMPLETE LINE
4040 REM
4050     FOR I=1 TO 42 : T$(R)=T$(R)+" " : NEXT I
4060     T$(R)=LEFT$(T$(R),42)
4070 REM
4080     RETURN
4090 REM
4100 REM
4110 REM SUBROUTINE : GET CHARACTER (UPPER CASE)
4120     R$=GET$()
4130     IF R$>"Z" THEN R$=CHR$(ASC(R$)-32)
4140 REM
4150     RETURN
```

Sample output

```
            If you feel you want to highlight,
                                      igh igh
        HILIGHTC is what you need.

        Even in the growing twilight
                                  igh

        Text is neat and clear to read
                    ea          ea        ea




    Type a command
    For a list of commands, type COMMANDS
    :█
```

```
If you feel you want to highlight,

HILIGHTT will take too long.

Though it may not strain your eyesight

You will curse when you go wrong!




Do you want to clear this (Y/N)
```

Discussion

What to notice: By running both versions – and only by running them – you can get a feel for the difference between their modes of control. You must decide which program you want to run first. While you are unfamiliar with the situation, you may find that HILIGHTT (tutorial) is the more reassuring in that it asks you questions; as you gain familiarity and confidence, you may appreciate the greater freedom offered by HILIGHTC (command), and find the continual questions of HILIGHTT increasingly irritating. To experience the greatest possible frustration, run HILIGHTC first and HILIGHTT second.

Program code: In the introduction to this section, it was pointed out that command mode encourages the use of subroutines, while tutorial mode can often be programmed without their use. Subroutines are obviously of use when the same piece of code needs to be available at different points in the main program, but subroutines can also be used to make the logic clear to the programmer, even if the code within them is in each case executed only once. HILIGHTC and HILIGHTT both use subroutines, and the subroutines are much the same.

The principal differences in the coding of the two versions are in the main programs, and concern the ways in which the user gains access to the facilities which are offered by the subroutines. If you are interested in writing your own programs in command mode, you should note that the main program and the first two subroutines in HILIGHTC can be used with very little modification in any such programs.

Note the use of graphics commands to enable the text on the screen to be modified, and see also the section below concerning portability.

Note also that code is provided to enable characters to be deleted during input of text, even when such deletions require the cursor to move back to the previous line.

Error-checking: The error-trapping in both programs is conditioned by the fact that space on the screen is severely restricted because text is being displayed. For this reason, in all cases where a choice is to be made by pressing a single key, all keys other than those associated with valid choices are deadened: the computer does nothing until an appropriate key is pressed.

While text is being entered, a minimal check is made to ensure that control characters entered inadvertently do not produce bizarre effects.

In each program, numbers are input in only one place: these numbers signify how many characters the user wishes to delete (while editing). They are checked to ensure that inappropriate input (such as negative or zero numbers) does not disrupt the program: no error message is issued, inappropriate input simply produces no deletion.

In HILIGHTC, each command is checked and an error message is issued if it is invalid.

On all occasions except where textual material or strings of characters to be highlighted are being entered, the effect of the 'CAPITALS LOCK' key is neutralized: commands may therefore be entered in upper or lower case.

What you could do: You could modify either of the programs to send the already highlighted text to the printer (a process called **screen dumping**). You could also modify either program so that highlighted text is sent to the printer *instead* of to the screen – in this case, you will probably find it useful to permit the user more than the present seven lines of text, and to permit the lines to be longer than the present forty characters.

If you wish to use long texts, it may be convenient to write these first to disc or to tape as separate files: you could devise a program to help you in this. You will then need to modify the highlighting program so that it can take text from the disc or cassette file, as well as or instead of from the keyboard.

You could modify the program's response to finding the required string of letters. At the moment, it highlights these occurrences by echoing the letters on the next line down. Instead, it could (for example) omit the string, either replacing it by the equivalent number of asterisks (easy to program) or replacing it by a single asterisk to indicate an omission of unspecified length (more difficult to program, especially if you close up the text from line to line). Text treated in this way could be sent to the printer, and students could be invited to suggest what might most appropriately fill the omissions.

Instead of highlighting the strings, or as well as doing so, their occurrences could be counted and various statistics compiled. Such a development might afford the basis of a tool for textual (lexical) analysis (see section 7.3).

Portability: These programs were written to run on the RML 380Z. Although they do not produce pictures, they do use graphics commands to lay out the screen and to permit the modification of the displayed text when it is changed or highlighted. If you have a different micro, it will almost certainly enable you to produce an identical screen display, to which end you will need to alter the lines of code which contain the words 'GRAPH', 'TEXT' or 'PLOT'. Your micro may not allow you to split the screen between printed and plotted text (see section 7.1), in which case you will need to change the 'PRINT' instructions (other than those in the 'title page' section) to 'PLOT' equivalents, and to change the 'INPUT' statements to equivalents using 'GET'. Most micros display forty characters on each line, so it is less likely that this aspect of the programs will need to be changed.

8 Case studies in teaching

The programs in Chapter 7 were chosen to illustrate specific programming techniques of the sort that might be used in teaching programs. In Chapter 8, we look at some of these techniques in action. Programs in this chapter are for use in teaching: we examine some of the different ways in which programs may be used, we consider the extent of student involvement with them, and we give ideas about their use in the classroom.

There are still points to be made about the coding of these programs, and in each section we give notes on the salient features of the code. Portability remains a problem and we continue to indicate the lines of the program which may need adaptation on your machine. There are few fresh difficulties in this respect, so you will again find it helpful to refer to section 7.1.

In the opening to Chapter 7, we stressed the importance of *running* the programs. It was important to see the differences in the results on the screen using alternative techniques; it is still *more* important to see the differences when alternative teaching philosophies are in question. To get the most out of this chapter, you will need to try out with students the programs in their varying forms and discover for yourself how the students react.

This chapter considers four major themes concerning the use of computers in teaching, and concludes with one full-blown teaching program. It contains:
- *a program that may be used by one student or by several;*
- *a program that may be used with students or away from them;*
- *a program that may stimulate discussion;*
- *a program (in two versions) that offers freedom to the student to learn as he wishes or constrains him to learn as the teacher wishes;*
- *a program that illustrates many of our points together – that is a tool, that is flexible, that is powerful, that does more easily something that is being done already, that may be used in a variety of ways, in a variety of subjects, with students of a variety of ages – and that is a realistic example of the type of program that can be written to aid teachers.*

8.1 Individual and group use

The aim of this section is to illustrate our point that some programs are useful both to individuals and to groups. Many programs written for group use are used successfully by individuals, and vice versa; but the program given here is, we feel, well suited to either kind of use.

Specification

The program, SCALES, will calculate the complete major scale from a supplied keynote. It will display this on the screen, indicating notes which are sharpened or flattened, and stating their positions in the musical scale.

Outline flowchart of SCALES

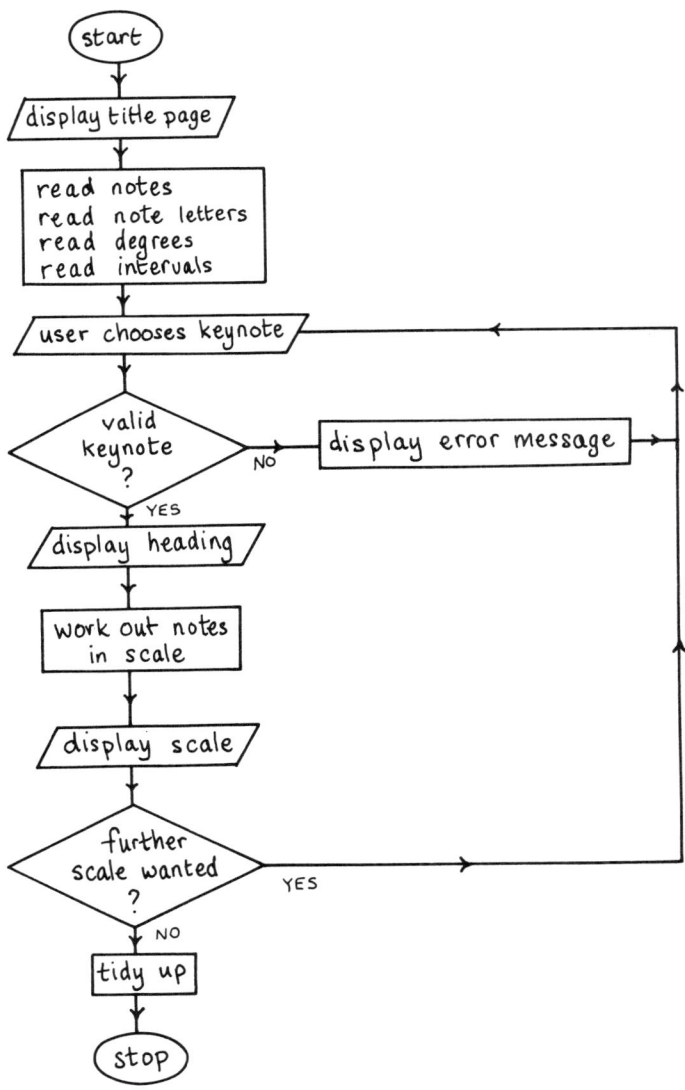

Listing of SCALES program code

```
1000 REM Program : SCALES
1010 REM
1020 REM
1030 REM Given a keynote, supply the major scale
1040 REM
1050 REM
1060     CLEAR 200
1070     DIM N$(12,4), D$(8), S(8)
1080 REM
1090     ON BREAK GOTO 2430
1100 REM   Deal with user's interruption
1110 REM
1120     TEXT : PRINT CHR$(12) : REM Clear the screen
1130     PRINT CHR$(17) : REM Disable paging
1140 REM
1150 REM
1160     PRINT TAB(17); "SCALES"
1170     PRINT
1180     PRINT TAB(4); "Supply major scale from keynote"
1190     PRINT : PRINT : PRINT
1200     PRINT TAB(19); "*"
1210     PRINT
1220     PRINT TAB(14); "Andrew Nash"
1230     PRINT
1240     PRINT TAB(15); "Derek Ball"
1250     PRINT
1260     PRINT TAB(19); "*"
1270     PRINT : PRINT : PRINT
1280     PRINT TAB(13); "Copyright 1982"
1290     PRINT
1300     PRINT TAB(10); "Hutchinson Education"
1310     PRINT
1320     FOR D = 1 TO 5000 : NEXT D : REM Delay
1330 REM
1340 REM
1350 REM >> ARRAY OF NOTES OF SCALE <<
1360 REM
1370     FOR I = 1 TO 12
1380       FOR J = 1 TO 2
1390         READ N$(I,J)
1400       NEXT J
1410     NEXT I
1420     DATA A,         null
1430     DATA A sharp,   B flat
1440     DATA B,         C flat
1450     DATA C,         B sharp
1460     DATA C sharp,   D flat
1470     DATA D,         null
1480     DATA D sharp,   E flat
1490     DATA E,         F flat
1500     DATA F,         E sharp
1510     DATA F sharp,   G flat
1520     DATA G,         null
1530     DATA G sharp,   A flat
1540 REM
1550 REM
1560 REM
1570     FOR I = 1 TO 7
1580       READ L$(I)
1590     NEXT I
1600     DATA A, B, C, D, E, F, G
1610 REM
```

```
1620 REM
1630 REM >> ARRAYS OF DEGREES AND OF INTERVALS (IN SEMITONES) <<
1640 REM
1650     FOR I = 1 TO 8
1660        READ D$(I), S(I)
1670     NEXT I
1680     DATA tonic, 0, supertonic, 2
1690     DATA mediant, 4, subdominant, 5
1700     DATA dominant, 7, submediant, 9
1710     DATA leading note, 11, tonic, 12
1720 REM
1730 REM
1740 REM >> INPUT AND IDENTIFY KEYNOTE <<
1750 REM
1760     PRINT CHR$(12) : REM Clear the screen
1770     PRINT "Enter the keynote - A B C D E F or G"
1780     PRINT "   (plus optional + for sharp"
1790     PRINT "                  or - for flat"
1800     PRINT
1810     PRINT "  Examples: F D+"
1820     PRINT
1830     PRINT : PRINT "Keynote";
1840     INPUT R$
1850 REM
1860     IF LEN(R$) < 1 OR LEN(R$) > 2 THEN 1980
1870 REM
1880     KN$ = LEFT$(R$,1)
1890     IF KN$ > "G" THEN KN$ = CHR$(ASC(KN$)-32)
1900 REM (Convert to upper case if necessary)
1910     IF KN$ < "A" OR KN$ > "G" THEN 1980
1920 REM
1930     IF LEN(R$) = 1 THEN 2060
1940     RE$ = RIGHT$(R$,1)
1950     IF RE$ = "+" OR RE$ = ";" THEN KN$ = KN$ + " sharp" : GOTO 2060
1960     IF RE$ = "-" OR RE$ = "=" THEN KN$ = KN$ + " flat" : GOTO 2060
1970 REM
1980     PRINT : PRINT "  ** Keynote not recognised - try again"
1990     PRINT : PRINT "Press SPACEBAR to continue"
2000     R$ = GET$() : IF R$ = " " THEN 1760 ELSE 2000
2010 REM
2020 REM
2030 REM >> OUTPUT THE SCALE <<
2040 REM
2050 REM Find position of keynote in dodecaphonic list
2060     FOR I = 1 TO 12
2070        IF KN$ = N$(I,1) OR KN$ = N$(I,2) THEN KN = I : GOTO 2110
2080     NEXT I
2090 REM
2100 REM Find position of keynote in letter list
2110     FOR I = 1 TO 7
2120        IF LEFT$(KN$,1) = L$(I) THEN L = I : GOTO 2160
2130     NEXT I
2140 REM
2150 REM Print heading in centre of screen
2160     PRINT CHR$(12) : REM Clear the screen
2170     H$ = "Scale of " + KN$ + " major"
2180     PRINT TAB((40-LEN(H$))/2); H$
2190     PRINT : PRINT
2200 REM
2210 REM Calculate and print scale
2220     FOR I = 1 TO 8
2230        RJ$ = "           " + D$(I)
2240        PRINT TAB(8); RIGHT$(RJ$,12); TAB(22);
2250        NN = KN + S(I) : REM Next note is keynote plus interval
2260        IF NN > 12 THEN NN = NN - 12
2270        NL = L + I - 1
```

Case studies in teaching

```
2280 REM       Find next letter: scale notes must have different letters
2290          IF NL > 7 THEN NL = NL - 7
2300          IF LEFT$(N$(NN,1),1) = L$(NL) THEN PRINT N$(NN,1) ELSE PRINT
2310       NEXT I                                                    N$(NN,2)
2320 REM
2330 REM
2340 REM >> NEW SCALE OR END <<
2350 REM
2360       FOR I = 1 TO 6 : PRINT : NEXT I
2370       PRINT : PRINT "Type S for a new scale or F to finish";
2380       INPUT R$
2390       IF (R$ = "S") OR (R$ = "s") THEN 1760
2400       IF (R$ = "F") OR (R$ = "f") THEN 2430
2410          PRINT "  ** Not understood - try again" : GOTO 2370
2420 REM
2430       PRINT CHR$(19) : REM Re-enable paging
2440       END
```

Sample output

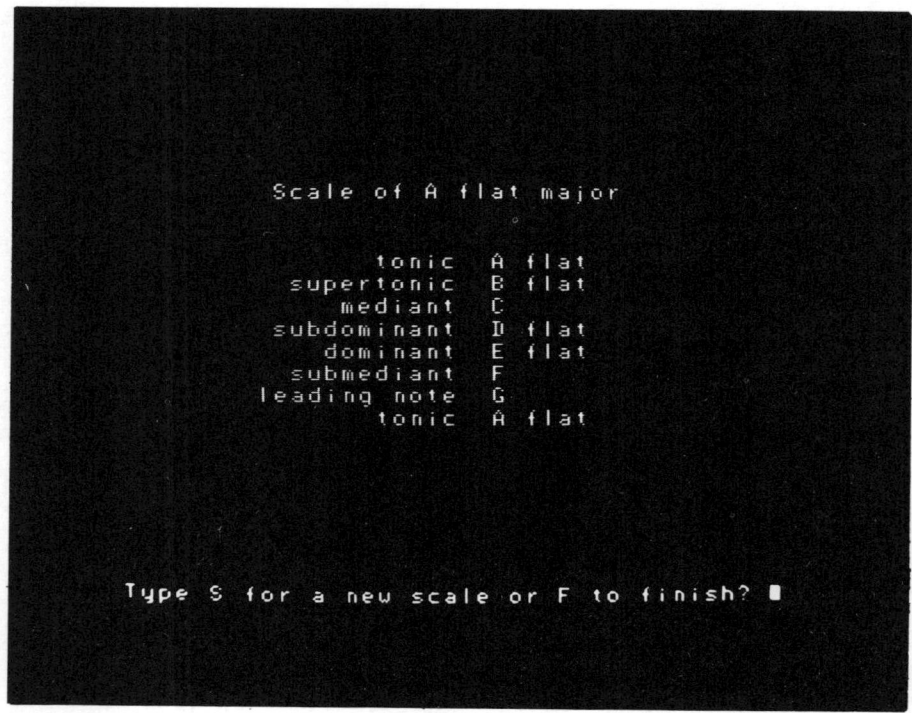

Discussion

What to notice: This program is in the 'simple-but-effective' category. The logic took some thought, especially in deciding whether a known note is, for example, 'A sharp' or 'B flat' in the context.

No proper ♯ or ♭ signs were available to us on our micro, and we debated using some other symbols to approximate. In the end, we decided that the words 'sharp' and 'flat' were simpler and more helpful. To input 'sharp' and 'flat', we made use of '+' and '−'. We do not want the user to be distracted by the setting of the 'SHIFT' key, so letters are accepted in upper and lower case, and we have also allowed the other characters on the '+' and '−' keys: in our case, these are ';' and '=' respectively.

Program code: Notes are stored in semitone intervals, so that there are twelve notes to the octave: the major scale is calculated by adding known intervals to the known keynote. A list of note letters is kept also, so that the program can guard against incorrect naming of the notes. In the scale of F♯ major, for example, the penultimate note is E♯, not F.

Note the way in which the program cycles round its two lists: if 'NL' exceeds 7, 7 is subtracted; if 'NN' exceeds 12, 12 is subtracted.

Note also the way in which the user's actual input ('R$') is converted into a usable keynote ('KN$'), irrespective of the case in which it was entered.

Error-checking: The most important piece of input is the keynote. This is obtained in one string and converted to another form in a different string. The input is rejected if it is not a note ('A' to 'G', in upper or lower case), or if it is followed by a symbol other than '+' or ';' for 'sharp', or '−' or '=' for 'flat'. Input which is of the correct form but which does not correspond to an allowable name for a scale ('F−', for example, since there is no scale of F♭ major) is not trapped as an error; the program continues to produce a 'scale' of sorts. The options at the end of the program (finish or new scale) may be entered in upper or lower case.

What you could do: You could do a great many things! You could modify the error-checking of the keynote supplied by the user, to reject inadmissible forms. You could modify SCALES to produce arpeggios instead of full scales. You could make the program produce downward scales, starting at the chosen keynote, either by calculating the downward scale directly, or by calculating and storing the *upward* scale and then displaying it in reverse order (which is quite an interesting programming exercise). You could make it produce minor scales as well as or instead of major scales; you could allow the choice between melodic and harmonic minors. (Note that you may have to deal with double sharps and flats!)

Another straightforward exercise is the transposition of a melody: the user supplies a tune in one (stated) key, and the program transposes it to a different (stated) key.

You could change the form of the output. For example, you could draw a staff and show the notes on this (for a scale or for a tune). (If you haven't got sharp and flat signs on your micro, you could consider using a hash sign as the sharp and a lower-case 'b' as the flat.) If you have a synthesizer, of course, you could make the micro *play* the output!

If you have confidence as a programmer *and* as a musician, you could write a program which provides a simple harmony for a supplied tune.

Portability: Apart from the usual remarks about the code which opens and closes the program, we note that you may need to change the symbols in the tests for 'sharp' or 'flat' in the input: ';' and '=' may need to be replaced by the symbols which are on the same keys as '+' and '−' on *your* keyboard.

Uses in teaching: SCALES – or your development of it – may be used either with individual students or with groups of them. Key progression is for some a difficult concept, and it may be helpful for them simply to be able to type keynotes and look at the scales produced. On this theme, we wondered about the order of the letters in the message which asks for the keynote: instead of being in alphabetic order, they could be in an order such as 'C G D A E B F'. We elected to use alphabetic order partly because any other order would imply the kind of key progression being discussed (the one above is for major scales, for example), and partly because it seems better to leave all choices completely open to the user.

SCALES is an example of a program where students may learn much from program development (that is, by taking the role of programmers) as well as from program use. Students who discuss the modifications needed to produce minor instead of major scales, or to transpose supplied melodies, will learn a great deal – whether or not they have sufficient expertise to enable them to carry these modifications through to a fully working program.

SCALES is an example of the fact that it is not always necessary for programs to be large and complicated simply to be worthwhile. We ourselves found it stimulating, both at the user level and at the programming level. Having started out to write a program to generate major scales, for individual or group use, we became aware of the breadth of possibilities which this program offers (some of which we have cited above). This diversity was not part of our original design specification, and was therefore exciting to us.

8.2 Overt and covert use

The aim of this section is to provide a program which can be used both overtly (by students or with students) or covertly (for students, but not in their presence). Most of the programs we have used in this book are intended for use with students or by students, but there are many programs which are used for administration and are not seen by the students. Examples include programs to mark tests, programs to keep class lists and programs to draw up timetables. The program given here could in fact be used either with students or away from them.

Specification

The program, CODE, will carry out simple substitutions of letters in a message. The message may be in mixed upper and lower case. The code setter will specify the message (in its uncoded form) of up to four lines, the number of lines, and the 'substitution number': these will all be given in the program as lines of 'DATA'. The program will print the supplied message, in each case substituting letters in the alphabet in accordance with the substitution number. Thus, if this number is '+3', 'A' will be replaced by 'D', 'B' by 'E' and so on. This number will be in the range −26 to +26.

At this point the program will offer two options: the message in its encoded form may be displayed on the screen or sent to the printer. If it is sent to the printer, the substitution number used will be printed also (but separated sufficiently far that it can be cut off without damaging the message). The printed message could, of course, be photocopied and distributed.

If the message is displayed on the screen, the user – the code breaker – will be able to supply a substitution number and have its effect calculated by the computer. (To succeed in decoding the message, the code breaker will need to supply the converse of the original number, which would be '−3' in the example given above.) He will not be told that he is 'correct' just because he invokes the converse of the original number. Code breakers know of their success only because a message becomes readable: it is conceivable (though unlikely) that a *wrong* substitution number might nevertheless yield a readable message. On the other hand, the user will be able to ask for the original number to be displayed.

Outline flowchart of CODE

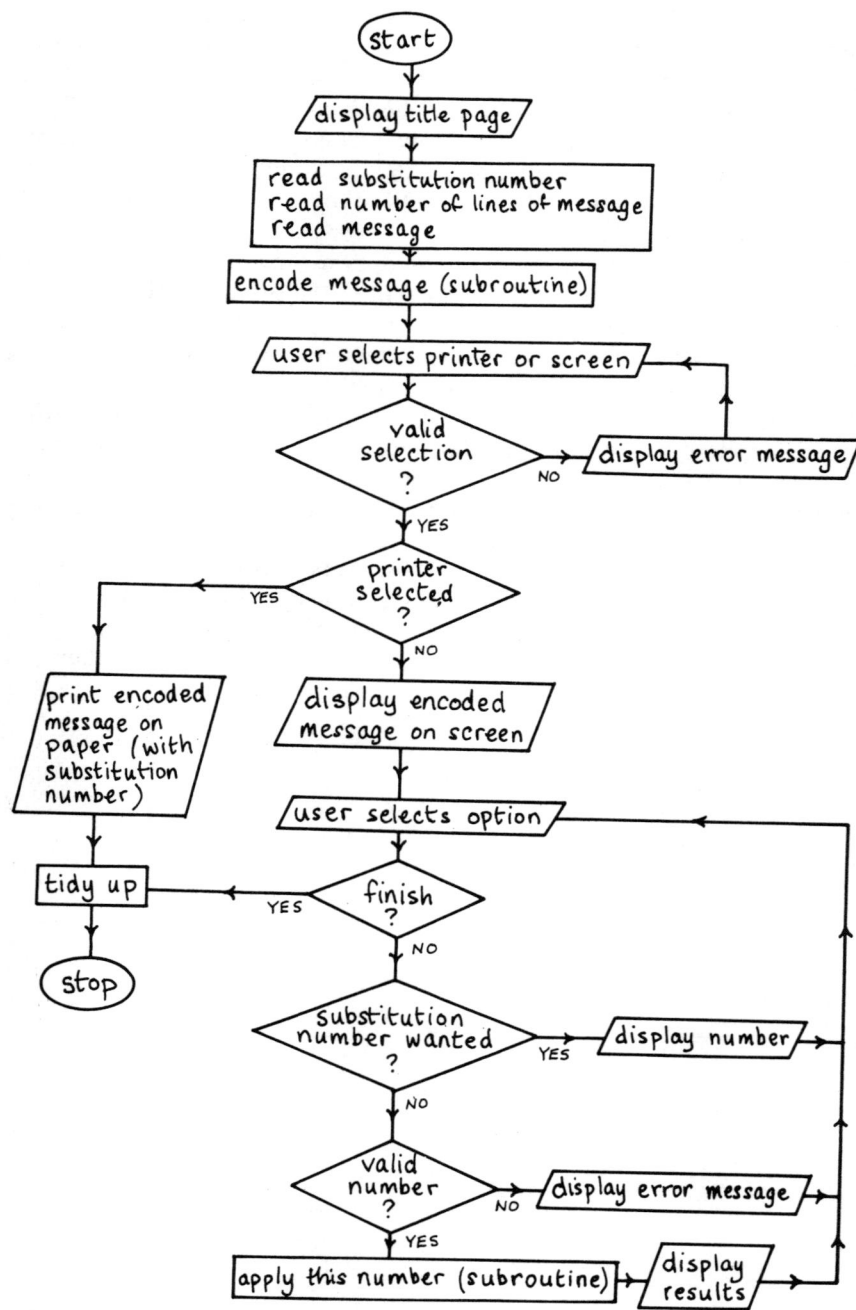

Listing of CODE program code

```
1000 REM Program : CODE
1010 REM
1020 REM
1030 REM Program to encode a message by simple
1040 REM     substitution. The message is supplied
1050 REM     by the code setter in DATA statements.
1060 REM     The alphabet (upper case and lower case
1070 REM     individually.) is considered as being
1080 REM     written in a circle; the code setter
1090 REM     gives a number between 0 and 26, which
1100 REM     may be positive or negative,
1110 REM     substitution is made by counting
1120 REM     round the circle that many letters.
1130 REM     (For example, with +3, 'D' becomes 'G'.)
1140 REM
1150 REM The program can be used in two ways:
1160 REM     PRINTER: The code is printed on paper
1170 REM         for the code breaker(s).
1180 REM     SCREEN: The code is displayed on the
1190 REM         screen, and the code breaker is
1200 REM         invited to supply a number; the
1210 REM         program then displays beneath the
1220 REM         message the result of applying this
1230 REM         number. It is for the code breaker
1240 REM         to decide whether or not he has
1250 REM         succeeded in breaking the code;
1260 REM         though he may ask to see the
1270 REM         number originally used.
1280 REM
1290 REM
1300     CLEAR (300)
1310     DIM CM$(4)
1320 REM
1330     ON BREAK GOTO 2610
1340 REM     Deal with user's interruption
1350     TEXT
1360     PRINT CHR$(12) : REM Clear the screen
1370     PRINT CHR$(17) : REM Disable paging
1380 REM
1390 REM
1400     PRINT TAB(17); "CODE"
1410     PRINT
1420     PRINT TAB(11); "Substitution code"
1430     PRINT : PRINT : PRINT
1440     PRINT TAB(19); "*"
1450     PRINT
1460     PRINT TAB(14); "Andrew Nash"
1470     PRINT
1480     PRINT TAB(15); "Derek Ball"
1490     PRINT
1500     PRINT TAB(19); "*"
1510     PRINT : PRINT : PRINT
1520     PRINT TAB(13); "Copyright 1982"
1530     PRINT
1540     PRINT TAB(10); "Hutchinson Education"
1550     PRINT
1560     FOR D = 1 TO 5000 : NEXT D : REM Delay
1570     PRINT CHR$(12) : REM Clear the screen
1580 REM
1590 REM
1600 REM ** DEFINE MESSAGE **
1610 REM
```

```
1620 REM Next line contains the substitution number (-26 to +26)
1630    DATA +5
1640 REM Next line contains number of lines of message (1 to 4)
1650    DATA 4
1660 REM That many lines below are lines of message.
1670 REM No line must exceed 40 characters.  Template:
1680 REM       V--------------------------------V
1690    DATA This is the first line of the message...
1700    DATA Second line
1710    DATA Third line
1720    DATA Fourth line
1730 REM
1740 REM
1750 REM ** IDENTIFY ASCII CODES **
1760 REM
1770    LET LA = 97  : REM ASCII code for 'a'
1780    LET LZ = 122 : REM ASCII code for 'z'
1790    LET UA = 65  : REM ASCII code for 'A'
1800    LET UZ = 90  : REM ASCII code for 'Z'
1810 REM
1820 REM
1830 REM ** SET UP CODE **
1840 REM
1850    READ S1 : REM Substitution number
1860    READ NL : REM Number of lines of message
1870    LET SN = S1
1880    FOR I = 1 TO NL
1890       READ UL$ : GOSUB 2680
1900       LET CM$(I) = CL$
1910    NEXT I
1920 REM
1930 REM
1940 REM ** PRINTER OR SCREEN **
1950 REM
1960    PRINT : PRINT "Would you like the coded message"
1970    PRINT "   printed (P) or displayed on the"
1980    PRINT "   screen (S)";
1990    INPUT R$
2000    IF R$="P" OR R$="p" THEN 2080
2010    IF R$="S" OR R$="s" THEN 2200
2020    PRINT ")) Response not understood - try again"
2030    GOTO 1960
2040 REM
2050 REM
2060 REM ** PRINTER SELECTED **
2070 REM
2080    LPRINT "This is the coded message:" : LPRINT
2090    FOR I = 1 TO NL
2100       LPRINT : LPRINT CM$(I)
2110    NEXT I
2120    LPRINT : LPRINT : LPRINT
2130    LPRINT : LPRINT : LPRINT
2140    LPRINT "Your substitution number was"; S1
2150    GOTO 2610
2160 REM
2170 REM
2180 REM ** SCREEN SELECTED **
2190 REM
2200    GRAPH
2210 REM
2220    FOR I = 1 TO NL
2230       PLOT 0,(69-I*15),CM$(I)
2240    NEXT I
2250 REM
2260    PRINT :PRINT "Enter 'F' for finish"
2270    PRINT "        'S' for original substitution no."
```

```
2280      PRINT "        or number between -26 and +26";
2290      INPUT R$
2300 REM
2310      IF R$="F" OR R$="f" THEN GOTO 2610
2320 REM
2330      IF R$()"S" AND R$()"s" THEN 2390
2340 REM
2350      PRINT "The substitution number was"; S1
2360      PRINT : PRINT "Press SPACEBAR to continue"
2370      LET R$ = GET$() : IF R$ () " " THEN 2370 ELSE 2260
2380 REM
2390      LET S2 = VAL(R$) : LET S2 = INT(S2)
2400      IF S2 )= -26 THEN 2440
2410         PRINT "))"; S2; " is below range"
2420         PRINT : PRINT "Press SPACEBAR to continue"
2430         LET R$ = GET$() : IF R$ () " " THEN 2430 ELSE 2260
2440      IF S2 <= +26 THEN 2510
2450         PRINT "))"; S2; " is above range"
2460         PRINT : PRINT "Press SPACEBAR to continue"
2470         LET R$ = GET$() : IF R$ () " " THEN 2470 ELSE 2260
2480 REM
2490 REM Apply this substitution number
2500 REM
2510      LET SN = S2
2520      FOR I = 1 TO NL
2530         LET UL$ = CM$(I) : GOSUB 2680
2540         PLOT 0,(63-I*15),CL$
2550      NEXT I
2560      GOTO 2260
2570 REM
2580 REM
2590 REM ** TIDY AND END **
2600 REM
2610      PRINT CHR$(19) : REM Re-enable paging
2620      TEXT : PRINT CHR$(12) : REM Clear the screen
2630      END
2640 REM
2650 REM
2660 REM ** SUBROUTINE TO ENCODE **
2670 REM
2680      LET CL$ = ""
2690 REM
2700      FOR J = 1 TO LEN(UL$)
2710 REM
2720         LET SC$ = MID$(UL$,J,1)
2730         LET AC = ASC(SC$)
2740 REM
2750         IF AC<LA OR AC>LZ THEN 2840
2760 REM
2770 REM Lower-case letter
2780 REM
2790            LET AC = AC + SN
2800            IF AC<LA THEN LET AC = AC + 26
2810            IF AC>LZ THEN LET AC = AC - 26
2820            GOTO 2920
2830 REM
2840         IF AC<UA OR AC>UZ THEN 2940
2850 REM
2860 REM Upper-case letter
2870 REM
2880            LET AC = AC + SN
2890            IF AC<UA THEN LET AC = AC + 26
2900            IF AC>UZ THEN LET AC = AC - 26
2910 REM
2920         LET SC$ = CHR$(AC)
2930 REM
```

214 *Case studies in teaching*

```
2940          LET CL$ = CL$ + SC$
2950 REM
2960          NEXT J
2970 REM
2980          RETURN
```

Sample output

```
Dpejoh boe efdpejoh bsf wfsz tjnqmf jg
Gshmrk erh higshmrk evi zivc wmqtpi mj

b dpnqvufs jt bwbjmbcmf! Cpui qspdfttft
e gsqtyxiv mu ezempefpi! Fsxl' tvsgiuuiu

gpmmpx wfsz dmfbs svmft, boe bsf
jsppsa zivc gpiev vypiu, erh evi

uifsfgpsf fbtz up qsphsbn.
xlivijsvi ieuc xs tvskveq.

Enter 'F' for finish
      'S' for original substitution no.
      or number between -26 and +26? ∎
```

Discussion

What to notice: Coding and decoding are very simple if a computer is available! Both processes follow clear rules, and are therefore easy to program. For many people, they are also quite fun.

'Code' is a word with various related meanings.

This program could be used by an individual (once the message had been set up by someone else), and he could simply work at it until he got a readable message or grew tired of it. It could also be used by a class (see below). Both are 'overt' uses, in our terms; but the program can be used to prepare coded messages in advance for use either by the teacher in the class or to be set as a quiz.

Program code: The code setter has actually to alter the code, since his data forms part of the program code (as opposed to being entered via 'INPUT' statements). The same subroutine is used to code and to decode, since the underlying process is identical.

Characters in the machine are stored not as actual characters, but as numeric codes: these codes are standard, and are known collectively as **ASCII code**. (ASCII code is described more fully in section 7.1.) In this program, it is useful to be able to exploit these numbers in doing the coding and decoding. Rather than refer on each occasion to the numbers in use (such as '97' for 'a'), it is convenient to assign certain values to suitably named variables. Thus there are variables called 'LZ' for 'lower-case z' and 'UA' for 'upper-case A'.

Error-checking: Data entered by the code *setter* is not checked at all, though he is given some help in ensuring that his message lines are of the right length (see lines 1670 and 1680).

Input from the code *breaker* is checked in the usual ways, and may be in either upper or lower case. In line 2390, string input required by the program to be a number is converted to a numeric form. No check is made that the string is appropriate to this, because there is no absolute need: if the 'VAL' function is applied to an empty string or to letters, it simply returns the value '0' (and hence the message remains coded). You may, of course, regard this as lazy programming, in which case you can correct the deficiency.

What you could do: You could develop the program in various ways. You could extend its range to take data from file rather from 'DATA' statements. You could make it count the occurrences of chosen (or of all) letters (see below).

Portability: Apart from the opening and closing instructions in the program, CODE (the code) is portable.

Uses in teaching: You could discuss how best to set about finding the substitution number. Trial and error is slow as a method, and inefficient. If there is enough text, it may be possible to make use of the fact that 'E' is the most common letter in English, and 'T' the second most common. Thus if you can identify the most common letter in your coded message, this may help you towards finding the substitution number. The program could be made to count letter frequencies for you, as we mentioned above. These ideas lead on naturally to a discussion of lexical analysis (see section 7.3).

8.3 Stimulation of discussion

The aim of this section is to provide an example of a program which may be used to stimulate discussion (in this case, of geometry and spatial awareness) and whose usefulness may be compared with that of other methods (such as films) of presenting a similar situation.

A subsidiary aim is to provide you with a routine for drawing circles quickly, which you can make use of in your own programs if you wish.

Specification

The program, CIRCLES, will require a micro with high-resolution graphics. The program will present a sequence of pictures in which a circle moves so that it always passes through one fixed point and so that it always touches a fixed circle. (In doing so, the moving circle will grow and diminish as implied by these criteria.) The effect produced by this program depends upon the fact that a circle is *moving*, to which end the drawing must be fast. The program will allow the user:

* to choose the radius of the fixed circle;
* to choose the position of the fixed point;
* to display either the moving circle as a whole or the path traced by its centre or both;
* to halt the drawing temporarily, and to restart it;
* to step through the drawing 'manually';
* to superimpose the paths obtained by varying the position of the fixed point.

Each command used to effect the options above will be issued using a single keystroke. Error messages will be given only in connection with the input of numbers.

Outline flowchart of
CIRCLES

Stimulation of discussion 217

```
start
   │
   ▼
display title page
   │
   ▼
[adapt machine code in routine to draw circles rapidly]
load into computer memory the routine to draw circles rapidly
   │
   ▼
user gives command ◄──────────────────────────────┐
   │                                               │
   ▼                                               │
finish? ──YES──► tidy up ──► stop                  │
   │NO                                             │
   ▼                                               │
go? ──NO──► other valid command? ──NO─────────────┤
   │YES              │YES                          │
   │                 ▼                             │
   │            carry out command ─────────────────┤
   ▼                                               │
user gives radius of fixed circle                  │
and distance of fixed point from centre            │
   │                                               │
   ▼                                               │
draw fixed circle and fixed point                  │
   │                                               │
   ▼                                               │
draw next bit of picture ◄─────────────┐           │
   │                                    │           │
   ▼                                    │           │
further command issued yet? ──NO───────┘           │
   │YES                                             │
   ▼                                                │
stop? ──YES──────────────────────────────────────►│
   │NO                                              │
   ▼                                                │
pause? ──NO──► other valid command? ──NO──────────┤
   │YES              │YES                           │
   │                 ▼                              │
   │            carry out command                   │
   ▼                                                │
user gives command ◄──────────────────────────────┤
   │                                                │
   ▼                                                │
stop? ──YES───────────────────────────────────────►│
   │NO                                              │
   ▼                                                │
resume? ──NO──► other valid command? ──NO─────────┤
   │YES              │YES                           │
   │                 ▼                              │
   │            carry out command ──────────────────┘
   ▼
(back to draw next bit of picture)
```

Listing of CIRCLES program code

```
1000 REM Program : CIRCLES
1010 REM
1020 REM
1030    CLEAR 20,,500
1040    TEXT : PRINT CHR$(12) : CALL "RESOLUTION",0,2 : REM Clear
1050 REM                                                    the screen
1060    ON BREAK GOTO 2520
1070 REM   Deal with user's interruption
1080 REM
1090    PRINT CHR$(17) : REM Disable paging
1100 REM
1110 REM
1120    PRINT TAB(16); "CIRCLES"
1130    PRINT
1140    PRINT TAB(9); "Locus-drawing program"
1150    PRINT : PRINT : PRINT
1160    PRINT TAB(19); "*"
1170    PRINT
1180    PRINT TAB(15); "Derek Ball"
1190    PRINT
1200    PRINT TAB(14); "Andrew Nash"
1210    PRINT
1220    PRINT TAB(19); "*"
1230    PRINT : PRINT : PRINT
1240    PRINT TAB(13); "Copyright 1982"
1250    PRINT
1260    PRINT TAB(9); "Hutchinson Education"
1270    PRINT
1280    FOR D = 1 TO 3000 : NEXT D : REM Delay
1290 REM
1300 REM
1310 REM PRELIMINARIES
1320 REM
1330    GOSUB 3310 : REM set up machine-code routine to draw circles
1340 REM                                                       rapidly
1350 REM Set constant and parameters
1360 REM
1370    PI=3.14159
1380    B1=0 : C$="shown"
1390 REM
1400 REM
1410 REM MAIN PROGRAM
1420 REM
1430    TEXT : PRINT CHR$(12) : CALL "RESOLUTION",0,2 : REM Clear
1440 REM                                                    the screen
1450    PRINT "Give a command"
1460    PRINT "For the list of commands, type C"
1470    PRINT : PRINT ":";
1480    A$=GET$()
1490    IF A$)="a" AND A$<="z" THEN A$=CHR$(ASC(A$)-32) : REM To
1500 REM                                                    upper case
1510    IF A$="F" THEN 2520 : REM Finish
1520    IF A$="G" THEN PRINT "GO" : GOTO 1570
1530    T$="stopped"
1540    GOSUB 2590 : REM Check options choice
1550    GOTO 1470
1560 REM
1570    S$="newstart" : T$="going"
1580    PRINT : PRINT
1590    PRINT "Give radius of circle and distance of"
1600    PRINT "  fixed point from centre"
1610    PRINT "   (e.g. radius=90, distance=60)"
```

```
1620      PRINT
1630 REM
1640      PRINT "   radius";
1650      INPUT LINE L$
1660      GOSUB 2830 : REM Check L$ is number; assign this to N
1670      IF E$="error" THEN 1640 ELSE R1=N
1680 REM
1690      PRINT "   distance";
1700      INPUT LINE L$
1710      GOSUB 2830 : REM Check L$ is number; assign this to N
1720      IF E$="error" THEN 1690 ELSE A=N
1730 REM
1740      IF R1>=0 THEN 1810
1750        PRINT "FIRST NUMBER MUST NOT BE NEGATIVE."
1760        PRINT "PLEASE INPUT BOTH NUMBERS AGAIN."
1770        GOTO 1590
1780 REM
1790 REM Prepare screen for graphics
1800 REM
1810      PRINT CHR$(12) : CALL "RESOLUTION",0,2
1820      CALL "OFFSET",-150,-90
1830      GRAPH
1840 REM
1850 REM Print message for user
1860 REM
1870      PRINT "To stop press S"
1880      PRINT "For the list of commands, type C"
1890 REM
1900 REM Plot circle if radius is less than 255
1910 REM
1920      IF R1>255 THEN 1970
1930        CALL"CIRCLE",0,0,R1,3
1940 REM
1950 REM Plot centre of circle and fixed point
1960 REM
1970      CALL"FILL",-1,-1,1,1,3 : REM Plot centre of circle
1980      GOSUB 2950 : REM Plot a dot
1990 REM
2000      FOR D = 1 TO 1000 : NEXT D : REM Delay
2010 REM
2020 REM Set logical brightness. This is varied not to change actual
2030 REM     brightness but to switch circle drawings on and off
2040 REM
2050      B=-2
2060 REM
2070 REM CREATE MOVING PICTURES
2080 REM
2090      S$="newstart"
2100      FOR I = 0 TO 10000
2110        A$=GET$(0) : REM Check whether user has issued command
2120        IF A$="" THEN 2210 : REM If not jump forward     ┌upper case
2130          IF ASC(A$)>96 THEN A$=CHR$(ASC(A$)-32) : REM Convert to
2140          IF A$="S" THEN I=10000 : GOTO 2480 : REM Stop picture sequence
2150          IF A$="P" THEN T$="pausing" : REM Pause
2160          IF A$="R" THEN T$="going" : REM Resume
2170          IF A$="N" THEN I=I+5: GOTO 2240 : REM Nudge
2180          IF A$="W" THEN 1730 : REM Wipe
2190          GOSUB 2590 : REM Check remaining options
2200 REM
2210        IF T$="pausing" THEN 2110 : REM If pausing do nothing
2220 REM
2230        A$="" : REM Clear user response
2240        T=2*PI*I/100 : REM Recalculate angle
2250 REM
2260 REM Determine centre and radius of next circle
2270 REM
```

```
2280        IF R1-A*COS(T)=0 THEN 2480
2290        R=(R1^2-A^2)/(2*(R1-A*COS(T)))
2300        R2=ABS(R1-R)
2310        IF R2>255   THEN 2480 : REM Circle not drawn if radius
2320        X0=R*COS(T):Y0=R*SIN(T)                        exceeds 255
2330 REM
2340        IF C$="not shown" THEN 2400 : REM Circle not drawn in this
2350 REM                                                               case
2360           CALL"CIRCLE",X0,Y0,R2,B
2370           CALL"COLOUR",-8,128 : REM Displays new circle
2380           CALL"COLOUR",3+B,0 : REM Blacks out old circle
2390 REM
2400           CALL"PLOT",X0,Y0,B1 : REM Plot centre of new circle
2410 REM
2420        IF C$="not shown" THEN 2480
2430           IF S$="newstart" THEN 2450                    record
2440              CALL "CIRCLE",X3,Y3,R3,-3-B : REM Remove old circle from
2450           R3=R2:X3=X0:Y3=Y0 : REM Save parameters of current circle
2460           S$="continue"
2470           B=-3-B : REM Change logical brightness (see line 1881)
2480        NEXT I
2490        GOTO 1430
2500 REM
2510 REM
2520        TEXT : CALL"RESOLUTION",0,2 : PRINT CHR$(12) : REM clear
2530        PRINT CHR$(19) : REM Enable paging              the screen
2540        CLEAR 100,,0
2550 REM
2560        END
2570 REM
2580 REM
2590 REM SUBROUTINE : CHECK OPTIONS
2600 REM
2610        M$=""
2620        IF A$="L" THEN M$="LOSE LOCUS" : C$="shown" : B1=0
2630        IF A$="O" THEN M$="ONLY LOCUS" : C$="not shown" : B1=3
2640        IF A$="A" THEN M$="ALL SHOWN" : C$="shown" : B1=3
2650        IF A$<>"M" THEN 2750
2660           PRINT
2670           PRINT "MOVE POINT"
2680           PRINT "How far";
2690           INPUT LINE L$
2700           GOSUB 2830
2710           IF E$="error" THEN 2690
2720           GOSUB 2950 : REM Plot a dot
2730           A=A+N
2740           GOSUB 2950 : REM Plot a dot
2750        IF T$="stopped" THEN PRINT M$
2760        IF A$="C" THEN GOSUB 3030
2770 REM
2780        RETURN
2790 REM
2800 REM
2810 REM SUBROUTINE : CHECK NUMBER INPUT
2820 REM
2830        E$="ok"
2840        IF L$="0" THEN N=0 : GOTO 2900
2850        N=VAL(L$)
2860        IF N<>0 THEN 2900
2870           PRINT "PLEASE GIVE A NUMBER IN FIGURES"
2880           E$="error"
2890 REM
2900        RETURN
2910 REM
2920 REM
2930 REM SUBROUTINE : PLOT A DOT
```

```
2940 REM
2950    IF A=0 THEN 2980
2960    CALL "FILL",A-1,-1,A+1,1,-3
2970 REM
2980    RETURN
2990 REM
3000 REM
3010 REM SUBROUTINE : PRINT COMMANDS
3020 REM
3030    IF T$()"stopped" THEN 3080
3040      PRINT TAB(15); "COMMANDS"
3050      PRINT TAB(15); "========"
3060      PRINT : PRINT
3070      PRINT "The following may be used at any time:"
3080    PRINT
3090    PRINT "  Commands            All shown"
3100    PRINT "  Lose locus          Only locus"
3110    IF T$()"stopped" THEN 3210
3120      PRINT
3130      PRINT "The following may be used only when"
3140      PRINT "the picture is NOT on the screen:"
3150      PRINT
3160      PRINT "  Go                 Finish"
3170      PRINT
3180      PRINT "The following may be used only when"
3190      PRINT "the picture is on the screen:"
3200      PRINT
3210    PRINT "  Pause       Resume       Nudge"
3220    PRINT "  Wipe screen Move point   Stop";
3230    IF T$()"stopped" THEN 3280
3240      PRINT : PRINT
3250      PRINT "TO GIVE COMMAND, TYPE ONLY FIRST LETTER"
3260      PRINT
3270 REM
3280    RETURN
3290 REM
3300 REM
3310 REM SUBROUTINE : SET UP MACHINE CODE TO DRAW CIRCLES RAPIDLY
3320 REM
3330    GOSUB 3990 : REM Adapt machine-code routine to this machine
3340    HM=PEEK(6)+256*PEEK(7)
3350    PI=3.14159
3360    A=HM-46
3370    FOR I=0 TO 11
3380      X=COS(I*PI/48+PI/96)*128 : Y=SIN(I*PI/48+PI/96)*128
3390      X=INT(X+0.5) : Y=INT(Y+0.5)
3400      POKE A,X : POKE A+1,Y
3410      A=A+2
3420    NEXT I
3430    N=HM-454
3440    A1=INT(N/256) : A0=N-256*A1
3450    POKE 53056,A0
3460    POKE 53057,A1
3470    N=HM-438
3480    A1=INT(N/256) : A0=N-256*A1
3490    FOR P=HM-454 TO HM-446
3500      READ Q
3510      POKE P,Q
3520    NEXT P
3530    DATA 0,0,6,67,73,82,67,76,69
3540    POKE HM-445,A0 : POKE HM-444,A1
3550    FOR P=HM-438 TO HM-81
3560      READ Q
3570      POKE P,Q
3580    NEXT P
3590    DATA 225, 34,248,108,225, 34,250,108,225, 34
```

```
3600    DATA 254,108,225, 34,252,108,253, 33,215,108
3610    DATA 205, 61,108, 33,192,108,205, 91,108,221
3620    DATA  33,147, 53,205,148,108,205, 91,108,221
3630    DATA  33, 27, 54,205,148,108, 62,216,189,194
3640    DATA 116,107, 43,205,100,108,205,133,108,221
3650    DATA  33, 27, 54,205,148,108, 62,191,189,194
3660    DATA 133,107, 35,205, 91,108,205,133,108,205
3670    DATA 140,108,221, 33, 27, 54,205,148,108, 62
3680    DATA 216,189,194,153,107, 43,205,100,108,205
3690    DATA 140,108,221, 33, 27, 54,205,148,108, 62
3700    DATA 191,189,194,176,107, 35,205, 91,108,205
3710    DATA 133,108,205,140,108,205,133,108,205,140
3720    DATA 108,221, 33, 27, 54,205,148,108, 62,216
3730    DATA 189,194,196,107, 43,205,100,108,205,133
3740    DATA 108,205,140,108,205,133,108,205,140,108
3750    DATA 205,133,108,221, 33, 27, 54,205,148,108
3760    DATA  62,191,189,194,225,107, 35,205, 91,108
3770    DATA 205,140,108,205,133,108,221, 33, 27, 54
3780    DATA 205,148,108, 62,216,189,194,  1,108, 43
3790    DATA 205,100,108,205,133,108,205,140,108,205
3800    DATA 133,108,221, 33, 27, 54,205,148,108, 62
3810    DATA 191,189,194, 24,108, 35,205, 91,108,221
3820    DATA  33, 27, 54,205,148,108,201,217, 30,  0
3830    DATA 253, 35,253,126,  0,237, 75,250,108,205
3840    DATA 109,108,205,128,108,253,119,232, 28, 62
3850    DATA  24,187,194, 64,108,217,201, 94, 22,  0
3860    DATA  35, 78,  6,  0, 35,201, 78,  6,  0, 43
3870    DATA  94, 22,  0, 43,201, 33,  0,  0, 22,  8
3880    DATA 203, 71, 40,  1,  9,203, 33,203, 16, 31
3890    DATA  21, 32,243,201,125, 23,124, 23,201,122
3900    DATA  80, 71,123, 89, 79,201,123, 47, 95,122
3910    DATA  47, 87, 19,201,213,197,229, 42,252,108
3920    DATA  25, 84, 93, 42,254,108,  9, 68, 77, 33
3930    DATA 177,108,229,213,197, 42,248,108,229, 14
3940    DATA   3,221,233,225,193,209,201,209
3950 REM
3960    RETURN
3970 REM
3980 REM
3990 REM SUBROUTINE : ADAPT MACHINE-CODE ROUTINE TO THIS MACHINE
4000 REM
4010    PRINT TAB(15); "CIRCLES"
4020    PRINT : PRINT
4030    PRINT "     The first time you run this program"
4040    PRINT "the machine code it contains will need"
4050    PRINT "to be adapted for your machine."
4060    PRINT "When you have finished running the"
4070    PRINT "program it is suggested that you"
4080    PRINT "delete line 3330 and lines 3970-4940"
4090    PRINT "and then save the program again on your"
4100    PRINT "disc or tape."
4110    PRINT "     If you do so, the program will"
4120    PRINT "not go through this process again next"
4130    PRINT "time it is run."
4140    PRINT : PRINT
4150    RESTORE 3590
4160    DIM A(400)
4170    PRINT "Please give address of SUBPTR"
4180    PRINT "    (might be &11A)";
4190    INPUT N
4200    SP=N
4210    PRINT "Please give address of BBUFV"
4220    PRINT "    (might be &118)";
4230    INPUT BB
4240    PRINT : PRINT
4250    PRINT "Please wait"
```

```
4260      N=PEEK(SP)+256*PEEK(SP+1)
4270      IF N=0 THEN 4350
4280      IF PEEK(SP+2)()4 THEN SP=N : GOTO 4260
4290      C$=CHR$(PEEK(SP+3))
4300      IF C$()"P" AND C$()"L" THEN SP=N : GOTO 4260
4310      A0=PEEK(SP+7) : A1=PEEK(SP+8)
4320      IF C$="P" THEN P0=A0:P1=A1
4330      IF C$="L" THEN L0=A0:L1=A1
4340      SP=N : GOTO 4260
4350      HM=PEEK(6)+256*PEEK(7)
4360      D=HM-&6D06
4370      FOR I = 0 TO 357
4380        READ A(I)
4390        IF I=0 THEN 4520
4400        IF A(I)()&6B AND A(I)()&6C THEN 4450
4410        N=A(I-1)+256*A(I)
4420        N=N+D
4430        A(I)=INT(N/256) : A(I-1)=N-256*A(I)
4440        GOTO 4520
4450        IF A(I)()&D8 AND A(I)()&BF THEN 4500
4460        N=A(I)+D
4470        N=N-256*INT(N/256)
4480        A(I)=N
4490        GOTO 4520
4500        IF A(I-1)=&93 AND A(I)=&35 THEN A(I-1)=P0 : A(I)=P1
4510        IF A(I-1)=&1B AND A(I)=&36 THEN A(I-1)=L0 : A(I)=L1
4520      NEXT I
4530      B=BB
4540      FOR I = 0 TO 357 STEP 10
4550        LM=3590+I : GOSUB 4860 : REM Find stored line
4560        PT=PT+4
4570        IF PEEK(PT)()ASC(",") THEN PT=PT+1 : GOTO 4570
4580        PT=PT-4
4590        FOR J = 0 TO 9
4600          IF I+J>357 THEN 4630
4610          A$=RIGHT$("   "+STR$(A(I+J)),3)
4620          FOR K=1 TO 3 ; POKE PT+4*J+K,ASC(MID$(A$,K,1)) : NEXT K
4630        NEXT J
4640      NEXT I
4650      B=BB
4660      LM=3450 : GOSUB 4860 : REM Find stored line
4670      X=SP : GOSUB 4770
4680      LM=3460 : GOSUB 4860 : REM Find stored line
4690      X=SP+1 : GOSUB 4770
4700      RESTORE
4710 REM
4720      RETURN
4730 REM
4740 REM
4750 REM SUBROUTINE : POKE PROGRAM CHANGE
4760 REM
4770      A$=RIGHT$("    "+STR$(X),5)
4780      IF PEEK(PT)()ASC(",") THEN PT=PT+1 : GOTO 4780
4790      FOR J=1 TO 5
4800        POKE PT-6+J,ASC(MID$(A$,J,1))
4810      NEXT J
4820 REM
4830      RETURN
4840 REM
4850 REM
4860 REM SUBROUTINE : FIND STORED LINE
4870 REM
4880      PT=B
4890      PT=PEEK(PT)+256*PEEK(PT+1)
4900      LN=PEEK(PT+2)+256*PEEK(PT+3)
4910      IF LN()LM THEN4890
```

224 *Case studies in teaching*

```
4920        B=PT
4930    REM
4940        RETURN
```

Sample output

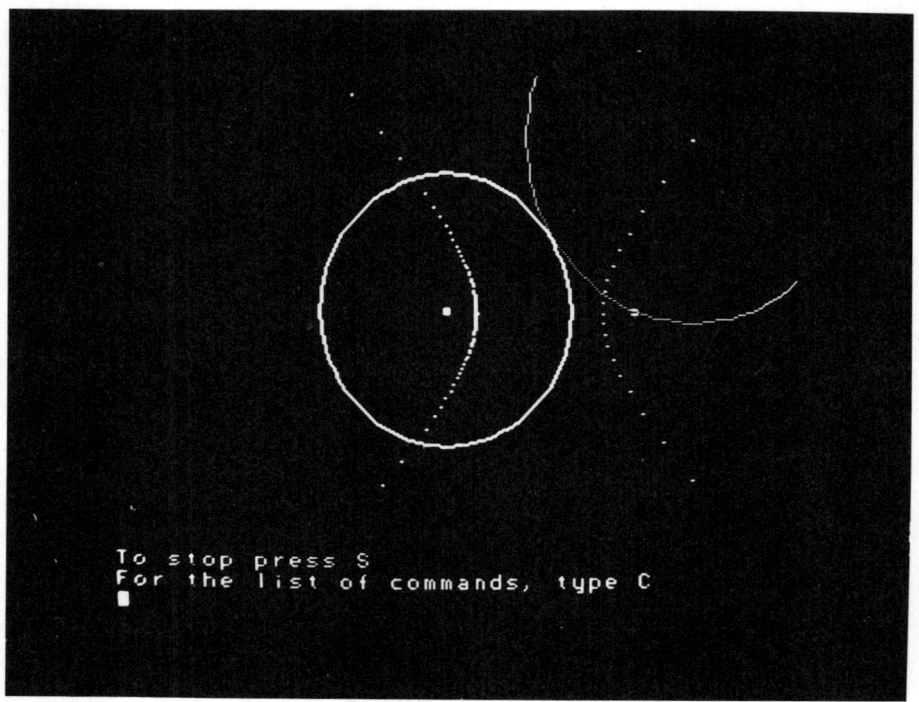

Discussion

Commands: Within the program itself, the commands are listed but not described. Short notes are given here for clarification.
* COMMANDS The computer lists the commands which are available.
* FINISH This ends the program.
* ALL SHOWN The moving circle is displayed and the locus of its centre is retained on the screen as the circle advances. The alternatives are 'LOSE LOCUS' and 'ONLY LOCUS'.
* LOSE LOCUS The moving circle is displayed, but not the locus of its centre. The alternatives are 'ONLY LOCUS'; and 'ALL SHOWN'.
* ONLY LOCUS The locus of the moving circle is displayed and retained as the circle advances, but the circle itself is invisible. The alternatives are 'LOSE LOCUS'; and 'ALL SHOWN'.

* GO Picture-drawing is initiated, with the new radius of the fixed circle and the new distance of the fixed point from the centre of this circle. See 'PAUSE' and 'NUDGE'.
* PAUSE Picture-drawing is suspended temporarily. The converse is 'RESUME'; see also 'NUDGE'.
* RESUME Picture-drawing is restarted (following 'PAUSE').
* NUDGE If used during a pause, this allows the user to step through the pictures one by one. If used while the circle is moving, some pictures are omitted from the sequence: this is useful during a slow-moving phase.
* WIPE SCREEN The screen is cleared without disturbing the choice of radius and distance.
* MOVE POINT The position of the fixed point is respecified, but the fixed circle is left unchanged. Subsequent pictures are superimposed on what is already on the screen.
* STOP The current picture sequence is curtailed. It is followed by 'FINISH', or – after adjustments – by 'GO'.

Each command is effected by typing its initial letter only.

What to notice: The program contains a machine-code routine to enable the circles to be drawn more rapidly than would otherwise be possible. Machine code, by definition, is machine-dependent, so that this program, written for the RML 380Z, will run only on RML 380Z or 480Z machines. If you have one of these machines, you may still need to make minor changes – see the section below concerning portability.

When you run the program, note the speed at which circles are produced. It may be that the circles do not look completely circular on your screen: this depends in part upon the ratio of height to width of the picture as displayed on your screen. The routine, as written, cannot easily be adapted to cope with this problem.

Note the flexibility available when running this program. Commands may be issued at three different stages: before starting the picture sequence (that is, before issuing 'GO'), while the picture sequence is running, and while the picture sequence has been temporarily suspended (by 'PAUSE'). The radius of the fixed circle may take any value between 0 and 255, and the distance of the fixed point from the centre of this circle may be positive or negative.

Note the very small variation between successive pictures in the sequence which occur at some stages and with particular choices of radius and distance. If the rate of movement on these occasions seems tedious, you may use 'NUDGE' to speed things up.

When the fixed point is *on* the fixed circle, the situation is insufficiently defined. What the program produces is disappointing rather than intriguing.

Program code: The most significant feature of the code for this program is obviously the machine-code routine used to produce the circles rapidly. You are invited to compare the speed of the drawing with that produced by any routine written simply in BASIC. If you can write one in BASIC that is as fast, please let us know!

The code, when adapted to your micro, can be used in other programs. You need to incorporate the subroutine as a whole (lines 3340–3960) and it is invoked by means of the command

```
3470     CALL "CIRCLE", X0, Y0, R, B
```

in which 'X0' and 'Y0' are the coordinates of the centre of the circle, 'R' is the radius of the circle, and 'B' is the brightness of the line drawn. Note that when invoking this command, you *must* specify the brightness.

The delay loop which keeps the title page visible for some seconds is shorter in this program than in some others: this is because the machine-code routine takes time to set up, and the title page is visible during this operation as well.

Error-checking: Each number that is input is fully checked; appropriate error messages are issued if necessary.

When a command is expected (as opposed to a number), no error messages are issued: only those keys which represent valid commands are 'live', and all other keys are simply ignored. This approach is justified, as the message

```
For the list of commands, type C
```

is always visible. More elaborate error-checking, especially during the drawing of the picture sequence, would be too intrusive and might cause unnecessary embarrassment when the program is used in front of a group of people – it is easy to hit a key in error.

What you could do: If the message displayed at the foot of the screen during the drawing of the picture sequence annoys you, you could easily remove this.

You could change the number of points used to trace the path of the centre of the moving circle. For example, you could increase the number when the program is in 'ONLY LOCUS' mode.

A more ambitious exercise would be to get the computer to select both the radius of the fixed circle and the position of the fixed point at random, with the option of making either or both invisible. The user could then examine the picture produced and attempt to deduce the position of the circle or point (or both). An idea similar to this is incorporated into the program GRAPH given in section 8.5.

You could write any program of your own which makes effective use of the subroutine to draw circles rapidly.

Stimulation of discussion 227

As a really difficult task, you could write your own machine-code routine for drawing circles rapidly. Ours could be improved by making it adjustable for screen height, by allowing the drawing of ellipses and of circular arcs, and by simply making it faster.

Portability: As with all the programs, this one was originally written for the RML 380Z micro. But it differs from most of the others in that it relies on machine code. High-level languages, as we have said elsewhere in the book, offer many advantages in ease of writing, in comprehensibility and in portability. But routines written in BASIC may, as here, function too slowly to fulfil their purpose: by writing the code directly in machine code, the time taken in execution is considerably reduced. If you have a 380Z or 480Z, CIRCLES should run subject to the remarks in the next paragraph; if you have a different micro, you will need either to write your own routine or to adapt the one provided (see below).

Even on micros made by one firm, in this case RML, there are differences between interpreters. The routine uses addresses in memory which may vary with the interpreter in use and the amount of memory available. Having supplied the addresses of 'SUBPTR' and of 'BBUFV', which you will find in the RML *Release Note* for your interpreter, the program itself will make the rest of the changes for you. If the addresses supplied are incorrect, the program will crash and you will have to reload it. Once the machine code has been successfully adapted to your machine, you are encouraged to follow the advice given on the screen at the start of the program: to delete line 3330 and lines 3970–4940, and then to save the program in its adapted form.

Some remarks about the machine code for those with machines other than the 380Z and 480Z. These two machines have Z80 processor chips, in common with some other makes of micro. If your machine has a Z80 chip, the routine may work with a few modifications. One change that you will need to make is in the mechanism by which the routine is called. On the 380Z this is elegant, but the method may not be available on your micro – you could substitute a more straightforward call by memory address, perhaps, but you would need to check how parameters are passed from BASIC code to machine-code routines. Another problem is that the machine-code routine, in its present form, calls a subroutine within the BASIC interpreter which plots points of high resolution. The address of this subroutine would be different on another micro, and the method of passing parameters to it might be different also.

CIRCLES uses high-resolution graphics and will run only on micros which have this. All high-resolution graphics instructions in the program begin with the word 'CALL', so they are easily identified: they will certainly need adapting for a different micro. On the 380Z and the 480Z screens, there are 192 rows each of 320 pixels: these numbers would be different on another machine, though these differences would not seriously affect the operation of the program. The 'CALL "OFFSET"' instruction is used to reposition the origin of coordinates at the centre of the screen: if this instruction were not available, adjustments would need to be made.

Uses in teaching: This program *could* be used by students individually: they could investigate what happens as the radius of the fixed circle and the position of the fixed point are varied, and they could ponder the nature of the intersections of the different paths taken by the centres of the circles. However, the program was written for use with a class rather than by an individual, and particularly to stimulate discussion among them and with the teacher. This entails a search on the part of the students for the language through which to communicate their ideas and images.

There are few restrictions about which students might most benefit from using the program: it can be used with eight-year-olds and with university mathematics students. To make profitable use of CIRCLES, it is not necessary for students to be familiar with words like 'ellipse', 'hyperbola' or 'asymptote' – before or after.

Similarly, there are few restrictions concerning the order in which images may be presented to a class. To date, CIRCLES has mainly been used in teaching classes of children in the 11–14 range; discussion has been encouraged and students have tried to forecast what would happen, before seeing it on the screen; and students themselves have suggested profitable directions in which to proceed.

Two quite different types of path are traced, depending on whether the fixed point is inside or outside the fixed circle. And there are three special cases: where the fixed point is at the centre of the fixed circle, where the fixed point is *on* the fixed circle, and where the radius of the fixed circle is zero.

Finally, a brief comment on the differences in teaching strategy when using computer programs as opposed to films. A teacher using a film to present the same concepts would first show this to the class, perhaps twice, and then invite discussion – recall what happened, interpretation, suggestions about what would have happened if things had been slightly different. At the end of the discussion, students might be asked to produce some written work based on the film and the ensuing discussion, and they might be shown the film once more.

If, on the other hand, the *program* is used with the class, the teacher intersperses discussion with the running of the program. He might start by showing a picture sequence and then invite a description of what had been seen or a suggestion about what might be done next and a forecast of what would happen. The blend of discussion and pictures enables interaction with the micro in two senses: students can make hypotheses and have them confirmed or rejected, and students can influence the course of events.

The main difference between the uses of film and micro is thus the degree of interaction, though there are other distinctions – for example, the picture sequence produced on a film may be of better quality. Interaction has advantages and disadvantages: if you have used both approaches in your

teaching, it is for you to decide where the balance lies.
This program is likely to stimulate discussion, in the classroom and outside it.

8.4 Freedom and constraint

The aim of this section is to provide two versions of one program to illustrate alternative ways in which the same basic idea can be presented to students. In one of the versions, facilities are presented as a set of options available in command mode, and the student is free to use the program as he chooses. In the other, some of these features are presented in a particularly closely defined tutorial mode without any choice being exercised by the student.

A subsidiary aim of the section is to demonstrate two approaches to the 'packaging' of programs: one version of the program is an open, unemotional tool; the other is a drill program in which the user is credited with no initiative or personal responsibility.

Specification

The program will aid in the teaching of students who have difficulties with their spelling. It will list ten words whose spelling is to be learnt by the user: he will then attempt to spell these words correctly. There will be two versions of the program, and they will have very little in common other than the task.

One version, SPELLC, will demonstrate a constrained approach to teaching. It will follow these principles:
* It will be written for the teacher, and will explain its purpose to him.
* It will be intended for use with children. It will address them by name, in an attempt to make them feel at ease.
* It will cycle through the list of ten words until the child gets all ten right. If he succeeds, he will be congratulated; if not, he will be told how many words he got wrong and advised of his current error rate.
* Each word to be spelt will be presented for the same set length of time.

The other version, SPELLF, will demonstrate a free and unconstrained approach to teaching. *It* will follow these principles:
* It will be written for the user, and will explain its purpose to him.
* It will be intended for use by anyone. It will not involve itself with the user personally in any way.
* It will go through the list of ten words once. Thereafter, it will offer the user a set of options. He will be able to go through the whole list again, or only those words which he spelt incorrectly, or only those words which he spelt correctly. He will be able simply to display and look at those words which he spelt incorrectly. He will be able to finish whenever he chooses.
* Each word to be spelt will be presented and will remain visible until the user presses the space-bar.

230 Case studies in teaching

Outline flowchart of SPELLC

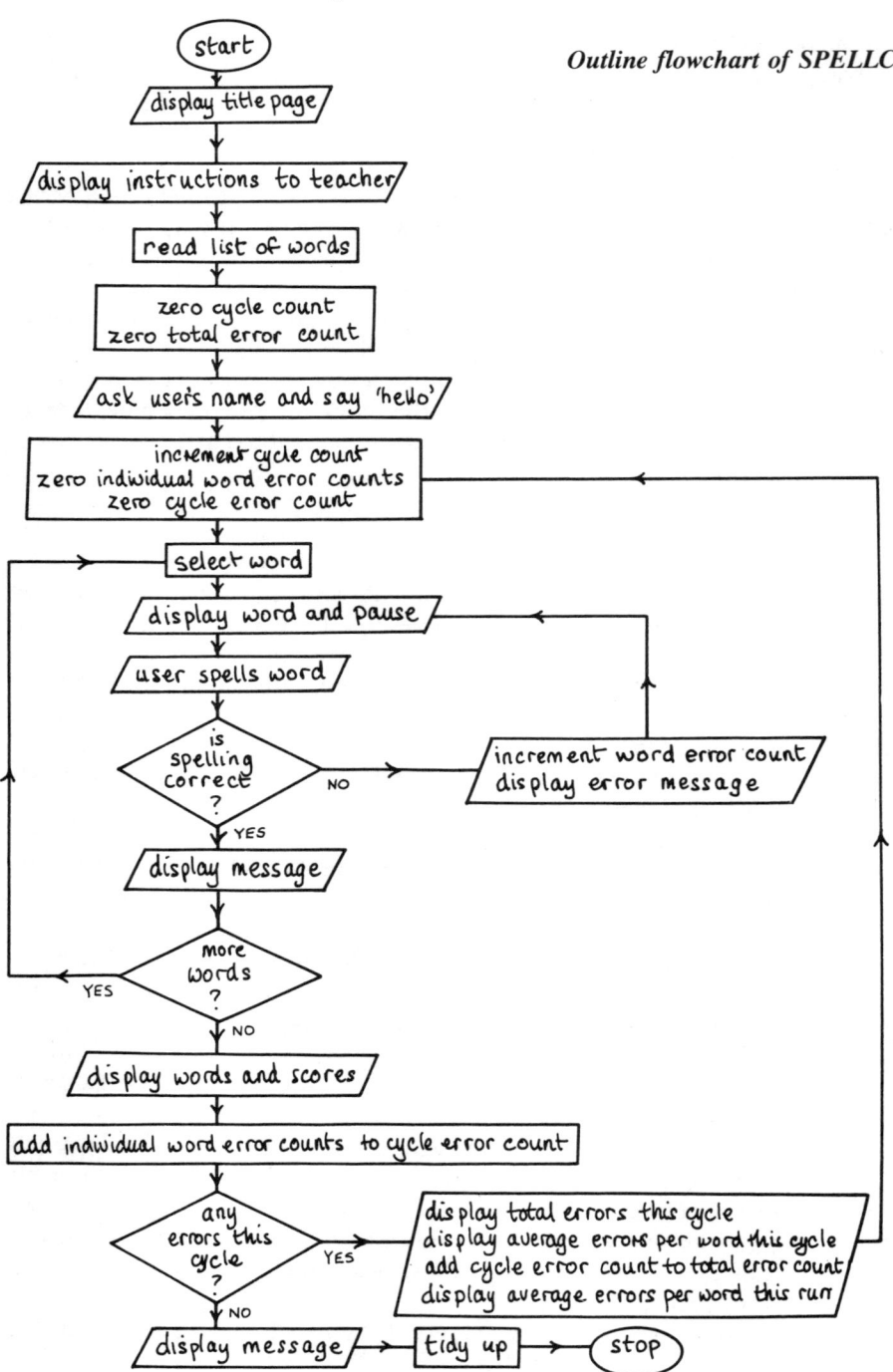

Outline flowchart of SPELLF

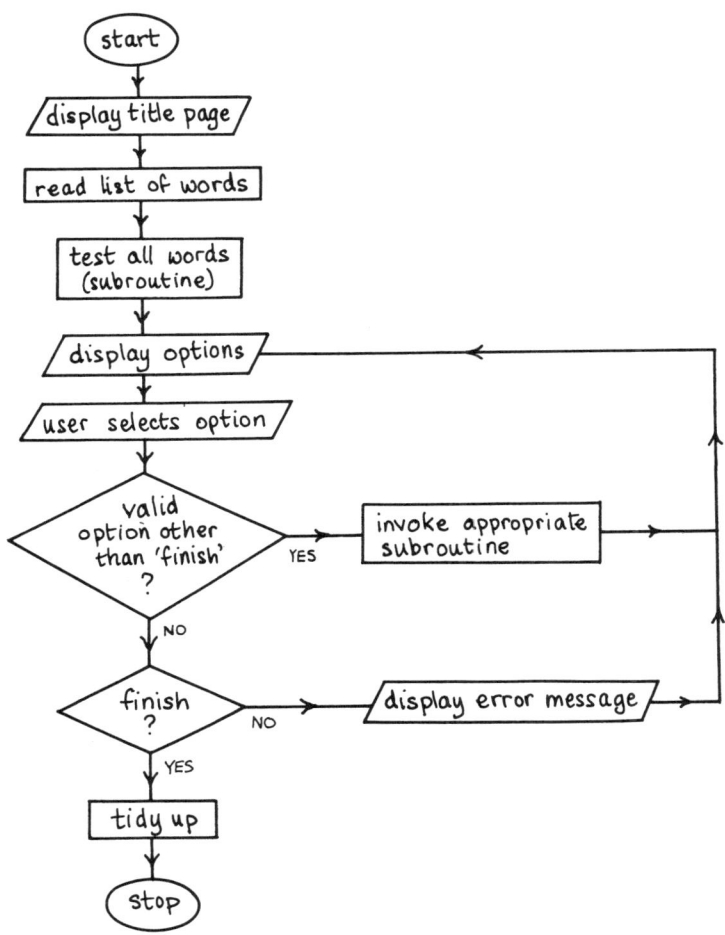

Listing of SPELLC program code

```
1000 REM Program : SPELLC
1010 REM
1020 REM
1030     CLEAR 100
1040 REM
1050     ON BREAK GOTO 2400
1060 REM    Deal with user's interruption
1070 REM
1080 REM
1090     TEXT : PRINT CHR$(12) : REM Clear the screen
1100     PRINT CHR$(17) : REM Disable paging
1110 REM
1120 REM
1130     PRINT TAB(17); "SPELLC"
1140     PRINT
1150     PRINT TAB(11); "Spelling practice"
1160     PRINT : PRINT : PRINT
1170     PRINT TAB(19); "*"
1180     PRINT
1190     PRINT TAB(14); "Andrew Nash"
1200     PRINT
1210     PRINT TAB(15); "Derek Ball"
1220     PRINT
1230     PRINT TAB(19); "*"
1240     PRINT : PRINT : PRINT
1250     PRINT TAB(13); "Copyright 1982"
1260     PRINT
1270     PRINT TAB(10); "Hutchinson Education"
1280     PRINT
1290     FOR D = 1 TO 5000 : NEXT D : REM Delay
1300     PRINT CHR$(12) : REM Clear the screen
1310 REM
1320 REM
1330 REM * INSTRUCTIONS *
1340 REM
1350     PRINT "INSTRUCTIONS TO TEACHER"
1360     PRINT "-----------------------"
1370     PRINT
1380     PRINT "This program, SPELLC, has been specially"
1390     PRINT "designed to help YOU with the"
1400     PRINT "unrewarding job of teaching SLOW"
1410     PRINT "CHILDREN who can't spell."
1420     PRINT
1430     PRINT "All you have to do is start it off for"
1440     PRINT "the child and leave him/her to work"
1450     PRINT "through it. He/she will be told how"
1460     PRINT "he/she is getting on, and will be"
1470     PRINT "ENCOURAGED when he/she gets a word"
1480     PRINT "RIGHT.  FULL STATISTICS are given at the"
1490     PRINT "end of each cycle through the list so"
1500     PRINT "that the child can assess his/her"
1510     PRINT "progress"
1520     PRINT
1530     PRINT "Ensure that the child is told to enter"
1540     PRINT "his/her answer in CAPITAL LETTERS."
1550     PRINT : PRINT
1560 REM
1570 REM
1580 REM * SET UP WORD LIST, ETC *
1590 REM
1600     DIM W$(10), E(10)
1610     FOR W = 1 TO 10
```

```
1620        READ W$(W)
1630      NEXT W
1640      LET T=0 : REM Total error count
1650      LET C=0 : REM Cycle count
1660 REM
1670 REM
1680 REM * FIND OUT USER'S NAME *
1690 REM
1700      PRINT "What is your name";
1710      INPUT N$
1720      PRINT "Hello, "; N$
1730      PRINT
1740 REM
1750 REM
1760 REM * CYCLE THROUGH THE LIST UNTIL USER GETS IT RIGHT *
1770 REM
1780      LET C=C+1 : REM Increment cycle count
1790      FOR I = 1 TO 10 : REM Empty individual error counts
1800        LET E(I)=0
1810      NEXT I
1820      LET E9=0 : REM Empty cycle error count
1830 REM
1840      FOR W = 1 TO 10
1850 REM
1860 REM * PRINT WORD AND PAUSE *
1870 REM
1880        FOR I = 1 TO 5 : PRINT : NEXT I
1890        PRINT "WORD"; TAB(10); W$(W) : REM display word
1900        FOR I = 1 TO 5 : PRINT : NEXT I
1910        FOR D = 1 TO 2000 : NEXT D
1920 REM
1930 REM * USER TO SPELL WORD *
1940 REM
1950        PRINT CHR$(12) : REM clear the screen
1960        PRINT "Now you spell it, "; N$; "!"
1970        PRINT
1980        INPUT A$
1990        PRINT
2000 REM
2010 REM * CHECK USER'S ATTEMPT, THEN NEXT WORD OR REPEAT
2020 REM
2030        IF A$ <> W$(W) THEN 2090
2040          PRINT "WELL DONE, "; N$; "!"
2050          IF W = 10 THEN 2130
2060          PRINT "Here's the ";
2070          IF W > 1 THEN PRINT "next ";
2080          PRINT "word" : GOTO 2130
2090        LET E(W) = E(W)+1
2100        PRINT "No, "; N$; ", you got that WRONG!"
2110        PRINT "Try that again" : GOTO 1880
2120 REM
2130      NEXT W
2140 REM
2150 REM * FINISHED ALL WORDS. PRINT REPORT *
2160 REM
2170      PRINT : PRINT : PRINT
2180      PRINT "O.K., "; N$; ", here's your score" : PRINT
2190      FOR W=1 TO 10
2200        IF E(W) = 0 THEN PRINT TAB(3); ELSE PRINT "** ";
2210        PRINT W$(W);
2220        IF E(W) > 0 THEN 2240
2230          PRINT TAB(20); "Excellent!" : GOTO 2260
2240        PRINT TAB(20); "WRONG"; E(W); " TIMES!"
2250        LET E9 = E9+E(W)
2260      NEXT W
2270      PRINT
```

234 *Case studies in teaching*

```
2280 REM
2290    IF E9 = 0 THEN 2380
2300       PRINT "You made a total of"; E9; " ERRORS that time"
2310       PRINT "Average that cycle ="; E9/10; " errors/word"
2320       LET T=T+E9
2330       PRINT "Average this run ="; ,T/(10*C); " errors/word"
2340       PRINT : PRINT "  Press SPACEBAR to continue"
2350       LET R$ = GET$() : IF R$ () " " THEN 2350
2360       PRINT : PRINT "Now try again" : GOTO 1780
2370 REM
2380    PRINT "Well done, "; N$; ", you made it."
2390    PRINT "Goodbye!"
2400    PRINT CHR$(19) : REM Re-enable paging
2410    END
2420 REM
2430 REM
2440    DATA BURGEON, DEPENDENT, HIRSUTE, PRESTIDIGITATION, QUINQUAGESIMA
2450    DATA INVOLUCRUM, BIPED, CASUISTRY, WYCH-HAZEL, PROCELEUSMATIC
```

Listing of SPELLF program code

```
1000 REM Program : SPELLF
1010 REM
1020 REM
1030    CLEAR 500
1040 REM
1050    ON BREAK GOTO 2000
1060 REM    Deal with user's interruption
1070 REM
1080 REM
1090    TEXT : PRINT CHR$(12) : REM Clear the screen
1100    PRINT CHR$(17) : REM Disable paging
1110 REM
1120 REM
1130    PRINT TAB(17); "SPELLF"
1140    PRINT
1150    PRINT TAB(11); "Spelling practice"
1160    PRINT : PRINT : PRINT
1170    PRINT TAB(19); "*"
1180    PRINT
1190    PRINT TAB(14); "Andrew Nash"
1200    PRINT
1210    PRINT TAB(15); "Derek Ball"
1220    PRINT
1230    PRINT TAB(19); "*"
1240    PRINT : PRINT : PRINT
1250    PRINT TAB(13); "Copyright 1982"
1260    PRINT
1270    PRINT TAB(10); "Hutchinson Education"
1280    PRINT
1290    FOR D = 1 TO 5000 : NEXT D : REM Delay
1300    PRINT CHR$(12) : REM Clear the screen
1310 REM
1320 REM
1330 REM * INSTRUCTIONS *
1340 REM
1350    PRINT "INSTRUCTIONS TO USER"
1360    PRINT "--------------------"
1370    PRINT
1380    PRINT "This program offers you practice in"
1390    PRINT "spelling certain words.   After the"
1400    PRINT "first pass through the list you will be"
1410    PRINT "offered several options and it will be"
1420    PRINT "left to you at all times to decide what"
1430    PRINT "to do next."
```

```
1440      PRINT
1450      PRINT "Please make sure you enter your words"
1460      PRINT "in CAPITAL letters."
1470      PRINT
1480      PRINT "Have fun"
1490      PRINT : PRINT
1500      PRINT "Press SPACEBAR to continue"
1510      LET R$ = GET$() : IF R$ () " " THEN 1510
1520      PRINT CHR$(12) : REM Clear the screen
1530 REM
1540 REM
1550 REM * SET UP WORD LIST, ETC *
1560 REM
1570      DIM W$(10,3)
1580      FOR W = 1 TO 10
1590         READ W$(W,1)
1600      NEXT W
1610 REM
1620 REM
1630 REM * FIRST PASS THROUGH LIST *
1640 REM
1650      LET O$ = "WL" : GOSUB 2060 : REM list all words
1660 REM
1670 REM
1680 REM
1690 REM
1700 REM * COMMAND OPTIONS *
1710 REM
1720      PRINT : PRINT
1730      PRINT "OPTIONS:"
1740      PRINT "  WL (whole list again)"
1750      PRINT "  CW (words spelled correctly)"
1760      PRINT "  IW (words spelled incorrectly)"
1770      PRINT "  DI (display incorrect words)"
1780      PRINT "  FI (finish)"
1790      PRINT "    Which option";
1800      INPUT O$
1810      PRINT CHR$(12) : REM Clear the screen
1820 REM
1830      IF O$ () "WL" THEN 1850
1840         GOSUB 2060 : GOTO 1720
1850      IF O$ () "CW" THEN 1890
1860         IF E = 10 THEN 1880
1870            GOSUB 2060 : GOTO 1720
1880         PRINT "No words spelled correctly!" : GOTO 1720
1890      IF O$ () "IW" THEN 1930
1900         IF E = 0 THEN 1920
1910            GOSUB 2060 : GOTO 1720
1920         PRINT "All words spelled correctly!" : GOTO 1720
1930      IF O$ () "DI" THEN 1970
1940         IF E = 0 THEN 1960
1950            GOSUB 2430 : GOTO 1720
1960         PRINT "All words spelled correctly!" : GOTO 1720
1970      IF O$ = "FI" THEN 1990
1980         PRINT "/";O$;"/ IS NOT AN OPTION  -  TRY AGAIN" : GOTO 1720
1990      PRINT "O.K. Goodbye"
2000      PRINT CHR$(19) : REM Re-enable paging
2010      END
2020 REM
2030 REM
2040 REM * SUBROUTINE TO TEST WORDS *
2050 REM
2060      IF O$ () "CW" THEN LET E=0 : REM Reset error count
2070 REM
2080      FOR W = 1 TO 10
2090 REM
```

```
2100      IF (O$ = "CW" AND W$(W,3) = "incorrect") THEN 2360
2110      IF (O$ = "IW" AND W$(W,3) = "correct") THEN 2360
2120 REM
2130      FOR I = 1 TO 5 : PRINT : NEXT I
2140      PRINT "WORD"; W; TAB(10); W$(W,1) : REM Display word
2150      FOR I = 1 TO 5 : PRINT : NEXT I
2160      PRINT "Press SPACEBAR to continue"
2170      LET R$ = GET$() : IF R$ () " " THEN 2170
2180 REM
2190 REM * ASK USER TO SPELL WORD *
2200 REM
2210      PRINT CHR$(12) : REM Clear the screen
2220      PRINT "Now you spell it"
2230      PRINT
2240      INPUT W$(W,2)
2250      PRINT
2260 REM
2270 REM * CHECK USER'S ATTEMPT *
2280 REM
2290      IF W$(W,2) () W$(W,1) THEN 2310
2300         LET W$(W,3) = "correct" : PRINT "Right" : GOTO 2330
2310      LET W$(W,3) = "incorrect" : PRINT "Wrong"
2320      LET E = E+1
2330      FOR D = 1 TO 2000 : NEXT D
2340      PRINT CHR$(12) : REM Clear the screen
2350 REM
2360      NEXT W
2370 REM
2380      RETURN
2390 REM
2400 REM
2410 REM * SUBROUTINE TO LIST WORDS SPELLED INCORRECTLY *
2420 REM
2430      PRINT : PRINT
2440      LET R$ = "CORRECT SPELLING" : GOSUB 2580 : REM Right-justify
2450      PRINT R$; "      YOUR SPELLING"
2460      PRINT
2470      FOR W = 1 TO 10
2480         IF W$(W,3) = "correct" THEN 2510
2490         LET R$ = W$(W,1) : GOSUB 2580 : REM Right-justify
2500         PRINT R$; "      "; W$(W,2)
2510      NEXT W
2520 REM
2530      RETURN
2540 REM
2550 REM
2560 REM * SUBROUTINE TO RIGHT-JUSTIFY TO COLUMN 18 *
2570 REM
2580      LET R$ = "                  "+R$
2590      LET R$ = RIGHT$(R$,18)
2600 REM
2610      RETURN
2620 REM
2630      DATA BURGEON, DEPENDENT, HIRSUTE, PRESTIDIGITATION, QUINQUAGESIM
2640      DATA INVOLUCELLUM, BIPED, CASUISTRY, WYCH-HAZEL, PROCELEUSMATIC
```

Sample output

```
WELL DONE, Derek!


O.K., Derek, here's your score
 ** BURGEON            WRONG 3   TIMES!
 ** DEPENDENT          WRONG 2   TIMES!
 ** HIRSUTE            WRONG 1   TIMES!
    PRESTIDIGITATION   Excellent!
    QUINQUAGESIMA,     Excellent!
    INVOLUCELLUM       Excellent!
 ** BIPED              WRONG 7   TIMES!
    CASUISTRY          Excellent!
 ** WYCH-HAZEL         WRONG 1   TIMES!
 ** PROCELEUSMATIC     WRONG 1   TIMES!

You made a total of 15 ERRORS that time
Average that cycle = 1.5 errors/word
Average this run  = 1.5 errors/word

   Press SPACEBAR to continue
■
```

```
OPTIONS
   WL (whole list again)
   CW (words spelled correctly)
   IW (words spelled incorrectly)
   DI (display incorrect words)
   FI (finish)
     Which option? ■
```

Discussion

What to notice: We are trying to convince you that, for a program of this type, the freer approach is vastly better than the constrained one. We are doing this by our choice of language ('free' and 'constrained', for example) and by the attitude adopted to the user of SPELLC, which is patronizing in the extreme (we hope). While both programs provide practice in accomplishing a straightforward task, there seems to us every reason for adopting an approach in which the user is free to choose what is for him the best route to memorizing spellings, rather than one in which he is constrained to follow that exact pattern deemed most appropriate by the teacher or programmer.

This is a rare occasion in the book when we consciously try to persuade you to one point of view rather than another, and so it is only fair to say that programs which retain tight control of the learning sequence do have their uses. To us, however, there seems to be no justification for the condescension typified by the language used in the SPELLC messages – *even* (or as we would say, *'especially'*) when the program is for use with younger children.

Note the assumptions made in the design of SPELLC: it is for the teacher, it is to be used by a child, words are displayed for a set time (irrespective of their length or complexity) and so on. Compare the attitudes shown by SPELLF, where everything is placed at the user's disposal. This includes the invitation to quit at any time: contrast that with the user of SPELLC, who must sit there going through the ten words until *every single one* is spelt right in one cycle. Having got number two wrong, he knows immediately that the rest of the list will be right in vain: he will still have to start from the top!

Note that one of the options in SPELLF is that of repeating only the words which were spelt *correctly*. If that strikes you as eccentric, consider the psychological value of this option to someone who keeps getting the same couple of words wrong: he can, in effect, go through a list of his own choosing and be able to get every one right.

Note that in SPELLF the user may look at each word for as long as he wishes before trying to spell it. He will know best how long he requires, especially with very complicated or unfamiliar words.

Note the kind of language used in the SPELLC messages, and note the use of capitals particularly. Compare 'Excellent!' with 'WRONG', for example. This version is *not* just a cynical parody; commercial programs have been produced in this style.

An interesting question concerns the use in SPELLC, but not in SPELLF, of the user's name. Having decided to keep SPELLF on an impersonal basis, it was natural to leave this bit out; yet we do not feel that the use of the user's name is of itself a good or a bad thing: it can be either. Some people find that being addressed by name throughout the course of a program is reassuring. On the other hand, people who are new to a particular program and who are asked for their name do not know the purpose of the question. Most probably, they suppose, records are being kept of their responses, so they had better be careful. This can have an inhibiting effect rather than an encouraging one, and they tend to reply in a form such as 'J. Bloggs' instead of 'Joe'. Thereafter, when they discover what the name is actually used for, they are forever being addressed as 'J. Bloggs'; and they still do not know that no records are being kept!

Finally, consider the statistics issued by SPELLC. Computers are incomparably efficient in the production of statistics. Do they really serve a purpose? As a user who kept getting the words wrong, would you find the statistics helpful or distressing?

In our view, as expressed on page 27, SPELLC represents a means of testing students, while SPELLF is perhaps a means of teaching them.

Program code: The code is very straightforward in both versions. Note the use in SPELLC of the variables 'C', 'T' and 'E9': 'C' records the current cycle number (used in calculating the average error rate); 'E9' records the number of errors made in any one cycle, and 'T' records the total number of errors.

In SPELLF, note the use of the space-bar delay: just two lines of code which we have used many times in the programs in this book, yet which make a disproportionate difference to the user in handing the control to him.

The last subroutine in SPELLF is a neat way of handling the right-justification on the screen of text whose length is unknown. The text is displayed in eighteen character positions: instead of counting the number of characters actually provided, the string variable 'R$' is preset to be eighteen spaces, the text is added to the right of these spaces, and the right-hand eighteen characters are printed. (A similar technique is used in SCALES, in section 8.1.)

Note that even at the level of the comments *within* the program, the attitude to the user in SPELLC is patronizing – see the first 'REM' statement.

Error-checking: SPELLC has only two kinds of input, the user's name and the attempted spellings of words. The user's name is unknown, so it cannot really be checked (though one could ensure at least that it comprised only letters). The spellings are, of course, the purpose of the program and so are subject to a particular form of checking.

SPELLF additionally allows the user to select an option, and this too is checked. If the input does not correspond to a valid selection, the user is simply invited to try again.

What you could do: You could change the words – those provided may not always be suitable!

For SPELLC, you could check that the entry corresponding to the user's name is alphabetic.

For SPELLF, you could allow the user to enter text – options or attempted spellings – in upper or lower case: at the moment, text issued correctly in lower or mixed case would nevertheless fail. You could allow the user to select how many words he is to be asked. You could allow him to retry words immediately,

240 *Case studies in teaching*

or to indicate which words he wishes to retry. You could, as a slightly more demanding exercise, pick the words to be asked from a longer list; selection being made by order of difficulty or at random. Note that you will have to record which words were asked, so that the user can go back to them.

Portability: With the exception of the groups of commands used at the beginning of the program and at the end, these programs should offer no difficulties at all on any micro.

Uses in teaching: These programs may or may not be useful to people with spelling difficulties. To you, however, they might be useful in comparing the differing approaches: try the two versions with two groups of students learning the same words, and see which group looks the happier at the end.

8.5 GRAPH: an illustration

The aim of this section is to provide an example of a program which demonstrates the power of the computer and is of considerable use in a variety of situations.

GRAPH is designed to be a tool. Like all tools, it has many uses, all concerned in some way with drawing on a screen the graphs of mathematical functions. The program's aims are:
* to provide teachers with the means of displaying graphs of their choice, either one at a time or several at once;
* to provide students with the opportunity of improving their ability to draw, to sketch or to identify graphs;
* to leave with the user as much freedom as possible in deciding how to use the program and in specifying what he wants;
* to be easy to use, so that the minimum of effort is required to obtain desired outcomes;
* to be coded as clearly as possible, so that adaptation to different micros, although it may not be easy, is at least as straightforward as it can be.

Specification

The program will require high-resolution graphics. The computer will draw graphs of mathematical functions such as '$y = 3x$', '$y = \sin x$' or '$y = x^2 + \tan 2x - \log x$'. The computer's task will be to do the necessary calculations and then to draw the graph. The user will be offered the greatest possible freedom in specifying what he wants. He will be free:
* to graph one function or several;
* to define the functions to be graphed or to ask the computer to choose a function at random;
* to choose the range of x-values;

* to choose the range of y-values, to leave it to the computer to choose a suitable range, or to specify that the scales on the two axes are to be equal;
* to add the graph of an extra function to a picture which has already been drawn;
* to have the graphs labelled or unlabelled;
* to change any of the individual factors in the situation – x-range, y-range, plotting density or labelling – without having to respecify the whole situation;
* to experiment with any of the commands as soon as the program has started, default values having been given to all parameters and variables.

In meeting the criteria above, it is essential that the program will be operated in command mode. The structure of the program will therefore be simple as far as the user is concerned, and this simplicity is reflected in the outline flowchart.

Outline flowchart of GRAPH

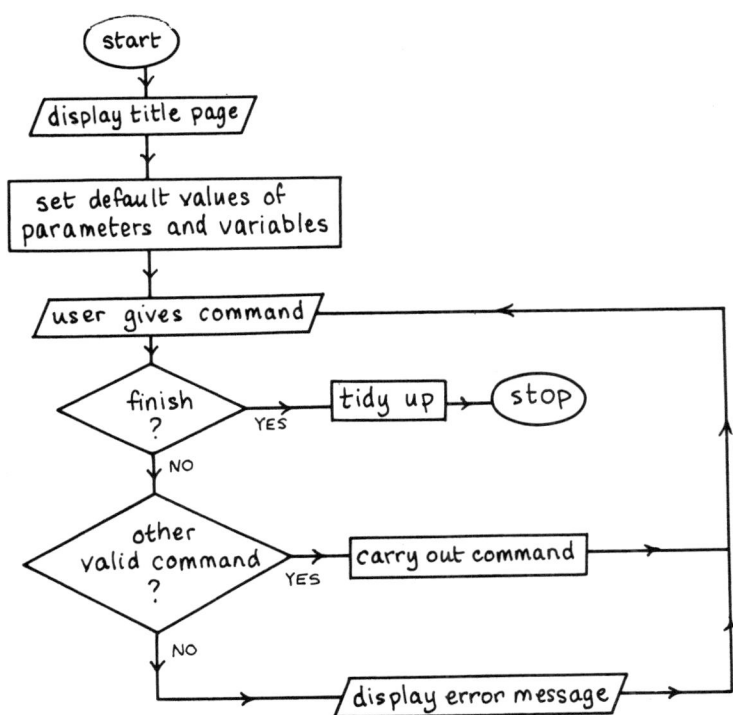

Listing of GRAPH program code

```
1000 REM Program : GRAPH
1010 REM
1020    CLEAR 300,,0
1030    GOSUB 5850 : REM Clear screen
1040    ON BREAK GOTO 1910
1050 REM Tidies screen and storage if program interrupted
1060    ON ERROR GOTO 5950
1070 REM Protects against bad function or bad value
1080    PRINT CHR$(17) : REM Disable paging
1090    PRINT TAB(17); "GRAPH"
1100    PRINT
1110    PRINT TAB(9); "Graph-drawing program"
1120    PRINT : PRINT : PRINT
1130    PRINT TAB(19); "*"
1140    PRINT
1150    PRINT TAB(15); "Derek Ball"
1160    PRINT
1170    PRINT TAB(14); "Andrew Nash"
1180    PRINT
1190    PRINT TAB(19); "*"
1200    PRINT : PRINT : PRINT
1210    PRINT TAB(13); "Copyright 1981"
1220    PRINT
1230    PRINT TAB(9); "Hutchinson Education"
1240    PRINT
1250 REM
1260 REM PRELIMINARIES
1270 REM
1280 REM Define storage
1290    DIM PT(3),F$(3),CM$(16),P$(3),X(16),Y(16),C(14),C$(14)
1300 REM Ensure a tidy run
1310 REM Find location of lines in core memory to be PEEKed or POKEd
1320    PT=PEEK(&118)+256*PEEK(&119) : REM &118 is address of BBUFV
1330    FOR I = 0 TO 3
1340       IF I=0 THEN LM=1460 ELSE LM=2000+10*I
1350       PT=PEEK(PT)+256*PEEK(PT+1)
1360       LN=PEEK(PT+2)+256*PEEK(PT+3)
1370       IF LN<>LM THEN 1350
1380       PT(I)=PT+3
1390       PT(I)=PT(I)+1
1400       C=PEEK(PT(I))
1410       IF I=0 AND C=ASC(" ") THEN 1390
1420       IF I>0 AND C<>ASC(":") THEN 1390
1430    NEXT I
1440 REM Load information to convert user's function to internal format
1450    GOTO 1470
1460    + - * / ^ SGN INT ABS SQR LOG EXP COS SIN TAN ATN
1470    FOR I = 0 TO 14
1480       C(I)=PEEK(PT(0)+2*I) : READ C$(I)
1490    NEXT I
1500    DATA  +,-,*,/,^,SGN,INT,ABS,SQR,LOG,EXP,COS,SIN,TAN,ATN
1510 REM Set option defaults
1520    F5=1 : F5$="not equal" : S5$="no surprise" : Y5$="computer"
1530    L5$="displayed" : X1=-5 : X2=5 : G$="off" : ST=1
1540    F$(1)="COS X" : F$(2)="SIN 2X" : F$(3)="(X+2)(X-1)"
1550    F1$="SINX"
1560 REM Read in commands
1570    L=16
1580    FOR I=1 TO L : READ CM$(I) : NEXT I
1590    DATA FINISH,LABEL,SUPPRESS,EQUAL,NOTEQUAL
1600    DATA XRANGE,YRANGE,DRAW,DEFINE,ADD,REDRAW
```

GRAPH: an illustration 243

```
1610    DATA SURPRISE,COMMANDS,TUTORIAL,MOREPOINTS,POINTSSTANDARD
1620 REM Read in locations for commands display
1630    FOR I = 1 TO L : READ X(I), Y(I) : NEXT I
1640    DATA 4,45,4,39,4,36,4,30,4,27,28,45,28,42,28,36,28,33
1650    DATA 28,30,28,27,48,45,48,39,48,36,48,30,48,27
1660 REM
1670 REM MAIN PROGRAM
1680 REM
1690    GOSUB 5850 : REM Clear screen
1700    PRINT "Type in a command"
1710    PRINT "For help, type TUTORIAL"
1720    PRINT "For a list of commands, type COMMANDS"
1730    GOSUB 3030 : REM Get a command
1740    IF CM$="FIN" THEN 1910
1750    IF CM$="LAB" THEN L5$="displayed"
1760    IF CM$="SUP" THEN L5$="suppressed"
1770    IF CM$="EQU" THEN E5$="equal"
1780    IF CM$="NOT" THEN E5$="not equal"
1790    IF CM$="XRA" THEN GOSUB 2390
1800    IF CM$="YRA" THEN GOSUB 2440
1810    IF CM$="DRA" THEN GOSUB 2050
1820    IF CM$="DEF" THEN GOSUB 2120
1830    IF CM$="ADD" THEN GOSUB 2220
1840    IF CM$="RED" THEN GOSUB 2310
1850    IF CM$="SUR" THEN GOSUB 2500
1860    IF CM$="COM" THEN GOSUB 2910
1870    IF CM$="TUT" THEN GOSUB 2770
1880    IF CM$="MOR" THEN ST=ST/2
1890    IF CM$="POI" THEN ST=1
1900    GOTO 1730
1910 REM ** FINISH
1920 REM
1930    GOSUB 5850 : REM Clear screen
1940    PRINT CHR$(19) : REM Re-enable paging
1950    CLEAR 100
1960    END
1970 REM
1980 REM * SUBROUTINES *
1990 REM
2000 REM ** INSPECT FUNCTIONS
2010    DEF FNA(X)=COS(X)                      : REM
2020    DEF FNB(X)=SIN(2*X)                    : REM
2030    DEF FNC(X)=(X+2)*(X-1)                 : REM
2040    RETURN
2050 REM ** DRAW
2060    GOSUB 2000 : REM Inspect functions
2070    IF PF=1 AND NF=1 THEN N=VAL(P$(1)) : IF N=1 OR N=2 OR N=3
                                                     THEN F5=N
2080    GOSUB 4190 : REM Plot axes
2090    IF UN=1 THEN 2110
2100    GOSUB 5020 : REM Plot graph
2110    RETURN
2120 REM ** DEFINE
2130    G$="off"
2140    IF PF=1 AND NF=1 THEN N=VAL(P$(1)) : IF N=1 OR N=2 OR N=3
                                                     THEN F5=N
2150    PF=0
2160    G$="off" : S5$="no surprise"
2170    FOR F=1 TO F5
2180       GOSUB 3560 : REM Choose function
2190    NEXT F
2200    GOSUB 5850 : GRAPH : REM Clear the screen
2210    RETURN
2220 REM ** ADD
2230    IF G$="off" THEN PRINT "SORRY! NO GRAPH TO ADD TO" : GOTO 2300
2240    L5$="displayed"
2250    IF F5<3 THEN F5=F5+1
```

```
2260      F=F5
2270      IF PF=1 THEN F$=P$(1)
2280      GOSUB 3560 : REM Choose function
2290      GOSUB 5020 : REM Plot graph
2300      RETURN
2310 REM ** REDRAW
2320      IF G$="off" THEN PRINT "SORRY! NO GRAPH TO REDRAW" : GOTO 2380
2330      Y1=Y3:Y2=Y4
2340      Y5$="computer"
2350      GOSUB 4190 : REM PLOT AXES
2360      IF UN=1 THEN 2380
2370      GOSUB 5020 : REM Plot graph
2380      RETURN
2390 REM ** XRANGE
2400      Z$="X"
2410      GOSUB 3310 : REM Choose axis range
2420      X1=Z1 : X2=Z2
2430      RETURN
2440 REM ** YRANGE
2450      Z$="Y" : Y5$="user"
2460      IF P$(1)="COMP" THEN Y5$="computer" : GOTO 2490
2470      GOSUB 3310 : REM Choose axis range
2480      Y1=Z1:Y2=Z2
2490      RETURN
2500 REM ** SURPRISE
2510      PRINT "COMPUTER CHOOSES SURPRISE FUNCTION"
2520      G$="off" : S5$="surprise" : F5=1
2530      PRINT
2540      PRINT "  How difficult?";
2550      PRINT "  Choose 1-4 (easy to"
2560      PRINT "     difficult)";
2570      INPUT LINE I$
2580      C=INT(VAL(I$))
2590      IF C<1 OR C>4 THEN 2550
2600      RANDOMIZE
2610         IF C=1 THEN H=1
2620         IF C=2 THEN H=1
2630         IF C=3 THEN H=2
2640         IF C=4 THEN H=4
2650      IF C>1 THEN H=H+INT(2*RND(1))
2660      D9=INT(RND(1)*6)+1
2670      SG=SGN(RND(1)-0.5)
2680      D9=D9*SG
2690      A9=INT(3*RND(1))+1
2700      A9=A9*SG
2710      Q9=INT(RND(1)*3)
2720      IF Q9=0 THEN B9=A9 ELSE B9=INT(9*RND(1))-4
2730      Q9=INT(RND(1)*3)
2740      IF Q9=0 THEN C9=B9 ELSE C9=INT(9*RND(1))-4
2750      GOSUB 5850 : GRAPH : REM Clear the screen
2760      RETURN
2770 REM ** TUTORIAL
2780      I5$="displayed"
2790      E5$="not equal"
2800      GOSUB 5850 : REM Clear screen
2810      PRINT "First choose the function you want the"
2820      PRINT "computer to graph."
2830      PRINT
2840      PF=0 : F5=1 : GOSUB 2120 : REM Define
2850      GOSUB 2390 : REM Xrange
2860      GOSUB 2440 : REM Yrange
2870      GOSUB 2050 : REM Draw
2880      PRINT "Now try using the other commands,"
2890      PRINT "or else type TUTORIAL again"
2900      RETURN
```

```
2910 REM ** COMMANDS
2920    GOSUB 5850 : REM Clear screen
2930    G$="off"
2940    PLOT 0,54, "Available commands are:"
2950    PLOT 0,51, "========================"
2960    FOR I=1 TO L
2970       PLOT X(I),Y(I),CM$(I)
2980    NEXT I
2990    PLOT 0,15, "Only the first three letters of command"
3000    PLOT 0,12, "   need be typed"
3010    PRINT
3020    RETURN
3030 REM ** INPUT COMMAND
3040 REM Input command and split into parts
3050    PF=0
3060    PRINT ":";
3070    I5$="show" : GOSUB 5680 : REM Input a string
3080    IF I$="" THEN 3070
3090    IF LEFT$(I$,1)=" " THEN I$=MID$(I$,2) : GOTO 3090
3100    I1$=I$:I$=""
3110    FOR I=1 TO LEN(I1$)
3120       IF MID$(I1$,I,1)<>" " AND MID$(I1$,I,1)<>"," THEN 3140
3130       I$=MID$(I1$,I+1) : I1$=LEFT$(I1$,I-1)
3140    NEXT I
3150    P$(PF)=I1$
3160    IF I$<>"" AND P<3 THEN PF=PF+1 : GOTO 3090
3170    CM$=P$(0) : NF=1
3180 REM Determine whether parameters are numbers
3190    IF PF=0 THEN 3250
3200    FOR I=1 TO PF
3210       IF P$(I)="0" THEN 3230
3220       IF VAL(P$(I))=0 THEN NF=0
3230    NEXT I
3240 REM Check command
3250    CM=0
3260    FOR I=1 TO L
3270       IF LEFT$(CM$,3)=LEFT$(CM$(I),3) THEN CM=I : CM$=LEFT$(CM$(I),3) : I=L
3280    NEXT I
3290    IF CM=0 THEN PRINT CM$;" not recognised" : GOTO 3050
3300    RETURN
3310 REM ** CHOOSE AXIS RANGE
3320    PRINT CHR$(12) : REM Clear bottom of screen
3330    IF PF<>2 OR NF=0 THEN 3360
3340    Z1=VAL(P$(1)):Z2=VAL(P$(2))
3350    GOTO 3500
3360    PRINT "RANGE OF VALUES FOR ";Z$;"-AXIS"
3370    IF Z$="X" THEN 3430
3380    PRINT "  Do you want Y-range chosen by"
3390    PRINT "  the computer (Y/N)?";
3400    GOSUB 5800 : REM Answer yes or no
3410    IF C=89 THEN Y5$="computer" : GOTO 3550
3420    PRINT "    OK"
3430    PRINT " Least ";Z$;"? ";
3440    GOSUB 5470 : REM Input a number
3450    Z1=N
3460    PRINT "Greatest ";Z$;"? ";
3470    GOSUB 5470 : REM Input a number
3480    Z2=N
3490    PRINT
3500    IF Z2>Z1 THEN 3540
3510    PRINT Z2;"IS NOT GREATER THAN";Z1
3520    PRINT "  TRY AGAIN"
3530    GOTO 3430
3540    PRINT CHR$(12) : REM Clear bottom of screen
3550    RETURN
```

```
3560 REM ** CHOOSE FUNCTION
3570   IF PF=1 AND CM$="ADD" THEN 3640
3580   PRINT "Function";
3590   IF CM$<>"ADD" AND F5>1 THEN PRINT F;
3600   PRINT "?   Y=";
3610   IF L5$="displayed" THEN I5$="show" ELSE I5$="hide"
3620   GOSUB 5680 : REM Input a string
3630   F$=I$
3640   F$(F)=F$
3650 REM CONVERT FUNCTION TO INTERNAL FORMAT
3660   FO$=""
3670   FOR I = 1 TO LEN(F$)
3680     C$=MID$(F$,I,1)
3690     IF C$="a" AND C$<="z" THEN C$=CHR$(ASC(C$)-32)
3700     IF C$<>" " THEN FO$=FO$+C$
3710   NEXT I
3720   F1$=""
3730   FOR I = 1 TO LEN(FO$)
3740     C$=MID$(FO$,I,1)
3750     IF C$="X" OR C$<("A" OR C$)"Z" THEN 3770
3760     C$=MID$(FO$,I,3) : I=I+2
3770     FOR J = 0 TO 14
3780       IF C$=C$(J) THEN C$=CHR$(C(J))
3790     NEXT J
3800     F1$=F1$+C$
3810   NEXT I
3820   F1$=LEFT$(F1$+"                    ",20)
3830 REM Convert algebra supplied into computer algebra
3840   I=0
3850   FOR J=2 TO 20
3860     C1$=MID$(F1$,J-1,1):C2$=MID$(F1$,J,1)
3870     IF (C1$)="A" AND C1$("X") OR C1$="=" THEN ERROR 3
3880     IF ASC(C1$))C(4) AND C2$<>"(" THEN I=J : J=20
3890   NEXT J
3900   IF I=0 THEN 4000
3910   F1$=LEFT$(F1$,I-1)+"("+MID$(F1$,I)
3920   I=I+1
3930   I=I+1
3940   C2$=MID$(F1$,I,1)
3950   IF I>18 THEN 3980
3960   IF C2$="0" AND C2$<="9" THEN 3930
3970   IF C2$="X" OR ASC(C2$)=C(4) OR C2$="." THEN 3930
3980   F1$=LEFT$(F1$,I-1)+")"+MID$(F1$,I)
3990   GOTO 3840
4000   I=0
4010   FOR J=2 TO 20
4020     C1$=MID$(F1$,J-1,1):C2$=MID$(F1$,J,1)
4030     IF C1$=")" AND (C2$="(" OR ASC(C2$)<C(4)) THEN I=J
4040     IF C1$="X" AND (C2$="(" OR C2$="X" OR ASC(C2$))C(4)) THEN I=J
4050     IF C1$<"0" OR C1$>"9" THEN 4070
4060     IF C2$="X" OR C2$="(" OR ASC(C2$))C(4) THEN I=J
4070     IF I=J THEN J=20
4080   NEXT J
4090   IF I>0 THEN F1$=LEFT$(F1$,I-1)+CHR$(C(2))+MID$(F1$,I) : GOTO 4000
4100   IF MID$(F1$,20,1)<>" " THEN PRINT "TOO LONG":GOTO 3580
4110   PT=PT(F)
4120   FOR I=1 TO 20
4130     C=ASC(MID$(F1$,I,1))
4140     POKE PT+I,C
4150   NEXT I
4160   GOSUB 2000 : REM Inspect functions
4170   GOSUB 5240 : REM Evaluate functions
4180   RETURN
4190 REM ** PLOT AXES
4200   LIN=0
```

```
4210    IF Y5$="user" OR CM$="RED" THEN 4240
4220    GOSUB 4760 : REM Computer choose Y-range
4230    IF Y1>Y2 THEN PRINT "FUNCTION UNDEFINED FOR WHOLE RANGE":UN=1:┐
                                                              └GOTO 4750
4240    SX=300/(X2-X1)
4250    IF Y1=Y2 THEN Y2=Y1+160/SX:Y1=Y1-160/SX
4260    SY=160/(Y2-Y1)
4270    RX=1:RY=1
4280    IF I5$="not equal" THEN 4310
4290    IF SY<SX THEN RX=SX/SY:SX=SY
4300    IF SX<SY THEN RY=SY/SX:SY=SX
4310    Z1=X1:Z2=X2:RZ=RX
4320    GOSUB 4870 : REM Find mark intervals for axes
4330    IX=IZ
4340    Z1=Y1:Z2=Y2:RZ=RY
4350    GOSUB 4870 : REM Find mark intervals for axes
4360    IY=IZ
4370    X0=(-300*X1)/(X2-X1)/RX+10
4380    Y0=(-160*Y1)/(Y2-Y1)/RY+15
4390    GOSUB 5850 : GRAPH : REM Clear screen
4400    IF X0<0 OR X0>319 THEN 4430
4410    CALL"PLOT",X0,0,1
4420    CALL"LINE",X0,200
4430    IF Y0<0 OR Y0>191 THEN 4460
4440    CALL"PLOT",0,Y0,1
4450    CALL"LINE",320,Y0,1
4460    XP=X0-1 : YP=Y0-5 : S$="0" : DX=1
4470    GOSUB 5390 : REM Plot labels
4480    FOR Y=INT(Y1/IY)*IY TO Y2+IY STEP IY
4490       IF ABS(Y)<(Y2-Y1)/100 THEN 4580
4500       YP=Y0+SY*Y
4510       IF X0<0 OR X0>319 THEN 4530
4520       CALL"PLOT",X0-1,YP,2
4530       S$=STR$(Y)
4540       DX=LEN(S$)
4550       XP=X0-1
4560       IF (XP-8*DX<0 OR X0>319) THEN XP=8*DX
4570       GOSUB 5390 : REM Plot labels
4580    NEXT Y
4590    FOR X=INT(X1/IX)*IX TO X2+IX STEP IX
4600       IF ABS(X)<(X2-X1)/100 THEN 4720
4610       XP=X0+SX*X
4620       IF Y0<0 OR Y0>191 THEN 4640
4630       CALL"PLOT",XP,Y0-1,2
4640       S$=STR$(X)
4650       DX=LEN(S$)
4660       IF X>0 THEN DX=DX-1
4670       S$=RIGHT$(S$,DX)
4680       DX=DX/2
4690       YP=Y0-5
4700       IF (YP<0 OR Y0>191) THEN YP=0
4710       GOSUB 5390 : REM Plot labels
4720    NEXT X
4730    IF X0<0 OR X0>319 THEN 4750
4740    IF Y0<2 OR Y0>191 THEN PLOT X0/4,0,ASC("0")
4750    RETURN
4760 REM ** COMPUTER CHOOSE Y-RANGE
4770    Y1=1E34 : Y2=-1E34
4780    FOR F=1 TO F5
4790       FOR X=X1 TO X2 STEP (X2-X1)/20
4800          GOSUB 5240 : REM Evaluate function
4810          IF NV=1 THEN 4840
4820          IF Y>Y2 THEN Y2=Y
4830          IF Y<Y1 THEN Y1=Y
4840       NEXT X
4850    NEXT F
```

```
4860    RETURN
4870 REM ** FIND MARK INTERVALS FOR AXES
4880    IZ=10000000 : J=(Z2-Z1)/5*RZ
4890    GRAPH
4900    IF J>IZ THEN 4930
4910    IZ=IZ/10
4920    GOTO 4900
4930    K=J/IZ
4940      IF K<1.25 THEN K=1
4950      IF K>=1.25 AND K<2.2 THEN K=2
4960      IF K>=2.2 AND K<3 THEN K=2.5
4970      IF K>=3 AND K<4.5 THEN K=4
4980      IF K>=4.5 AND K<7 THEN K=5
4990      IF K>=7 THEN K=10
5000    IZ=IZ*K
5010    RETURN
5020 REM ** PLOT GRAPH
5030    Y3=1E34 : Y4=-1E34
5040    PRINT CHR$(12) : REM Clear screen
5050    G$="on"
5060    FOR F=1 TO F5
5070      IF CM$="ADD" AND F<F5 THEN 5220
5080      IF S5$="surprise" AND F=1 THEN 5100
5090      IF L5$="displayed" THEN PRINT "Y=";F$(F)
5100      FOR XP=X0+SX*X1 TO X0+SX*X2 STEP ST
5110        C=GET(0)
5120        IF C=32 THEN XP=X0+SX*X2 : GOTO 5210
5130        X=(XP-X0)/SX
5140        GOSUB 5240 : REM Evaluate function
5150        IF NV=1 THEN 5210
5160        YP=Y0+Y*SY
5170        IF YP<0 OR YP>200 THEN 5190
5180        CALL "PLOT",XP,YP,B
5190        IF Y<Y3 THEN Y3=Y
5200        IF Y>Y4 THEN Y4=Y
5210      NEXT XP
5220    NEXT F
5230    RETURN
5240 REM ** EVALUATE FUNCTION
5250    NV=0
5260    IF S5$="no surprise" OR F>1 THEN 5340
5270      B=1
5280      IF H=1 THEN Y=D9*X/2+C9
5290      IF H=2 THEN Y=D9*(X-A9)*(X-B9)
5300      IF H=3 THEN Y=D9*(X-A9)*(X-B9)*(X-C9)
5310      IF H=4 THEN Y=D9*COS(X-A9)+C9
5320      IF H=5 THEN Y=D9*ATN(X-A9)+C9
5330    GOTO 5380
5340    IF L5$="suppressed" THEN B=2 ELSE B=3
5350    IF F=1 THEN Y=FNA(X)
5360    IF F=2 THEN Y=FNB(X)
5370    IF F=3 THEN Y=FNC(X)
5380    RETURN
5390 REM ** PLOT LABELS
5400    XQ=XP/4-2*DX:YQ=YP*29/96+2
5410    IF XQ<0 OR XQ+2*LEN(S$)>79 THEN 5460
5420    IF YQ<0 OR YQ>59 THEN 5460
5430    FOR J=1 TO LEN(S$)
5440      PLOT XQ+2*J,YQ,ASC(MID$(S$,J,1))
5450    NEXT J
5460    RETURN
5470 REM ** INPUT A NUMBER
5480    C1=1 : DP=0 : S$=""
5490    GOSUB 5910 : REM Get character
5500    L1=LEN(S$)
```

```
5510      IF C<127 THEN 5560
5520      IF L1=0 THEN 5490
5530      IF RIGHT$(S$,1)="." THEN DP=0
5540      PRINT CHR$(127);
5550      S$=LEFT$(S$,L1-1)
5560      IF C>47 AND C<58 THEN 5610
5570      IF L1=0 AND (C=43 OR C=45) THEN 5610
5580      IF DP=0 AND C=46 THEN DP=1:GOTO 5610
5590      IF C=13 AND L1>0 THEN 5650
5600      GOTO 5490
5610      C1=0
5620      S$=S$+CHR$(C)
5630      PRINT CHR$(C);
5640      GOTO 5490
5650      N=VAL(S$)
5660      PRINT " ";
5670      RETURN
5680 REM ** INPUT A STRING
5690      I$=""
5700      GOSUB 5910 : REM Get character
5710      IF C<32 THEN PRINT : GOTO 5790
5720      IF C<127 THEN 5750
5730         IF I$<>"" THEN PRINT CHR$(127); : I$=LEFT$(I$,LEN(I$)-1)
5740         GOTO 5700
5750      C$=CHR$(C)
5760      IF I5$="show" THEN PRINT C$; ELSE PRINT "*";
5770      I$=I$+C$
5780      GOTO 5700
5790      RETURN
5800 REM ** ANSWER YES OR NO
5810      GOSUB 5910 : REM Get character
5820      IF C<>78 AND C<>89 THEN GOTO 5810
5830      IF C=78 THEN PRINT "NO" ELSE PRINT "YES"
5840      RETURN
5850 REM ** CLEAR SCREEN
5860      TEXT
5870      G$="off"
5880      PRINT CHR$(12)
5890      CALL"RESOLUTION",0,2
5900      RETURN
5910 REM ** GET CHARACTER
5920      C=GET()
5930      IF C>96 AND C<123 THEN C=C-32
5940      RETURN
5950 REM ** ERROR HANDLING
5960      ON ERROR GOTO 5950
5970      IF ERR >3 THEN NV=1 : GOTO 5380
5980      PRINT "FUNCTION NOT RECOGNISED"
5990      PRINT "TRY AGAIN"
6000      GOTO 3560
```

250 Case studies in teaching

Sample output

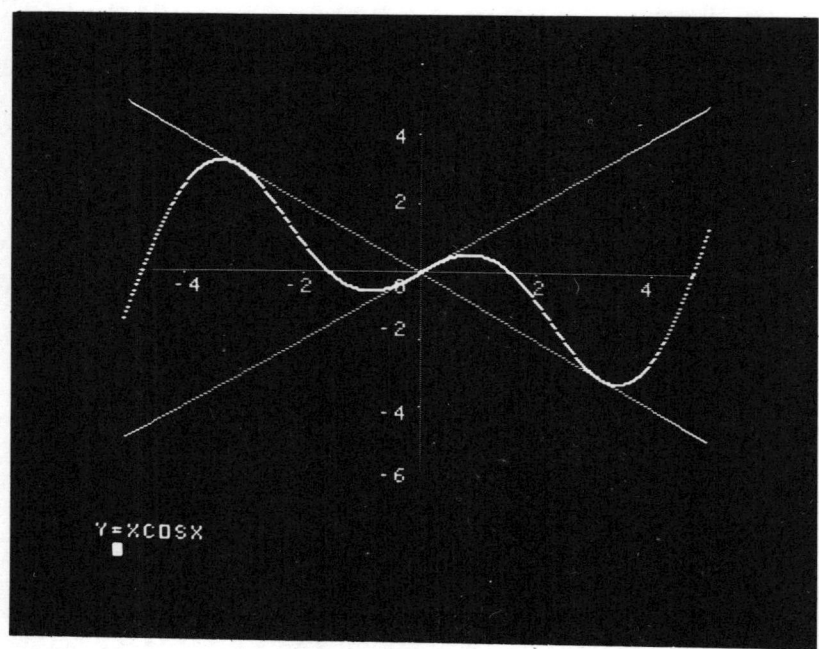

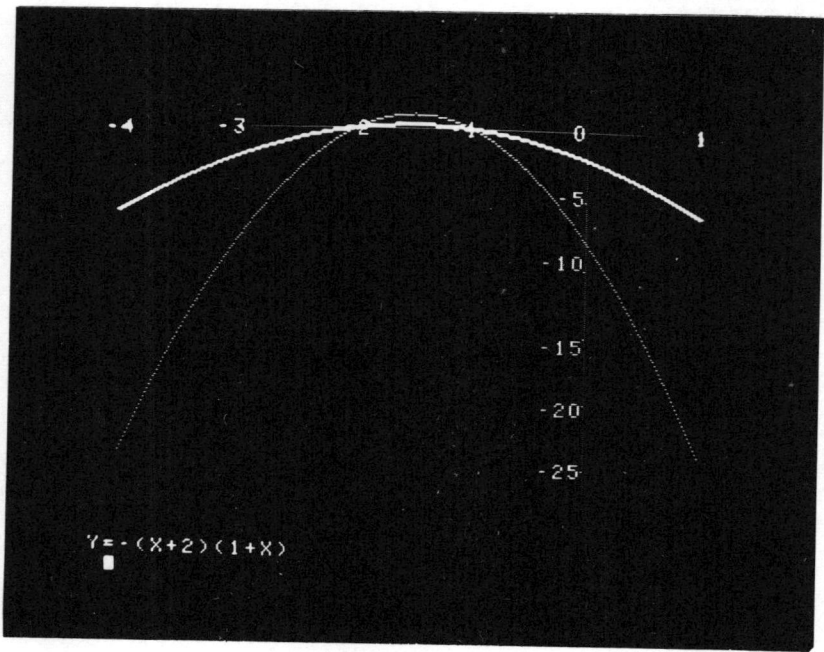

GRAPH: an illustration 251

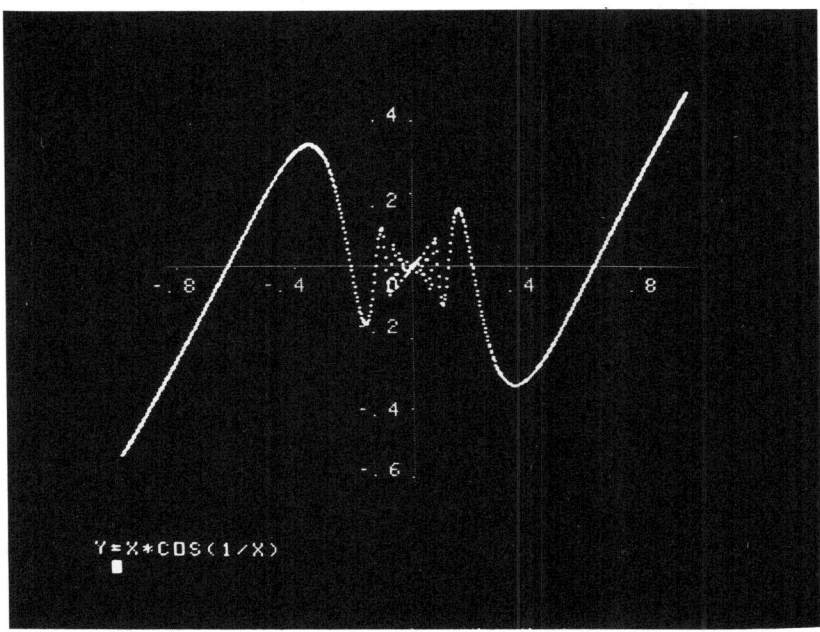

Discussion

Commands: Within the program itself, commands are listed but not described; the program is large and there is a consequent shortage of space. Each command may be issued by typing the first three letters of its name. Notes about the commands are given here, and we recommend that you read them before using the program.
* COMMANDS The computer lists the commands that are available.
* FINISH This ends the program.
* LABEL When the user defines functions, what he types is displayed on the screen. When the computer draws graphs, the graphs are labelled. By default, 'LABEL' is set. The converse is 'SUPPRESS'.
* SUPPRESS When the user defines functions, what he types is echoed on the screen by asterisks so that the actual text is not visible. When the computer draws graphs, these are not labelled. The converse is 'LABEL'.
* EQUAL When graphs are drawn, the scales on the two axes are made equal. The converse is 'NOTEQUAL'.
* NOTEQUAL When graphs are drawn, the scales on the two axes are not adjusted so that they are equal. By default, 'NOTEQUAL' is set. The converse is 'EQUAL'.
* XRANGE The user chooses the range of x-values required for the graph. By default, the range is set as -5 to $+5$. To vary this, the user

may type 'XRA' and then supply the values in answer to the questions that follow; or he may simply type the command and values together (e.g. 'XRA –34'), which saves time.

* YRANGE The user chooses the range of y-values required for the graph, or asks the computer to make the choice for him. By default, the computer makes the choice. To specify the values, the user may type 'YRA' and supply the values in answer to the questions that follow; or he may simply type the command and values together (e.g. 'YRA -17'), which saves time. To return the choice to the computer, the user may type 'YRA COMP'.

* DRAW The computer draws the graph or graphs of the function or functions defined. Predefined functions – namely, cos x, sin $2x$ and $(x+2)(x-1)$ – are available at the beginning of the program, so 'DRAW' *may* be used as the first command. The user specifies how many graphs are to be drawn, by typing 'DRA1', 'DRA2' or 'DRA3'. If the number is omitted ('DRA'), it remains unchanged. By default, the number of functions drawn is 1. If the space-bar on the keyboard is pressed while a graph is being drawn, the computer abandons its drawing of the present function and either moves on to the next function, if there is one, or awaits the next command.

* DEFINE The user defines functions whose graphs are required. Considerable latitude is given to the user concerning the use of brackets, multiplication signs and the like when defining functions. However, when typing indices, the user must type 'X↑2' for 'x^2' and so on. The user specifies how many functions he wishes to define by typing 'DEF1', 'DEF2' or 'DEF3'. If the number is omitted ('DEF'), it remains unchanged. By default, the number of definitions is 1.

* ADD The user defines a function whose graph is to be added to the graph which has already been drawn. The user may type 'ADD' and then supply the function in response to the request to do so, or he may type the command and function together (for example, 'ADD 3X↑2').

* REDRAW Sometimes the range of y-values chosen by the user, and occasionally that chosen by the computer, results in one or more of the graphs disappearing off the top or bottom of the screen. 'REDRAW' causes the picture to be redrawn so that this does not happen.

* SURPRISE The computer chooses at random a function to be graphed, and does not tell the user what it is. There are four levels of difficulty: linear functions ('1'); linear and quadratic functions ('2'); quadratic and cubic functions ('3'); and trigonometric and inverse trigonometric functions ('4'). The user can attempt to identify the function that has been drawn, and may supply his idea as a function to be drawn on the same picture; but it is for him to decide whether the function he has supplied is likely to be that which was chosen by the computer – he is not told that he is 'right' or 'wrong'.

* TUTORIAL The computer asks questions which enable it to draw the graph required by the user.
* MOREPOINTS When plotting the graph of a function, the computer plots twice as many points as previously (that is, the increment in the *x*-direction is halved). The command may be issued repeatedly to increase the number of points still further. This is useful where functions are oscillating rapidly, so that the standard number of points results in gaps on the screen. The converse is 'POINTSSTANDARD'.
* POINTSSTANDARD The computer reverts to the standard number of points to be plotted. By default, 'POINTSSTANDARD' is set. The converse is 'MOREPOINTS'.

What to notice: The program offers the user great flexibility. Some very different suggestions for the program's use are given in detail at the end of this section.

The speed at which graphs are plotted is fairly low: this is to enable the program to cope with graphs of functions whose values change in a rapid or bizarre fashion. If the graph being drawn is not quite what you want, you need not wait for it to be drawn completely: simply press the space-bar, and the computer will move on to the next function or to the next command.

Considerable freedom is given to the user in defining functions. For example, you can type '(2*X+3)*(3*X−4)' or simply '(2X+3)(3X−4)'. Similarly, 'SIN(2*X)', 'SIN(2X)', 'SIN 2X' and 'SIN2X' are treated as identical. But if your brackets do not match, the computer makes no attempt to interpret your intentions: it invites you to retype the function. If what you type is ambiguous, the computer may come to the wrong conclusion.

Program code: The code for this program is long. We could have made it shorter by offering fewer facilities or by documenting the code less adequately: we did not want to do either. As it is, we have been unable to space out the code as fully as we would have liked.

If you have an RML 380Z with a 32 K system, the program will load and run; but you will have to load it so that the lines of code are not indented as they are in the listing here. (This means that to fit GRAPH into only 32 K, you may not make use of the BLANKRML program given in Appendix A.2.)

The program uses high-resolution graphics: this means that clearing the screen involves clearing high-resolution graphics too. A subroutine is provided to do this.

The program uses a subroutine to allow the user to enter numbers. This subroutine prevents the cursor from moving to the next line after the number has been entered.

The functions entered by the user are POKEd into lines of program in the 'INSPECT FUNCTIONS' subroutine. Before this happens, the code needs to be converted into the format used to store functions and must also be 'corrected' so that the syntax accords with that used in BASIC statements rather than that normally written (thus 'SIN 2X' is converted to 'SIN(2*X)'). The user's functions are then POKEd into 'DEF' statements because this method works equally well with disc and cassette operating systems. When the program is input, it is necessary to save space in the 'DEF' lines (lines 2010–2030) for functions later supplied by the user that are of the maximum allowed length. The spaces in lines 2010–2030 achieve this, and the 'REM' statements at the ends of these lines serve to show the form that the lines must take. They appear to be of variable length, but this is simply because 'COS' and 'SIN' are each *stored* as a single byte although each is *listed* as three characters. If you modify GRAPH and renumber the lines, you may need to alter line 1340: this refers to what is at present line 1460 (where internal codes for '+', '−', 'COS' and so on are obtained) and to the lines which hold the 'DEF' instructions.

Since the user's input actually modifies lines of program code, bizarre input can produce syntactic errors in these lines. Usual methods of error-checking will therefore not work in this context. The instruction 'ON ERROR' is used to prevent problems which might arise from this: if an error is encountered, 'ON ERROR' transfers control to a particular point in the program instead of interrupting the program's execution.

In this program, 'ON ERROR' guards against two kinds of error. The first is a syntax error in one of the lines in the 'INSPECT FUNCTIONS' subroutine, caused by the user entering functions of an unrecognizable form. The second is an error caused by trying to evaluate a function with a value of x for which the function is undefined. An example is the function 'FNA(X) = 3/(X−2)' if evaluated when x has the value '2', since this results in dividing 3 by zero.

Error-checking: The method used to deal with errors in the input of functions is described above. If the user's attempt produces a syntax error, the message 'FUNCTION NOT RECOGNISED. TRY AGAIN' is displayed. Much of the other error-trapping is simplified by the use of 'dead' keys: only keys which correspond to allowable responses produce any effect at all. This method is used for two reasons, both concerned with saving space. First, the code is very long and there is no room in the micro (in 32 K) for elaborate error messages. Second, much of the data is entered in response to messages printed in the bottom four lines of the screen, below the graph; there is no room on the screen for longer messages.

What you could do: The first two suggestions are of changes that you could make to the program without substantially increasing its length and thereby requiring more space in core. You could change the type of function selected by the computer in response to the 'SURPRISE' command: this entails changes to the 'EVALUATE FUNCTION' subroutine. This may well be the most straightforward and the most useful change to make. You could also speed up the plotting of graphs (with a consequent loss of accuracy for those functions which oscillate rapidly) by using the BASIC instruction 'CALL "LINE"' instead of the present instruction 'CALL "PLOT"' in the 'PLOT GRAPH' subroutine and by using a larger step in the loop.

If you have more space in core – because you have more than 32 K of memory, perhaps, or because you are prepared to sacrifice some of the features or some of the documentation – you might try to devise a more sophisticated system for diagnosing errors in function input, so that the user is given more explicit information about *why* the function he suggested was not recognized. This, however, is a difficult exercise in programming.

You could add more options, such as these:
* the option of displaying grid lines with the graph;
* the option of requesting other features to be drawn on the graph (such as tangents, chords, vertical and horizontal lines from graph to axis);
* the option of requesting information about such things as the co-ordinates of points of intersection of graphs.

In addition, you could provide packages for the user who is interested in particular subjects or situations, such as wave motion, Fourier series, solutions of equations, numerical analysis or the meaning of 'derivative'.

Portability: GRAPH uses high-resolution graphics and will therefore run only on micros that have this facility. High-resolution graphics instructions are easily identified, as they all begin with the word 'CALL': they will certainly need adapting for a different micro. On the RML 380Z, there are 192 rows of pixels and 320 pixels in each row; on a different micro, these numbers would probably be different also, so that you would need to change the numbers '300' and '160' in the 'PLOT AXES' subroutine. The 380Z permits text to be mixed on the screen with the high-resolution graphics: if your micro does not, you will not be able to label the axes of the graph.

Near the beginning of the program is a special section of code whose purpose is to locate in the micro's memory those lines of code into which alterations are to be POKEd. Most micros use broadly similar methods of storing program code, so that this block of code will probably work on your micro, though you will certainly have to change the address in core (given in line 1320) from which the chain is initiated.

A note for 380Z users: The program we provide assumes that the address of 'BBUFV' is '&118' (or '118H'). If the interpreter that you are using has a different address for 'BBUFV' – see the RML *Release Note* for your interpreter – you will need to modify both addresses in line 1320.

Uses in teaching: GRAPH is a teaching and learning tool; it does not prescribe teaching methods. Thus its use can involve several of the different functions of the computer described in section 5.3. In this respect, it is less a set of resource material than a teaching or learning aid – as is a geometry set, a bunsen burner or a map table. Its usefulness will be apparent to anyone who already finds himself drawing graphs and who would like to have them drawn quickly and painlessly.

This use for the program is likely to present itself in a number of subjects. Instead of merely listing them here, we describe below some of the modes in which GRAPH may be used.

Mode 1: The program may be used simply to display graphs for discussion. In this case, the most likely sequence of commands is:

```
DEFINE
XRANGE
YRANGE
DRAW
```

'YRANGE' might be omitted. After discussion, extra graphs could be added to the picture, using 'ADD'.

Mode 2: The program may be used by the teacher to display a graph for students to identify. In addition, suggestions made by the students may be displayed on the screen and compared with the original graph. This might involve a sequence such as:

```
SUPPRESS
DEFINE
XRANGE
DRAW
LABEL
ADD
```

The 'ADD' instruction may be repeated indefinitely.

Mode 3: Students may try to identify a function chosen by the computer. This kind of use is suitable for a class or for an individual student.

```
SURPRISE
XRANGE
DRAW
ADD
```

If the first choice of *x*-range is unsuitable, the 'XRANGE' and 'DRAW' commands may be repeated. The 'ADD' command may also be repeated indefinitely.

Mode 4: The program may be used to identify the root of an equation by trial and error. This can be done by a class or by an individual student. The sequence is:

```
DEFINE
XRANGE
DRAW
```

'DEFINE 2' may be used in place of 'DEFINE'. The 'XRANGE' and 'DRAW' commands may be repeated indefinitely.

Mode 5: the program may be used in discussing derivatives of functions. The straightening-out effect obtained by focusing on a smaller and smaller portion of its graph may be illustrated clearly in this way.

```
EQUAL
DEFINE
XRANGE
DRAW
```

The 'XRANGE' and 'DRAW' commands may be repeated indefinitely.

Mode 6: The program may be used in discussing waves and combinations of waves:

```
DEFINE 3
XRANGE
DRAW
```

and in discussing Taylor or Maclaurin series:

```
DEFINE
XRANGE
DRAW
ADD
```

with indefinite repetition of the 'ADD' instruction.

Mode 7: The program may be used for discussing so-called 'pathological' functions, such as '$y = x \cos(1/x)$'.

```
DEFINE
XRANGE
DRAW
MOREPOINTS
```

The 'DRAW' and 'MOREPOINTS' commands may be repeated indefinitely.

9 Microcomputers

You may now care to know a little about the machines and the way they work: such is the aim of this chapter. If you are new to computing, this chapter should give you a good grounding in the subject; if you are familiar with computing, the chapter will show you what *we* mean when we mention particular items, and you can judge our remarks accordingly.

Computing is riddled with **jargon**. While we have tried to avoid unnecessary use of it, we have also tried to introduce the useful words; some knowledge is essential to your understanding, and many technical terms are quite self-explanatory in any case. Less understandable, perhaps, are the innumerable **acronyms**, words formed from the initial letters of other words. The language BASIC, for instance, derives its name from 'Beginner's All-purpose Symbolic Instruction Code'!

This chapter is the most technical, yet its contents may be important to you. We hope that you find it is also enjoyable. In it, we provide a technical guide to micros – not an exhaustive one, by any means, but sufficient for most purposes. We examine:

- the nature of a computer, and that of a computer system;
- the individual elements of a computer system (processing, storage, input, output, programs);
- the computer system as a combination of these elements;
- the differences between microcomputers, and how these affect your choice of one.

9.1 Computers: what are they?

A **computer** is a machine which can take information in a prescribed form, process it in a prescribed way, and produce results in a prescribed form. If the computer takes the information as discrete digits or characters, it is a **digital computer**. If it takes the information as some continuously varying physical quantity – such as electrical voltage – and not as a digital representation thereof, the computer is an **analog** (or **analogue**) **computer**. There are a few computers which use a combination of these and are called **hybrid computers**. This book deals with microcomputers: all microcomputers are digital computers.

All computers have **processors** which cope with the logical decisions, control the flow of information, do the arithmetic and so on. In many computers, the processors are **microprocessors**: all of their electrical circuitry is very small – it is etched onto a piece of silicon. The tiny fragment of silicon, which contains a complete processor, is known as an **integrated circuit (IC)** or **chip**. Many pieces of equipment which are not thought of as computers, such as cash registers and traffic lights, make use of microprocessors.

Computers, like washing machines, come in different sizes for different applications. The smallest is the **microcomputer**, and this may be likened to the domestic washing machine: each household has its own. It can do several types of washing, but only one type at a time. It is relatively cheap, and there when you want it. The microcomputer, or **micro**, incorporates integrated circuits. Not all of these are processors: one probably will be, in a microcomputer, while others may serve as memory chips in which information can be stored. The chips are mounted on **boards**.

The next size up is the **minicomputer**, similar perhaps to the washing machine found in a launderette. It can do more work than is required by one person, and is therefore shared by several.

Next comes the **mainframe computer**, named after the frameworks on which the earlier models were mounted. Mainframes correspond to the machines held by laundries: they can do much more 'washing' than is created by any one person, and are made available to many people. They cost a lot to buy and to run, and are often kept running continuously. Because the machine is housed centrally, individual users need not be troubled by maintenance and the like.

Finally, there are **supercomputers**: machines which are so big, so fast, that they do everyone's 'washing' for a year in about two minutes. They are *very* expensive to buy, maintain and run; to make economic sense, they must operate all the time. They are used by organizations such as the Meteorological Office, whose forecasting requires extensive analysis of past weather records; the calculation required for tomorrow's forecast, if performed by other means, might take a week to do.

Although this book is about microcomputers, much of what is said in it applies equally to other sorts of computer.

In this section, we look at:
- the elements of a computer system;
- the nature of information;
- instructions and programs of instructions.

The computer in a context

The computer by itself is of little use; it becomes useful only when associated with other bits of equipment which together constitute the **computer system**.

At the heart of any system is the **processor**. To be able to use it, we must be

260 Microcomputers

The computer by itself is of little use; it becomes useful only when associated with other bits of equipment which together constitute the computer system.

able to get information in (**input**) and out (**output**). There are two kinds of input: information which is to be processed and information about *how* this is to be processed – these can be thought of as 'data' and 'instructions' respectively.

It is often convenient to construct in advance a sequence of instructions about how to perform the processing, and to keep these instructions together: such a sequence is a **program**.

Programs are not the only sort of information found in a computer, as we have seen, but all information is *stored* in the same way within it. So it is important to remember that to the computer, any set of information is simply a string of characters. It will try to make of these what sense it can when you tell it what to do with them. So if you tell it to use what you know to be a program *as a program*, it will probably produce the kind of result you want. But if you inadvertently tell it to use what you know to be a program *as input data*, the machine will not know that you are wrong, and will try to comply with your instructions. It may even produce some quite plausible output!

Some people use 'information' and 'data' to mean subtly different things: the one as a loose term connoting that which humans use, the other an exact term for that which machines use. We do not think this distinction particularly helpful, and use the terms interchangeably. This ambiguity is a useful reminder that it is not only the information which is important, but also the way that you use it.

Output also is of two kinds: there is the sort which is information derived from your input according to your instructions, and there is the sort which consists in **messages** from the computer telling you what is going on. Output of the second kind may tell you about some mistakes you have made: messages of this sort are called **error diagnostics**, and should by their nature assist you in getting it right next time.

There are machines to help with the input (**input devices**) and machines to help with the output (**output devices**). There are machines to store information (**storage devices**), and media upon which to store information (**storage media**).

The flow of information from one place to another is controlled by the processor, which is at the centre of the system, and is thus often called the **central processor** (or **CP**). All other machines are peripheral to it, and are therefore known as **peripheral devices**, or just 'peripherals'. All the machines and all the media are known collectively as **hardware**.

The instructions to the computer, as has been mentioned, can be grouped together to form **programs**. Programs are collectively known as **software**, by analogy with 'hardware'. In some microcomputers there are facilities which, though they are programs (and hence 'software'), are permanently stored in the memory of the machine (the 'hardware'): these are known as **firmware**.

We now look at each of these items in greater detail.

9.2 Processing

The first item for detailed consideration is processing, since this underlies all other aspects of the use of computers. Processing affects the design of the machine itself; it influences the design of storage and other equipment; it dictates the limitations of programs. So this section introduces the following topics:

- *holding information in the machine;*
- *the nature of processing itself;*
- *efficient ways of using computers to do jobs;*
- *speed as an aspect of using a computer.*

How is information held?

The thing that does the processing, the processor, comprises many **elements** of storage, each of which can be set to either of two states. (A storage element is often likened to a switch, which can be set either to 'on' or to 'off'.) Only two states are possible, so the elements are said to be **binary**; and custom has it that the two alternative states are represented by 0 and 1, each of these being a **binary digit** or **bit**.

Any data which is to be processed, and any instructions about how to do the processing, must be represented simply in terms of bits. Using only 0 and 1, therefore, we must be able to represent (at least): a complete alphabet, in upper and lower case (52 characters); the digits 0 to 9 (10 characters); punctuation, arithmetic operators and the like (another 20 or so characters); and have a few spare for contingencies. This gives a total of at least 85 different characters, yet the processor consists of elements each of which can have only one of two different states.

The solution is to look at the bits not individually but in groups, in sequences of standard length. *One* element can take either of two **bit patterns** (0 or 1). *Two* elements can take any one of four patterns (00, 01, 10 or 11). *Three* elements can take any one of eight patterns (000, 001, 010, 011, 100, 101, 110 or 111). This progression can be continued indefinitely: each additional element doubles the number of possible bit patterns.

Number of elements	Number of patterns possible		
1	2	(2^1)	2
2	2×2	(2^2)	4
3	2×2×2	(2^3)	8
4	2×2×2×2	(2^4)	16
5	2×2×2×2×2	(2^5)	32
6	2×2×2×2×2×2	(2^6)	64
7	2×2×2×2×2×2×2	(2^7)	128
8	2×2×2×2×2×2×2×2	(2^8)	256

You can see from this table that to achieve our 85 different characters, we need at least seven bits. In practice, most microcomputers use eight bits to represent each character; and this group of bits – the bits which correspond to one character – is known as a **byte**. Using an eight-bit byte, we can have a **character set** of up to 256 characters – enough to accommodate those specified above, and a variety of graphics characters in addition. For details about how the 256 different values are used in one micro (the RML 380Z), see section 7.1.

Where is information held?

Historically, each element in the processor consisted of a minute magnetic ring around a piece of wire; the ring was used to magnetize the wire with one or the other polarity. The wire was at the core of the ring, and in time all such elements came collectively to be called **core store**, **core memory** or simply **core**: the name has stuck, though core now may comprise microelectronic circuitry. (Other names in use are **main store** and **main memory**.)

All computer users are interested in the size of their processors. One way to measure this is to count the number of elements in core, which is the number of bits which the machine can hold. In practice, however, it is more useful to know the number of *bytes* of store, which is the number of *characters* which the machine can hold.

The numbers of characters held by different machines are very large. It is convenient to have a basic 'unit of storage', and to express core sizes as multiples of this unit. The unit chosen is 2^{10}, which is 1024, characters: this unit is designated by the letter **K**. Chips, of which we spoke earlier, usually contain 4 K bytes of storage; so one chip can hold 4×1024, which is 4096, characters.

Microcomputers have store sizes which are multiples of 4 K, according to how many such chips they hold. Typical sizes are 16 K (16×1024 bytes, hence 16 384 characters) and 32 K (32×1024 bytes, hence 32 768 characters), but sizes such as 20 K, 48 K and 56 K are also used. It is usually possible to increase the size of your store by adding extra chips.

Actual processing

We have been talking about *storing* information, but we wish to do more than that; we wish to *process* it. Again we must remember that there are the two types of information – that which is processed, and that which gives instructions about the processing. Both are held in core memory.

The processor therefore needs to perform a **control function**: it needs to know where things are and to fetch information of either type as it is required. Some actions simply consist in moving information from one part of store to another. Others, though, examine the information, or change it, according to the instructions. Examining information often means comparing the contents of two pieces of store to see if they are the same. Changing information often means treating the contents of store as numbers (even though they may actually correspond to letters or symbols), and adding or subtracting them.

The processor, then, has an **arithmetic function** also; and this is made possible by reserving parts of the store as **registers**. One such register is known as the **accumulator**: this is used for adding, subtracting and comparing data. Other registers provide a **work area**, in which data that is to be used repeatedly is stored temporarily. (One instruction may be repeated ten times, for example, and it is necessary to count how many times it has been executed so far – this count is kept in such a register.)

In microcomputers, the control function and the arithmetic function, with the associated registers, are often housed on one chip: the **CPU (central processing unit) chip**. The rest of the processor's storage is housed on other chips, called **memory chips**. A new microcomputer, as bought, contains one CPU chip and a few memory chips; processor size is increased as described above by adding extra memory chips as your requirement grows.

During processing, the computer needs to be able to find its way around the store, to record where information is held. To do this, it uses **addresses**, which are very like map references. Each byte is at a particular **location** in core, and has its own, unique, address.

It is important, of course, to know when individual locations are in use and when they have served their purpose and are again available. From time to time, new information is inadvertently 'written' to locations whose contents were still needed; the machine then grinds to a halt sooner or later. Precautions are taken to prevent this kind of mishap, and particular care is taken to protect certain of the programs which are essential to the working of the computer.

In microcomputers, most of the memory can be accessed at will, simply by specifying the address and putting data there. Such store is called **RAM** (**random access memory**). But part of the store may be written to only when the machine is used for the first time: this **ROM** (**read-only memory**) cannot later be overwritten, so programs, once they are in ROM, are safe. Another distinction between ROM and RAM is what happens when the machine is switched off; again, the contents of ROM are protected, and are there intact when the machine is switched on again. In everyday use of a microcomputer, one is using different programs at different times, and these must therefore be loaded into, and taken out of, the processor. Such programs use RAM. But a few special programs, such as the overall operating system (described on page 279), are used all the time, and it can be helpful to have these in ROM. It is these programs in ROM that are software but that are permanently 'resident' in the processor which are called **firmware**.

Ways of working

When you give a computer a piece of work to do, such as running a program, you are giving it a **job**. If you are using a microcomputer, you are likely to have the machine to yourself, so you can go to it when you wish and run your job.

Sometimes, the job will be complete in itself; you will simply need to initiate it and sit twiddling your thumbs for the **execution time** or **run time** – the time taken for the micro to do that job. Such a job, which runs without intervention once started, is a **batch job**. Other jobs, on the other hand, will need you there even as they execute – to supply further information for them to process, or further instructions about what to do next. These jobs are **interactive**; you, as the user, interact with the machine as it executes the job. (Computers operating on this basis are said to be working in **interactive mode** or **conversational mode**.)

In terms of micros, 'batch' is not a very helpful word; it was used originally in the context of mainframe computers. Mainframes are big enough to do the work of several people, and they have programs which schedule the use of their processors by assembling jobs in batches, hence the name. This approach is rarely used with microcomputers.

On the other hand, it is still possible for a micro to have more computing 'power' than is needed by any one person, even if he uses it continually. For example, you may have a program which draws pictures (a program such as the GRAPH program in section 8.5). The purpose of the program is to draw the pictures, so that you can look at them and perhaps interpret them; you may thus use the micro a great deal for drawing and displaying the pictures (and thus prevent anyone else using it) but use very little time in the processor itself.

This idea that the processor stands **idle** for some of the time has led to the notion of **multiaccess systems**, systems in which several people can use the same processor at the same time. Each user has a **terminal** (a screen and a keyboard) connected to the one processor, and the processor attends to these terminals in rotation. Allocation of processor time must now be a little different; if each job was run complete (batch processing), other users might have to wait a long time. So jobs are split up, and the processor does a bit of one person's job, a bit of the second person's, a bit of the third person's, and so on round the terminals and back to the first to do another bit of that job. If this process of **timesharing** is organized properly, the users will be oblivious of it: their own speed of working is so much less than that of the processor. Timesharing is uncommon with micros, though usual with mainframes. Machines which operate independently of others, as micros often do, are said to be **stand-alone** machines.

Speed of working

Computer users need to know how fast they can get their work done. There are various measures of time taken: one is the time from initiation of a job to completion of that job – **turnaround time**, or **response time**. **Run time** (or **execution time**), which we met earlier, is only part of turnaround time; it is the part for which the processor is actually working. The other part of the time is taken in moving information in and out of core, interpreting the strokes on the keyboard, writing the results on the screen. Another useful measure of time is **access time**, the time taken to locate and fetch a piece of information from store. How fast information can be copied to and from locations in store is just one of many factors which contribute to the ill-defined concept of computer **efficiency**.

9.3 Storage

Storage plays so intimate a part in processing that it was central to the discussion of processing in the previous section. In this section, we draw a distinction between the storage in the machine itself – core storage – and that available elsewhere – backing storage. We ask:
- how much storage do you need?
- what sorts of storage are there?
- how is the information accessed from the different types of storage?

Storage and extra storage

Core storage, as we explained on page 263, is so designed that any location within it can be accessed simply by specifying the appropriate address. The ease with which individual locations may be accessed has given rise to various names for this type of store – **immediate access**, **fast access** and **direct access**. Any location, chosen at random, can be accessed in the same time with the same ease, which has given rise to the alternative and confusing name, **random access**. In fact, access is not in the least random; it is very highly specific.

As your use of the computer grows, so will the number of programs and files of text. So you need to store them; not just while you are using them, but until tomorrow, until next week, until next year. It takes very little time to create more text than can be accommodated in your processor – remember that a 16 K processor stores only 16 384 characters. The core store can be increased, as we mentioned, by adding extra memory chips to it; but you will not want the computer to grow indefinitely in this fashion, because of physical limitations – you need to house it, move it and so on. There is also the question of addressing all parts of the store: the more locations there are, the more difficult the addressing becomes (and this in turn could effect the 'efficiency' of the machine). And finally, there is the problem that the contents of store, except those in ROM, are lost when you switch off the machine. (You may wonder why this is not solved by making all core store into ROM store. This would indeed mean that no programs were lost when the machine was switched off, but it would also mean that you couldn't change your applications program when you wanted to. RAM store and its contents are accessible to you to use as you wish; ROM store and *its* contents are fixed.)

Indefinite extension of core store is not only inadequate as a solution, it is unnecessary. You need to store files which you have created, but you do not need them in the processor unless they are being processed. Storage has been developed which is external to the core store, and this is called **secondary** or **backing store** (causing the core store to be called 'primary' or 'main' store).

There are several types of backing store, principally consisting either of magnetic tape or magnetic disc. Magnetic tape, for use with micros, comes in the form of ordinary domestic **cassettes**. **Magnetic discs** are flat, circular plates; information is stored on the magnetic coating on the surface of each disc. Each surface is considered as a number of concentric **tracks**, and each track is divided into **sectors**. Information can thus be stored at an address which denotes the surface, track and sector. Discs may be either hard or soft: the latter are known as **floppy discs** or **diskettes**, and when in use rotate so fast that they attain a kind of rigidity.

Information can be **transcribed** from one storage medium to another at will. Cassettes and discs are easy to obtain. You need devices on which to mount them – cassette players or **disc drives** – which support the media and enable you to **write** information to them and **read** information from them by means of **read/write heads**. Because the media are magnetic, you can use them repeatedly with different information, the new data **overwriting** the old. It may be possible to link more than one such device to your micro.

Access to stored information

Backing store has one main disadvantage compared with main store. Consider a cassette tape. One day you create a program you want to keep: you save it by copying it from core to a cassette. The next day you create another program and copy this onto the same cassette – at the end of the first program, being careful not to overwrite the first. And the third day.... Each time you add a new program, you must position the tape to the end of the current recording. Similarly, if you wish to read the programs back, from the tape into core, you must position the tape correctly first. This means that you must **wind** or **rewind** the tape until you find the beginning of the program which you want. Tape, then, unlike core store, has **serial** or **sequential access** – all the information recorded on it is in a line, and you must physically move the tape until the piece that you want lies beneath the read/write head. Access to information stored on disc is much more direct, since you can address the right sector of the right track of the right surface of the right disc. But even so, it is not truly direct as with core; access is still sequential within a given sector. In addition to the access time mentioned before (the time taken to copy data when found), there is the **seek time** taken to find this information. It is this which makes core store so much faster than secondary store.

(A note about cassettes: though, for a given amount of tape, one large cassette may be cheaper than several smaller ones, the smaller ones have the advantage that information contained on them may be accessed more easily.)

Backing store allows you to increase your total storage enormously, and so encourages you to take duplicate (backup) copies of anything you value.

Comparison of types of storage

To close the section, here is a brief summary of the two types of store, and of the technical terms associated with each.
* Main store
    Alternative names: core, core store, core memory, internal store, memory, primary store.
    Access: direct, immediate, fast (random).
    Storage capacity: limited by physical constraints such as addressibility.
    Duration of storage: permanent if in ROM; otherwise only until the machine is switched off.
* Backing store
    Alternative names: secondary store, external store.
    Access: indirect, slow, serial, sequential in the case of cassette; direct for disc (though not as fast as main store).
    Storage capacity: unlimited.
    Duration of storage: permanent.

9.4 Input

To use processors and secondary storage, we must be able to feed information into the machine in the first place, both data to be operated upon and instructions about the operations. In the case of batch processing, as described on page 264, input will be at the start of the job only; but micros are usually operated interactively, with the program asking the user for instructions as it executes. Input must therefore be via some simple, accessible medium, and preferably one which is easily understood by unskilled users. This section deals with:

- input of new information, using a keyboard;
- input of existing information, from storage;
- input of new information, using relatively sophisticated input devices.

Input from keyboard

Most input to a computer is by means of a **keyboard** similar to that of an ordinary typewriter. Letters are arranged in the standard 'QWERTY' layout, and the keyboard also includes numbers, punctuation, symbols, arithmetic operators and **function keys**. Function keys serve various ends: there is the **SHIFT** key, for example, which makes letters upper or lower case; there is the **RETURN** key, which is pressed at the end of each line of text and causes the line to be 'sent' to the processor; and there is the **control (CTRL)** key which changes the meaning of other keys on the keyboard. Each key, when depressed, generates a unique bit pattern in temporary storage; these are sent to the processor only when the line is complete.

As an aside, it is interesting to note that the keyboard is frequently the most expensive part of a microcomputer. This is because it is the piece which gets the roughest treatment; it is the piece which has the most mechanical parts. In an attempt to cut the cost of micros, those designed for the home enthusiast often have **touch-sensitive keypads**. These are much smaller than mechanical keyboards (about the size of a pocket calculator), and respond to gentle pressure from a fingertip. They are somewhat fragile; because of their size, they are fiddly to use and it is impossible to type using the whole hand (or hands) – but they are cheap. It is curious that the 'QWERTY' layout of the typewriter keyboard survived the advent of computer keyboards; the reason is presumably that trained typists can touchtype at a computer. Such an argument does not apply to touch-sensitive keypads, because of their size and fragility; and since the 'QWERTY' layout is unhelpful to most novice computer users, its use on keypads seems indefensible. It would be more sensible to have keys laid out in alphabetic order.

Input from storage

Not all information comes each time from the keyboard. Programs, for example, are used over and over again; they are stored in ROM or on backing store (disc or cassette), and thus it is from there that they must be retrieved for use. Data to be processed may also be assembled and stored on backing store.

To use input from secondary store, one must know where it is and have attached to the computer devices suited to reading it. This may seem

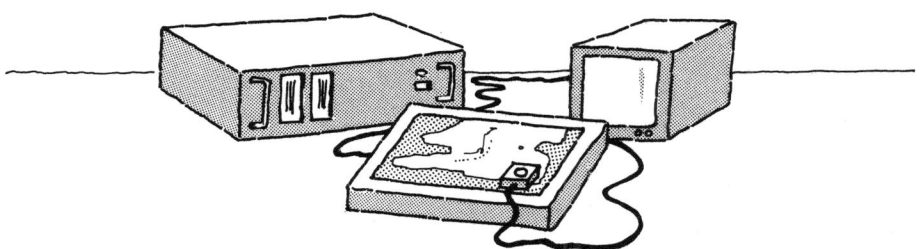

One input device is the digitizer.

self-evident; after all, you must have had such devices to write the files out to backing store in the first place. Well, not necessarily: when you start buying programs, or exchanging them with your friends, you may be sent programs on tape or disc and have to read them. It is vital when you acquire a program in this way to be sure that it will be sent to you in a form which you can use.

Input from other sources

The two most commonly used input sources are undoubtedly the keyboard and backing store. A variety of other devices is also available or becoming so; if any of them appeal to you particularly, you can check whether they are available with your micro.

One such device is the **digitizer**. This enables you to produce a set of coordinates corresponding to a picture; it enables you to turn pictorial information into numbers, which you can then operate upon mathematically. A neat example is that of a map of a country: this is laid flat on the digitizer table, and you then trace round edges, rivers, roads and so on with a **cursor** – a piece of glass with cross hairs for sighting. As you trace, the computer notes the coordinates of the centre of the cross hairs, and hence produces a digital representation of the map. This information can then be used selectively: for example, you could produce a map showing only the rivers (not the roads or towns) or an enlargement of a part of the map. The digitizer is an input device, but is probably of little use without a corresponding output device – a graph plotter, which we shall describe later, or alternatively a screen with high-resolution graphics.

Another input device which makes use of an output device is the **light pen**. This is used in conjunction with a screen, probably an ordinary television screen. Its purpose is to select a part of the screen; so a typical use would be to display on the screen a list of options (different things which the executing program could do) and invite the user to select one. With a keyboard, you would

270 *Microcomputers*

With a pressure pad, the programmer defines areas of the pad and ascribes to them certain functions: the user then presses anywhere in the drawn area to exercise the specified function.

type some letter or word which corresponded to the chosen option. With a light pen, you would point the pen at the chosen option and simply press a button. A light pen is a pen-like wand with a photocell at the end: when the button is pressed, the computer calculates which part of the screen the pen is pointing at: it knows what it is displaying there, and so acts accordingly.

Touch-sensitive screens are becoming more widespread. In this case, the input and output devices are one and the same. Information is displayed on the screen, again as a set of options for the user, and selection is made by pressing the bit of the screen which displays the chosen option. Each screen has embedded within it a fine mesh of wires: pressure causes an electrical signal to be generated from which the coordinates of the point pressed can be calculated.

The potential of such devices, and their way of working, is perhaps clearer in the case of **pressure pads**, which are very similar. A pressure pad is an independent input device, of various sizes, and flat like a book. It contains a mesh of horizontal and vertical wires; like the screen described above, pressure at some point enables the computer to determine the coordinates of that point. The programmer defines areas of the pad and ascribes to them certain functions: the areas are drawn on a piece of paper, and the function written in the middle of each area: this piece of paper is laid on top of the pressure pad. The user then simply presses anywhere in the drawn area to exercise the specified function. This is a very powerful and versatile facility.

For example, suppose you have a program which draws chosen shapes on the screen. You can control its execution by means of a pressure pad which has areas labelled 'up', 'down', 'right', 'left', 'circle', 'square', 'bigger', 'rub out' and so on.

Earlier we argued that for those who are not trained typists, the 'QWERTY' keyboard layout is unhelpful. With a pressure pad, you can create a touch-sensitive keyboard that has 'keys' in alphabetical order. Indeed, for the purposes of programming, as for instance in the language BASIC, the programmer can have areas on the pad which correspond to whole words – 'PRINT', 'GOSUB', 'GOTO' and so on – a technique which can greatly reduce the time taken at the keyboard, as well as enabling the novice programmer to concentrate on the intended skill (programming) rather than a peripheral skill (typing).

Pressure pads can be made to any size, and can be made of washable materials. They open all sorts of possibilities for disabled computer users, who can operate the computer using a whole hand, a toe or a nose. Indeed, all sorts of computer equipment have now been successfully adapted for use by the disabled. For example, for those who are visually handicapped, there are braille keyboards and braille printers. For those with gross movements only, there are keyboards on which the keys are deeply recessed: keys are operated by means of a stick held in the hand or mouth, or attached to the forehead. And for those with restricted movement, there is a whole range of devices which select characters on a grid. Instructions are given simply by counting: the sequence '1, 2, 3, end; 1, 2, end; select' selects the character in the second row up of the third column from the left. Control can therefore be exercised by use of two signals only – one for counting, one for marking the end of the count – and this can be done using a rocker switch (for fingers, hands or feet). Other controls use breath in a pipe (sucking and puffing) or gross movements of parts of the body, such as the chin.

9.5 Output

As there are special devices for input, so there are special devices for output. The choice of output device depends on what use you wish to make of the output subsequently, since the screen – which is by far the most commonly used output device for micros – displays its information only transiently. This section considers:
- *output displayed on a screen;*
- *output printed on paper (text or graphics);*
- *output sent to storage.*

Output to screen

The output device usually associated with a microcomputer is a **visual display unit** (**VDU**), a screen. Very often this is an ordinary television set, though sometimes the screen and the processor are integral.

The printers most frequently used with micros are dot-matrix printers.

Screens can display characters in defined positions (**cells**) – so many characters per line, so many lines on the screen. Thus a given character may be displayed only in these defined positions, and all characters on the screen will line up vertically and horizontally. (As we explain in Chapter 4 in our discussion of graphics, it is often possible to subdivide individual cells into small units called **pixels**. Although this increases the number of possible printing positions on the screen, they are still in defined rows and columns.)

Characters are displayed on the screen in response to bit patterns sent from the processor. Usually, each fresh character is printed to the right of the last one, and new lines are thrown automatically as necessary. The programmer can override this, however, and print characters on the screen wherever he chooses. (See for example the program in section 7.4.) The screen can display all the characters shown on the keyboard (letters, numbers, punctuation, symbols and so on), and may be able also to display additional graphics characters, as discussed in Chapter 4.

Output to paper

The main disadvantage of a screen – and it has many advantages – is that information displayed on it is lost from view when new information is displayed. If the display is a table of numerical data or a picture, this can be a nuisance: you may wish to keep a record of your results, and must therefore transcribe the output to paper by hand. Two kinds of output device are available to solve this: printers, for text, and plotters, for pictures. Each performs the transcription from screen to paper, and provides thereby what is called **hard-copy output**.

The **printers** most frequently used with micros are **dot-matrix printers**. These do not have characters embossed on slugs of type (as do typewriters), with one slug per character; they *create* all the characters using just one printing head.

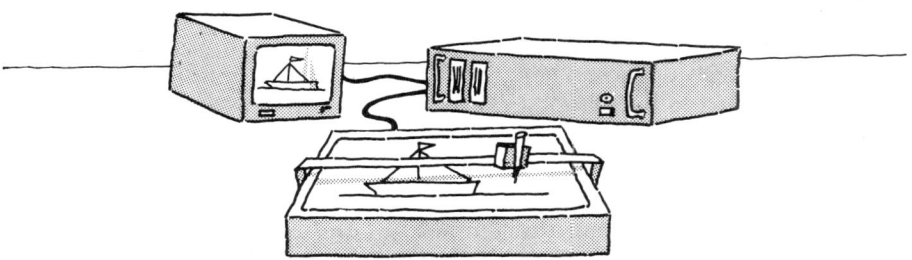

Graph plotters have one or more pens that can be moved over the surface of a sheet of paper.

The head has an array of very fine wires, protruding end on. Characters are printed using patterns made with selected wires, and thus appear as arrays of fine dots on the paper. Dot-matrix printers print characters one at a time, and are slower than **line printers**, which – as their name implies – print whole lines one at a time. Printers can usually take paper in the form either of single sheets or of **continuous stationery**. The latter may be rolled or folded backwards and forwards alternately (**fan-fold**). Paper is held either by friction or by sprocket holes at the sides. It is possible to use **pre-printed stationery**, such as notepaper with letterheads.

Many printers print characters only, and are of no use in printing output that is graphical or pictorial. Some printers can deal also with high-resolution graphics, copying the contents of the screen, top to bottom, onto paper (so-called **screen dumping**). And there are **graph plotters**, which have one or more pens that can be moved over the surface of a sheet of paper, according to instructions from the computer. Movement will usually be restricted to eight directions (up, down, sideways, and diagonally), so that curves are imperfect. Nevertheless, plotters are of great assistance, especially in conjunction with digitizers.

Output to storage

Plotters and printers are useful in giving a permanent, written record of output which can be referred to later as needed. Often you will not want to *look* at the output from your program, but to keep it for use again later – for example, you may produce large amounts of data as the output from one program, and wish to use this data as input to another program. In such cases, you will be able to direct the output to one of the usual storage media (magnetic tape or disc), in duplicate if you value it, and retrieve this information later when you want it.

9.6 Software

Computers are both powerful and versatile: they can work fast, accurately and consistently. They are capable of a vast range of complex operations.

Yet each of these processes, no matter how sophisticated, is reduced in the machine to a long sequence of very simple operations, operations which make use of the registers in the CPU chip (page 263). These simple tasks are setting registers to particular values, clearing registers, comparing the contents of registers, shunting the contents from one register to another, adding and subtracting contents of registers and so on. Multiplication, for example, is a process of repeated addition; division is a process of repeated subtraction, comparing the remainder each time with zero. This section assesses:

- *instruction (the way in which the computer is told what to do);*
- *languages (the way in which instructions are written);*
- *the differences between low-level and high-level languages;*
- *the differences between alternative high-level languages;*
- *the differences between micros, as these affect languages;*
- *the differences between applications programs and systems programs.*

Instructing the computer

The basic operations outlined above constitute the **instruction set** or **instruction repertoire** of the machine: the complete list of the few operations of which the machine is actually capable. Each instruction is represented by a unique bit pattern, the **instruction code** or **machine code**. (At this level, it is interesting to note that despite the large number of different microcomputers, there are only two or three different CPU chips and these are used by all manufacturers – the differences in the machines built from them arise from the ways in which the chips are used.)

Each instruction is very limited and very explicit; it comprises one of the instruction codes and the names of one or more registers. Thus: 'move the contents of register A into register B'. To perform the simplest sum will require several such instructions; most operations will require many instructions. It is vital, of course, that the steps are executed in the correct order, and one register (the 'sequence control register') is used to keep track of this order.

Talking to the computer

A computer can perform any task which can be reduced to machine instructions of this kind. To reduce tasks to this level is not an easy job for the programmer! He has to *understand* each step in the utmost detail, and to *remember* at all times what he is trying to do and which instructions are needed to achieve this. On top of this, the instructions must be given in a form which the machine can understand.

Programming has been made simpler by several developments. The first was the introduction of **mnemonic codes** which the programmer could use instead of the instruction code which the machine itself needed (for instance, 'MBY' for 'multiply by'): these mnemonics were turned into machine codes *by the machine*. The various mnemonics make up a limited language, a means of talking to the machine. The language is still very like that used by the machine, machine code, and is thus called a **low-level language**.

Mnemonics are turned into machine-code equivalents, then; a process called **translation**. Computers do a lot of translating, due to the fact that the meanings of bit patterns may vary according to the context, and that bit patterns have to be turned into characters for display, and so on. At this level, the translation of mnemonics into machine codes, the translation is also known as **assembly**; and the particular low-level language is an **assembly language**. Translation – which is done by the machine – follows a set of rules (if the mnemonic is this, the machine code is that), and the set of rules is a program, an **assembly program**.

It is much easier to write a program in assembly language than to write one in machine language, but it is still hard work, and the result doesn't look like English. When you look at a program that you wrote some time ago, you may have some difficulty in understanding it. (This problem can be reduced by using the facility of writing comments with the assembly language instructions, comments that are ignored when the program is assembled.)

The second stage of the development was to represent several low-level language instructions by one **high-level language** instruction. High-level instructions can be chosen to be helpful; the words can be ordinary English words. High-level programs can therefore be a lot more intelligible than low-level ones. They are also simpler to follow by virtue of their being shorter.

There are now many different high-level languages, such as BASIC, PASCAL, PILOT and PROLOG. Each language comprises a set of **reserved words**, which can be translated into machine code by the computer. The language BASIC, for example, uses words like 'LET', 'IF', 'NEXT' and 'TO'. PASCAL uses words like 'DO', 'WHILE', 'UNTIL' and 'END'. And so on.

When talking in terms of high-level languages, it is usual to speak of **statements** rather than instructions. (For example, 'LET N = 5' is a *statement* in the BASIC language; the single word 'LET' is the *instruction*.) Programs are sequences of statements, and these statements may be laid out in several ways, making use of the lines of the program text. A **line of program** may contain one statement, several statements – even no statements. Each line may be used once or repeatedly during execution of the program.

(One view is that you should never put more than one statement on a line. Our view, illustrated in the programs in this book, is that statements should normally be on separate lines but that they may be combined to advantage if, and only if, they are in any case indissolubly linked. See for example page 94, where a single line of code invokes a subroutine after pre-setting three parameters.)

In order to execute programs in high-level languages, you must have a **translator** which will convert each high-level statement into the appropriate sequence of machine instructions. Each high-level language needs its own translator. There are two types of translator.

One sort of translator is the **interpreter**, and this is the sort most frequently used with microcomputers. The interpreter works by reading each line of the program in turn, as it is used (bear in mind that this may be more than once), and generating the machine code which corresponds to the high-level statements on that line. (If the line is executed ten times, therefore, the translation will be done ten times.) This approach makes it possible to modify the program easily, and even to execute only part of the program.

The other sort of translator is the **compiler**, which is most frequently used on mainframe computers but which is increasingly available on micros also. The compiler works by looking at the whole program as a piece: it creates from the high-level program (the **source program**) a complete low-level program (the **object program**). The object program can be executed again and again without translating it each time (provided that it is not altered in any way). Indeed, the object program can be stored in that form, and brought back for use when required.

Why the choice? There are two facets to the explanation. The first concerns alterations to the program. A program can be altered in either system; it may be argued that translating the new versions (which happens frequently when you are developing a program, and keep finding faults in it) is simpler and quicker with an interpreter. This is particularly true of interpreters on micros which contain editing facilities to help the programmer make such alterations; the editing function is actually part of the interpreter, whereas it would be quite separate from a compiler.

The second facet concerns space in main memory. Main memory, to remind you, consists of some multiple of 4 K bytes; that is, it holds some multiple of 4096 characters. A typical machine with 16 K can therefore hold up to 16 384 characters. In practical working, that's not a lot, so some effort must be made to minimize the space required by all the programs you need in core at one time. A compiler is a program, as is the source program which you are translating *using* the compiler, and the compiler produces an object program – a total of three programs, all of which take up core. An interpreter, on the other hand, never produces a complete object program, only fragments corresponding to individual statements, so less core is required. (This is a simplified explanation; interpreters can make other economies also.) So why doesn't everyone use an interpreter? Well, because it's inefficient in that it has to keep translating statements each time they are used, and each time the program is run. And besides, once a compiler has been used to generate an object program, it is no longer required, and neither is the source program – at the time of execution, therefore, you need only the object program in core. The best way of working, then, if the program once developed is to be used many times, would be to develop it using an interpreter, and when it is finalized, compile it once and for all and save the object program. (As well as the source program!)

Talking to different computers

Computers actually *operate* in terms of machine language. Machine languages depend on the inner workings of the CPU; and we said that for micros, there are only two or three different CPU chips in a variety of different machines. But although there are only a few CPU chips, they are *used* in subtly different ways, and so there are several slightly different machine languages.

Programmers usually operate in terms of a high-level language, such as BASIC; there are several of these also. When the programs are executed, however, they must be translated (using an interpreter or a compiler) into machine code – machine code which works on the particular machine. So each computer may need a translator of its own to turn each high-level language into the machine language which *it* uses. Thus we need not one BASIC interpreter for all micros, but one for each machine language.

The machine language itself is individual to the machine: it is **machine-dependent**. So is the translator, since it translates into machine code for that machine. But the *high-level* language is **machine-independent** – it is in no way constrained by an individual machine. Again, a source program is machine-independent; an object program is machine-dependent.

So, that's quite easy, isn't it, from the programmer's point of view? All he has to do is pick a language (say, PASCAL), write his program, and take it to any machine anywhere which has a PASCAL translator. All the rest, the translation and so on, is done automatically; he need know nothing about all that. There is a slight drawback to this excellent principle, and it is called competition between manufacturers. If all machines could use all languages (high-level ones, that is), if a program written on one machine could run happily on any other, then – then there wouldn't be much to choose between different makes, would there? (Apart from 'efficiency', of course, but few users understand the subtle differences there.) In practice, therefore, each manufacturer devises his own version of a language, a **dialect**, which has minor variations from the dialects of his competitors. These minor differences are often a considerable nuisance to programmers, and we discussed the problems in Chapter 3.

Types of program

It is time we drew a distinction between two types of program. The one with which you are primarily concerned is the **applications program**. This is the sort which you write, or buy, or acquire from your friends, the sort which has to do in your case with helping people to learn.

However, you cannot simply start with an empty machine and write your applications program. As we have seen, you also need translators, editors, and programs to operate the hardware (to send characters to the printer, for example). These extra programs are called **systems programs**, and you need them whether or not you write programs of your own.

Keeping control

With the increasing number of programs – applications programs and systems programs – there is a growing need for orderly ways of keeping track of everything.

On microcomputers (and on most mainframes), programs are kept as files. A **file** is any group of related information which can usefully be treated as a single entity – each program is a separate file, and so is each set of data (you might have a file of names and addresses, perhaps, or of the numbers which are the result of digitizing a map). Each file has its own **filename**, a name chosen by the user. Filenames can be useful in reminding you of the contents of the files, so always choose meaningful names, not just serial numbers – a program to depict population growth could be called 'POPGROW', for example, and not 'RBT0034'.

Files, when not actually in use, are stored on backing store: tape or disc. It is useful to have a **directory** or **catalogue** of files stored on each medium. With discs, this is done for you by the computer; part of each disc is allocated to keeping notes about the files stored on it – their names, their addresses (in terms of sectors of tracks), their lengths, how much disc space is still free. This information can all be listed on the screen when required. With cassettes, unfortunately, you must do the job for yourself. Before starting to wind a tape from its beginning, always set the tape counter to zero. You can then write on the cassette the names of the files stored on it, and with each name, the tape count at the start of that file.

Another form of control is the ability to **modify** files. Files need changing because they are out of date, or inadequate, or incorrect. While it would of course be possible to effect such alterations by retyping the entire file in each case, such a technique would be time-consuming and error-prone. Most microcomputers support **editors**, programs which make it relatively easy and relatively safe to alter the contents of existing files using a few simple instructions. Text can be added, deleted or moved in this way. Editors are often available at two levels of sophistication. The simpler is a primitive form of editing provided within the interpreter, useful in correcting misspellings or inserting omitted letters. The more sophisticated editor is a separate program which manipulates whole chunks of text, makes a consistent alteration throughout a file acting on one instruction, and so on.

The programs which create disc directories and allocate disc space to new files (**file management** programs) and those which edit existing files are examples of **utility programs**. They are not critically necessary to the use of the computer, but make such use a great deal simpler.

You have now got a great deal to keep track of in using your micro! There are all the files – the programs, the utilities, the data. And there are all the bits of hardware – the printer, the disc drives, the cassette player. And there is the processor itself – how do the files get moved in and out of that? How does it talk to the hardware? And when you issue a command to the processor, such as 'fetch the file called WARGAME, I want to use it' or 'right, you can make WARGAME work now', what looks at your command? What executes the command?

Each computer has one program, one really clever, exceptionally complete program which runs the whole computer. This indefatigable administrator is variously known as the **supervisor**, the **executive**, the **monitor** or the **operating system**. It is this program which controls absolutely everything, most of it unseen by you, the user. The operating system organizes core store. The operating system oversees transfer of information from core to backing store, and vice versa. The operating system sends and receives data from peripherals such as keyboard and screen, making sure that data is transferred at the right speed and to the right place. The operating system asks you for information when it needs it, gives you messages when you make mistakes, tells you what is going on, assesses your commands and obeys them if it understands them. A clever operating system can even protect you from your own most damaging mistakes (like erasing files unintentionally).

9.7 Computer systems

Having considered the various components of a **computer system** independently, we now take a look at them assembled. First we put them together, then we switch on. There may be some problems to deal with, especially in the early stages. But when we've sorted these out, we can develop the system as confidence and ambition grow.

We need to think about:
- *the practicalities of connecting bits of equipment to each other;*
- *what is in the machine when you switch it on;*
- *problems encountered, and what to do about them;*
- *development of programs;*
- *documentation.*

Putting the bits together

A system comprises quite a few bits of hardware – certainly you will have a processor, screen and keyboard, which may be combined or separate. And you will have a cassette player, perhaps disc drives, probably a printer. So that an early task for you is to connect them all together.

Usually this is quite straightforward: you simply follow the manufacturer's instructions. (Keep components in bags until identified; don't throw away labels, especially those attached to lengths of wire.) Work slowly, and check as you go along.

Sometimes the bits of hardware will have been made by different manufacturers. This is not often a problem; again, the instructions will tell you how to connect them, and each manufacturer – or retailer – should be able to tell you which bits are **compatible** with which.

We explained that micros often use eight-bit bytes, that is, eight bits in store are used to represent each character. We also said that each character has a unique pattern of bits, its **character code**. But not all machines use the *same* character codes, and not all machines use *eight* bits for each byte. If the equipment to be connected together is consistent in these respects, the components should be able to 'talk' to each other. But if components differ, it is necessary to perform some conversion as characters pass between them. The conversion may be done by hardware or by software, or by a combination of the two; a device to *do* the converting is provided by the manufacturer, and this device is called an **interface**.

('Interface' is a term used somewhat loosely to denote the bit-in-the-middle that enables any two items to understand each other. The items may be two machines, or a machine and a person! Thus the way in which the computer *appears* to the user – its messages, instructions, questions and so on – constitutes the **user interface**. When this is easy to understand and helpful in times of trouble, the machine is said to be 'user-friendly'.)

A few terms concerning the relationships between bits of equipment. All the bits in one place (**site**) form an **installation**. They are connected one to another in an arrangement called a **configuration**. Microcomputers are usually used singly (**stand-alone**) but may be connected to others, or even to bigger computers, to form a **network**. Network members may all be in one place (in one installation), or geographically separate (**remote**).

Switching on

Main memory is of two basic types – RAM and ROM (pages 263–4). RAM (random access memory) is used over and over again by the various systems and applications programs. RAM is **volatile**: when the processor is switched off, information contained in RAM is lost. ROM (read-only memory) is **non-volatile**: information in ROM is retained even when the machine is switched off. ROM is therefore used to house the programs which are *always* wanted, whatever the computer is being used for: such programs are permanently **resident** in ROM and form the **firmware** of the machine.

There is one obvious candidate for ROM: the operating system or monitor. Many micros have the complete operating system in ROM, others have a slimmed-down version of it. A common distinction is between use of cassettes and use of discs: if discs are used, there is much more work for the computer to do – keeping the discs running, distinguishing between them if there are several, making directories, allocating storage space. So the **disc operating system (DOS)** may be bigger than the **cassette operating system (COS)**. If you are going to use cassettes only, it is wasteful of your main memory to have it cluttered up with disc-handling programs. In this arrangement, then, the cassette operating system is firmware (in ROM) and the disc operating system is loaded from backing store if required – and loaded into RAM.

The disc operating system, since it is there to help you use discs, can conveniently be kept on a disc. There is thus a paradox: to load the system which enables you to use discs, you must be able already to use the disc on which the system is stored! The explanation is that there are sufficient instructions in firmware (with COS) to enable the computer to read the disc operating system from disc – but the disc must be in the right place (usually one particular drive, even if you have several) at the outset. This computing phenomenon – using a limited ability so as to acquire a greater ability, and perhaps using the greater ability to acquire an even greater one – is called **bootstrapping** or simply **booting** (from the notion of pulling oneself up by one's own bootlaces).

To recap: when the machine is switched off – when it is new or when it has been out of use, for no matter how short an interval – it contains firmware intact in ROM, and random bits in RAM. Switching on may give you a complete operating system, or you may have additionally to load part of it (or a fuller version of it) from backing storage. COS is likely to be in firmware, DOS is likely to kept on backing store. Interpreters might be in either place.

Things which can go wrong

Sooner or later (probably both), something will go wrong. There are different kinds of error, with more or less damaging consequences. The better constructed the operating system, the less damaging the consequences of errors.

An **execution error**, a mistake made while a program is running, may be trivial. It will probably produce a diagnostic message, such as 'ILLEGAL DATA AT 570' (which means that when the program was at a particular line, number 570, it asked you for a number and you supplied a letter or word). Such an error is simple to deal with: you simply supply the right ('legal') data, and the program continues.

More damaging than this sort of execution error is the sort where the computer is asked to do something it can't do. A common problem is that one number is divided by zero: this produces an error, and the execution of the whole program is terminated. This is a **program crash**, and the user must start the program again.

Occasionally, files in the processor (in RAM) become **corrupted**, often because the same part of memory has been used for two different purposes and the original information has been **overwritten**. A well-designed system may be able to sort this mess out for you, to **recover** your files in their earlier states. If this is not possible, you will have to **reset** the machine (clear out the main

Occasionally, files in the processor become corrupted.

memory) and reload the system and the program. This is obviously a nuisance, not just because it wastes time, but because if you are developing a program, recent modifications will be lost. It is as well, therefore, to save modified versions of files on backing store from time to time. This kind of crash is a **system crash**.

Development

As your interests and confidence grow, you will want to develop your system. Adding hardware is straightforward: you decide what you want, buy the model best suited to your needs (or to your pocket), and plug it in and test it as described above.

Adding software is more problematic. Much of what you use will be written by other people; the operating system and the interpreters, for example, will be written by the manufacturer. You will have to check that it loads and runs in your own micro, a process called **implementation**. You will need to check that it does what is claimed of it, and consistently, the process of **testing**. Not all programs work properly first time! Most contain **bugs**, little problems which should be sorted out by careful checking and correction (**debugging**). Of course, software provided by the manufacturer should have been tested very thoroughly and should contain no bugs, but inevitably some slip through the net – if so, let him know!

All programmers, especially manufacturers, modify their programs from time to time. One reason is to correct bugs. Another is to produce a better version of the program, more powerful, more versatile, easier to use, more in keeping with new requirements. New **versions** of programs may thus be **revisions**, **updates** or **enhancements** – and probably all at the same time. One of the least exciting but most necessary parts of running a computer system is looking after all the files, modifying and updating them as necessary: **program maintenance**.

Another form of development is to join (or start!) a **user group**, a group of people with a shared interest in computing, perhaps with the same kind of machine, who meet occasionally to exchange ideas and programs. One of the most worthwhile functions of such groups is to set standards – to agree common practices or ways of tackling particular problems, and perhaps to pass on such group views, and group complaints, to manufacturers. (Standards can be a great help. But they are there to serve; they should not continue unquestioned, and should sometimes be ignored.)

Which leaves one last item, critical at all stages, more and more critical as your system develops: **documentation**. Documentation is crucial in the fight for survival: documentation from the manufacturer on how to use hardware and software, documentation from programmers about how best to use their brainchildren, documentation from your friends about which file is on which cassette, documentation of your own about where things are and in what state, documentation within programs about how they work, what they do, why they were written. Documentation about where to get help.

You will not remember everything: write it down.

9.8 Choice of microcomputer

There are many makes of microcomputer. Which one should *you* use? Well, the decision may not be yours; you may have to use what is already available, or buy one chosen for you by some higher authority. Even so, the contents of this section may prove useful to you.

Unfortunately, we cannot give you a simple list of recommended makes. For one thing, the choice depends on what you want, what you wish to do, and how much you are prepared to pay. For another, the equipment and programs marketed by manufacturers change so fast that any recommendation would soon be out of date.

Certain makes lead the field. This is partly because they are good, but does not mean that they are (or will remain) the best. Once a particular make has been around for a while, people develop programs and techniques for using it, and pass these on to their friends. And there are certain advantages in having a machine of the same make as your friends and colleagues. So a given machine can acquire a market lead, especially within a locality or education authority. It is important to remember, however, that quantity and quality are not the same. That many people near you have the same machine may be convenient, but does not make that machine the best.

In this final section, we consider:

- *the range of hardware available;*
- *the range of software available;*
- *maintenance of hardware;*
- *support for the programmer;*
- *mobility of the micro.*

Range of hardware

Your capabilities as a programmer are to some extent limited by hardware. Some things you need; some things are exciting optional extras. Individual pieces of hardware may or may not be made by the same manufacturer.

You *need* a processor. How big is it? Can you increase the size? How easily – can you do it yourself, or do you need a mechanic? Does it give you graphics (the ability to draw pictures)? How sophisticated are these? Are they in colour? Are graphics part of the basic processor, or do they come separately? How much does the processor cost? How much do graphics cost?

You *need* a screen. Is this part of the same unit as the processor? If not, is an ordinary television adequate? Do you need a specially big screen for class use? Is this possible? Do you need to be able to show colour?

You *need* a keyboard. Is this part of the same unit as the processor? Is it resilient? Have your friends any experience of this make?

You *need* backing storage. Are you limited to cassettes or can you use discs? How many cassettes at a time? How many discs at a time? If both, can they talk to each other? For discs: are the discs single- or double-sided?

You would use a printer. What sorts are there? How fast do they print? What size of paper do they use? How much does the paper cost? Is the processor free to do other things while a file is being printed?

You might use a plotter. How many pens? How well can it draw a circle? What size of paper does it use? How fast is it? Do you really need it? You might use a digitizer, pressure pad and all the rest. Think about what you will use them for, before you buy them.

Range of software

Your capabilities as a programmer will be limited also by software. In daily use of a micro, you will be heavily dependent on things like the operating system and the disc handler; if these are slow or inconvenient, they will drive you to distraction. They will in practice all do much the same things, probably in much the same way, but they will differ vastly in their 'user interfaces': the appearance of the system to you, the user; the kind of messages you get. Two kinds of unpleasantness: one, manufacturers sometimes try to protect you from your own incompetence to such an extent that everything you do has to be spelled out in full, so that the simplest task becomes tedious; and two, some manufacturers make their user interfaces either unhelpful or light and jocular, with merry quips and jests to make you feel at ease. Either is hard to tolerate day after day.

Languages have recurred through the book. At the outset, if you are new to the game, you will need interpreters (or compilers) for the programs which you wish to use: these programs will very probably be in BASIC. And if you start programming, BASIC is a good first language, as is PASCAL. Rather like the choice of machine, the most popular is not necessarily the best. BASIC is most common on micros, and has built up a following; much software is now written in BASIC, and so it is unlikely that there will be a sudden mass move to another language. We have mentioned dialects: each manufacturer has his own version of BASIC (or any other language), and this differs marginally from the versions of his competitors. If you know enough about it, which you probably don't when buying, compare the dialects and choose one you like. A given dialect will be specific to a given machine: the two go together. That said, though, each manufacturer is probably developing and enhancing his version. And perhaps we should stress that 'acquiring a language' actually *means* 'acquiring a translator of that language, specific to your machine'. It is the translator – interpreter or compiler – which enables the machine to turn statements in, say, PASCAL into sequences of machine-code instructions.

Maintenance and support

Both hardware and software require **maintenance**. Hardware needs to be checked routinely, especially the moving parts of it, and to be cleaned: you can do much of this for yourself. Software, as we have pointed out, needs to be kept up to date and to have any bugs removed.

What is the manufacturer's part in this? Well, he should provide revised software for you, if it was he who supplied the original. This applies to operating systems, interpreters and so on. If his revisions are corrections, you may expect to get them automatically. If they are 'upgrades', producing a service superior to the original though the original is still working satisfactorily, you may expect to have to pay. Either way, he will doubtless tell you about his new products.

You will not have bought your hardware from the manufacturer but from a retailer, and it is to him that you should turn with your problems and faults. You will probably get some kind of warranty with your equipment, which will entitle you to free repairs within a certain period. Thereafter, you will have to pay. You should find out who will perform such repairs, whether it will be on your premises or whether you will have to send the machine back (and who will pay the carriage). You should find out how quickly repairs will be carried out from the time of your distress call. If the machine has to be taken away, do you get the use of a replacement?

The equipment requires maintenance; *you* require **support**. This is the name given to the help and encouragement you can get from a variety of sources. You can get help from your dealer or the manufacturer, help with problems of hardware limitations or inadequate software. You can also get from them information about new developments planned or on the way, and how long these will be. And you can make use of people locally who have more or different experience, by attending user groups to compare notes.

Transport

Finally in our considerations about choice of micro, a brief glance at transport. Many users simply install their equipment and leave it there ever after, with the dust accumulating around it. Others, though, need to move it about a lot – to take it to another classroom, perhaps, or to demonstrate it at a public lecture.

If this is a need for you, consider how easy it will be to carry your micro. There are those for which processor, keyboard and screen are three separate units; these are cumbersome. There are those for which all three are combined; these can be bulky and heavy. Microcomputers and their peripherals are usually pretty resilient, so there is not a great likelihood of breakage in transit. On the other hand, there may be quite a lot of equipment and a lot of wires to unplug and then reassemble later, so if you are to move the machine often in one area, it may be worthwhile to build some sort of special trolley and leave everything set up permanently on this.

10 Epilogue

Chapter 9 contained hard fact, and we invited you to skip it if you were not particularly interested in the technicalities of the micro. Chapter 10, on the other hand, is largely speculative, and we hope that you will read this. No doubt that says a great deal about our own view of education. In this final chapter, we look to the future of microcomputers in teaching, and consider what might happen and what we hope will not happen.

While talking in this book about a variety of equipment, we have tended to assume that your micro consists of the processor itself, a keyboard, a screen (probably black-and-white), tape or disc storage, perhaps a printer and perhaps high-resolution graphics.

This situation is likely to change, but we can make a few informed guesses about the future. It seems fairly certain that high-resolution graphics will become widely available, and quite soon. Disc-based systems (as opposed to cassette-based systems) will become more common than hitherto, with far-reaching implications for the way micros are used: applications involving the rapid retrieval of stored information (including the provision of extensive support for the user) will become possible in more educational contexts. Such applications will be made even easier in some institutions by the introduction of networks, whereby several micros are linked together and can use the same disc storage – an arrangement which reduces the need to copy discs and which means that a single file of information may be updated for several users, each with his own machine. A suitable combination of hardware and software may even be produced to 'interface' one micro to another, completely different micro (as, for example, an APPLE to an RML 380Z): this would remove many of the existing problems of portability.

One of us, who is colour-blind, will have to adjust to the increasingly widespread use of colour on screens. The more specialized methods of input and output – pressure pads, light pens, voice synthesizers and so on – are likely to become cheaper and more widely available, with the result that new uses of micros will become possible and existing uses will become easier. Even the use of relatively simple and inexpensive devices, where they are available, will greatly enhance the value and ease of use of some learning programs. Joysticks and games paddles – two examples of hand-operated controls commonly used with television games – may be more appropriate than keyboards for controlling some interactive programs. Analogue-to-digital (A–D) converters, which translate continuous smooth movement into a numeric representation of this, will enable computer simulations to be controlled in a realistic way – it will be possible for the user of a program about driving to operate the program via a steering wheel, for example, and for the user of a program about welding to hold an oxyacetylene torch.

Although new gadgets are exciting and look both colourful and enticing in computer magazines, it is developments in software which are likely to be more significant in the use of computers in education. Communication of ideas and information will remain important: a great deal of time can be wasted by some teachers in producing programs which are almost identical to – but perhaps not quite as good as – those produced by other teachers. Efforts to coordinate and publicize the production of software, so that the right material is available at the right price, will need to be very imaginative; the various information systems available on domestic television (which themselves make extensive use of computers) may have much to offer in this respect. Teachers will have relatively little time to spare for computing, and need to be free to use this precious computing time for activities other than simply writing and typing programs.

Over the next few years, a considerable number of teaching programs will become available: we hope that most of these will be designed by teachers rather than programmers. At the time of writing, the distribution of programs, across both the country and the curriculum, is rather uneven. Geographical distribution is affected by local expertise and communication, hence our repeated references to the importance of 'user groups'. Subject distribution is affected by the ways in which teachers consider the computer to be relevant. One or two subjects are relatively well provided for; in others the use of the computer, especially with younger students, has yet to be explored. It will help greatly if teachers of those subjects for which little material is available are encouraged to design teaching and learning programs. Such encouragement will require that time and money be made available; and teachers may need to be helped in understanding more clearly what is involved in designing computer software, but without having preconceived design concepts imposed upon them. This difficult task is well worth attempting; it will be relatively easy to find programmers to implement the teachers' designs.

Almost all teaching programs written for micros – except perhaps in higher education – are written in BASIC. In one sense, choice of language is immaterial: it makes no difference to the user which language has been used to write the program as long as the resulting program is adequate. But in another sense, the language which is available conditions firstly the type of program written, and therefore secondly the type of application considered.

It may be that programs to help in teaching mathematically based subjects such as the sciences, geography and economics can easily be written in programming languages like BASIC or PASCAL, whereas programs to teach subjects such as languages and the arts cannot. These are general-purpose languages: *one* of the fields in which they are useful is education, but they were not designed specifically to be useful there. Other languages *have* been specially designed; and their usefulness is most apparent when we consider the teaching and learning of the art of programming itself. Neither BASIC nor PASCAL is ideally suited to the teaching of programming: BASIC may encourage bad programming habits; PASCAL is too difficult for young beginners.

BASIC has many good features, but (as we discussed on page 57) it is difficult to write really clear, structured BASIC programs in which modules are independent and 'protected' from each other. Extensions of BASIC, such as COMAL, may improve this situation.

But there are also new languages, designed specifically to be learnt by young children. One such language is LOGO. LOGO has been described briefly earlier in the book: it was invented a few years ago to teach young children not only programming, but also logical thinking and mathematics; indeed, it has been claimed to be useful in teaching a variety of other subjects. LOGO, unlike BASIC, is a language which uses the idea of procedures to the full, and so encourages tidy thinking and planning; and unlike PASCAL, for example, the payoff from a LOGO program is immediate and may be spectacular, even for the beginner writing his short first program.

LOGO was designed originally to drive a mechanical 'turtle' around the floor; a pen carried by the turtle left a trace on the paper over which the turtle moved. Students writing LOGO programs were encouraged to be inventive and exploratory: how could the turtle be made to do this or that? LOGO is now more widely known in its 'screen turtle' version, in which the picture is drawn on the screen rather than the floor: although this version may have less impact than that of the earlier one, the invitation to explore is just as pressing. There is a more serious drawback to the screen version: many implementations of LOGO are not interpreters written in machine code, but merely simulators written in BASIC; and these are slower and more limited than the real thing.

Another language whose use is appropriate in teaching (including the teaching of programming) is PROLOG. PROLOG has been described as a 'declarative' language: its largest divergence from most other languages is that statements in a PROLOG program are not ordered – extra statements may be added at will and the program may be run at any stage. The distinction between 'typing the program' and 'running the program' is considerably more blurred than is usually the case. Because of the way in which PROLOG allows statements to be considered as a group after they have been made independently and without order, it is particularly suited to the teaching of natural languages and the humanities. Here is an example on the subject of the programs given in Chapter 8.

290 *Epilogue*

```
SCALES is-about music
CODE is-about words
CIRCLES is-about pictures
SPELLC is-about words
SPELLF is-about words
GRAPH is-about pictures
X uses high-res-graphics if
        X is-about pictures
X runs-on standard-machine if
        X is-about Y and
        Not (X uses high-res-graphics)
```

To run this program, a question such as this is typed in:

```
Which ((You can run X on a standard machine) X runs-on standard-machine)
```

The computer then responds:

```
Answer is (You can run SCALES on a standard machine)
Answer is (You can run CODE on a standard machine)
Answer is (You can run SPELLC on a standard machine)
Answer is (You can run SPELLF on a standard machine)
No (more) answers
```

It is much easier to write useful programs in PROLOG than in languages like BASIC, and, even with young children, the understanding of a new topic may often be helped by writing a PROLOG program to represent it.

PROLOG programs are often successfully written by groups of students, and indeed groups are frequently more successful than individuals in writing such programs; in this, too, PROLOG differs from other programming languages. LOGO programs are usually written by individuals, though they lend themselves readily to group discussion. Both LOGO and PROLOG are suitable for use with young students, including children in primary schools. Whether or not they become widely used in the future will depend largely on their availability.

Some manufacturers are delighted to cooperate with users of their equipment in producing what is needed, so it is useful to draw their attention to software requirements of the kinds described above. It is also useful to make them aware of the ways in which their hardware and software fall short of the purposes you have in mind. Some manufacturers sponsor or liaise with users' groups set up for just this reason; and the extent to which manufacturers care about and are sensitive to the emerging needs of teachers is one factor that you may like to consider when choosing your micro.

Our own recommendations as regards choice of micro are concerned more with software than with hardware, and specifically with the documentation which accompanies it. Documentation produced by manufacturers is often far from clear and easy to read: it may be obscured by the use of unnecessary technical terms, or it may be ambiguous. Clarity in documentation is preferable to humour. Systems should be designed, where possible, to permit rather than to restrict. One example of the restrictive nature of many systems is the way in which the blanks that are so useful in laying out a program clearly are removed from the beginnings of lines of code: this is something which is imposed on the user, not a feature which he can adopt if he chooses.

The justification for removing leading blanks, for skimping on the comments and blank lines within a program, and for writing short pieces of code where longer pieces would be easier to understand, is the alleged need to save space in the machine. We have said that this problem is reduced by adding additional memory chips to your machine, so increasing the size of core store. These chips are somewhat expensive (though becoming cheaper) and for this reason many people prefer to manage with the amount of store that they have, despite the disadvantages. Yet the cost of the time spent grappling with badly laid out programs – compare the two versions of the marmalade recipe, on pages 49–50 and 52 – must vastly outweigh the cost of a little extra store.

In Chapter 9, we mentioned the value of pressure pads, rocker switches, suck-and-blow controls and braille keyboards. Such devices do not simply enable physically handicapped people to become programmers, or to teach in the ways discussed in this book: they may actually extend the power of the handicapped person enormously. A person who can control a computer can control anything controlled *by* the computer – light switches, telephones, televisions, radios, cookers, electronic libraries and so on. They may be helped in producing written or even spoken language, not least by the ability to operate a typewriter, albeit indirectly. Many people expect that the education of the mentally handicapped also will be helped in the future by computers; some work is already being done in this area. As in many other applications of the computer, it is probably much easier to offer mundane support than imaginative help. Computers are certainly useful in providing the necessary practice in skills which must be painfully acquired; but surely they can be useful far beyond this in giving new power to mentally handicapped students as well as to those whose handicaps are physical. This is an area of growth where we feel particularly strongly that it is not the professional programmers employed by commercial software houses, but practising *teachers* who are likely to design the really useful programs.

There may well come a time when most educational institutions are equipped with laboratories full of micros, so that each student may have prolonged access to his own machine as a continuing part of his education. Such a development would encourage the use of learning through programming, and would underline the need for suitable languages to be readily available. It would no doubt also encourage the computer to be seen in the role of tutor, where its success would depend (in our view) on what was seen to be the role of a tutor. A few years ago it was predicted that a future use of the computer would be in giving millions of school-children access to a *well-informed* and *responsive* 'tutor'. If this is what is now meant by the term, and if it proves practicable, it will be very exciting. Another use of the computer is in helping a student to pick his way through a new topic for which no teacher is available. But the computer could simply be fed with the equivalent of a set of unimaginative workcards, thereby ensuring that the gloomy straitjacket in which he finds himself is even more effective: this is one of the things that we hope will *not* happen.

Teachers approach computing with various emotions – reluctance, enthusiasm, disinterest and eagerness are all in evidence. Is the computer just a passing fad? It is difficult to predict the changing fortunes of any piece of educational technology. Teaching machines have come and gone; overhead projectors, filmstrip projectors, cassette recorders and the like are all used extensively in some institutions but hardly at all in many others. Perhaps some teachers dismissed the newly-invented blackboard as a gimmick which would not last.

The computer has many of the disadvantages of most other teaching equipment: it is expensive, difficult to move about, frightening to the uninitiated and difficult to use well on the spur of the moment. We have argued that it has several advantages over the others: it is very flexible, it should become easier to use, and the fact that its use is already widespread and not confined to education may enhance its credibility in the minds of both teachers and students.

Computers will take and retain their place in education, as a significant resource for teachers, only if teachers are thereby offered real support in educating their students. It is our belief that education is a process of seduction. First you seduce your students into believing that they are interested in what is being learnt, then you seduce them into believing that they are as capable as you of operating with the material being learnt, and then they no longer need you.

Our task in this book has been to educate you in the use of microcomputers in teaching. If we have succeeded, you no longer need us.

Appendices

A.1 Program evaluation checklist

A list of things to look at and for when assessing software. Add your own as you think of others.

* Program design
    Is it what you want? Have you seen something better elsewhere?
    Is it attractive? To you? To the learner?
    What skills are required? What skills are taught?
    Has the learner to provide data – must this be collected in advance?
    Is operation in command mode or in tutorial mode?
    Is the program flexible: does it leave the initiative with the learner, does it give him options, are these clear to him at all stages?
    Does it fit in with the teaching scheme or syllabus?
    Does it fit in with other teaching programs?
    Is it for individual use or for group use?
    Does it require tutorial support?
* Program code
    Is it clear?
    Is it modular?
    Is it readable?
    Are identifiers (names of modules and of variables) chosen to reflect their purposes?
    Are errors trapped to your satisfaction?
    Does it use special language features? If so, have you got these?
    Can you alter it if you wish?
    Can you develop it if you wish?
* Program requirements
    How much space does it need?
    Does it need cassette or disc drives? If so, how many?
    Does it use graphics? If so, does it require high-resolution graphics?
    Does it use colour?
* Documentation
    Is this in the code?
    Is there external documentation about the program as well?

294   *Appendices*

    Is there an explanation of the objectives?
    Is there a flowchart?
    Is there a copy of the code?
    Are there suggestions for class use? Are there worksheets?
* Maintenance and support
    How is the program to be supplied?
    What guarantees do you get with it?
    What happens when it goes wrong, when you find bugs? Whose responsibility are these?
    What happens when you want further advice?
    Do you get offered enhancements and updates? Do they cost more? How are they supplied?
    For how long do these things apply?

A.2 Program to prevent the stripping of leading blanks

In preparing the programs for this book, we made continual use of our own modified form of RML's disc BASIC, version 5.0A. The purpose of this modification is to prevent the interpreter from stripping the leading blanks from lines of program code. Since we feel that this facility might be useful to you also, this appendix offers you our modification.

The interpreter is modified by means of a BASIC program, BLANKRML. We have tried to make this program apply to as many different versions of the interpreter as possible. We regret that we have not yet had time to discover how to modify cassette BASICs in this way, though we see no reason in principle why the process should be intrinsically more difficult than modifying disc BASICs. We know that the program offered works for BASICS V5.0A and for BASICSG V5.0A: we do not know about other disc BASICs, so you will have to try it and hope.

We have spoken elsewhere in the book of our reasons for wanting to use indentation: we hope that the code provided in the book illustrates our argument. We are not aware of any cogent argument against allowing the user to indent, if he so wishes. Since *we* can modify the interpreter by means of a program, it would seem that RML themselves could make the necessary alterations to their interpreters if they thought it worthwhile. RML, indeed, could produce interpreters which preserve indentation but do not show the one known defect of our modification, described below, or any other defects at present unknown to us. Such a modification to the interpreter would produce a negligible increase in *its* size: the only appreciable loss of space in memory would result from the inclusion in applications programs of the leading blanks themselves – and this choice could safely be left to the individual user. In any case, since well laid-out programs are more quickly developed and modified, economy of space must at all times be set against economy of programming time.

Program to prevent the stripping of leading blanks 295

The aim of BLANKRML, then, is to adapt as many RML disc BASICs as possible so that they no longer strip leading blanks from lines of program code when listing, saving and loading programs. It is offered for your use until such time as RML produce a better version of their own – soon, we hope.

Specification

The program will make the adaptation described above to BASICS V5.0A and to BASICSG V5.0A. It will be written in such a way that it may possibly make a similar modification to other versions of disc BASIC.

How to use the program

First load your BASIC interpreter, then type:

```
LOAD "BLANKRML"
RUN
NEW
```

You may then type your programs with leading blanks as required. Listing, saving and loading the programs will not result in the loss of these blanks.

Listing of BLANKRML program code

```
1000 REM Program : BLANKRML
1010 REM
1020 REM
1030 REM This program modifies some RML disc BASIC interpreters to
1040 REM     prevent them from stripping leading blanks from lines
1050 REM     of program code. The user needs to supply the address
1060 REM     of B8UFV.
1070 REM
1080 REM No attempt is made within the program to document the
1090 REM     function of the different sections of code, since
1100 REM     explanations are too complicated to make this
1110 REM     practical. This program is provided as a useful
1120 REM     tool rather than as an example of programming.
1130 REM
1140 REM
1150     CLEAR 100
1160 REM
1170     TEXT : PRINT CHR$(12) : REM Clear the screen
1180     PRINT CHR$(17) : REM Disable paging
1190 REM
1200 REM
1210     PRINT TAB(16); "BLANKRML"
1220     PRINT
1230     PRINT "Modifies BASIC to retain leading blanks"
1240     PRINT : PRINT : PRINT
1250     PRINT TAB(19); "*"
1260     PRINT
1270     PRINT TAB(15); "Derek Ball"
1280     PRINT
```

```
1290      PRINT TAB(14); "Andrew Nash"
1300      PRINT
1310      PRINT TAB(19); "*"
1320      PRINT : PRINT : PRINT
1330      PRINT TAB(13); "Copyright 1982"
1340      PRINT
1350      PRINT TAB(10); "Hutchinson Education"
1360      PRINT
1370      FOR D = 1 TO 5000 : NEXT D : REM Delay
1380      PRINT CHR$(12) : REM Clear the screen
1390 REM
1400 REM
1410 REM MAIN PROGRAM
1420 REM
1430      DIM L(4)
1440 REM
1450      PRINT "Please give the address of BBUFV"
1460      PRINT "    (might be &118)";
1470      INPUT BB
1480 REM
1490      PRINT CHR$(12) : REM Clear the screen
1500      PRINT "Please wait"
1510      PRINT : PRINT : PRINT
1520 REM
1530      EB=PEEK(BB)+256*PEEK(BB+1)-1
1540 REM     EB is the address of end of BASIC
1550      X=EB+12 : GOSUB 2220
1560 REM     X points to byte beyond new end of BASIC
1570      C0=A0 : C1=A1
1580 REM
1590 REM Find various strings of bytes in BASIC interpreter
1600 REM
1610      N=2 : V(1)=PEEK(BB) : V(2)=PEEK(BB+1) :    ST=&2A00
1620      GOSUB 2300
1630      L0=I
1640 REM
1650      N=4 : V(1)=&23:V(2)=&7E : V(3)=&FE : V(4)=&3A : ST=&500
1660      GOSUB 2300
1670      X=I
1680      GOSUB 2220
1690      B1=A1 : B0=A0
1700 REM
1710      N=4 : V(1)=B0 : V(2)=B1 : V(3)=&B7 : V(4)=&F5 : ST=&200
1720      GOSUB 2300
1730      L(1)=L
1740 REM
1750      N=3 : V(1)=&3D : V(2)=&28 : V(3)=&D4 : ST=&1700
1760      GOSUB 2300
1770      L(2)=L-3
1780 REM
1790      N=4 : V(1)=B0 : V(2)=B1 : V(3)=&D0 : V(4)=&E5 : ST=&500
1800      GOSUB 2300
1810      L(3)=L
1820 REM
1830      N=3 : V(1)=&E : V(2)=&20 : V(3)=&CD : ST=&1900
1840      GOSUB 2300
1850      L(4)=L+2
1860 REM
1870 REM Poke address of alternative subroutine in three places
1880 REM
1890      X=EB
1900      GOSUB 2220
1910      FOR I=1 TO 3
1920         POKE L(I),A0
1930         POKE L(I)+1,A1
1940      NEXT I
```

```
1950 REM
1960 REM Remove call to a subroutine which inserts leading blanks
1970 REM     into lines when saving a program
1980 REM
1990     POKE L(4),0 : POKE L(4)+1,0 : POKE L(4)+2,0
2000 REM
2010 REM Poke new version of subroutine (for reading lines of program)
2020 REM    which does not read over blanks
2030 REM
2040     FOR P = EB TO EB+11
2050         READ Q
2060         POKE P,Q
2070     NEXT P
2080     DATA &23,&7E,&FE,&3A,&D0,&FE,&30,&3F,&3C,&3D,&C9,0
2090 REM
2100 REM Poke new value of BASIC buffer vector
2110 REM
2120     POKE BB,C0
2130     POKE BB+1,C1
2140 REM
2150     POKE L0,C0
2160     POKE L0+1,C1
2170 REM
2180     PRINT CHR$(19) : REM Re-enable paging
2190     END
2200 REM
2210 REM
2220 REM SUBROUTINE TO SPLIT ADDRESS BETWEEN TWO BYTES
2230 REM
2240     A1=INT(X/256)
2250     A0=X-256*A1
2260 REM
2270     RETURN
2280 REM
2290 REM
2300 REM SUBROUTINE TO FIND STRING OF BYTES IN THE INTERPRETER
2310 REM
2320     L=ST
2330     L=L+1
2340     IF L<ST+2000 THEN 2390
2350         PRINT "Sorry! This program will not work with"
2360         PRINT "your interpreter"
2370         PRINT CHR$(19) : REM Re-enable paging
2380         STOP
2390     A=PEEK(L)
2400     IF A<>V(1) THEN 2330
2410 REM
2420     FOR I = 2 TO N
2430         IF V(I)<>PEEK(L+I-1) THEN 2330
2440     NEXT I
2450 REM
2460     RETURN
```

Discussion

What to notice: If you use our modification, you will soon notice that when *listing* your program (on the screen or the printer), an *extra* blank is inserted at the start of each line of code, after the line number. These extra blanks are not stored, but added to each line as it is listed, so happily they do not accumulate. This additional blank is not much of a nuisance until you come to add lines of code. When using existing lines as reference for alignment, you must remember that there is this extra blank, and so stop your new lines one space short of the text that you wish it to match. When you next list the program, all the lines – including the new ones – will have the extra blank inserted, and the text will now be properly aligned.

Program code: The code of this program is highly specific: it applies only to disc BASIC interpreters on the RML 380Z. Its workings depend on the workings of the interpreter, and on some relatively sophisticated programming. For detailed 'REM' statements in the program to make any sense to you, you would have to invest an unwarranted amount of time in understanding the underlying principles, so we have decided in this case simply to list the code for you to use as it stands.

Portability: Of all the programs in the book, it is this one – not surprisingly – that is the least portable: it modifies the machine code of a specific interpreter. Attempts have been made to enable the program to modify as many RML disc BASIC interpreters as possible, though we do not know how successful we have been in this endeavour.

Obviously, this program is totally inappropriate for those who wish to make similar modifications to an interpreter provided by a different manufacturer. It is possible that some of the principles used in adapting the RML 380Z interpreter might apply elsewhere, but such principles are too technical to be described here in the necessary detail. In any case, the modification relies on the fact that the RML 380Z interpreter is held in RAM, and may therefore be changed by the program; considerably greater difficulty would be experienced by anyone trying to modify an interpreter held in ROM.

A.3 Programs to aid design in low-resolution graphics

This appendix offers two programs: the first helps in preparing the data required to display pictures in low-resolution graphics; the second is a machine-code routine which enables these pictures to be displayed on the screen more rapidly than is possible by other means.

In designing pictures in low-resolution graphics, you probably start with a piece of squared paper and colour in squares until you have created the picture you require. When satisfied with your efforts, you have the task of converting your design into data which can be interpreted by a computer program.

You can calculate all the graphics codes for yourself if you wish, though the task may be tedious and liable to errors which can be rectified only with difficulty. Alternatively, you can make the computer do the calculations for you: this will be easier and less prone to error. We were faced with this choice when we created the data required for the program BIGLET (section 7.2), and we devised the program DESIGN given below. It is an interesting example of a point made in section 6.3: we devised the program simply to create characters, but after a minor modification it is equally good at producing complete pictures.

The version of DESIGN that *we* used produced characters which were all of the same size; we have since adapted it so that you can specify the size of picture that you require. It has also been modified so that graphics codes are produced by reading along the rows of the screen, rather than up the columns: this simplifies the machine-code routine in the program FASTPLOT that displays the picture again.

When you have produced data for your picture by means of DESIGN, you will need to incorporate this data into your program. The approach adopted with BIGLET is first to read the data into an array (here called 'C'):

```
1430        FOR Y = 1 TO Y8
1490          FOR X = 1 TO X8
1500            READ C(X,Y)
1510          NEXT X
1520        NEXT Y
```

and then to plot the picture with a block of BASIC code such as this:

```
2370        FOR Y = 1 TO Y8
2380          FOR X = 1 TO X8
2390            PLOT X0+2*X, Y0+3*Y, C(X,Y)+192
2400          NEXT X
2410        NEXT Y
```

This approach produces the picture rather slowly. A simple machine-code routine can be written to make the picture appear almost instantaneously: the program FASTPLOT given below includes such a routine, written for an RML 380Z. You may care to use this routine in your programs, particularly if you wish to make your pictures move.

Specification of DESIGN

The program will require data files, and hence will required either a disc-based system or a cassette-based system that includes an automatic cassette controller.

The program will provide a design frame whose dimensions will be specified by the user and within which he can move a cursor to create the design of his choice. When the design is complete, it will be converted into data consisting of graphics codes suitable for use within a program: these will be stored in a file on disc or tape. The user will be able to include more than one design within the same file. Each design will be given a name chosen by the user.

300 *Appendices*

Outline flowchart of DESIGN

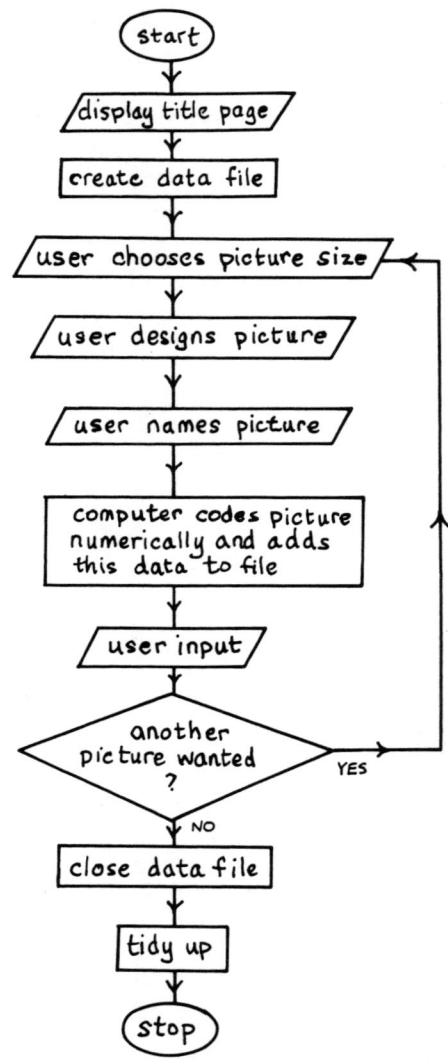

Listing of DESIGN program code

```
1000 REM Program : DESIGN
1010 REM
1020 REM
1030 REM This program is a tool whch may be used to design
1040 REM      low-resolution graphics pictures. The graphics codes
1050 REM      are calculated by the program and stored in a data
1060 REM      file as BASIC 'DATA' statements. Either a disc system
1070 REM      or a cassette system with automatic tape control is
1080 REM      required tro enable the data file to be created.
1090 REM
1100 REM
1110      CLEAR 100
1120 REM
1130      ON BREAK GOTO 2520
1140 REM    Deal with user's interruption
1150 REM
1160      TEXT : PRINT CHR$(12)   : REM Clear the screen
1170      PRINT CHR$(17) : REM Disable paging
1180 REM
1190 REM
1200      PRINT TAB(17); "DESIGN"
1210      PRINT
1220      PRINT TAB(6); "Create data file for picture"
1230      PRINT : PRINT : PRINT
1240      PRINT TAB(19); "*"
1250      PRINT
1260      PRINT TAB(15); "Derek Ball"
1270      PRINT
1280      PRINT TAB(16); "Andrew Nash"
1290      PRINT
1300      PRINT TAB(19); "*"
1310      PRINT : PRINT : PRINT
1320      PRINT TAB(13); "Copyright 1982"
1330      PRINT
1340      PRINT TAB(10); "Hutchinson Education"
1350      PRINT
1360      FOR D = 1 TO 5000 : NEXT D : REM Delay
1370      PRINT CHR$(12) : REM Clear the screen
1380 REM
1390 REM
1400 REM PRELIMINARIES
1410 REM
1420      DIM G(38,18) : REM G is array to record user's picture
1430      LN=1000 : REM First line number for data file
1440 REM
1450 REM Set up file
1460 REM
1470      PRINT "Please give the filename";
1480      INPUT N$
1490      CREATE £10,N$ : REM Create data file on disc or tape
1500 REM
1510 REM
1520 REM MAIN PROGRAM
1530 REM
1540 REM Decide picture size
1550 REM
1560      PRINT
1570      PRINT "Please give the size of the picture"
1580      PRINT
1590      PRINT "How many pixels across"
1600      PRINT "    (must be a multiple of 2)";
1610      INPUT N$
```

```
1620      I$="across" : GOSUB 3070 : REM Check input
1630      IF E$="error" THEN 1580
1640      X9=N : REM X9 is number of pixels across
1650 REM
1660      PRINT
1670      PRINT "How many pixels up"
1680      PRINT "   (must be a multiple of 3)";
1690      INPUT N$
1700      I$="up" : GOSUB 3070 : REM Check input
1710      IF E$="error" THEN 1660
1720      Y9=N : REM Y9 is number of pixels up
1730 REM
1740 REM Empty array used to record picture
1750 REM
1760      FOR X = 1 TO X9
1770          FOR Y = 1 TO Y9
1780              G(X,Y)=0
1790          NEXT Y
1800      NEXT X
1810 REM
1820 REM Plot frame
1830 REM
1840      GRAPH
1850      PLOT 0,0,191
1860      LINE 2*X9+2,0
1870      LINE 2*X9+2,3*Y9+3
1880      LINE 0,3*Y9+3
1890      LINE 0,3
1900 REM
1910      PRINT "Use the following commands:"
1920      PRINT "Left     Fill    Up"
1930      PRINT "Right    Empty   Down    Complete"
1940      PRINT "Type only the first letter of a command"
1950 REM
1960 REM Set up cursor
1970 REM
1980      X=1 : Y=1 : X0=1 : Y0=1
1990 REM   Position cursor at bottom left of frame
2000 REM
2010      GOSUB 2580 : REM Display cursor
2020 REM
2030 REM User designs picture
2040 REM
2050      R$=GET$()
2060      IF R$>"Z" THEN R$=CHR$(ASC(R$)-32) : REM Convert to upper case
2070      X=X0 : Y=Y0
2080      IF R$="L" THEN X=X-1 : GOSUB 2580 : REM Move cursor left
2090      IF R$="R" THEN X=X+1 : GOSUB 2580 : REM Move cursor right
2100      IF R$="U" THEN Y=Y+1 : GOSUB 2580 : REM Move cursor up
2110      IF R$="D" THEN Y=Y-1 : GOSUB 2580 : REM Move cursor down
2120 REM
2130      IF R$="F" THEN GOSUB 2750 : REM Fill cell
2140      IF R$="E" THEN GOSUB 2830 : REM Empty cell
2150      IF R$()"C" THEN 2050 : REM Go back if design not complete
2160 REM
2170 REM Create lines of code
2180 REM
2190      PRINT CHR$(12) : REM Clear the bottom of the screen
2200      PRINT "Please name this picture"
2210      INPUT PN$
2220      GOSUB 2910 : REM Create 'REM' line
2230      CT=0 : REM Set to zero the counter for number of
2240 REM      codes on current line of data
2250      FOR Y = 1 TO Y9 STEP 3
2260          FOR X = 1 TO X9 STEP 2
2270              IF CT=0 THEN GOSUB 2990 : REM Start creating 'DATA' line
```

```
2280            C=G(X,Y+2)+2*G(X+1,Y+2)+4*G(X,Y+1)
2290            C=C+8*G(X+1,Y+1)+16*G(X,Y)+32*G(X+1,Y)
2300 REM         Calculate graphics code for each block of six pixels
2310 REM
2320            CT=CT+1
2330            PRINT £10, STR$(C); : REM Send graphics code to file
2340            IF CT=10 THEN PRINT £10 : CT=0 : GOTO 2390
2350 REM         If there are 10 codes on this line of data,
2360 REM         complete this line and start another
2370            IF X<X9-1 OR Y<Y9-2 THEN PRINT £10, ",";
2380 REM         Separate codes on data line with commas
2390          NEXT X
2400       NEXT Y
2410       PRINT £10 : REM Complete the line of data
2420 REM
2430       PRINT "Do you want to design another picture"
2440       PRINT "   (Y/N)";
2450       INPUT R$
2460       IF R$="Y" OR R$="y" THEN GRAPH : TEXT : GOTO 1560
2470       IF R$="N" OR R$="n" THEN 2520
2480       PRINT "Please reply Y or N" : GOTO 2430
2490 REM
2500 REM FINISH
2510 REM
2520       CLOSE £10 : REM Close the data file
2530       PRINT CHR$(19) : REM Re-enable paging
2540       TEXT
2550       END
2560 REM
2570 REM
2580 REM SUBROUTINE : MOVE CURSOR
2590 REM
2600 REM Don't move cursor outside frame
2610 REM
2620       IF X<1 OR X>X9 THEN 2720
2630       IF Y<1 OR Y>Y9 THEN 2720
2640 REM
2650 REM Show cursor move on screen
2660 REM
2670       IF G(X0,Y0)=1 THEN PLOT 2*X0,3*Y0,255 ELSE PLOT 2*X0,3*Y0,192
2680       IF G(X,Y)=0 THEN PLOT 2*X,3*Y,67 ELSE PLOT 2*X,3*Y,191
2690 REM
2700       X0=X : Y0=Y : REM Record new position of cursor
2710 REM
2720       RETURN
2730 REM
2740 REM
2750 REM SUBROUTINE : FILL CELL
2760 REM
2770       PLOT 2*X,3*Y,191 : REM Display cell on screen
2780       G(X,Y)=1 : REM Enter cell in record
2790 REM
2800       RETURN
2810 REM
2820 REM
2830 REM SUBROUTINE : EMPTY CELL
2840 REM
2850       PLOT 2*X,3*Y,67 : REM Replace cell on screen by C
2860       G(X,Y)=0 : REM Remove cell on record
2870 REM
2880       RETURN
2890 REM
2900 REM
2910 REM SUBROUTINE : CREATE REM LINE
2920 REM
2930       PRINT £10,MID$(STR$(LN),2); " REM "; PN$
```

```
2940     LN=LN+10
2950 REM
2960     RETURN
2970 REM
2980 REM
2990 REM SUBROUTINE : START DATA LINE
3000 REM
3010     PRINT £10,MID$(STR$(LN),2); " DATA";
3020     LN=LN+10
3030 REM
3040     RETURN
3050 REM
3060 REM
3070 REM SUBROUTINE : CHECK INPUT
3080 REM
3090     N=INT(VAL(N$))
3100     IF I$="across" THEN M=2 : N9=38 ELSE M=3 : N9=18
3110     IF N>0 AND N=M*INT(N/M) AND N<=N9 THEN E$="ok" : GOTO 3250
3120       E$="error"
3130       PRINT
3140       IF N>0 THEN 3180
3150         PRINT "You must have at least"; M; "pixels"
3160         PRINT "Please give number in figures"
3170         GOTO 3250
3180       IF N<=N9 THEN 3210
3190         PRINT "number of pixels must not exceed"; N9
3200         GOTO 3250
3210       PRINT "The number of pixels must be a multiple"
3220       PRINT "    of"; M
3230       PRINT "Please give new number"
3240 REM
3250     RETURN
```

Sample output from DESIGN

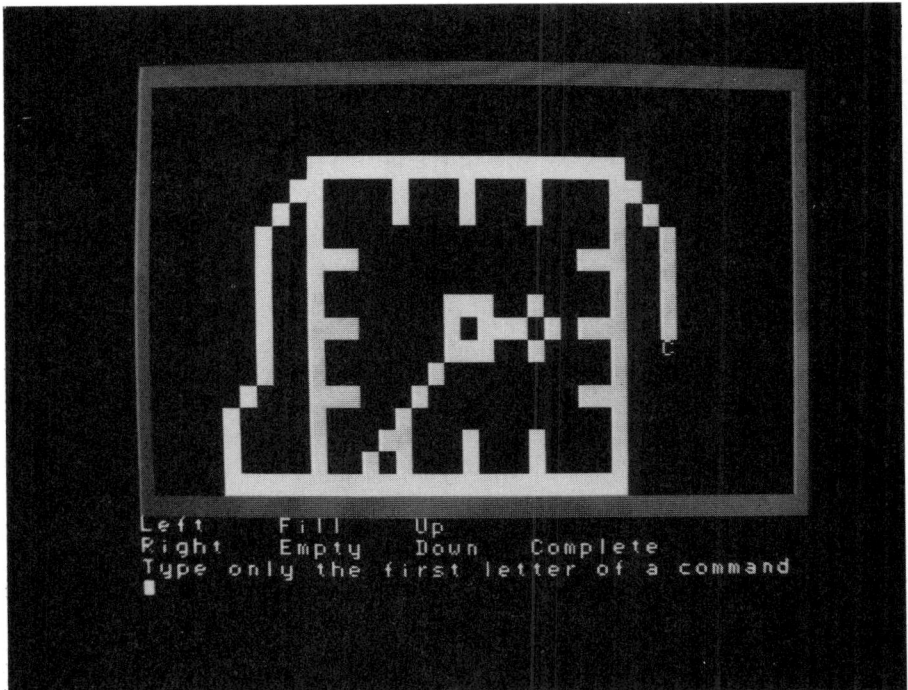

Discussion of DESIGN

What to notice: The frame within which you create your design is considerably larger than the area that your design will occupy when plotted by your program on the screen. It is also somewhat different in shape, being twice as long but three times as high. To know in advance exactly what your picture will look like without this distortion, you must draw it first on squared paper; but even then, DESIGN offers a much simpler route to creating the necessary data.

Once the file of data has been created, it can be merged into the program which is to use it. The lines of data produced by DESIGN are prefaced in each case by the word 'DATA' and a line number: you may, of course, need to renumber this data file before merging it into your program.

Program code: Lines 2280 and 2290 are the ones that convert each group of six pixels, displayed or undisplayed, into the appropriate graphics code number.

Error-checking: During execution of DESIGN, the user is asked to provide a filename for the data file. To be legal on the RML 380Z, the filename must not exceed eight characters (for disc) or six characters (for cassette) in length, and each of these characters must be a letter or a digit. (Other micros may have different rules.) This program does not check the legality of the filename as supplied.

While the user is designing his picture, keys other than those appropriate to commands are deadened; the computer does nothing until one of the permitted keys is pressed.

When the user specifies the size of the design, the data he provides for the numbers of pixels across and up the screen is checked to ensure that it satisfies the requirements of the program. Where numbers are inappropriate, error messages are displayed.

What you could do: You could check that the filename supplied by the user is valid for your system: the program as supplied does not do this.

You could use DESIGN to produce data for your own pictures. These might be modifications of the BIGLET characters, or smaller versions of them; or they might be pictures which are quite unrelated, either static or moving.

If you have a cassette-based system *without* an automatic cassette controller, you could amend DESIGN so that the data is sent to a printer rather than to a data file – or even to the screen, if you do not have a printer.

Portability: Although this program produces data specifically for the RML 380Z or 480Z, the ideas and most of the code can be applied just as well to other micros. Lines 2280 and 2290 will need to be adapted so that the graphics codes produced are appropriate to your micro; and the pixels may need to be grouped differently (not necessarily in sixes). The code for creating and writing to data files will almost certainly need modification; but equally certainly these modifications, for any micro that allows the use of data files, will consist in writing exactly equivalent lines of code.

Specification of FASTPLOT

The program will make use of the machine-code routine and will demonstrate how two designs (in this case the words 'MOVES' and 'FAST') may be first produced on the screen and then moved around it. The machine-code routine will be written so that it runs equally well on micros with different amounts of core memory, and on cassette-based and disc-based systems.

Listing of FASTPLOT program code

```
1000 REM Program : FASTPLOT
1010 REM
1020 REM
1030 REM This program uses a machine-code routine for plotting
1040 REM      low-resolution graphics rapidly on the screen.  The
1050 REM      data for the pictures are POKEd into user memory just
1060 REM      below the machine-code routine.
1070 REM
1080 REM X8 and Y8 give the dimensions of the graphics block
1090 REM      measured in characters (not pixels).   X0 and Y0
1100 REM      are the coordinates of the bottom left of the
1110 REM      graphics block counted in pixels (the coordinate
1120 REM      system used by the PLOT command).  DS is the address
1130 REM      of the start of POKEd data for a block of graphics.
1140 REM
1150 REM The machine-code routine is useful in any program
1160 REM      requiring rapid display of a block of graphics.
1170 REM
1180 REM
1190     CLEAR 100,,301
1200 REM
1210     ON BREAK GOTO 1960
1220 REM  Deal with user's interruption
1230 REM
1240     TEXT : PRINT CHR$(12) : REM Clear the screen
1250     PRINT CHR$(17) : REM Disable paging
1260 REM
1270 REM
1280     PRINT TAB(16); "FASTPLOT"
1290     PRINT
1300     PRINT TAB(2); "Plots pictures on the screen rapidly"
1310     PRINT : PRINT : PRINT
1320     PRINT TAB(19); "*"
1330     PRINT
1340     PRINT TAB(15); "Derek Ball"
1350     PRINT
1360     PRINT TAB(14); "Andrew Nash"
1370     PRINT
1380     PRINT TAB(19); "*"
1390     PRINT : PRINT : PRINT
1400     PRINT TAB(13); "Copyright 1982"
1410     PRINT
1420     PRINT TAB(10); "Hutchinson Education"
1430     PRINT
1440     FOR D = 1 TO 5000 : NEXT D : REM Delay
1450     PRINT CHR$(12) : REM Clear the screen
1460 REM
1470 REM
1480 REM MAIN PROGRAM
1490 REM
1500     HM=PEEK(6)+256*PEEK(7) : REM Address of high memory
1510 REM
1520     RS=HM-33 : REM Routine start address
1530     GOSUB 2000 : REM Load fast-plot routine
1540 REM
1550     X8=24 : Y8=4 : DS=RS-172
1560     GOSUB 2170 : REM Load first data block
1570 REM
1580     X8=19 : Y8=4 : DS=RS-76
1590     GOSUB 2170 : REM Load second data block
1600 REM
```

```
1610      X8=24 : Y8=4 : DS=RS-268
1620      GOSUB 2170 : REM Load data block to clear graphics
1630 REM
1640 REM Display the words 'MOVES' and 'FAST'
1650 REM
1660      X8=24 : Y8=4 : DS=RS-172
1670      X0=0 : Y0=27
1680      GOSUB 2340 : REM Plot 'MOVES'
1690      FOR D=1 TO 3000 : NEXT D : REM Delay
1700 REM
1710      X8=19 : Y8=4 : DS=RS-76
1720      X0=0 : Y0=12
1730      GOSUB 2340 : REM Plot 'FAST'
1740      FOR D = 1 TO 3000 : NEXT D : REM Delay
1750 REM
1760 REM Move the word 'MOVES' across screen
1770 REM
1780      X8=24 : Y8=4
1790      FOR X = 0 TO 30 STEP 2
1800         X0=X : Y0=27 : DS=RS-268
1810         GOSUB 2340 : REM Erase "MOVES'
1820         X0=X+2 : Y0=27 : DS=RS-172
1830         GOSUB 2340 : REM Plot 'MOVES'
1840      NEXT X
1850 REM
1860 REM Move the word 'FAST' across screen
1870 REM
1880      X8=19 : Y8=4
1890      FOR X = 0 TO 40 STEP 2
1900         X0=X : Y0=12 : DS=RS-268
1910         GOSUB 2340 : REM Erase 'FAST'
1920         X0=X+2 : Y0=12 : DS=RS-76
1930         GOSUB 2340 : REM Plot 'FAST'
1940      NEXT X
1950 REM
1960      PRINT CHR$(19) : REM Re-enable paging
1970      END
1980 REM
1990 REM
2000 REM SUBROUTINE : LOAD FAST-PLOT ROUTINE
2010 REM
2020      AD=RS
2030      FOR I = 1 TO 33
2040         READ C
2050         POKE AD, C
2060         AD=AD+1
2070      NEXT I
2080 REM
2090      RETURN
2100 REM
2110      DATA &F7, &0B, &21, &00, &00, &11, &00, &00, &0E, &00
2120      DATA &06, &00, &7D, &90, &D6, &40, &6F, &7C, &DE, &00
2130      DATA &67, &1A, &77, &13, &23, &10, &FA, &0D, &20, &EC
2140      DATA &F7, &0C, &C9
2150 REM
2160 REM
2170 REM SUBROUTINE : LOAD DATA BLOCK
2180 REM
2190 REM DS is address of start of data block
2200 REM X8, Y8 are number of characters across and up
2210 REM
2220      AD=DS
2230      FOR Y = 1 TO Y8
2240         FOR X = 1 TO X8
2250            READ C
```

```
2260            POKE AD, C+192
2270            AD=AD+1
2280         NEXT X
2290      NEXT Y
2300 REM
2310      RETURN
2320 REM
2330 REM
2340 REM SUBROUTINE : PLOT PICTURE RAPIDLY
2350 REM
2360 REM X8, Y8 are number of characters across and up
2370 REM X0, Y0 are coordinates of bottom left-hand corner of picture
2380 REM
2390 REM Subroutine protects against bad values of X0 and Y0
2400 REM but not against bad values of X8 and Y8
2410 REM
2420 REM US is the address of the start of the data block to be used
2430 REM
2440      X1=INT(X0/2) : Y1=INT(Y0/3)
2450 REM
2460      IF X1<0 OR X1>39 THEN 2660
2470      IF Y1<0 OR Y1>19 THEN 2660
2480      IF X1+X8>40 THEN 2660
2490      IF Y1+Y8>20 THEN 2660
2500 REM
2510      SS=&F000+64*(20-Y1)+X1+X8
2520 REM    SS is address of bottom left of
2530 REM    graphics block in screen memory
2540      P=RS+3 : Q=SS
2550      GOSUB 2690 : REM Poke address of screen start
2560      P=RS+6 : Q=US
2570      GOSUB 2690 : REM Poke address of data start
2580 REM
2590 REM Poke picture size
2600 REM
2610      POKE RS+11, X8
2620      POKE RS+9, Y8
2630 REM
2640      CALL RS : REM Call fast-plot routine
2650 REM
2660      RETURN
2670 REM
2680 REM
2690 REM SUBROUTINE: POKE CHANGE OF ADDRESS
2700 REM
2710      Q1=INT(Q/256)
2720      Q0=Q-256*Q1
2730      POKE P, Q0
2740      POKE P+1, Q1
2750 REM
2760      RETURN
2770 REM
2780 REM
2790 REM Data for 'MOVES'
2800 REM
2810      DATA 63, 0, 0, 63, 0, 11, 61, 62, 7, 0
2820      DATA 0, 43, 23, 0, 0, 63, 60, 60, 60, 0
2830      DATA 11, 61, 62, 7, 63, 42, 21, 63, 0, 63
2840      DATA 0, 0, 63, 0, 10, 61, 62, 5, 0, 63
2850      DATA 3, 3, 0, 0, 50, 3, 3, 63, 63, 47
2860      DATA 31, 63, 0, 63, 0, 0, 63, 0, 47, 20
2870      DATA 49, 31, 0, 63, 48, 48, 0, 0, 63, 52
2880      DATA 48, 19, 61, 16, 32, 62, 0, 56, 31, 47
2890      DATA 52, 0, 63, 0, 0, 63, 0, 63, 15, 15
2900      DATA 15, 0, 56, 31, 47, 52
```

```
2910 REM
2920 REM
2930 REM Data for 'FAST'
2940 REM
2950    DATA 63, 0, 0, 0, 0, 63, 0, 0, 63, 0
2960    DATA 11, 61, 62, 7, 0, 0, 42, 21, 0, 63
2970    DATA 3, 3, 0, 0, 63, 60, 60, 63, 0, 50
2980    DATA 3, 3, 63, 0, 0, 42, 21, 0, 63, 48
2990    DATA 48, 0, 0, 63, 0, 0, 63, 0, 63, 52
3000    DATA 48, 19, 0, 0, 42, 21, 0, 63, 15, 15
3010    DATA 15, 0, 56, 31, 47, 48, 0, 56, 31, 47
3020    DATA 52, 0, 15, 47, 31, 15
3030 REM
3040 REM
3050 REM Data for clearing screen
3060 REM
3070    DATA 0, 0, 0, 0, 0, 0, 0, 0, 0, 0
3080    DATA 0, 0, 0, 0, 0, 0, 0, 0, 0, 0
3090    DATA 0, 0, 0, 0, 0, 0, 0, 0, 0, 0
3100    DATA 0, 0, 0, 0, 0, 0, 0, 0, 0, 0
3110    DATA 0, 0, 0, 0, 0, 0, 0, 0, 0, 0
3120    DATA 0, 0, 0, 0, 0, 0, 0, 0, 0, 0
3130    DATA 0, 0, 0, 0, 0, 0, 0, 0, 0, 0
3140    DATA 0, 0, 0, 0, 0, 0, 0, 0, 0, 0
3150    DATA 0, 0, 0, 0, 0, 0, 0, 0, 0, 0
3160    DATA 0, 0, 0, 0, 0, 0
```

Discussion of FASTPLOT

What to notice: By running the program, you can see how rapidly the words 'MOVES' and 'FAST' are displayed on the screen. Compare this with the speed at which characters are displayed by BIGLET.

Note that both words stay completely on the screen (neither appears partly on it and partly off it at any stage). This is a limitation of the particular machine-code routine being used.

Program code: If you want to make use of the machine-code routine in your own programs, the code in FASTPLOT will require careful study. In particular, you will need to know how to load and how to call the blocks of data used for the pictures.

FASTPLOT contains three blocks of data: the first produces 'MOVES', the second produces 'FAST', and the third blanks out a portion of the screen. The chart given below indicates where these blocks of data are stored in computer memory, and should help you in deciding what numbers to put where. Note that the space required for both machine-code routine and data blocks is reserved by means of the second number in the 'CLEAR' statement at line 1190. Once you have understood the principle involved, you may use in your own programs as many blocks of data as you wish.

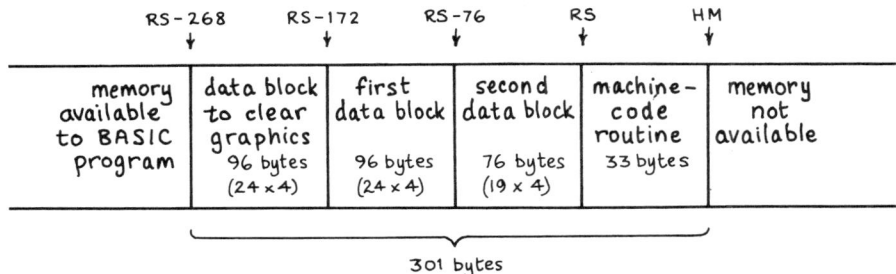

Error-checking: The program does not require any data to be input from the user, so there is no need for error-checking. If you change the data to produce your own pictures, it is possible that you may make mistakes while modifying the program which produce errors when it is run – but that is another matter.

What you could do: You could design your own picture and use the FASTPLOT routine to plot it. As a first step, you could try to substitute a design of your own in place of either 'MOVES' or 'FAST': this would not entail any other alteration to the code.

The machine-code routine in FASTPLOT is limited in that it cannot cope with pictures which partly disappear off the edge of the screen. As a *relatively* simple exercise in machine-code programming, you could write a routine to improve on the one given.

Portability: While the exact form of the machine-code routine works only with the RML 380Z or 480Z, it would need little adaptation to run on any machine with a Z80 microprocessor chip. A similar routine could also be written without any great difficulty for a microcomputer based on a different microprocessor chip.

A.4 Addresses

Below is a select list of organizations which we feel may be of interest to you: some provide hardware, some software; all provide information. Many publishers of books now market software also: watch their catalogues. We suggest that before buying any software, even that recommended by friends and colleagues, you try it for yourself if at all possible.

Advisory Unit for Computer-Based Education (AUCBE)
   Endymion Road, Hatfield, Hertfordshire AL10 8AU
     Suppliers of a variety of software for school use (including microQUERY, an excellent information-retrieval package which runs on the RML 380Z)

Appendices

BBC Microcomputer Systems
PO Box 7, London W3 6XJ
Suppliers of the BBC Microcomputer

Computers in Education as a Resource (CEDAR)
Imperial College of Science and Technology, London SW7 2AZ
Suppliers of information and suggestions concerning the use of computers in teaching a variety of subjects

Educational Computing Section, Chelsea College, University of London
Pulton Place, London SW6 5PR
Suppliers of information about the Schools Council's 'Computers in the Curriculum' project and about the 'Chelsea Science Simulations'

Council for Educational Technology in the United Kingdom (CET)
3 Devonshire Street, London W1N 2BA
Suppliers of various publications concerning the use of computers in education

Department of Artificial Intelligence, University of Edinburgh
Old College, Edinburgh EH8 9YL
Suppliers of publications describing research into the use of computers in education

Geographical Association Package Exchange (GAPE)
Department of Geography, University of Technology, Loughborough LE11 3TU
Suppliers of software for use in the teaching of geography

Investigations on Teaching with Microcomputers as an Aid (ITMA)
College of St Mark and St John, Derriford Road, Plymouth PL6 8BH
Suppliers of excellent software for use in teaching a variety of subjects at a variety of levels, and of a regular newsletter and other publications

Logic Programming Associates Ltd
36 Gorst Road, London SW11 6JE
Suppliers of PROLOG to run on CP/M-based machines (including the RML 380Z)

Micros and Primary Education (MAPE)
St Helens County Primary School, Bluntisham, Cambridgeshire
Suppliers of information and ideas about the use of computers in primary schools

Microelectronics Education Programme (MEP)
Cheviot House, Coach Lane Campus, Newcastle-upon-Tyne NE7 7XA
Suppliers of information about the availability of software and other materials to support the use of computers in schools – information is also available from the various MEP Regional Information Centres

Minicomputer Users in Secondary Education (MUSE)
Freepost, Bromsgrove, Worcestershire B61 0JT
Suppliers of a marketplace for the exchange of software among teachers; also run courses

PCD-Maltron Ltd
219 Sycamore Road, Farnborough, Hampshire GU14 6RQ
Suppliers of superb two- and one-handed (right or left) keyboards for use with microcomputers (including the RML 380Z and the BBC Microcomputer), with word processors or directly with printers – unlike the QWERTY keyboard, the Maltron keyboards are designed with a view to comfort, speed and ease of use, and they are very light: they should appeal to all those who need to type, including the handicapped

Rehabilitation Engineering Movement Advisory Panels (REMAP)
Thames House North, Millbank, London SW1P 4QG
Suppliers of specially designed equipment for handicapped people – each job is tackled individually by voluntary technical specialists

Research Machines Ltd (RML)
Mill Street, Oxford OX2 0BW
Suppliers of the 380Z and 480Z microcomputers

A.5 Books

There are many books and magazines which provide information of possible interest to you: information about kinds of hardware, kinds of software, programming languages, the electronics of your equipment, and so on. In this book, we have discussed evaluation of hardware and software, and we feel that the same principles should be applied to the selection of books: is the book attractive, well-organized, readable, accessible and does it seem to contain the information that you want? Here are five books of a different kind: we have enjoyed them and found them useful and stimulating.

Hermann Hesse: *The glass bead game*
Penguin Books
ISBN 0-14-003438-2

John Holt: *How children fail*
Penguin Books
ISBN 0-14-021115-2

John M Nevison: *The little book of BASIC style*
Addison-Wesley Publishing Company
ISBN 0-201-05247-4

Seymour Papert: *Mindstorms: children, computers and powerful ideas*
The Harvester Press Ltd
ISBN 0-85527-163-9

I D H Shepherd, Z A Cooper and D R F Walker: *Computer-assisted learning in geography*
CET *with* Geographical Association
ISBN 0-86184-012-7

Programs in this book

This book contains the following programs:
  AUGURY (pages 70–4)
  BIGLET (pages 143–9)
  LEXICAL1 (pages 154–5), LEXICAL2 (page 156) and LEXICAL3 (pages 156–8)
  EXHIBIT1 (pages 164–5) and EXHIBIT2 (pages 165–7)
  CANALOCK (pages 171–5)
  AIRLINE1 (page 179) and AIRLINE2 (pages 180–2)
  HILIGHTC (pages 188–93) and HILIGHTT (pages 193–8)
  SCALES (pages 204–6)
  CODE (pages 211–4)
  CIRCLES (pages 218–24)
  SPELLC (pages 232–4) and SPELLF (pages 234–6)
  GRAPH (pages 242–9)
  BLANKRML (pages 295–7)
  DESIGN (pages 301–4) and FASTPLOT (pages 307–10)

The programs in the book were written originally for a Research Machines Ltd (RML) 380Z microcomputer, with a BASIC version 5 interpreter and 32K RAM. However, all of them should also run on RML 480Zs, and all are readily adaptable to RML 380Z micros with other interpreters; most of them can be adapted to micros from other manufacturers. On page 123, we invite you to use these programs, to show them to your friends, and to adapt them to your own needs. You are welcome to modify them in any way you wish, to improve them as we have suggested (or in other ways), and to incorporate parts or all of them into other programs that you yourself write. The programs are all copyright, and we would like you always to acknowledge us as the original authors.

To make it easier for you to use them (see page 62), and to save your time in typing them from the book, the programs are available in machine-readable form. For an up-to-date list of the machines and interpreters for which versions of these programs have been prepared, please write to:
  Bob Osborne
  Hutchinson Education
  17–21 Conway Street
  London W1P 6JD

Index

acceptability of computers in teaching, 97
access time, 265
accountancy, 123
accumulator, 263
acknowledgements, 15
acronyms, 258
adapting program code (to micros other than the RML 380Z), 75, 134–42
   'CALL' instruction, 227–8
   display of text, 201
   files, 306
   high-resolution graphics, 152, 176, 255, 306
   'INPUT' instruction, 201
   machine code, 227, 311
   'PLOT' instruction, 152
   'POKE' instruction, 255
   'PRINT' instruction, 169
A–D converters, 288
addresses, useful, 311–3
addresses in core memory (*see also* 'POKE' instruction in BASIC), 35, 263
   problems in use of, 266
administration, 107, 112
advertising of programs, 54–5, 122
aims, success in achieving, 113–6
AIRLINE programs, 177–84
algorithmic languages, 49
algorithms, 49
   turning into code, 124
alphabetic order in relation to keyboards, 268
amnesia, 119
analogue computer, 258
analogue-to-digital converters, 288
angles, estimating size of, 99
ANIMAL program, 107
annotation in code, 131
ANSI, 61–2
answers, checking with computer, 109

anticipation (by user of program), 45
applications programs, 54
approximation, teaching of, 25
archaeology, teaching of, 111
architecture, teaching of, 125
arithmetic function (of processor), 263
arpeggios, 207
arrows (as error indicators), 183
art, teaching of, 105, 106
arts, teaching of, 289
ASCII code, 137, 215
assembly, 275
assembly language, 275
assembly program, 275
assistance to user *see* help
'attitudes' displayed by computers, 18
attitudes of learners, 99–100
AUGURY program, 66–75
   modification for machines other than the RML 380Z, 75
   specification of, 38–42, 43–6, 47
author languages, 98
availability of programs, 121–3

backing store, 10, 266
   directory of files on, 278
barter, obtaining programs by, 123
BASIC programming language, 12
   compared with other languages, 32
   derivation of name, 258
   pros and cons of, 115
   standard for, 61–2
batch job, 264
BIGLET program, 142–52
binary digits, 261
binary states, 261
biology, teaching of (*see also* sciences), 108, 111
bits, 261
   bit patterns, 261–2
   bit patterns from keyboard, 268

blank lines in code *see* code, program
BLANKRML program, 294–8
  defect in, 297–8
  not to be used with GRAPH in 32 K, 253
block structure, 57
board, 10, 259
bomb symbols, 79
book, this
  comparison with computers in learning, 18–9
  evaluation of, 28
  programs in, 315
  purpose of, 7, 8
  running programs in, 129
  structure of, 7
  use of, 8
  validity of ideas in, 8
  value of pictures in, 76
books, information from, 127–8
books, interesting, 313
bootstrapping, 281
bounds of loop, 132
braille, 271
'BREAK' key, 135
bugs, programming, 11, 65, 282
bus drivers, output, 125
byte, 262

'CALL' instruction in BASIC, 140
CANALOCK program, 82, 107, 169–76
'CAPITALS LOCK' key (*see also* 'SHIFT' key)
  neutralizing of, 149, 200
card-suit symbols, 79
case sensitivity, 47, 149
  neutralizing of, 149, 200
cassette operating system, 281
  core memory occupied by, 141–2
  where stored, 281
cassettes, magnetic, 10, 266
  interfaces between cassette systems, 63
  length of, 119–20
  limited storage on, 101
  overwriting of, 119
  problems in use of, 62, 101, 119–20, 266–7
  transferring information to disc, 10
  use of tape counter with, 278
catalogues, 9
  of files, 278
cells of screen, 272
central processor, 261, 263

chance (in programs), 102–3
character code, 137
  differences between machines, 280
character set, 262
  what is needed, 261
chemistry, teaching of (*see also* sciences), 108
chess, coding of moves in, 111
chips, 10, 259
  addition of, 263–4, 291
  CPU chips, 10, 263
  memory chips, 10, 263
choice (*see also* freedom)
  'correct' choice implied by message, 208
  effected by light pen, 269–70
  effected by pressure pad, 270–1
  freedom of, 21, 23
  made at random, 102–3
  of filenames, 278
  of hardware, 284, 287–8
  of identifiers, 119, 150, 215
  of microcomputer, 283–6
  of program flags, 150
  of programming language, 284–5, 288–90
  problems caused by, 104
CIRCLES program, 216–29
  commands in, 224–5
circuitry in micros, 259
clarity (*see also* code, program; screens)
  portability and, 122
classification, teaching of, 107
classroom, uses of micro in, 97–116
cleaning of equipment, 121
'CLEAR' instruction (on RML 380Z), 134, 139, 310
clever, being, 124
code, cryptic, 111
code, program (*see also* adapting program code; statements), 11, 32, 48–53
  adaptation of, 61–2, 75, 95
  ideals versus practicalities, 50
  indentation in, 51, 131–2, 150, 291, 294–8
  instruction code, 274
  intelligibility of, 12, 158–9
  layout of, 32–3, 130–4, 150–1, 152–60
  machine code, 274
  modification by a user, 215
  reducing length of, 51, 152–60
  running-on of text in, 160
  sectioning of, 131, 150
  spacing in, 132, 133, 159

318   *Index*

code, program – *cont.*
   structure of, 56–8, 142–52
   style in, 48–53, 130–4
code, useful (in other programs)
   in centring of text, 183
   in clearing high-resolution graphics screens (RML 380Z), 253
   in command-mode programs, 200
   in controlling a cursor, 200, 253
   in controlling execution, 176
   in converting input, 207
   in cycling around lists, 207
   in deadening keys, 200
   in displaying large characters, 142
   in displaying pictures rapidly, 216, 226, 298–9, 310–1
   in marking character errors, 183
   in right-justifying text, 239
   in searching text, 185
CODE program, 208–15
colour, use of, 86, 287
COMAL programming language, 57
command-mode programs, 43
   examples of, 152, 184–201, 216–29, 229–40, 240–57
comments (in code), 32–3, 65
   deletion of, 151
common sense, use of, 118, 121, 128
compatibility of hardware, 280
competition, 24
compilers, 276
   use in increasing speed, 96
   versus interpreters, 96, 276–7
computer (*see also* microcomputer), 258
computerese, 125
computer-managed learning, 109
computer system, 259–61, 279–83
confidence
   building through mistakes, 26
   in learning, 22
   in programming, 55–6
configuration, 280
consistency, 133–4, 184
   in choice of micros, 283
   in programs, 46
constants, 35
context for programs, design of, 27
continuous stationery, 273
control by micro
   of equipment, 103, 126
   of user, 104
control function (of processor), 263
control key, 268

control of learning, 19
control of micro
   by equipment, 126, 291
   by games paddle, 287
   by joystick, 287
   by mouth, 271
   by rocker switch, 271
   by space-bar, 170, 176, 229, 238, 239, 252
   by system, 278–9
   by user, 238
   by voice, 111
   transfers within programs, 31
conversational mode (of working), 264
coordinates, origin of, 227–8
copies, backup, 118, 127, 267
copyright of programs, 55, 120, 122–3
   in this book, 150, 315
core memory (*see also* user memory; workspace), 10, 262
   addresses in, 263
   locations in, 263
   resetting of, 281–2
   shortage of space in, 41, 152, 276, 291
   size of, 60, 141–2, 262, 263, 266
   types of, 280–1
corruption of files, 281–2
COS *see* cassette operating system
cost, mistaken view of, 291
counting, 113
   of errors, 239
counts, 35
CP, 261
CPU chips, 10, 263
   similarity of, 274
crash, program, 11, 281
   recovery from, 281–2
crash, system, 281–2
'CTRL' key, 268
curriculum, areas where computer applicable to, 97
cursor, 10, 135, 141
   backward movement of, 149–50, 200
   control of, 149–50, 253
   use during input, 91, 142
   use in designing pictures on a screen, 299
   use with digitizer, 269

damage
   accidental, 117–8
   wilful, 120
danger, avoidance of, 100

Index

data (*see also* information)
  availability in parts of program, 57
  clear use of, 150
  storage for, 152
  tabulation of, 9
databanks, 127
databases, 31, 107
  example of use of, 161
'DATA' statements in BASIC, use of, 209
data transfer standards, 62–3
daydreams, 24
debugging, 282
decision (in a program), 31
decrement, 35
defaults, 46–7
definition (precision) (*see also* resolution), 87
degradation, graceful, 125
degrading of system, 63
delay (in execution), 132–3, 150, 226
demonstrations, pre-recording of, 105
design, 106
DESIGN program, 298–306
devices *see* hardware
diagnostics, error, 260
dialects, 53, 277
  pros and cons of, 60
dialogue between computer and user, 39–42
digital computer, 258
digitizer, 269
direct access store, 265
directory of files, 278
disabled users *see* handicapped users
disc drives, 266
disc operating system, 281
  core memory occupied by, 141–2
  loading of, 281
  where stored, 281
discs, magnetic, 10, 266–7
  needed with large amounts of information, 101
  transferring information to cassette, 10
discussion, stimulation of, 216–29
diskettes, 266
documentation (*see also* manuals), 11, 283
  example of, 66–75
  external to program, 33
  in programs, 33, 93
  manufacturers', 290
  need to update, 119
  versus facilities, 253
DOS *see* disc operating system

dot-matrix printers, 272–3
drawing, 114, 115
drill programs, 99, 105
  example of, 229–40
duplication, value of (*see also* copies, backup), 118
dynamics of process, demonstration of, 82

echoing, 47
  example of, 185
  of keyboard to screen, 141
economics, teaching of, 100, 103, 106, 108, 289
economy of time as well as money, 294
editing, 111–2
  of text, 112, 195
editors, 278
educational equipment
  connected to micros, 103
  micros as, 97
efficiency of computer, 265
electronic blackboard, 106–7
electronics (of hardware), 126
elements (of storage), 261
engineering, teaching of, 103
English, teaching of, 97, 185
  essay writing in, 108
  letter frequencies, 215
  spelling, 229–40
  textual analysis, 152
enhancement of programs, 53, 282
'ENTER' key *see* 'RETURN' key
equipment
  connected to micros, 103, 126
  monitoring of, 126
erasure of files, 119
error diagnostics, 260
  clear use of (example), 177–84
  not always helpful, 151
errors
  execution errors, 281
  counting of, 239
error-trapping, 40, 104, 140
  dangers of oversimplifying this, 52
  difficulties in establishing occurrence of error, 98
  examples of, 151, 160, 169, 176, 200, 207, 215, 226, 239, 254
  in numeric input, 140, 177–84
  in text, 66–75
  levels of, 64–5
  need for, 41
  use of 'ON ERROR', 254

Index

essays, writing of, 108
estimation of sizes of angles, 99
evaluation
   of learning, 26–8
   of learning situations, 20
   of micros, 100–4
   of programs, 48–53, 63–6, 75, 97, 160, 293–4
   of teaching methods, 202
   of this book, 28
examples in this book, general applicability of, 97
examples within programs, 104
execution, 11
execution error, 281
execution time, 264, 265
executive *see* operating system
exercises, checking answers to, 109
EXHIBIT programs, 160–9
experiment, opportunity to, 100, 109
experimenting, with own micro, 125
experiments
   simulations of, 80–1
   usefulness of, 114
explanation, 82
exploration, 81

facts, teaching of, 98
   general-purpose programs to test, 98
   need for disc system, 101
   storage of, 98, 101
   versus teaching of, 99
fan-fold stationery, 273
fast access store, 265
FASTPLOT program (in machine code), 298–9, 306–11
faults
   in hardware, 121
   in software, 276
feelings of learner, 99–100
files, 10, 278
   corruption of, 281–2
   data in, 299
   directory of, 278
   maintenance of, 282
   management of, 278
   marks in, 63
   modifying, 278
   names of, 10, 119, 278, 305–6
films
   projector connected to micro, 103
   versus programs on micros, 87–9
firmware, 261, 264, 280

flags (in programs), 150
   example of, 176
   numbers versus strings, 150
flexibility
   in approach, 123–5
   in hardware, 124
   in planning, 124–5
   in programs, 253
   in teaching, 125
floppy disc (*see also* discs, magnetic), 266
flowcharts, 35, 68
   examples of, 69, 143, 153, 162, 163, 171, 178, 186, 187, 203, 210, 217, 230, 231, 241, 300
FORTRAN programming language, example of, 32
freedom
   in exploration, 82
   in input, 253
   in programs, 23, 229–40
friendly environment, 90
function (as a module), 35
function keys, 268

gadgets *see* hardware
games, 21, 100, 105
geography, teaching of, 100, 105, 106, 108, 109, 289
'GET' instruction in BASIC, 141
global, 57
grapefruit marmalade, 49–50
graphics (*see also* high-resolution graphics; low-resolution graphics; pictures), 10, 76–96
   clarity of, 93
   ease of use of, 84, 89–90, 92
   meaning of term, 79
   portability of programs containing, 85–6, 93
   problems with, 91–6
   reversed field in, 79
   special characters in, 79, 138
   standard commands for, 95
   unnecessary use of, 92
   use of, 79–83, 83–7, 287
   use on micros versus use elsewhere, 87–91
   use with displayed text, 169–76, 200
   use with large classes, 142
graphics codes calculated from individual pixels, 305
'GRAPH' instruction (on RML 380Z), 139

graph plotters, 273
GRAPH program, 240–57
   commands in, 251–3
   different uses in teaching, 255–7
graphs, 9
   on screens versus on printers, 83
groups, local, 123

Hahlwud, 38
handicapped users, 291
   pressure pads and, 271
hard-copy output, 272–3
hardware, 261
   choice of, 124, 284, 287–8
   connecting together, 279–80
   for input, 260, 268–71
   for output, 260, 271–3
   for storage, 260, 266
   maintenance of, 121, 285
   not always necessary, 117
   packaging of, 121
hazard, yourself as a, 118–20
hazards, 117–8
headings (in code), 131
help to user (*see also* consistency), 25–6, 39–42, 48, 104
   different kinds of, 99
   difficulty in providing, 99
   for teachers, 109
   use of defaults, 46–7
Hertfordshire County Council Advisory Unit for Computer-Based Education, 184
high-level language *see* languages, programming
high-resolution graphics, 78–9
   example of use, 216–29, 240–57
   limitations of, 86–7
   need for, 86
   speed of display of, 95–6
HILIGHT programs, 107, 184–201
history, teaching of, 9, 100, 105, 106
humanities, teaching of, 289
humidity, 118
humour, questionable value of, 290
hybrid computer, 258
hypotheses, testing of, 25

IC *see* integrated circuit
ideas
   receptivity to, 125–8
   teaching of, 100
identification, teaching of, 107

identifiers, 56
   choice of, 119, 150, 215
   listed in program, 176
   of data, 35, 150
   of modules, 34
idle time, 264
'IF...GOTO' instruction in BASIC, 62
'IF...THEN' instruction in BASIC, 62
illness, catching up after, 105
imagination, need for, 288, 291
immediate access store
implementation of programs, 282
increment, 35
indentation *see* code, program
information
   distinction from data, 260
   kinds of access to, 266–7
   presentation of, 101
   processing of, 263
   retrieval of, 31, 98, 101, 267, 287
   sources of, 127–8
   storage of, 10, 31, 98, 101, 107–8, 261–2
   transfer between media, 10, 266, 262–3
'INKEY' instruction *see* 'GET' instruction
innovation in teaching, 100, 125
   opportunity for, 97
   possible problems of, 18
input (*see also* error-trapping), 259–60, 267–71
   conversion of form of, 207
   devices for, 260, 268–71
   freedom in form of, 253
   from storage, 268–9
   of numbers, 140, 177–84
'INPUT' instruction in BASIC, 140
'INPUT LINE' instruction (on RML 380Z), 141
installation, 280
instruction code, 274
instructions (in a program), 30
instruction set, 274
integrated circuit, 10, 259
interaction
   of factors, 114–5
   pros and cons of, 228
interactive mode (of working), 264
interfaces, 280
   between cassette systems, 63
   between micro and user, 284
   between micros, 287
   between pieces of equipment, 126
interpreters (*see also* compilers; translators), 10, 276

322 *Index*

interpreters – *cont.*
  core memory occupied by, 141–2
  modifying, 95, 298
  versus compilers, 276–7
  where stored, 10–1
interruption of program, 135–6
iteration (looping), 30–1
ITMA (Investigations into Teaching using Microcomputers as an Aid), 184

jargon; 258
job, 264
joystick control, 287
jumps (in programs)
  conditional, 31
  destination of, 150–1
  unconditional, 31

K, 262–3
keyboards, 9, 268
  braille, 271
  non-QWERTY layout of, 271
  touch-sensitive, 268
keys, deadening of, 41, 200, 226
  to save core memory, 254
kinetic theory of gases, 81
knowledge, 20

languages (natural), teaching of (*see also* English), 107, 289
languages (programming) (*see also* BASIC; COMAL; LOGO; PASCAL; PROLOG), 31–3
  algorithmic languages, 49
  assembly language, 275
  author languages, 98
  choice of, 56, 58, 284–5, 288–90
  development of, 274–5
  dialects of, 277
  high-level, 10, 30, 275, 277
  low-level, 10, 30, 275, 277
  machine language, 10
  portability and, 122
  reserved words in, 33, 275
  standards in, 61–2
  statements in, 33
  structured languages, 56–8
  syntax of, 33
  unclear definition of, 115
layout *see* code, program; screens
leap-frog tests, crippled, 125
learners (*see also* users), 22–6
  appearance of programs to, 18
  gaining interest of, 100
  individuals and groups, 202–8
  motivation of, 99–100
  needed in evaluating teaching methods, 202
  needs of, 16, 23
  number of, 105
  teachers as, 20
  value of printed copy to, 108, 112
  young, 112
learning, 16–28, 97–100
  by programming, 89–90, 208
  competition in, 24
  computer-managed, 109
  confidence in, 22
  evaluation of, 19, 26–8
  freedom in, 16–9, 20–1, 100
  from interactions, 114–5
  management of, 19, 23–4, 109
  mistakes during, 21, 24–6
  motivation in, 16
  objectives in, 21, 26–7
  open situations in, 23
  testing in, 27
  tutorial computer-assisted, 101, 107–8
'LET' instruction in BASIC, 133
letters
  enlarged on screen, 142–52
  upper-case versus lower-case, 47
lexical analysis, 152, 201
LEXICAL programs, 152–60
liability, 123
library
  of programs, 35–6
  of routines, 35–6, 57, 94–5
light pen, 269–70
'LINE' instruction in BASIC, 137
line numbers, 32
  shortage of core memory and, 159
line of program, 275
line printer, 273
listing of program, 34
local, 57
locations in core memory, 263
  direct allocation of data to, 93
logical operators, 183
logical thinking, teaching of, 289
LOGO programming language, 90, 115, 289
loops, program, 30–1, 132, 150
  nesting of, 31
low-level language *see* languages, programming

Index

low-resolution graphics, 78–9
  designing pictures in, 298–306
  differences between machines, 84–5
  rapid display of pictures in, 298–9, 306–11
  use in tabulating data on screen, 45

machine code, 274
  example of, 225, 306
  in increasing speed in graphics, 95
  pros and cons of, 96
machine dependence, 59, 277
machine independence, 59, 277
machine instructions, 30
machine language *see* languages, programming
machine operations, 30
machine-readability, 62
magazines (*see also* information), 127
magic, computer's lack of, 128
magnetic cassette *see* cassette, magnetic
magnetic disc *see* disc, magnetic
mainframe computer, 259
main memory *see* core memory
main routine, 35
maintenance
  of hardware and software, 285
  of programs, 52–3, 65, 282
manuals, 62
manufacturers
  attitude to copyright, 120
  competition between, 277
  contact with, 66, 125, 290
  documentation from, 290
  maintenance and, 285
  reporting program bugs to, 282
  support from, 285
  user groups and, 282–3
maps, 9, 106, 269
  screen displays versus other media, 90–1
marketing, 121–3
marmalade, grapefruit, 49–50
mastery of situations, 97–100
mathematical model, 80
mathematics, teaching of, 106, 107, 109, 289
  drawing graphs in, 240–57
  estimating angles in, 99
  freedom in exploration of, 82
  tracing paths of loci in, 216–29
mazes, 114
medium-resolution graphics, 79

media, storage, 10
memory *see* backing store; chips; core memory
memory (human), testing of, 98
memory-mapping (of screen), 78, 86, 93–4
menu-driven operation, 45
menus, 33–4, 45
  examples of, 152
  irritation caused by, 45, 168
  modifying on screen, 160–9
messages, 10, 260
  encoding of, 208–15
  need to keep screen clear, 254
  wording of, 177, 238
microcomputers (see also RML 380Z microcomputer), 7, 9, 258–86
  abundance of, 291–2
  as a solution to all problems, 21–2
  as a threat to teachers, 17
  characteristics in teaching, 18
  choice of, 59, 283–6
  connected to other equipment, 103, 126
  day-to-day use of, 117–28
  efficiency of, 265
  flexibility of, 20, 228
  handicapped users and, 291
  in dialogue with user, 39–42, 47, 100
  in education, 7, 97, 100–4, 287
  information stored in, 101, 107–8
  maintenance of, 117
  parts of, 9–10
  processing in, 261–5
  pros and cons of, 17, 91, 292
  roles of, 9, 79–83, 97–116, 126–7, 291–2
  speed of, 102
  subjects in which useful, 9, 97
  transport of, 286
  word processing on, 112
  working with, 134, 274, 278–9
microprocessors, 259
minicomputers, 259
mistakes, 21, 24–6
  as a source of confidence, 26
  during run of program, 38–42
  protection by operating system, 279
  use in debugging, 282
mnemonic codes, 275
model, mathematical, 80
modelling, 9
modules (*see also* library of routines), 34–5, 43, 56
  as an aid to portability, 60
  graphics, 85–6

modules – *cont.*
　in command-mode programs, 184–5
monitor *see* operating system
monitoring of equipment, 126
monitor screens, 105
motivation (of learners), 99–100
multiaccess system, 126, 264–5
museum catalogue, 127, 161
music, teaching of, 105, 110–1, 202–8
　programming as an aid in, 208

name of user, use of, 238–9
names *see* identifiers
narrative *see* comments
nesting (of program loops), 31
networks, 126, 280, 287
non-volatile storage, 280
nuclear reactor, 100
null response, 47
null strings, 134
numbers, 113
　checking input of, 140, 177–84
　translation into pictures, 113

object program, 276
objectives of learning, influence on program design, 26–7
'ON BREAK' instruction in BASIC, 135–6
'ON ERROR' instruction in BASIC, 254
operating system (*see also* cassette operating system; disc operating system), 10, 279
　held in processor, 264
　system crash, 281–2
　where stored, 11
options (*see also* choice; freedom; menus)
　for the user, 42–8
　invocation of, 152
order
　importance in teaching, 20–1
　in programs, 20, 76–7
oscilloscopes, 126
output, 259–60, 271–3
　devices for, 260
　documentation of, 33
　kinds of, 260
　to paper, 272–3
　to storage, 273
　visibility of, 105–6
overhead projectors, 87
overwriting
　of backing store, 119, 266

　of core memory, 281–2
　protection from, 263

package, 11
　design of, 90
packaging (of hardware), 121
paddle, games, 287
paging (on screen), 135
paper *see* stationery
parameters, 43, 57–8
PASCAL programming language, examples of, 32, 49–50
patronizing program, example of, 229–40
peripheral devices (*see also* hardware), 261
permanence of information in store, 266
physics, teaching of (*see also* sciences), 108
pictures (*see also* graphics), 78, 106–7
　extent of detail in, 78–9, 87
　facilities for drawing of, 78–9
　in interpreting numbers, 113
　modifying on screen, 169–76
　moving, 9, 86–7, 216–29, 298–9, 306–11
　static, 9
　value of, 76, 108
　versus text, 76–7, 105–6
PILOT programming language, 98
pixels, 84–5, 136, 272
　ease of use of, 85
　number of, 140
　used in groups, 138–9, 305
　variation in size and use, 85
plagiarism, 120
planning, flexibility in, 124–5
'PLOT' instruction in BASIC, 136–9
plotters, graph, 273
'POKE' instruction in BASIC, 93–4
　example of, 253–4
　subroutine to use, 94
portability of programs, 59–60, 122, 134–42
　with graphics, 85–6, 140
power, computers as givers of, 291
practice in skills, 99
precautions, 118
preconceptions, avoidance of, 288
pre-printed stationery, 273
presentation, 82–3
　of information, 106–7
pressure pads, 270
　handicapped users and, 271
primary teaching, 105
　display of large characters in, 142–52

principles, teaching of, 100
printed text, 112
　value to learners of, 108, 112
printers (*see also* plotters), 9, 272–3
　braille, 271
　dot-matrix, 272–3
　limited mode of working of, 83
　line printer, 273
　optional use of, 209
'PRINT' instruction in BASIC, 33, 65, 136, 139
　use of '?' instead of, 159
print layout, 101
　cost of, 83
problems in use of micros, 281–2
problem-solving, teaching of, 108
procedure (as a module), 34–5
'PROCEDURE' instruction in PASCAL, 50
processing, 261–5
　speed of, 265
processor, 9, 259
　CPU chip in, 263
　size of, 262
program code *see* code, program
programming, 12–4
　as an aid in teaching other subjects, 115, 208
　bugs in, 11
　case studies in, 129–201
　demand on time of, 58
　desirability of doing it yourself, 12, 55
　done anywhere, 58–9
　flexibility in, 123–5
　instruction in, 55
　labyrinthine, 43
　pressure pads as an aid to, 271
　problem-solving as a form of, 81–2
　unclear nature of definition of, 289
programming, teaching of
　error-trapping, 177–84
　in teaching other subjects, 115, 208
programming languages *see* languages, programming
programming practice (*see also* adapting program code)
　in changing screen rewriting to screen updating, 169
　in checking input, 169, 183, 207, 215, 255, 306
　in checking logic, 75
　in condensing code, 160
　in converting tutorial to command mode, 75
　in increasing the user's control, 176, 239–40, 255
　in interfacing with other equipment, 208
　in manipulating text, 160, 200–1, 215
　in music, 207–8
　in packaging a program, 255
　in reversing the order of output, 207
　in use of data blocks, 310–1
　in use of files, 160, 169, 200, 215, 305
　in use of graphics, 151, 176, 207–8, 254–5, 306
　in use of lists, 239–40
　in use of printers, 169, 200, 306
　in use of random numbers, 240
　in use of tables, 169
　in using machine code, 226, 310–1
　in writing machine code, 225–6, 227, 311
program operation *see* command mode; tutorial mode; menus
programs (*see also* code, program; copyright; portability; software), 10, 29–75, 260
　adapted from mainframes, 82–3
　appearance to user of, 18, 229–40
　applications programs, 54, 277
　availability of, 53–9, 115–6, 121–3, 127, 268–9, 284–5, 288
　bugs in, 65
　chance in, 102–3
　clarity of operation of, 33–5, 275
　completeness of, 35
　consistency in, 35, 46
　cost of, 54, 58–9, 63
　designing context for, 27
　design of, 36–53, 63, 76–8, 90, 288, 291
　drill programs, 99, 105
　evaluation of, 63–6, 293–4
　flexibility in, 35–6, 104, 229–40
　implementation of, 282
　kinds of use of, 37–8, 104–9, 202–8, 208–15, 228, 229–40, 240
　library of, 35–6, 127
　maintenance of, 52–3, 117–21, 282, 285
　modules in, 34–5
　on different micros, 59–63
　realism in, 288
　reliability of, 102
　size of, 141–2, 208
　systems programs, 54, 277–8, 278
　utilities, 278
　versions of, 53, 65, 119, 282

326 *Index*

programs – *cont.*
  what else is needed, 11, 53
  wording of messages in, 238
PROLOG programming language, 289–90
prompt (to user), 47
protection of programs, 117–21
publicity, importance of, 288

qualifications, 125–6
QWERTY keyboard layout, 268
  alternative to, 271
  survival of, 268
questions
  choice of answer to, 39–42, 46–7
  unnecessary, 39

RAM *see* random access memory
random access memory, 263–4, 265, 280–1
  size of, 141–2
  use in RML 380Z micro, 141–2
random numbers, 102–3
read-only memory, 263–4, 280–1
  use in RML 380Z micro, 141–2
read/write head, 266
realism in programs, 288
real-time programs, 80
recipe for grapefruit marmalade, 49–50
recovery (after overwriting), 281–2
registers (in processor), 263, 274
reliability of programs, 102
remedial teaching, 105
remote (of machines), 280
'REM' statements in BASIC, 32–3, 65
  deletion of, 151
repairs, 285
repertoire, instruction, 274
reserved words (in programming languages), 33, 275
resetting (of microcomputer), 134
  after crash, 281–2
  even after interruption, 135–6
resident programs, 280
resolution (*see also* high-resolution graphics; low-resolution graphics), 78–9
response time, 265
retrieval of information *see* information
'RETURN' instruction in BASIC, 159
'RETURN' key, 47, 141, 268
  code sent by, 138
reverse-field characters, 79
revisions of programs, 282

right answers
  not provided, 114
  obsessive need for, 25
RML 380Z microcomputer, 129–30, 134–42
  modification to disc BASIC to prevent loss of blanks in code, 294–8
  use of core memory in, 141–2
rocker switch, control by, 271
role of microcomputer in teaching *see* microcomputer
ROM *see* read-only memory
routines *see* subroutines
run time, 264, 265

sales (of programs), 122–3
SCALES program, 202–8
sciences, teaching of, 97, 100, 105, 106, 109, 289
  drawing graphs in, 240–57
screen layout, 101, 170
  division into text and picture areas, 139
  flexibility in, 45
  need to consider whole screen, 83
  problems caused by scrolling, 41, 44
screens (*see also* graphics; pictures; pixels), 9–10, 124, 271–2
  big letters on, 142–52
  cells of, 272
  colour on, 287
  coordinate systems on, 136
  copying of contents to printer, 200, 273
  light pens used with, 269–70
  modifying pictures on, 169–76
  modifying text on, 160–9, 200
  monitor screens, 105
  shading on, 136–7
  touch-sensitive screens, 270
scrolling (of text on a screen), 41, 44–5, 77, 135
searching for characters in text, 185
secondary storage *see* backing store
sectors (of disc), 266
seek time, 267
sequence (in a program), 30–1
sequence control register, 274
sequential access *see* serial access
serial access, 266–7
  problems of, 119–20
servicing of equipment, 121
shading (on screen), 79, 136–7
'SHIFT' key (*see also* 'CAPITALS LOCK' key), 268

Index 327

avoiding problems caused by, 207
silicon, 259
simulation, 9, 80–1
　avoiding danger by, 100
　chance in, 102–3
　games based on, 100, 114–5
site (of computer), 280
skills, teaching of, 99, 125
Slalewic, 38
snapshot dumps, 125
social sciences, teaching of, 109
software (*see also* programs), 10, 261, 274–9
　systems programs, 276, 277–8
software houses, 63
source program, 276
space-bar *see* control
speech, 111
speed
　controlled by space-bar, 170, 253
　increased by use of compiler, 96
　in high-resolution graphics, 95–6, 253
　in low-resolution graphics, 310
　in moving pictures, 86–7, 225
　need to reduce, 132–3
　of microcomputer, 102
　of working, 265
　pressure pads as an aid to, 271
spelling, automatic correction of, 112
SPELL programs, 229–40
stand-alone machines, 265, 280
standards, 283
　in command structure, 184
　in programming languages, 61–2
　of data transfer, 62–3
　user groups and, 282–3
statements (in a program), 33, 275
　how many on one line, 133, 159–60, 275
stationery
　continuous, 273
　fan-fold, 273
　pre-printed, 273
statistics, 9
　questionable value of, 239
stimulation
　of discussion, 216–29
　of imagination, 81–2
stock market prices, 127
storage (*see also* backing store; core memory), 265–7
　access to, 265, 266–7
　devices for, 260
　duration of, 266

elements of, 261
input from, 268–9
insufficiency of, 119
types of, 265–6, 267
strategies, teaching of, 99
string variables
　emptying of, 134
　use as program flags, 150, 176
　use in numeric input, 140
structured languages, 56–8
students *see* learners
style *see* code, program
subjects in which micros are useful, 9, 97
subroutines, 34–5
　as an aid to clarity, 199
　as an aid to portability, 85–6, 94
　examples of, 152, 165, 167
　in machine code, 95
　library of, 35–6, 57, 94–5
substitution
　of letters, 208–15
　of words, 112
suck-and-puff controls, 271
supercomputers, 259
supervisor *see* operating system
support (for microcomputer owner), 285
　with programs, 65
swings-and-roundabouts principle, 60
switching on, 281
symbols, special *see* graphics
syntax (in a programming language), 33
synthesizer, 103
system, computer, 279–83
　control of, 278–9
　degrading of, 63
　development of, 282–3
systematic working, value of, 119
systems programs, 54, 277–8

tabulated data (*see also* menus), 9
　modifying on screen, 160–9
　use in printed output, 44
talents of computers, 101
tape, magnetic *see* cassettes
tape recorder, 103
teachers (*see also* users), 19–22, 292
　as program designers, 102, 288, 291
　computers seen as a threat to, 17, 101
　support for, 109
　time well used by, 288
teaching
　case studies in, 202–257
　flexibility in, 125

328 Index

teaching – *cont.*
  of facts, 98
  of ideas, 100
  of identification, 107
  of principles, 100
  of skills, 99
  of strategies, 99
  of trial-and-error methods, 215
  qualifications and, 125–6
  questionable value of statistics in, 239
  roles of computers in, 97–116
  through programming, 115, 208
  using computers in, 37–8, 66, 109, 228
  varied styles in, 20
  versus testing, 27, 239
technology, educational, 91
temperature, extremes of, 118
terminal, 264
testing
  of learners, 9, 27, 98
  of programs, 35–6, 64–5, 282
text, 10
  amount on screen, 101
  analysis of, 107, 152, 201
  layout of, 112
  preparation of, 9
  right-justification of, 239
  visibility of, 105
'TEXT' instruction (on RML 380Z), 139
time, saving of, 294
timesharing, 265
title page (in programs), 150
tools, programs as, 240
touch-sensitive keypads, 268, 270
tracks (of disc), 266
transcription, 266
transfer of control, 31
  computer to user, 47
  user to computer, 47
transfer of data
  between storage media, 266
  standards in, 62–3
transfer of programs by network, 126
translation, 110–3
  between programming languages, 62
  of programming languages, 275
translators (*see also* compilers; interpreters), 10, 276
  types of, 276

transport of machines, 286
trial-and-error (*see also* experiments), 25
  inefficiency of, 215
tuning (of systems programs), 63
turnaround time, 265
turtle *see* LOGO
tutorial computer-assisted learning, 101, 107–8
tutorial-mode programs, 42–3
  examples of, 184–201, 229–40
typesetting, 112

updates (of programs), 282
upward compatibility, 130
usefulness of computers, 97
user authority, 19, 43
user-friendly, 90, 280
user group, 282–3
user interface, 280
user memory, 141
users (*see also* learners; teachers), 37
  help for, 39, 104
  leaving control with, 238, 239
  use of user's name, 238–9
utility programs, 278

'VAL' function in BASIC, 140, 215
variables (*see also* identifiers), 35
  names listed in program, 176
VDU, 271–2
versions of programs, 53, 65, 282
  problems caused by, 119
visibility of microcomputer screen, 105–6
visual display unit, 271–2
volatile storage, 280

warranty, 285
word processing, 112
working
  different ways of, 264–5
  speed of, 265
workspace, 141, 263
'WRITE' instruction, 34
writing, teaching of, 108

young learners, 112

Z80 microprocessor chip, 227, 311